OXFORD COMMENTARIES ON INTERNATIONAL LAW

General Editors: *Professor Philip Alston*, Professor of International Law at New York University, and *Professor Vaughan Lowe*, Chichele Professor of Public International Law in the University of Oxford and Fellow of All Souls College, Oxford.

Sub-Series:

OXFORD COMMENTARIES ON THE GATT/WTO AGREEMENTS

General Editor: *Professor Robert Howse*, Professor of International Law at the University of Michigan.

The WTO Anti-Dumping Agreement

The WTO
Anti-Dumping
Agreement

A Commentary

EDWIN VERMULST

*This book has been printed digitally and produced in a standard specification
in order to ensure its continuing availability*

OXFORD
UNIVERSITY PRESS

Great Clarendon Street, Oxford OX2 6DP

Oxford University Press is a department of the University of Oxford.
It furthers the University's objective of excellence in research, scholarship,
and education by publishing worldwide in

Oxford New York

Auckland   Cape Town Dar es Salaam   Hong Kong   Karachi
Kuala Lumpur Madrid Melbourne Mexico City Nairobi
New Delhi Shanghai Taipei Toronto
With offices in
Argentina Austria Brazil Chile Czech Republic France Greece
Guatemala Hungary Italy Japan South Korea Poland Portugal
Singapore Switzerland Thailand Turkey Ukraine Vietnam

ISBN 978-0-19-927707-0

For Jiae, Juni and Alix

Foreword

This book provides an analytical overview of the WTO Anti-Dumping Agreement, as interpreted by WTO Panels and the Appellate Body up to May 2005. The Anti-Dumping Agreement is often perceived as the most technical – and, some would say, most controversial – WTO agreement. While the basic concepts of dumping and resulting injury may appear deceptively simple, complex calculation methods related to the calculation of dumping and injury margins as well as the very detailed procedural requirements that authorities need to comply with before taking anti-dumping action make the Anti-Dumping Agreement difficult to apply – and understand – in practice.

This book of necessity goes into great detail about the intricacies of anti-dumping law and practice, but at the same time it attempts to explain the various concepts in a relatively non-technical manner by means of simplified examples that are easy to grasp for experts and non-experts alike.

The book also pays extensive attention to interpretations of the various provisions of the Anti-Dumping Agreement by WTO panels and the Appellate Body. There have been more WTO dispute settlement cases under the Anti-Dumping Agreement than under any other WTO Agreement, reflecting both the increased recourse to anti-dumping measures by WTO members all over the world and the complexity of abiding by the WTO rules. Panels and the Appellate Body, called upon to review administrative determinations and – on several occasions – aspects of national legislation, have done a remarkable job in interpreting the WTO rules. For WTO members wishing to impose anti-dumping measures in a WTO-consistent manner, knowledge not only of the Agreement itself, but also of such interpretations, is therefore a must.

The Anti-Dumping Agreement is on the agenda of the Doha Round. At the time of writing, however, it is too soon to predict how these negotiations will turn out. Nevertheless, it seems unlikely that the basic concepts will significantly change.

The author would like to thank Jochen Beck, James Durling, Folkert Graafsma, Gary Horlick, John Louth, Francesca Sgritta and Daniel Tarullo for various forms of input.

Edwin Vermulst
Brussels, June 2005

Contents

WTO ADA Panel and Appellate Body Reports

WTO ADA Panel and Appellate Body Reports (Alphabetical)

Short Title	Full Case Title and Citation	Page Reference
Argentina–Ceramic floor tiles (from Italy)	Argentina–Definitive anti-dumping measures on imports of ceramic floor tiles from Italy, WT/DS/189/R of 28 September 2001	47–8, 58, 125, 137–9, 151, 152–3, 156–7, 159–60, 161, 163–4, 227–8, 256
Argentina–Poultry (from Brazil)	Argentina–Definitive anti-dumping duties on poultry from Brazil, WT/DS241/R of 22 April 2003	10, 47–8, 62, 67, 75, 82, 83, 87, 105–6, 107, 108, 109, 116–8, 127, 130–1, 134, 156, 161, 164–6, 171, 174, 208, 211, 227–8, 232, 240, 243, 244, 255, 260, 261
EC–Bed Linen (from India)	EC–Anti-dumping duties on imports of cotton-type bed linen from India, WT/DS141/R of 30 October 2000	13, 34, 38, 40, 41, 42, 43, 69, 79, 86, 88, 89, 113, 200, 211, 216–7, 223, 231, 241, 242, 246, 257, 259, 263
EC–Bed Linen (from India) AB	EC–Anti-dumping duties on imports of cotton-type bed linen from India, WT/DS141/AB/R of 1 March 2001	41, 53, 56, 58, 59 231
EC–Bed linen (from India) 21.5	EC–Anti-dumping duties on imports of cotton-type bed linen from India, WT/DS141/RW of 29 November 2002	79, 181–2, 199
EC–Bed linen (from India) 21.5 AB	EC–Anti-dumping duties on imports of cotton-type bed linen from India, WT/DS141/AB/RW of 8 April 2003	75, 81, 82, 228, 231
EC–Malleable cast iron tube or pipe fittings (from Brazil)	EC–Anti-dumping duties on malleable cast iron tube or pipe fittings from Brazil, WT/DS219/R of 7 March 2003	13, 124, 211, 244

WTO ADA Panel Reports (chronological from date of circulation)

WTO ADA Appellate Body Reports (chronological from date of circulation)

GATT AD Panel Reports (in alphabetical order)

List of Abbreviations

AB	Appellate Body
AD	anti-dumping
ADA	Anti-Dumping Agreement (Agreement on Implementation of Article VI of GATT 1994)
ADD	anti-dumping duties
ADP	Committee on Anti-Dumping Practices
ASCM	Agreement on Subsidies and Countervailing Measures
ASG	Agreement on Safeguards
BIA	best information available
CCDP	car compact disc player
CDSOA	Continued Dumping and Subsidy Offset Act ('Byrd amendment')
CIF	cost, insurance and freight
CVD	countervailing duty
DDA	Doha Development Agenda
DRAMS	dynamic random access memory semiconductor
DSB	Dispute Settlement Body
DSU	Dispute Settlement Understanding
G&A	general and administrative (costs)
GAAP	generally accepted accounting principles
GATS	General Agreement on Trade in Services
GATT	General Agreement on Tariffs and Trade
HS	Harmonized System
IIP	injury investigation period
IP	investigation period
ITC	International Trade Commission
L/C	letter of credit
MEG	monoethylene glycol
NOI	notice of initiation
NV	normal value
PCN	product control number
PET	polyethylene terephthalate
POI	period of investigation
PSF	polyester staple fibres
PTA	purified terephthalic acid
PTY	polyester textured yarn
REP	request for establishment of a panel
SGA	selling, general and administrative expense

SPB	Sunset Policy Bulletin
USDOC	US Department of Commerce
USITC	US International Trade Commission
VCLT	Vienna Convention on the Law of Treaties
WTO	World Trade Organization

INTRODUCTION

This book will analyse the 1994 WTO Agreement on Implementation of Article VI or the Anti-Dumping Agreement (ADA), as interpreted by Panels and the Appellate Body.[1] It is divided into three main parts: the dumping determination (Chapter 1), the injury determination (Chapter 2) and procedural rules (Chapter 3). A shorter fourth part will analyse non-ADA specific WTO jurisprudence that nevertheless has direct consequences for ADA disputes (Chapter 4).[2]

The ADA is often considered to be the most complex and technical agreement of the WTO.[3] In this book I will attempt to explain the provisions of the ADA in a relatively non-technical manner. Experts in the field are referred to more technical treatises, such as the *Handbook on Anti-Dumping Investigations*, co-authored by three experts in the WTO's Rules Division.[4] I will also pay extensive attention to important interpretations of the ADA provisions by the WTO dispute settlement bodies.[5]

Dumping has traditionally been defined as the type of *price discrimination* between national markets,[6] in which a producer sells at a lower price abroad than in his home market (*price dumping*). It is often considered *unfair*[7] that a producer

---

[1] See also the recently published WTO Appellate Body Repertory of Reports and Awards 1995–2004, pp 42–101 (2005).

[2] Chapter 4 is based on Chapter 1 of Vermulst and Graafsma, *WTO Disputes with respect to Anti-Dumping, Subsidies and Safeguards* (2002).

[3] Durling and Nicely, *Understanding the WTO Anti-Dumping Agreement: Negotiating History and Subsequent Interpretation* (2002) 2, note that the ADA may be the most important substantive agreement from the Uruguay Round negotiations.

[4] Czako, Human and Miranda, *A Handbook on Anti-Dumping Investigations* (Cambridge University Press, 2003).

[5] Interested readers are also referred to the excellent and always up-to-date Dispute Settlement Commentaries, reported on-line by WorldTradeLaw.net, available at *http://www.worldtradelaw.net/dsc/dscpage.htm*). It is to be noted that where I quote excerpts from panel or AB reports, I have used the term ADA in the quotes for the sake of consistency. I have further deleted footnotes in quotations.

[6] Viner, *Dumping, A Problem in International Trade* (1966 edn) 3; Dale, *Anti-Dumping Law in a Liberal Trade Order* (1980) 1.

[7] As originally envisaged by economists such as Viner, note 6 above, anti-dumping action would be justified against *predatory dumping* only. However, predatory dumping has never been proven to exist. Anti-dumping laws have also seldom contained a predatory intent requirement, presumably because of recognition of the difficulty of proving such intent.

who benefits from protection in his home market and therefore can charge high prices there, subsequently uses the artificially high profits generated on the protected home market to subsidize low-priced export sales. He is perceived to thereby *unfairly* compete with domestic producers in the – open – importing country market which cannot afford such low prices.[8] Over time, a second form of dumping, so-called *cost dumping*, has been treated as objectionable.

The focus on the effects of dumping on the domestic industry in the importing country led to the early realization that protective measures against dumping should only be permissible if such dumping causes injury in the importing country. This conclusion was drawn almost from the date of enactment of the first national anti-dumping laws at the beginning of the twentieth century.[9] Therefore, the national anti-dumping laws required two tests before the importing country could impose so-called anti-dumping duties: there had to be dumping and such dumping had to cause injury in the importing country.

However, the methods used to assess dumping and injury as well as investigatory procedures differed substantially among the countries that used such laws. This divergence, and the growing realization that anti-dumping laws, as applied, had the potential to become significant barriers to international trade, created international interest in dumping as early as the 1920s, a mere 20 years after the passage of the first anti-dumping laws. It was not until the end of the Second World War, however, that binding international rules were developed. Such rules were implemented as part of the 1947 General Agreement on Tariffs and Trade (GATT).

The GATT rules do not prohibit injurious dumping, although they condemn it.[10] However, they do allow the country in which a product is dumped to take protective action if it can establish that the product is dumped and thereby causes injury to the domestic industry of that product. To a certain extent this importing country emphasis follows logically from the definition of dumping as price discrimination practised by private individuals. The WTO addresses *governmental* behaviour and therefore could not possibly prohibit dumping by private enterprises.[11] Moreover, importing countries

---

[8] For a more sceptical view, see, for example, Kerr and Loppacher, 'Anti-Dumping in the Doha Negotiations, Fairy Tales at the World Trade Organization' (2004) 38 Journal of World Trade 211, 212–214.

[9] See for more detail Vermulst, (1986) 7 New York Law School Journal of International and Comparative Law 301–421.   [10] Art VI:1 GATT 1994.

[11] Compare GATT Analytical Index, 223 (vol 1 1995):

'[i]n discussions at the Review Session in 1954–55, in connection with the rejection of a proposal to add a clause specifically obligating contracting parties to prevent dumping by their commercial enterprises, it was agreed to add the following statement to the Working Party's Report:

"In connexion with the effect of Article VI on the practice of dumping itself, they agreed that it follows from paragraph 1 of Article VI, that contracting parties should, within the framework of their

may welcome dumped imports because their user industries and consumers will benefit from the low prices.

GATT 1947 applies only to goods. This implies that dumping of services is not covered.[12] It has furthermore long been accepted by the GATT signatories that neither Article VI nor the Agreement cover exchange dumping, social dumping, environmental dumping or freight dumping.[13] On the other hand, the *reasons* why companies dump are considered irrelevant as long as the technical definitions are met.[14] Dumping therefore potentially equally[15] covers predatory dumping,[16] cyclical dumping,[17] market expansion dumping,[18] state-trading dumping[19] and strategic dumping.[20]

Since 1947, anti-dumping has received elaborate attention in the GATT/WTO on several occasions. Following a 1958 GATT Secretariat study of national anti-dumping laws, a Group of Experts was established that in 1960 agreed on certain common interpretations of ambiguous terms of Article VI. Moreover, in an ambitious move, an Anti-Dumping Code was negotiated during the 1967 Kennedy Round and signed by 17 parties. The Code was revised during the Tokyo Round. The Tokyo Round Code had 25 signatories, counting the EC as one.[21] Although the 1979 Code was not explicitly mentioned in the Ministerial Declaration starting the Uruguay Round,[22] fairly early in the negotiations a number of GATT Contracting Parties, notably the United States,

---

legislation, refrain from encouraging dumping, as defined in that paragraph, by private commercial enterprises." '

See also, Jackson, *World Trade and the Law of GATT* (1969) 401–424.

[12] ibid 404–405. It may be noted that the WTO General Agreement on Trade in Services (WTO GATS) does not contain provisions on dumping of services.

[13] See EPCT/C.II/48, at 1, as quoted in GATT Analytical Index, at 222 (vol I (1995). Compare Stewart, 'Antidumping' in *The GATT Uruguay Round: A Negotiating History (1986–1992)*, Vol II, 1383–1711, pp 1406–1407 (1993). [14] Compare *United States–1916 Act (EC)*, AB, para 107.

[15] The distinctions are made by Willig, *Competition Policy and Anti-Dumping*, Ch 1: 'The Economic Effects of Anti-Dumping Policy' (OECD 1995).

[16] Dumping in order to drive competitors out of business and establish a monopoly.

[17] Selling at low prices because of over-capacity due to a downturn in demand.

[18] Selling at a lower price for export than domestically in order to gain market share.

[19] Selling at low prices in order to earn hard currency.

[20] Dumping by benefiting from an overall strategy which includes both low export pricing and maintaining a closed home market in order to reap monopoly or oligopoly profits.

[21] See GATT, B.I.S.D., 36th Supp., at 435 (1990). The Parties were: Australia, Austria, Brazil, Canada, Czechoslovakia, Egypt, the EC, Finland, Hong Kong, Hungary, India, Japan, Korea, Mexico, New Zealand, Norway, Pakistan, Poland, Romania, Singapore, Spain, Sweden, Switzerland, the USA and Yugoslavia.

[22] GATT/1396, Ministerial Declaration on the Uruguay Round (1986). For a brief background of the preparatory activities that led to the adoption of the Declaration, see GATT Activities 1985, 6–10 (1986).

Japan, Korea, Hong Kong and the EC proposed changes – sometimes radical ones – to the 1979 Code. These led to the new ADA.[23]

As the ADA forms part of the single package, all WTO members are automatically members of and bound by the ADA. This occasionally leads to the misunderstanding that the WTO rules oblige WTO members to adopt anti-dumping legislation. This is not correct. However, WTO members that do adopt and utilize anti-dumping legislation, must do so in accordance with the provisions of the ADA:

Article 1 ADA: Principles
An anti-dumping measure shall be applied only under the circumstances provided for in Article VI of GATT 1994 and pursuant to investigations initiated[24] and conducted in accordance with the provisions of this Agreement. The following provisions govern the application of Article VI of GATT 1994 in so far as action is taken under anti-dumping legislation or regulations.

It is significant that international regulation has always focused more on the trade-distorting effects of *anti*-dumping action than on the effects of the dumping itself; most GATT refinements of the anti-dumping regime over the past 60 years have limited the ability of the importing country to take protective action.

Until 1990, there were four GATT members that actively used their anti-dumping laws as a means of protecting domestic industries against injuriously dumped imports: Australia, Canada, the European Communities and the United States.[25] These four developed countries mostly applied measures against developing countries.

In the course of the last 15 years, however, more and more countries have adopted anti-dumping laws and started using them.[26] According to WTO data, thus far 104 WTO members, counting the EC as one, have submitted notifications of anti-dumping legislation and/or regulations to the WTO

---

[23] For an overview of the negotiating history, see Koulen, 'The New Anti-Dumping Code Through Its Negotiating History' in Bourgeois, Berrod and Gippini Fournier (eds), *The Uruguay Round Results* (1995) 151–233; Stewart, 'Antidumping' in *The GATT Uruguay Round: A Negotiating History (1986–1992)*, Vol II, 1383–1711 (1993). For a shorter summary, see Horlick and Shea, 'The World Trade Organization Anti-Dumping Agreement' (1995) 29 Journal of World Trade 5–31. Durling and Nicely, *Understanding the WTO Anti-Dumping Agreement: Negotiating History and Subsequent Interpretation* (2002) contains all of the negotiating drafts.

[24] Fn 1 in ADA: The term 'initiated' as used in this Agreement means the procedural action by which a Member formally commences an investigation as provided in Article 5.

[25] Compare Stewart, 'Antidumping' in *The GATT Uruguay Round: A Negotiating History (1986–1992)*, Vol II, 1383–1711, p 1395 (1993) who reports that from 1980 to 1989 these four members accounted for 95 per cent of the 1,456 anti-dumping cases reported to the GATT during the 1980–1989 period. See also Jackson and Vermulst, *Anti-Dumping Law and Practice: A Comparative Study* (1989).

[26] Compare Kerr and Loppacher, 'Anti-Dumping in the Doha Negotiations, Fairy Tales at the World Trade Organization' (2004) 38 Journal of World Trade 211, 211.

Secretariat.[27] During the period from 1 January 1995 to 31 December 2004, 38 WTO members applied a total of 1,656 anti-dumping measures.[28]

Anti-dumping measures by WTO member from 01/01/95 to 31/12/04:

Argentina (139)	Australia (54)	Brazil (62)	Canada (80)
Chile (6)	China (52)	Colombia (11)	Costa Rica (1)
Czech Republic (1)	EC (193)	Egypt (30)	Guatemala (1)
India (302)	Indonesia (23)	Israel (15)	Jamaica (4)
Japan (3)	Korea (43)	Latvia (1)	Lithuania (7)
Malaysia (18)	Mexico (69)	New Zealand (14)	Nicaragua (1)
Pakistan (4)	Paraguay (1)	Peru (34)	Philippines (9)
Poland (9)	Singapore (2)	South Africa (113)	Taiwan (2)
Thailand (23)	Trinidad & Tobago (7)	Turkey (77)	United States (219)
Uruguay (1)	Venezuela (25)		

As will be clear from the table, the 10 major users now are India, the United States, the EC, Argentina, South Africa, Canada, Turkey, Mexico, Brazil and Australia.

Details on the 40 major victims of these measures are provided in the table below:

Anti-dumping measures by victim from 01/01/95 to 31/12/04:

Argentina (9)	Australia (8)	Belarus (10)	Belgium (13)
Brazil (57)	Bulgaria (10)	Canada (13)	Chile (14)
China (297)	Czech Republic (14)	EC (38)	France (24)
Germany (35)	Hong Kong (12)	Hungary (7)	India (60)
Indonesia (54)	Italy (25)	Japan (82)	Kazakstan (18)
Korea (118)	Latvia (7)	Malaysia (34)	Mexico (21)
Netherlands (13)	Poland (18)	Romania (24)	Russia (76)
Singapore (21)	Slovak Republic (7)	South Africa (33)	Spain (21)
Sweden (6)	Taiwan (89)	Thailand (63)	Turkey (22)
Ukraine (47)	UK (20)	United States (83)	Venezuela (12)

Thus, the 10 major victims have become China, the EC-25 and its Member States, Korea, Taiwan, the United States, Japan, Russia, Thailand, India and Brazil. Anti-dumping disputes therefore are no longer mainly conflicts

---

[27] WTO Annual Report, pp 45–47 (WTO Geneva 2004).
[28] WTO website, consulted on 4 June 2005. See Annex 5 for more details.

between developed country WTO members as users and developing country WTO members as victims. Many important WTO members are both!

In the framework of the Doha Development Agenda, WTO members are once again negotiating about possible revisions of the ADA. At the time of writing (June 2005), it is too soon to predict how these negotiations will turn out.

However, it seems unlikely that the basic concepts will significantly change. Indeed, the 4th Ministerial WTO Conference in Doha decided in relevant part that:

DDA negotiating mandate
28. In the light of experience and of the increasing application of these instruments by Members, we agree to negotiations aimed at clarifying and improving disciplines under the Agreement[s] on Implementation of Article VI of the GATT 1994 ... while preserving the basic concepts, principles and effectiveness of these Agreements and their instruments and objectives, and taking into account the needs of developing and least-developed participants.

Paragraph 28 of this Ministerial Declaration[29] is clearly the result of a carefully drafted compromise between two factions. On the one hand, negotiations are to be '*aimed at clarifying and improving disciplines*', reflecting the desire of victim (including some developing) countries and, on the other hand, such negotiations will have to '*preserv[e] the basic concepts, principles and effectiveness of these Agreements*' reflecting the concerns of other WTO members[30] that the instrument might be tinkered with too much.

The widespread and ever-expanding use of the anti-dumping instrument makes it imperative that the ADA is *transparent, fair* and *predictable*.[31] A foreign supplier should be able to make in advance his own calculations regarding normal value and export price so that he can determine whether he is dumping and take steps to avoid it, if he wants to. The artificiality of dumping calculations would appear to mandate such an interpretation.

---

[29] WTO, Ministerial Declaration adopted on 14 November, WT/MIN(01)/DEC/1 (20 November 2001).

[30] Compare Tarullo, 'Paved with Good Intentions: The Dynamic Effects of WTO Review of Anti-Dumping Action' (2003) 2 World Trade Review 373, 388.

[31] Compare Horlick and Vermulst, 'The 10 Major Problems with the Anti-Dumping Instrument: An Attempt at Synthesis' (2005) 39 Journal of World Trade 67.

Chapter 1

DUMPING

Introduction

Article 2 ADA covers the determination of dumping. The fact that only one – albeit long – article of the ADA is devoted to this complex issue shows that the ADA continues to function as a framework agreement, leaving substantial discretion to the WTO members. Nevertheless, the ADA provisions on dumping are much more detailed than previous ones and have been further clarified by WTO and Appellate Body reports.

The *Thailand–H-Beams* case established early on that Article 2 contains *multiple obligations* with respect to the determination of dumping.[1] As a result, a WTO member wishing to challenge a dumping determination made by another member must take great care that it describe in sufficient detail in its request for establishment of a panel exactly which provisions it considers to have been violated. Failure to do so may lead the panel/Appellate Body to reject dumping claims on the ground that they were too vague. This confirms the practice of earlier GATT panels, such as *EC–Cotton yarns*:

[F]or a claim to be before the Panel it would have to be specified in the document requesting establishment of a panel . . . The panel found that Brazil's claim that the EC had made an 'incorrect determination that certain domestic sales were not in the ordinary course of trade' was not expressly referred to anywhere in document ADP/121, and accordingly dismissed Brazil's argument on this point.[2]

Article 2.1 sets out that for the purpose of the ADA, a product is to be considered as being dumped, i.e. introduced into the commerce of another country at less than its normal value, if the export price of the product exported from one country to another is less than the comparable price, in the ordinary course of trade, for the like product when destined for consumption in the exporting country:

Article 2.1 ADA
For the purpose of this Agreement, a product is to be considered as being dumped, i.e. introduced into the commerce of another country at less than its normal value, if

---

[1] *Thailand–H-Beams from Poland*, Panel, para 7.35.
[2] *EC–Cotton yarns from Brazil*, paras 449–456, ADP/137, 4 July 1995.

the export price of the product exported from one country to another is less than the comparable price, in the ordinary course of trade, for the like product when destined for consumption in the exporting country.

This definition of dumping introduces four important concepts, in order of appearance: normal value, export price, ordinary course of trade and like product. These concepts are discussed in more detail in the following paragraphs.

The comparison between prices or costs in different markets is normally performed during a period of time set by the authorities at the outset of the investigation. This is typically called the investigation period (IP) or the period of investigation (POI). It is noteworthy that Article 2 does not contain any rules on the selection of this period, which may sometimes have ramifications for the outcome of the proceeding.

However, a recommendation adopted by the Committee on Anti-Dumping Practices in 2000 provides that the investigation period for dumping purposes should normally be 12 months, and in any case no less than 6 months, ending as close to the date of initiation of the investigation as is practicable.[3]

1.1 The Like Product

As referred to in Article 2.1 the 'like product' is the product sold on the domestic market that is like the exported – dumped – product.[4]

Article 2.6 ADA stipulates more in general that throughout the ADA the like product is a product which is identical, ie alike in all respects to the product under consideration, or in the absence of such a product, another product which, although not alike in all respects, has characteristics closely resembling those of the product under consideration. Thus Article 2.6 both defines the like product and clarifies that the definition applies throughout the ADA:

Article 2.6 ADA
Throughout this Agreement the term 'like product' ('produit similaire') shall be interpreted to mean a product which is identical, i.e. alike in all respects to the product under consideration, or in the absence of such a product, another product which, although not alike in all respects, has characteristics closely resembling those of the product under consideration.

---

[3] Committee on Anti-Dumping Practices, Recommendation concerning the periods of data collection for anti-dumping investigations, G/ADP/6 (16 May 2000), reproduced in Annex 3.
[4] Compare *United States–Softwood lumber from Canada II*, Panel, para 7.152.

The panel in *United States–Softwood lumber II* noted that Article 2.6 is a definitional article, and then appeared to draw the conclusion that it does not contain in itself obligations on Members, or in any event that it could not be the basis for an *independent* violation.[5] In a similar vein, the panel in *Guatemala–Cement II* found that Guatemala had violated Articles 3.1, 3.2 and 3.5 by wrongly characterizing some imports by MATINSA as not of the like product and failing to take into account these imports in its determination of injury and causality.[6]

These approaches may be contrasted with *Mexico–HFCS*, where the panel noted[7] that the United States had not claimed that imported HFCS was not 'like' domestically produced sugar and therefore would not rule on this (in application of the WTO principle of *non ultra petita*).

In my view, there is no reason why Article 2.6 cannot form the basis for an independent claim, whether it is a definitional article or not.[8] If an authority treats imported coffee as a like product to domestically-produced tea, he violates the like product definition, in addition to any other ADA articles that may have been violated.[9]

For dumping purposes, the like product is to be compared with the allegedly dumped product, which is referred to in Article 2.6 as the *product under consideration*. In the context of the *injury* determination, on the other hand, the term refers to the product produced by the domestic industry allegedly being injured by the dumped product.[10] As a result, the 'like product' has a different meaning, depending whether it is used for the dumping or for the injury determination.

In both cases, the two products should ideally be identical. Only in the absence of identical products may products with closely resembling characteristics be compared with each other.

The 'like product' concept in the ADA and, indeed, the ASCM must be distinguished from the concept of 'like or directly competitive product' used in the

---

[5] *United States–Softwood lumber from Canada II*, Panel, para 7.146.

[6] *Guatemala–Cement from Mexico II*, Panel, para 8.272.

[7] *Mexico–HFCS from the United States*, Panel, para 7.59, fn 555.

[8] Compare *Argentina–Poultry from Brazil*, Panel, paras 7.331; 7.338, with respect to the Article 4.1 definition of the domestic industry, discussed in section 2.2, below. But see WorldTradeLaw.net, *Dispute Settlement Commentary on Argentina–Poultry from Brazil*, p 24, checked on 23 April 2005.

[9] Durling and Nicely, *Understanding the WTO Anti-Dumping Agreement: Negotiating History and Subsequent Interpretation* (2002) 113, implicitly take the same approach.

[10] Compare *United States–Softwood lumber from Canada II*, Panel, para 7.152.

> **Dumping:**
>
> - like product   = product sold in exporting country
>
>   to be compared with:
>
> - product under consideration = allegedly dumped product
>
> **Injury:**
>
> - like product   = product sold by domestic industry
>
>   to be compared with:
>
> - product under consideration = allegedly dumped product

ASG which is obviously broader.[11] In order for products to be considered like, they must have identical or closely resembling (physical) characteristics, while the focus for directly competitive products is the extent to which they compete in the marketplace. As the objective of the ADA is to protect the domestic market against *unfairly* traded imports while the objective of the ASG is to protect the market against *fairly* traded imports, it is surprising that the product definition in the ASG is in fact broader than the one in the ADA and the ASCM.

When an anti-dumping investigation is initiated, the product under consideration is often defined both by descriptive language and by reference to Harmonized System (HS) numbers, or national versions thereof. If, for example, the product under consideration is certain types of PET film, it could be defined as non-self-adhesive film of polyethylene terephthalate (PET film), excluding film for the manufacture of flexible magnetic discs and classifiable within HS numbers 392062. This definition will then be provided to all interested parties both in the notice of initiation of the investigation and in the questionnaires that are sent out.

The accuracy of the initial definition is important because it sets the parameters of the investigation and, at the end of the day, arguably limits the scope of the application of anti-dumping measures. If in the example above, the administering authorities exclude PET film for the manufacture of flexible magnetic discs at the outset of the investigation, they cannot impose anti-dumping measures on this type of film when the time comes to impose such measures, among others, because they would not have investigated whether such PET film in fact has been injuriously dumped.

---

[11] *Argentina–Footwear (EC)*, AB, para 94.

1.1.1 Sub-dividing the Like Product (Product Control Numbers)

For the purpose of dumping (and injury) margin calculations, it is customary in most countries to sub-divide the like product in various types or models, often on the basis of product control numbers (PCNs).[12] Such sub-divisions are normally prepared by the administering authorities before the case is initiated and then communicated to all interested parties in the various types of questionnaires.[13]

If, for example, the like product is polyester textured yarn (PTY), different types of PTY could be distinguished on the basis of quality, denier, filament count, flame retardance, colouring and number of twists. If the like product is steel fasteners, it could be sub-divided on the basis of type (eg nuts, bolts and screws), raw material, Department Idenfification Number (DIN), diameter (10th of mm) and length (10th of mm):

Field description	Explanation	
Type of fastener	Indicate the type of the fastener	
	Wood screws	1
	Self tapping screws	2
	Other screws without head	3
	Slot and cross-recessed screws	4
	Hexagon socket head screws	5
	Hexagon bolts	6
	Nuts	7
Raw material	Indicate the raw material used for producing the product concerned:	
	Austenitic steel	A1
	Austenitic steel	A2
	Austenitic steel	A4
	Chromium ferritic steel	C2
	Chromium ferritic steel	C4
	Chromium martensitic steel	C1
	Chromium martensitic steel	C3

(*Continued*)

---

[12] Compare Czako, Human and Miranda, *A Handbook on Anti-Dumping Investigations* (2003) 99.
[13] See section 3.2.5.2, below.

Field description	Explanation
	Other combination **D1** (please specify the components in a separate note)
DIN number	Indicate the corresponding DIN number
Diameter	Indicate the diameter of the product concerned, in 10th of millimetres, e.g. 045, or 120, etc.
Length	Indicate the length of the screw/bolt or the height of the nut in 10th of millimetres

If the like product is fish, one might distinguish different types on the basis of quality, fresh/chilled or frozen, presentation (whole, gutted, with/without head, off-cuts and fillets) and weight of presentation.

Such sub-divisions are arguably necessary in order to make accurate type-by-type comparisons before calculating producer-specific margins. Thus, for example, one cannot compare for dumping purposes carbon steel nuts sold by Chinese producers in China with their exports of stainless steel bolts to Canada. Similarly, for injury purposes, one should not compare frozen whole salmon exported from Chile to the EC with fresh salmon fillets produced in Scotland.

The ADA is silent on the legality of such sub-divisions. This is perhaps not surprising as the need to make them seems so obvious. However, as we will see below, administering authorities will apply many rules[14] also on a type-by-type, model-by-model basis, although this does not necessarily appear foreseen by the ADA. This may make the calculation of particularly dumping margins a very artificial and speculative exercise.

1.2 Export Price

The key product in an anti-dumping case is the allegedly dumped product, often referred to as the product under consideration. Not only is this the product which is allegedly dumped, but it is also the product which is allegedly causing injury to the domestic industry producing the like product. This product

---

[14] For example the 5% home market viability test, the ordinary course of trade test, the 20% sales below cost test and the concept of inter-model zeroing. As we will see in section 1.4.3.1, below, the AB ruled that inter-model zeroing is not allowed under the ADA in *EC–Bed linen from India*, *EC–Malleable cast iron tube and pipe fittings from Brazil* and *United States–Softwood lumber from Canada II*.

under consideration is, in other words, the product exported by the producers or exporters in the exporting country to importers in the importing country. As a result, it is logical to start the discussion with the analysis of the price of this product,[15] ie the export price, as we will do here, although this is not the order followed by the ADA, which starts with the analysis of the price of the product sold on the domestic market of the foreign producers, the so-called normal value.

Article 2.1 merely provides indirectly that the export price is the price of the product exported from one country (the exporting country) to another (the importing country). If, for example, producer x in country X sells T-shirts to importer y in country Y, then the price charged by producer x to importer y is the export price. At this stage, the terms and conditions agreed upon by the buyer and the seller do not matter yet, although they will need to be taken into account later on. If, for example, producer x sells his T-shirts to importer y ex-warehouse, cash at delivery, for $1 per T-shirt, then this is the export price. If producer x sells to importer y delivered, duty-paid, 90 days' credit, for $2 per T-shirt, then this is the export price. In other words, what matters at this stage is the price agreed upon between the buyer and the seller.

As this is virtually always an international transaction, the price is normally well documented in various transaction documents, such as the commercial invoice, the letter of credit, the bill of lading, the packing list, duty drawback claims, etc. Furthermore, the accuracy of these documents in theory[16] can be verified both at the exporter and at the importer. Consequently, it generally is not complicated to establish the export price.

1.2.1 Traders

It may happen that foreign producers sell the product under consideration to other parties, typically traders, in the exporting country which then resell it to the importing country. On the basis of Article 2.1 it seems clear that the export price then is the price charged by the trader to the importer. Indeed, the transaction between the producer and the trader is an internal sale in the exporting country and in many cases the producer may not even know whether the trader will export the product under consideration,[17] let alone to which destination.

---

[15] Compare *United States–Softwood lumber from Canada II*, Panel, paras 7.152–7.153.

[16] In practice, most authorities verify the export price during the verification of the exporter.

[17] For the producer it may not always be evident how to report such sales to traders. If, for example, he does not know whether the trader will resell the product on the domestic market or for export, should he then report it as a domestic sale or as an export sale? If the producer knows that the trader will export the product, but he does not know the destination, should he then report the transactions as an export sale to the importing country or as third country exports? Obviously, the answer to such questions is highly fact-specific.

Furthermore, it is the trader that sets the export price and therefore possibly engages in dumping.

On the other hand, it may be administratively difficult for administering authorities to make individual calculations for traders. Even if this can be done, the imposition of anti-dumping duties on traders is of limited use because traders can easily switch sources of supply. Presumably for these reasons, some countries normally do not calculate separate margins for traders.

A different approach is often taken when the producer and the trader qualify as *related parties*.[18] Administering authorities may then take the position that they belong to a single economic entity as a result of which, on the one hand, prices between the two may be unreliable and, on the other hand, actions by one may be attributed to the other. The authorities may then require the producer and the related trader to cooperate to ensure that all the producer's export sales to the importing country, whether direct or indirect through the related trader, are reported in the questionnaire response of the producer. In the example below, the relevant export price would then be the price of 105 charged by the related trader to his independent customers in the importing country:

Producer → Related trader → Independent customer
100 **105**

1.2.2 Constructed Export Price

There may be cases where the exporter and the importer do not establish an export price, for example in the case of barter, or where the export price that they agree upon is unreliable. The latter might be the case if the exporter and the importer are *related parties*[19] (in which case the price agreed upon by them might not be an arm's length price) or if the administering authorities have reason to believe, for example, that while the importer pays a high invoiced price, he receives compensation from the exporter in some other manner. Articles 2.3 and 2.4 (second part) contain important rules for such situations.[20]

Article 2.3 ADA authorizes the authorities to *construct* the export price on the basis of the price at which the imported products are first resold to an independent buyer, or if the products are not resold to an independent buyer, or not

---

[18] See section 2.2.2, below. [19] See section 2.2.2, below.
[20] Compare *United States–Stainless steel plate in coils and stainless steel sheet and strip from Korea*, Panel, para 6.90.

resold in the condition as imported, on such reasonable basis as the authorities may determine in cases where there is no export price or where it appears to the authorities concerned that the export price is unreliable because of association or a compensatory arrangement between the exporter and the importer or a third party.

By far the most common of these situations is the one where a foreign producer sells the product under consideration to a related party which then resells to unrelated customers. In application of Article 2.3 ADA many administering authorities will then almost automatically[21] proceed to *construct* the export price on the basis of the resale price to the first independent customer. However, authorities are under no obligation to do so, as the use of the word 'may' makes clear.

Producer   →   Related importer   →   Independent customer
100   **140**

Thus, in the example above, most administering authorities will use the price of 140 charged by the related importer to the independent customer. The construction of the export price on the basis of the price to the first independent customer is not problematic in and of itself because it is a market price.

However, the construction of the export price may become problematic because Article 2.4 ADA provides in relevant part that in such cases allowances for costs, including duties and taxes, incurred between importation and resale, and for profits accruing, should also be made.

Thus, Article 2.4 authorizes administering authorities to deduct all costs incurred between importation and resale as well as profits accruing from the price to the first independent customer.

Producer   →   Related importer   →   Independent customer
100   Duty: 14   **140**
Freight: 5
Storage: 2.8
SGA: 14 (10%)
Profit: 4.2 (3%)

---

[21] This automaticity may be questioned as the authorities must technically establish that the export price is *unreliable*.

In the example above, the costs[22] incurred between importation and resale are 35.8 while the 3 per cent profit realized by the related importer on his turnover amounts to 4.2. If such costs and profit were to be deducted by the administering authorities, the constructed export price would be 100. In other words, it would be the same as the export price charged by the exporter to the related importer and the construction of the export price therefore would be 'neutral'.

In practice, however, some administering authorities will not consider the profit margin realized by the related importer on the ground that it is influenced in part by the unreliable purchase price. They will therefore impute a profit margin to the related importer, supposedly based on the profit margins generated by independent importers cooperating in the same proceeding. While it is not clear whether the imputation of such profit is allowed, the ADA in any event provides no guidance on how to do this, as a result of which different administering authorities use different methods.

In *United States–Stainless steel plate in coils and stainless steel sheet and strip*, the panel ruled that administering authorities on the one hand are not required to make these special allowances, but on the other hand in no event may make allowances that are not provided for in Article 2.4 when they construct the export price:[23]

The term 'should' in its ordinary meaning generally is non-mandatory, i.e., its use in Article 2.4 indicates that a Member is not required to make allowance for costs and profits when constructing an export price. We believe that, because the failure to make allowance for costs and profits could only result in a higher export price – and thus a lower dumping margin – the ADA merely permits, but does not require, that such allowances be made.

. . . Article 2.4 provides an authorization to make certain specific allowances. Allowances not within the scope of that authorization cannot be made. If a Member were free to make any additional allowances it desired, there would be no effective disciplines on the methodology for construction of an export price and the provision in question would be reduced to inutility.[24]

---

[22] In the case of multi-product importers, SGA (selling, general and administrative expense) will normally need to be allocated between the product under consideration and other products.

[23] Cunningham and Cribb, 'Dispute Settlement Through the Lens of "Free Flow of Trade": A Review of WTO Dispute Settlement of US Anti-Dumping and Countervailing Duty Measures' (2003) 6 Journal of International Economic Law 155, 157–158 criticize this aspect of the panel report: 'In plain-speak, the panel's conclusion was "When it says you 'should' examine these things, it means you 'may' examine these things and when we say you 'may' examine these things, you may examine only these specifically enumerated things and no other things." '

[24] *United States–Stainless steel plate in coils and stainless steel sheet and strip from Korea*, Panel, paras 6.93–6.94.

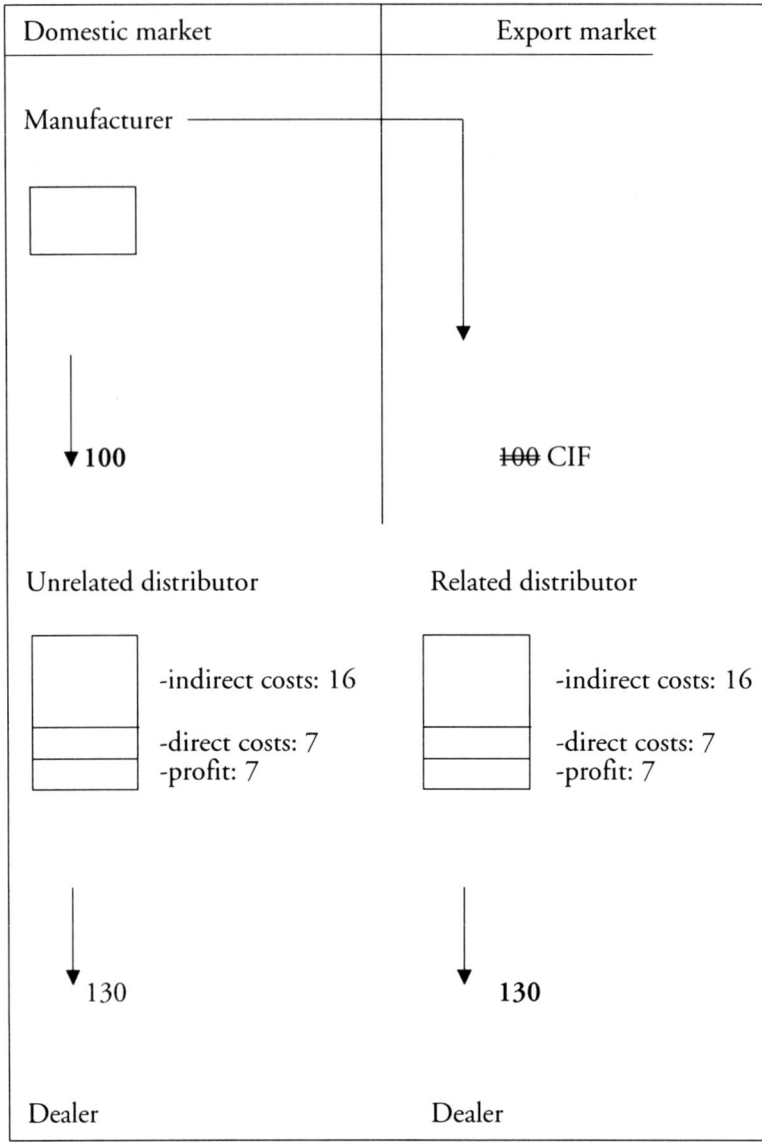

In the same case, the panel ruled that the concept of 'costs incurred between importation and resale' cannot be stretched to include costs, *in casu* bad debt as a result of bankruptcy, that not only were not incurred in an accounting sense until after the date of resale but which were entirely unforeseen at that time.[25]

---

[25] *United States–Stainless steel plate in coils and stainless steel sheet and strip from Korea*, Panel, para 6.100.

Article 2.4, fourth and fifth sentences, provides that in cases where price comparability has been affected by the construction of the export price, the authorities shall establish the normal value at a level of trade equivalent to the level of trade of the constructed export price, or shall make due allowance as warranted under Article 2.4.[26]

It seems clear that after all costs incurred between importation and resale, as well as profits accruing, have been deducted from the price to the first independent customer, what is left is the price of the product under consideration *as if* it had been sold *to* an *unrelated* importer. In the distribution chain, such an unrelated importer effectively functions as a distributor and therefore this constructed export price is the price *to* an unrelated distributor.

Thus, Article 2.4 would appear to require that where such costs and profits are deducted, the remaining price must be compared with a normal value, similarly established at the level of sale *to* a domestic distributor or, alternatively, that due allowance for the level of trade difference be made on the normal value side.

Thus, in the example on page 18, the constructed export price of 100 $(130 - 7 - 7 - 16 = 100)$ should be compared with the domestic price to the unrelated distributor of 100.[27]

1.3 Normal Value

1.3.1 Normal Value: Based on Domestic Sales

Article 2.1 indirectly defines *normal value* as the comparable price in the ordinary course of trade for the like product when destined for consumption in the exporting country. Thus, the normal value is normally the price of the like product in the exporting country, as long as the *product* is destined for consumption there and the *price* is in the ordinary course of trade.

1.3.1.1 Destined for Consumption

The requirement that the like product be *destined for consumption* in the exporting country thus far has not given rise to WTO disputes. However, this does not mean that it may not be problematic in practice. Some countries, for example, track imported raw materials all the way to exportation of the finished

---

[26] This sentence was added during the Uruguay Round negotiations and has been called a '*significant change*', see Koulen, 'The New Anti-Dumping Code Through its Negotiating History', in Bourgeois, Berrod and Gippini Fournier (eds), *The Uruguay Round Results* (1995) 151–232.

[27] Note that at this stage we are only discussing the special level of trade adjustment of Art 2.4 ADA. Direct selling costs included in both prices will still need to be taken out later on, see section 1.4.1, below.

product. If the like product is an intermediate product to be used in a final product which will be exported, some authorities may then question whether the intermediate product is destined for consumption in the country of export, particularly in situations where the producer of the intermediate product knows at the moment of sale to a domestic customer that the processed product will eventually be exported. The following example may clarify this:

| PTA/MEG | → | **Polyester staple fibres** | → | Polyester yarns |
| Imported | | Produced & sold domestically | | Produced/exported |

In this example the like product is polyester staple fibres (PSF). The producer under investigation imports the raw materials PTA and MEG from which he manufactures PSF. He then sells this PSF to domestic companies which produce polyester yarns which they export. On the basis of the wording of Article 2.1 ADA it seems clear that the like product under investigation, PSF, is destined for consumption in the exporting country as it is consumed in the product of the processed product polyester yarn which is equally manufactured in the exporting country market. Nevertheless, some administering authorities will exclude such domestic sales of the like product on the ground that they are incorporated in a processed product which is exported.

1.3.1.2 *Ordinary Course of Trade*

The ADA does not define the concept 'ordinary course of trade'.[28] However, Article 2.1 appears to establish that only domestic prices in the ordinary course of trade are to be used as normal value. This implies that administering authorities would normally need to check whether domestic sales are or are not made in the ordinary course of trade. While there may be various reasons why domestic sales are not made in the ordinary course of trade, two situations are most common:

- Some or all domestic transactions are sold below cost; or
- Domestic sales are made to related parties.

Exclusion of sales below cost   Many authorities consider that under certain circumstances sales below cost are not in the ordinary course of trade. In order to determine whether domestic sales are in the ordinary course of trade, the authorities therefore will need not only information on domestic prices, but also on the costs of the domestic transactions concerned in order to determine

---

[28] Compare *United States–Hot Rolled Steel from Japan*, Panel, para 7.108.

whether domestic prices are above or below cost. While many authorities routinely request cost information in the questionnaires and then check such cost information during the investigation, others will only request and check cost information if there are allegations by the domestic industry that the exporters have been selling below cost. In this context, the panel in *Guatemala–Cement II* held that nothing in the ADA prevents an investigating authority from requesting cost information, even if the domestic industry does not allege sales below cost.[29] Thus, the authorities are free to proactively seek information in this regard.

It is important to note that the ADA does not *require* authorities to treat domestic sales below cost as not in the ordinary course of trade.[30] Article 2.2.1 ADA merely provides that such sales *may* be treated as not in the ordinary course of trade and *may* be disregarded only if the authorities determine that sales below cost are made:

- within an extended period of time (normally one year, but never less than six months);
- in substantial quantities (meaning that either the weighted average selling price of the transactions under consideration for the determination of the normal value is below the weighted average per unit costs, or the volume of sales below per unit costs represents not less than 20 per cent of the volume sold in transactions under consideration for the determination of the normal value);
- at prices which do not provide for the recovery of all costs within a reasonable period of time.

Article 2.2.1 ADA
Sales of the like product in the domestic market of the exporting country or sales to a third country at prices below per unit (fixed and variable) costs of production plus administrative, selling and general costs may be treated as not being in the ordinary course of trade by reason of price and may be disregarded in determining normal value only if the authorities[31] determine that such sales are made within an extended period of time[32] in substantial quantities[33] and are at prices which do not provide for the recovery

---

[29] Compare *Guatemala–Cement from Mexico II*, Panel, para 8.183.

[30] Compare Czako, Human and Miranda, *A Handbook on Anti-Dumping Investigations* (2003) 152.

[31] Fn 3 in ADA: When in this Agreement the term 'authorities' is used, it shall be interpreted as meaning authorities at an appropriate senior level.

[32] Fn 4 in ADA: The extended period of time should normally be one year but shall in no case be less than six months.

[33] Fn 5 in ADA: Sales below per unit costs are made in substantial quantities when the authorities establish that the weighted average selling price of the transactions under consideration for the determination of the normal value is below the weighted average per unit costs, or that the volume of sales below per unit costs represents not less than 20 per cent of the volume sold in transactions under consideration for the determination of the normal value.

of all costs within a reasonable period of time. If prices which are below per unit costs at the time of sale are above weighted average per unit costs for the period of investigation, such prices shall be considered to provide for recovery of costs within a reasonable period of time.

It is important to bear in mind that many authorities apply these tests on a PCN-specific basis. This is therefore an area where the PCN classification[34] may play an important role.

In practice, the second test is often the most important. In applying this test, the authorities will normally first check whether the weighted average domestic selling price of a PCN is *lower* than its weighted average per unit cost. If this is the case, the domestic sales of that PCN will be ignored and recourse will be had to constructed normal value. This alternative manner of establishing normal value is discussed in more detail in section 1.3.2, below. Where the weighted average domestic selling price of a PCN is *higher* than its weighted average per unit cost, the authorities will then check whether the volume of sales below per unit costs represents 20 per cent or more of the volume sold in transactions under consideration for the determination of the normal value.

Where sales below cost represent *less* than 20 per cent of the total domestic sales of the PCN, such sales below costs *must* be *included* in the calculation of normal value, based on domestic prices. However, where sales below cost represent 20 per cent or more of the total domestic sales of the PCN, such sales below cost *may* be *excluded* and normal value may then be based on the remaining domestic sales of the PCN *above* cost. As domestic sales below costs are obviously lower-priced than sales at or above cost, such exclusion will increase the dumping margin, compared with inclusion of the below cost sales, as the following example may show:

Suppose the PCN cost is 90 and four transactions of equal weight took place in the domestic and the export market as follows:

	Domestic	Export
(1) 1 June	50	50
(2) 10 June	100	100
(3) 15 June	150	150
(4) 20 June	200	200

(Continued)

---

[34] See section 1.1.1, above.

The weighted average domestic price after the exclusion of the domestic sale below cost made on 1 June is: **150** [(100 + 150 + 200) / 3 = 150]. Compared with a weighted average export price of **125** [(50 + 100 + 150 + 200) / 4 = 125], this gives a dumping amount of **100** [(150 − 125) × 4 = 100] and an approximate dumping margin of **20%** (100 / 500 × 100 = 20%).

Suppose that the authority would include the domestic sale below cost, the weighted average domestic price would be 125 [(50 + 100 + 150 + 200) / 4 = 125], as a result of which no dumping would be found.

Despite the discretion that Article 2.2.1 grants investigating authorities, many authorities will exclude sales below costs as a matter of course where such sales represent 20 per cent or more of total domestic sales.

Domestic sales to related parties   Some authorities also consider that domestic sales *to* related parties may not be in the ordinary course of trade. Typically this occurs if a producer sells to a related domestic distributor which then resells to an unrelated dealer or end-user.

Producer	→	Related distributor	→	Unrelated customer
100		**130**		

As is the case on the export side, domestic sales to related parties in fact may or may not be made on an arm's length basis and arguably – rather than the qualification of the purchaser (ie related or unrelated) – the reliability of the prices charged ought to be the focus of the enquiry. In practice, however, some authorities assume as a matter of course that sales between related parties are unreliable and therefore will automatically treat them as not being in the ordinary course of trade. Thus far, this extreme interpretation has not been challenged in the WTO.

Ironically, however, a less radical interpretation by the American Department of Commerce was successfully challenged by Japan in *United States–Hot rolled steel*.[35] Under the so-called arm's length test, the Commerce Department tested whether there were differences in domestic

---

[35] *United States–Hot Rolled Steel from Japan*, Panel, paras 7.108–7.112.

pricing to affiliated customers as compared with domestic pricing to unaffiliated customers:

The USDOC 99.5% test

Under this test, the DOC checked whether the weighted average sales price of domestic sales to an affiliated party was lower than the weighted average sales price to all non-affiliated customers. If it was more than 0.5% lower, the domestic related party sales concerned were automatically excluded from the calculation of normal value. However, the DOC did not check whether affiliated party sales were higher-priced.

The panel considered this test objectionable and therefore not a permissible interpretation of the ADA because of its one-sided nature: the arm's length test only checked whether prices to affiliated customers were *lower*, on average, than prices to unaffiliated customers and therefore would treat only the lower-priced sales to affiliates as not in the ordinary course of trade. Relatively high-priced sales to affiliates, on the other hand, were not tested for and would be treated as ordinary course of trade sales by the Commerce Department. The panel considered this one-sided test result-oriented:

The result of application of the 'arm's length' test . . . is the exclusion from the determination of normal value of prices that are, on average, lower. As a result, the application of the 'arm's length' test cannot but skew the normal value upward, thereby making a finding of dumping, or a higher margin of dumping, more likely.[36]

On appeal, the Appellate Body (AB) upheld the conclusion of the panel, albeit for partially different reasons.

In our view, the duties of investigating authorities, under Article 2.1 of the ADA, are precisely the same, whether the sales price is higher or lower than the 'ordinary course' price, and irrespective of the reason why the transaction is not 'in the ordinary course of trade'. Investigating authorities must exclude, from the calculation of normal value, all sales which are not made 'in the ordinary course of trade'. To include such sales in the calculation, whether the price is high or low, would distort what is defined as 'normal value'.

. . . Although . . . the ADA affords WTO Members discretion to determine how to ensure that normal value is not distorted through the inclusion of sales that are not 'in the ordinary course of trade', that discretion is not without limits. In particular, the discretion must be exercised in an even-handed way that is fair to all parties affected by an anti-dumping investigation. If a Member elects to adopt general rules to prevent distortion of normal value through sales between affiliates, those rules must reflect,

---

[36] *United States–Hot Rolled Steel from Japan*, Panel, para 7.112.

even-handedly, the fact that both high and low-priced sales between affiliates might not be 'in the ordinary course of trade'.[37]

Thus, both the panel and the AB rejected the 99.5 per cent test because it was one-sided and not even-handed.[38]

Assuming that authorities do apply an appropriate test for determining whether sales to related parties in the domestic market are in the ordinary course of trade and find, on the basis of the application of the test, that this is *not* the case, the consequence of this finding will be that they may then conclude that the domestic sales *to* the related parties are not in the ordinary course of trade. However, on what basis should they then determine normal value? The obvious answer might appear to be: on the basis of domestic sales to *unrelated* customers.[39] However, such sales may not exist, may be unrepresentative[40] or may lead to exclusion of a significant portion of domestic sales. Possibly for such reasons, some authorities will not in fact exclude sales *transactions* to related parties, but will rather ignore the prices charged between the related parties and instead move down the distribution chain and base normal value on the resale price by the related party to independent customers.

Producer	→	Related distributor	→	Independent customer
100		**130**		

Thus, in the example above, the intra-group price of 100 will be ignored and instead normal value will be based on the price of 130 charged by the related distributor to its independent customer. In most cases, this price will be higher because it is a level down the distribution chain. The independent customer will typically be a dealer or an end-user who pays a higher price than the distributor because the distributor should normally cover its costs as well as a reasonable profit from the difference between its purchase price and its resale price.

In fact, there is conceptually a certain symmetry with sales to related parties on the export side, where Article 2.3 *jo.* 2.4 ADA provide special rules for

---

[37] *United States–Hot Rolled Steel from Japan*, AB, paras 141–148. WorldTradeLaw.net *Dispute Settlement Commentary on US–Hot rolled steel*, p 19, checked 23 April 2005, considers that 'the fact that the Appellate Body did not rely on specific language in Article 2.1 as support for these statements suggests that this principle [of fundamental fairness] applies throughout' the ADA.

[38] Durling, 'Deference, But Only When Due: WTO Review of Anti-Dumping Measures' (2003) 6 Journal of International Economic Law 125, 135.

[39] Czako, Human and Miranda, *A Handbook on Anti-Dumping Investigations* (2003) 150.

[40] See section 1.3.1.3, below.

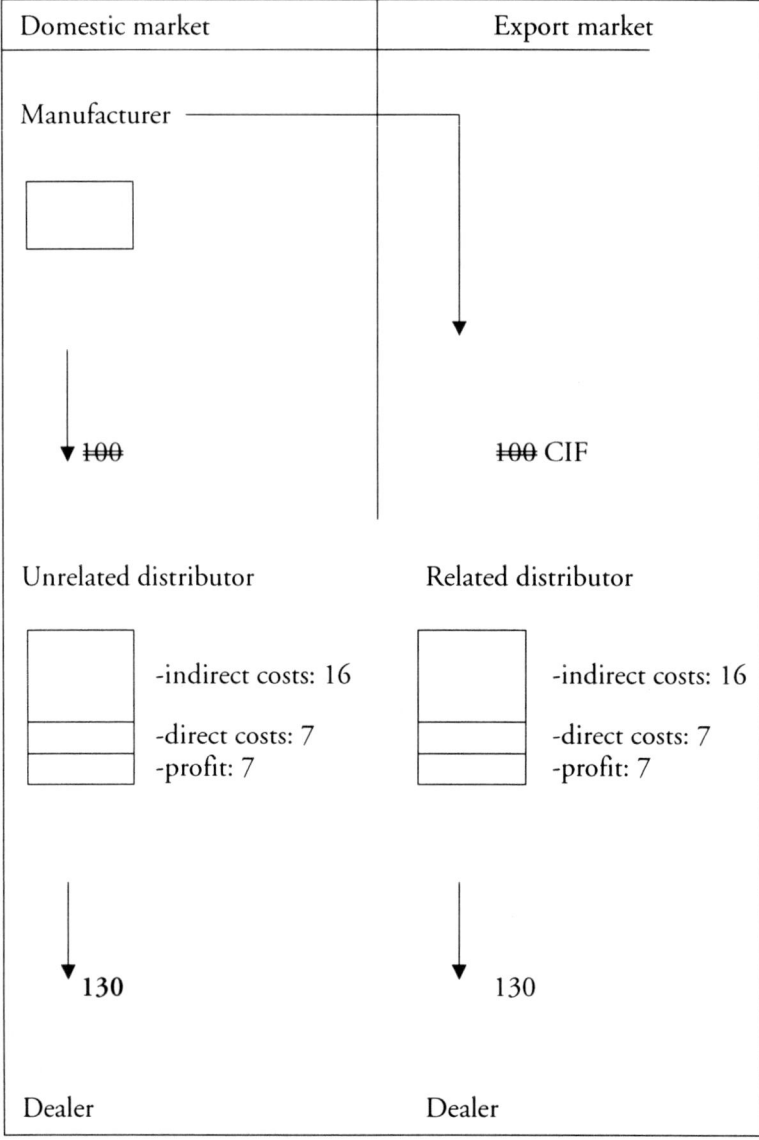

Domestic market	Export market

Manufacturer

▼ ~~100~~   ~~100~~ CIF

Unrelated distributor   Related distributor

-indirect costs: 16   -indirect costs: 16

-direct costs: 7   -direct costs: 7
-profit: 7   -profit: 7

▼ 130   ▼ 130

Dealer   Dealer

handling this situation through the constructed export price mechanism.[41] On the normal value side, however, a similar provision is lacking.

In *United States–Hot rolled steel*, the panel had determined that the ADA does not allow for the possibility of using such 'replacement sales' because the

---

[41] See section 1.2.2, above.

ADA is producer/exporter based and because a provision similar to Article 2.3 does not exist for the normal value side.[42] This reasoning was arguably too simplistic because it treated the producer and its related distributors as different entities although – not contestedly – they belong to the same corporate group. To treat group members as a *single economic entity* is in fact quite normal, not only for dumping, but also for other purposes including accounting,[43] taxation, corporate law, etc.

The AB did indeed overrule the panel by holding that the use of downstream domestic sales by the USDOC constituted a *permissible interpretation* of Article 2.1 ADA. However, it followed different reasoning:

> The text of Article 2.1 is...silent as to who the parties to relevant sales transactions should be. Thus, Article 2.1 does not expressly mandate that the sale be made by the exporter for whom a margin of dumping is being calculated. Nor does Article 2.1 expressly preclude that relevant sales transactions might be made downstream, between affiliates of the exporter and independent buyers. In our view, provided that all of the explicit conditions in Article 2.1 of the ADA are satisfied, the identity of the seller of the 'like product' is not a ground for precluding the use of a downstream sales transaction when calculating normal value. In short, we see no reason to read into Article 2.1 an additional condition that is not expressed.[44]

Like the panel, the AB therefore treated the producer and the related party as different entities, but considered that as Article 2.1 is silent as to who should sell the product on the domestic market, it was not necessary that the domestic seller be the same as the producer/exporter. It therefore proceeded from the same assumption (different parties) as the panel, but drew the opposite conclusion from the 'silence' of Article 2.1 as to the identity of the seller.

While one may have doubts about the correctness of this two-step approach (indeed, the single economic entity approach avoids this quagmire), the AB's subsequent reasoning makes it clear that the AB understood the underlying problems inherent in the use of downstream sales very well:

> ... The use of downstream sales prices to calculate normal value may affect the comparability of normal value and export price because, for instance, the downstream sales may have been made at a different level of trade from the export sales. Other factors may also affect the comparability of prices, such as...the costs and profits of the reseller. Thus, we believe that when investigating authorities decide to use downstream sales to independent buyers to calculate normal value, they come under a particular

---

[42] *United States–Hot Rolled Steel from Japan*, Panel, paras 7.114–7.118.
[43] Thus, for example, results of different group members will normally be consolidated for accounting purposes.   [44] *United States–Hot Rolled Steel from Japan*, AB, para 166.

duty to ensure the fairness of the comparison because it is more than likely that
downstream sales will contain additional price components which could distort the
comparison.[45]

... By making the allowances required under Article 2.4 of the ADA, the
investigating authorities should, in effect, arrive at a price which corresponds to the
'ex-factory' price of the 'like product' for the specific exporter concerned, as required by
that provision.[46]

Thus without explicitly saying so, the AB essentially instructs investigating
authorities that where they use domestic downstream sales, they must deduct
the same price components, notably the *reseller's costs and profit*, that are
deducted in a constructed export price situation, in order to arrive at an *ex
factory* domestic price. The AB thereby took the same line that a previous
GATT panel had taken in the – unadopted – panel report *EC–Audio tapes in
cassettes*.[47] While the Article 2.4 allowances will be discussed in more detail
below,[48] at this juncture the application of the AB's reasoning to the facts in the
flowchart opposite may indicate its importance.

On the export side, the starting point on the basis of Article 2.3 will be the
price charged by the related distributor to the unrelated dealer of 130. From
this price, the investigating authority *ex* Article 2.4 will then deduct both direct
(7) and indirect (16) costs as well a reasonable profit (eg 7) of the reseller in
order to arrive at a CIF price of 100. From this price, similarly *ex* Article 2.4,
ocean freight (eg 4), insurance (eg 0.2) and inland freight (eg 0.8) will then be
deducted to arrive at an *ex factory* export price of **95** (130 − 16 − 7 − 7 −
4 − 0.2 − 0.8 = 95).

The AB has now clarified that on the domestic side investigating authorities
may also use the price charged by the related distributor to the unrelated dealer
of 130, but they should then *ex* Article 2.4 *effectively* deduct the same price
components that they deduct on the export side, ie in the example above, both
direct (7) and indirect (16) costs as well as a reasonable profit (eg 7) of the
reseller and the inland freight paid by the producer (eg 0.8) in order to arrive at
an *ex factory* domestic price of 99.2 (130 − 16 − 7 − 7 − 0.8 = **99.2**). This
would lead to a dumping margin, expressed as a percentage of the CIF price, of:
99.2 − 95 = 4.2 / 100 = **4.2%**, a result that most of us would consider fair
on the basis of the facts above.

---

[45] *United States–Hot Rolled Steel from Japan*, AB, para 168
[46] *United States–Hot Rolled Steel from Japan*, AB, para 170.
[47] *EC–Audio tapes in cassettes*, GATT panel report, paras 374 and 377.
[48] See section 1.4.1, below.

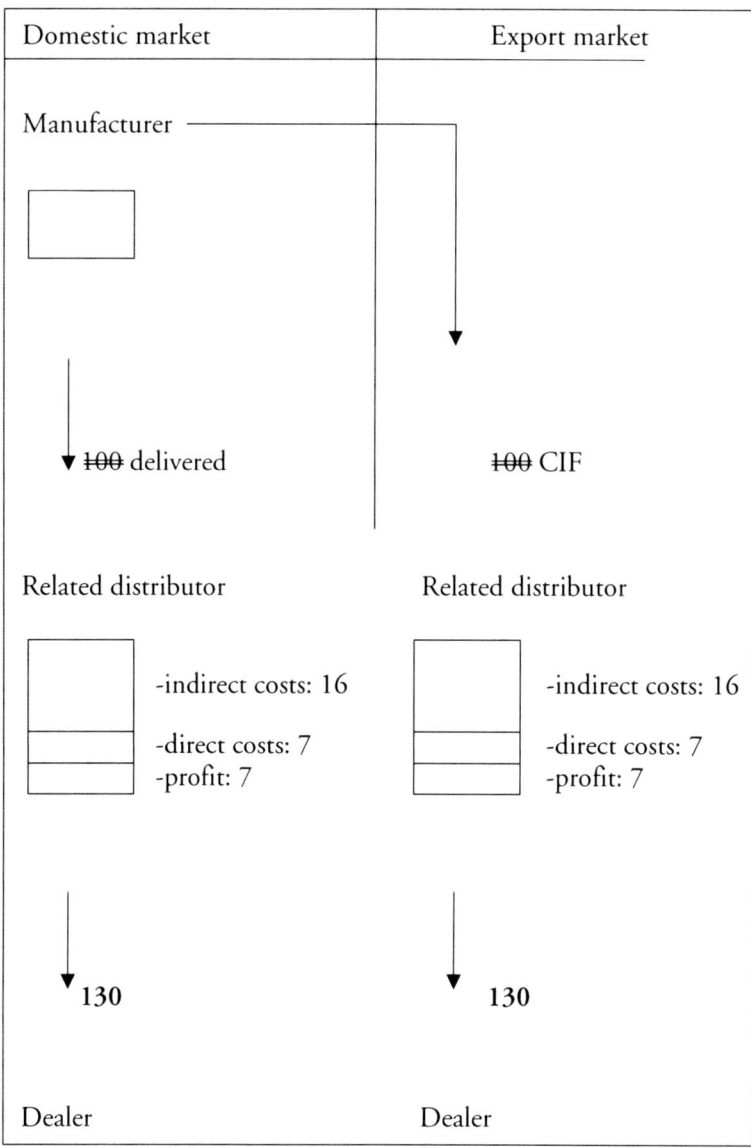

Prior to the AB's clarification, some investigating authorities would, on the domestic side, indeed have used the price charged by the related distributor to the unrelated dealer of 130, but they would then have deducted only direct selling expenses incurred by either the related distributor (7) or the producer (0.8) to arrive at a domestic price of **122.2** (130 − 7 − 0.8 = 122.2). In the example above, this would have resulted in a dumping margin, expressed as a percentage of the CIF export price, of: $122.2 - 95 = 27.2 / 100 = \mathbf{27.2\%}$. It may therefore be clear that the ruling of the AB is of significant practical importance.

1.3.1.3 Five per cent rule

Normal value obviously cannot be based on domestic sales where there are no domestic sales. Thus, if a producer sells only for export, his normal value will have to be determined on another basis. Similarly, if a producer sells frozen shrimp for exports (for example because of geographical distance between the markets), while he only sells fresh shrimp domestically, the two different types cannot be compared with each other and again export prices of frozen shrimp will have to be compared with a normal value for frozen shrimp, established on a different basis. These alternative bases are the subject of the next section. However, it is also possible that a producer does sell the like product on both markets, but that the quantity sold on the domestic market is relatively small. This happens often in countries with small home markets such as Singapore or Hong Kong.

Even in larger markets, however, it may happen frequently that while the like product is sold in sufficient quantities on both markets, certain types are sold more on the export market, while other types are sold more domestically, for example, because of differences in consumer tastes, technical specifications, etc. It may then occur that the exported types are sold only in small quantities on the domestic market.

Footnote 2 ADA
Sales of the like product destined for consumption in the domestic market of the exporting country shall normally be considered a sufficient quantity for the determination of the normal value if such sales constitute 5 per cent or more of the sales of the product under consideration to the importing Member, provided that a lower ratio should be acceptable where the evidence demonstrates that domestic sales at such lower ratio are nonetheless of sufficient magnitude to provide for a proper comparison.

Footnote 2 ADA provides as a general rule that domestic sales of the *like product* are sufficient to base normal value on if they account for 5 per cent or more of the sales of the product under consideration to the importing country market. This is often called the *five per cent* or *home market viability test*. It is important to note that footnote 2 clearly contemplates that this test be applied on a *global* basis by comparing sales of the like product in the domestic market with sales of the product under consideration in the importing market. Despite this clear admonition, many investigating authorities apply the five per cent test not only on a global basis, but also on a type-by-type, model-by-model basis.[49] This is therefore one of the areas where PCNs[50] have gained great importance.

Suppose, for example, that the product under consideration is farmed salmon, whether fresh or frozen, and that quantities sold in the two relevant markets are as follows:

Type	Export market	Domestic market
Frozen	199,000	3,000
Fresh	1,000	9,000
Total	200,000	12,000

In the example above, the global five per cent test is met because sales of the like product on the domestic market account for 6 per cent of export sales of the product under consideration (12,000 / 200,000 × 100 = **6%**). However, when applied to each type of salmon (fresh and frozen), the five per cent test is met only for the relatively small quantity of exported fresh salmon (9,000 / 1,000 × 100 = **900%**), but not for the far larger quantity of exported frozen salmon (3,000 / 199,000 × 100 = **1.51%**). Many investigating authorities will therefore consider that domestic sales of frozen salmon are not representative and refuse to base normal value on these domestic sales.

In this context, it is to be noted that administering authorities will typically apply *both* tests, with the global test operating as an overall benchmark test and the PCN-based test coming into play only in cases where the global test has been met. Needless to say, the more detailed the PCNs, the higher the likelihood that one or more exported PCNs are not sold in sufficient quantities on the domestic market, as a result of which recourse must be had to one of the alternative bases for calculating normal value for such PCNs. Much depends, therefore, on the level of classification details requested by the investigating authorities.

An example may clarify this. If the product under investigation is colour televisions from Korea, the investigating authorities might determine that colour televisions with different broadcasting standards constitute different types and require a different PCN for each. Such determination would almost certainly result in a finding that colour televisions with the NTSC broadcasting system

---

[49] Compare Didier, 'The WTO Anti-Dumping Code and EC practice' (2001) 35 Journal of World Trade 33, 36.   [50] See section 1.1.1, above.

sold in Korea cannot be compared with colour televisions exported to the EC with the PAL/SECAM broadcasting system, as a result of which *none* of the colour televisions sold in Korea would be viable.

However, an investigating authority could just as – if not more – plausibly determine that the differences in broadcasting standards constitute a minor physical difference, for which an allowance can be made on the basis of Article 2.4 ADA. Such a determination, in turn, might well lead to a finding that most exported television types have a viable domestic equivalent.

As the practice of sub-dividing the like product into PCNs is not discussed in the ADA, this is an area where investigating authorities have almost unfettered discretion. One could argue that the fact that the ADA is silent on the practice, coupled to repeated ADA references to the concepts of 'like product' and 'product under consideration', evidences that the ADA in fact does not allow such sub-divisions.

Such a broad claim, however, seems too blunt. A certain level of precision is required in order to effect a fair comparison between normal value and export price and the intermediate steps of sub-dividing the like product into PCNs and calculating margins *per PCN* before calculating a weighted average margin *per producer* are often a justifiable means to attain that objective.[51] Thus, rather than attacking the practice as such, it may be more appropriate to challenge case-specific, result-oriented PCNs devised by shrewd investigating authorities with a view to inflating dumping margins on the ground that unbiased and objective authorities would not have established such PCNs.

1.3.2 Normal Value: Based on Constructed Normal Value

Article 2.2 ADA provides that normal value may be based on third country exports or constructed normal value in three situations:

- no domestic sales of the like product in the ordinary course of trade;
- insufficient (less than 5 per cent) domestic sales of the like product; or
- particular market situation in the domestic market.

Article 2.2 ADA
When there are no sales of the like product in the ordinary course of trade in the domestic market of the exporting country or when, because of the particular market situation or the low volume of the sales in the domestic market of the exporting country,[52] such

---

[51] Compare the discussion by the AB in the context of inter-model zeroing in *United States–Softwood lumber from Canada II*, discussed below in section 1.4.3.1.

[52] Fn 2 in ADA: Sales of the like product destined for consumption in the domestic market of the exporting country shall normally be considered a sufficient quantity for the determination of the

sales do not permit a proper comparison, the margin of dumping shall be determined by comparison with a comparable price of the like product when exported to an appropriate third country, provided that this price is representative, or with the cost of production in the country of origin plus a reasonable amount for administrative, selling and general costs and for profits.

While the third situation does not occur very often, it happens frequently that investigating authorities determine that one of the first two situations exists. As we have seen above, such findings are facilitated by the practice of many investigating authorities to apply the tests both on a global basis and on a PCN-specific basis.

With respect to the third country exports alternative, Article 2.2 merely provides that export sales to an appropriate third country may be used, provided that the price is representative. Use of third country export sales is relatively rare, with only the United States using it on a regular basis. Many other investigating authorities prefer to use the second alternative, constructed normal value, without even checking third country exports' data.[53]

At least some investigating authorities have expressed a reluctance to use third country exports as the basis for normal value on the ground that, if exports are allegedly dumped into their market, it cannot be precluded that such exports are dumped into third country markets also. As the very definition of dumping depends in part on the price of the third country exports, one may wonder whether such simplistic reasoning passes muster. However, as the ADA leaves investigating authorities a full choice between the two methods, without even a motivation requirement, use of one rather than the other method seems difficult to challenge, unless one could make a case that the methodology used does not lead to a fair comparison.

Article 2.2 defines constructed normal value as the cost of production[54] in the country of origin plus a reasonable amount for administrative, selling and general costs and for profits. *Cost of production* in this sense is often called cost of manufacture and typically includes all the costs incurred in the factory. *Administrative, selling and general costs* are often called SGA and include both direct and indirect selling costs as well as administrative and other general costs

---

normal value if such sales constitute 5 per cent or more of the sales of the product under consideration to the importing member, provided that a lower ratio should be acceptable where the evidence demonstrates that domestic sales at such lower ratio are nonetheless of sufficient magnitude to provide for a proper comparison.

[53] Compare Durling and Nicely, *Understanding the WTO Anti-Dumping Agreement: Negotiating History and Subsequent Interpretation* (2002) 35.

[54] Art 2.2.1 clarifies that costs include both fixed and variable costs.

incurred after the product leaves the factory. If, for example, a company has a factory and a headquarters, the SGA costs will normally be the costs incurred by the headquarters.

It is important to bear in mind that the purpose of the constructed normal value is to construct a price of the *exported* product, as *if* it would have been sold on the domestic market. This has two consequences. First, as far as cost of production is concerned, one should calculate the cost of production of the exported product. If, for example, a car compact disc player (CCDP) is sold for export with an anti-theft device, while the domestically sold CCDP is sold without such a device,[55] the cost of production of the CCDP should include the cost of the anti-theft device. Similarly, if, for example, the country of export uses a duty drawback system, the cost of production of the exported product would normally be reported exclusive of import duties because the exported product does not include import duties.

Second, one should add to this cost of production of the exported product the SGA and profit on the domestic market. With regard to the reasonable profit requirement, explored in more detail below, it may be noted at this stage that WTO panels have repeatedly held that Article 2.2 does not provide an overarching reasonableness requirement and that where one of the methods provided in Article 2.2.2 is used in a legitimate manner, the result will *qualitate qua* be reasonable for purposes of Article 2.2.[56] Thus, in *EC–Bed linen*, the use of a profit margin of 18.6 per cent was not considered illegal as such.[57] In *Thailand–H-Beams*, a profit margin of 36.3 per cent was used.[58]

1.3.2.1 Cost Calculations and Allocations

With regard to the calculation of constructed normal values, Article 2.2.1.1 sets out two important general principles, applicable to both cost of manufacture and SGA:

- Costs must normally be *calculated* on the basis of records kept by the exporter or producer under investigation, provided that such records:
  - are in accordance with the generally accepted accounting principles (GAAP) of the exporting country; and
  - reasonably reflect the costs associated with the production and sale of the product under consideration;

---

[55] It is assumed that the domestically sold and the exported CCDP fall under the same PCN. If a different PCN has been assigned to each type, the problem does not arise.

[56] Compare *Thailand–H-Beams from Poland*, Panel, para 7.121; *EC–Bed linen from India*, Panel, para 6.96.   [57] *EC–Bed linen from India*, Panel, para 6.100.

[58] *Thailand–H-Beams from Poland*, Panel, paras 7.109 and 7.128.

- Authorities must consider all available evidence on the proper *allocation* of costs, including that which is made available by the exporter or producer in the course of the investigation, provided that such allocations have been historically utilized by the exporter or producer, in particular in relation to establishing appropriate amortization and depreciation periods and allowances for capital expenditures and other development costs.

Compared to a price-based normal value, constructed normal value calculations are often controversial because the ADA offers investigating authorities substantial leeway to calculate and allocate costs and profits and it happens frequently that the authorities do not agree with the calculations made by the exporters concerned. Not surprisingly, therefore, these issues have come up in a number of dispute settlement cases.

Article 2.2.1.1 ADA
For the purpose of paragraph 2, costs shall normally be calculated on the basis of records kept by the exporter or producer under investigation, provided, that such records are in accordance with the generally accepted accounting principles of the exporting country and reasonably reflect the costs associated with the production and sale of the product under consideration. Authorities shall consider all available evidence on the proper allocation of costs, including that which is made available by the exporter or producer in the course of the investigation provided that such allocations have been historically utilized by the exporter or producer, in particular in relation to establishing appropriate amortization and depreciation periods and allowances for capital expenditures and other development costs. Unless already reflected in the cost allocations under this sub-paragraph, costs shall be adjusted appropriately for those non-recurring items of cost which benefit future and/or current production, or for circumstances in which costs during the period of investigation are affected by start-up operations.[59]

In *United-States–DRAMS*, the panel ruled that the rules concerning GAAP and reflection of costs of production and sale *only* apply to records kept by the exporter or producer under investigation. The USDOC rejection of projections for future costs, prepared by an outside consultant on behalf of one of the Korean producers, therefore did not violate Article 2.2.1.1.[60]

United States–Softwood lumber II raised an interesting cost *allocation* issue. The panel had determined that Article 2.2.1.1 simply provided that investigating authorities must consider all available evidence on the proper allocation of

[59] Fn 6 in ADA: The adjustment made for start-up operations shall reflect the costs at the end of the start-up period or, if that period extends beyond the period of investigation, the most recent costs which can reasonably be taken into account by the authorities during the investigation.

[60] *United States–DRAMS from Korea*, Panel, para 6.66.

costs, including that made available by respondents, in so far as such allocations have been historically utilized by the exporter or producer[61] and that it therefore did not require the authorities to compare various possible allocation methods. On appeal, the AB considered this too categorical. The AB held that the term *consider* means that an investigating authority must 'reflect on' and 'weigh the merits of' all available evidence on the proper allocation of costs,[62] which may have to include a comparison between allocation methods:

... the parameters of the obligation to 'consider all available evidence' will vary case-by-case. It may well be that, in the light of the facts of a particular case, the requirement to 'consider all available evidence' may be satisfied by the investigating authority without comparing allocation methodologies or aspects thereof. However, in other instances – such as where there is compelling evidence available to the investigating authority that more than one allocation methodology potentially may be appropriate to ensure that there is a proper allocation of costs – the investigating authority may be required to 'reflect on' and 'weigh the merits of' evidence that relates to such alternative allocation methodologies in order to satisfy the requirement to 'consider all available evidence'. Thus, although ... Article 2.2.1.1 does not, as a general rule, require investigating authorities to compare allocation methodologies to assess their respective advantages and disadvantages in each and every case, there may be particular instances in which the investigating authority may be required to compare them ... [63]

In *Egypt–Steel rebar*, Turkey had claimed that the failure of the Egyptian authorities to offset short-term interest income against interest expenses violated Article 2.2.1.1.[64] The panel determined that it must consider the evidence on the record in order to decide whether there was evidence that short-term interest income was reasonably related to the cost of producing and selling rebar, as a result of which it should have been taken into account by the Egyptian authorities in the cost of production calculation.[65] The panel noted that the Turkish exporters had offset the interest income in their questionnaire responses, but that Turkey had not identified, nor had the panel found, any evidence that would demonstrate a relationship between the short-term interest income and the cost of producing rebar.[66] As a result, Turkey had not established a *prima facie* case.

---

61 *United States–Softwood lumber from Canada II*, Panel, para 7.237.
62 *United States–Softwood lumber from Canada II*, AB, para 133.
63 *United States–Softwood lumber from Canada II*, AB, paras 137–139.
64 *Egypt–Rebar from Turkey*, Panel, para 7.389.
65 *Egypt–Rebar from Turkey*, Panel, para 7.393.
66 *Egypt–Rebar from Turkey*, Panel, paras 7.422, 7.426.

1.3.2.2 SGA and Profits

One of the most complex – and arbitrary – aspects of constructed normal value calculations concerns the selection of appropriate SGA and profits. It is recalled that the objective of constructing a normal value is to calculate a price of the exported product, as if it has been sold on the domestic market.[67]

As the product *has* been exported, a *cost of manufacture* of the exported product will therefore exist, although the allocation of this cost, for example, to specific PCNs, may create controversy. On the other hand, it will happen often that the producer under investigation does not sell the like product or specific PCNs on the domestic market or that he does not sell in the ordinary course of trade. Indeed, these will tend to be the very reasons why normal value had to be constructed in the first place. The question then becomes which domestic SGA and profits to use.

Article 2.2.2 technically provides four possibilities:

- [Actual data pertaining to production and sales in the ordinary course of trade of the *like product* by the exporter or producer under investigation; or, when this is not possible:]
- the actual amounts incurred and realized by the exporter or producer in question in respect of production and sales in the domestic market of the country of origin of the *same general category of products*;
- the weighted average of the actual amounts incurred and realized by *other* exporters or producers subject to investigation in respect of production and sales of the *like product* in the domestic market of the country of origin;
- any other reasonable method, provided that the amount for profit so established shall not exceed the profit normally realized by *other* exporters or producers on sales of products of the *same general category* in the domestic market of the country of origin.

Article 2.2.2 ADA

For the purpose of paragraph 2, the amounts for administrative, selling and general costs and for profits shall be based on actual data pertaining to production and sales in the ordinary course of trade of the like product by the exporter or producer under investigation. When such amounts cannot be determined on this basis, the amounts may be determined on the basis of:

(i) the actual amounts incurred and realized by the exporter or producer in question in respect of production and sales in the domestic market of the country of origin of the same general category of products;

---

[67] *Thailand–H-Beams from Poland*, Panel, para 7.112.

(ii) the weighted average of the actual amounts incurred and realized by other exporters or producers subject to investigation in respect of production and sales of the like product in the domestic market of the country of origin;

(iii) any other reasonable method, provided that the amount for profit so established shall not exceed the profit normally realized by other exporters or producers on sales of products of the same general category in the domestic market of the country of origin.

Under the first method, the investigating authority sticks with the like product data of the producer/exporter concerned. This method *must* therefore be used where a producer has viable domestic sales in the ordinary course of trade of at least one exported PCN. The SGA and particularly the profit will then be based on the SGA incurred and the profit realized on the viable domestic sales in the ordinary course of trade of this PCN. It does not require much imagination to understand that the profit thus calculated may be very arbitrary.

In *EC–Malleable cast iron tube or pipe fittings*, the AB upheld the panel finding that SGA/profit calculations made per the Article 2.2.2 chapeau may include SGA/profits on low volume domestic sales.[68] The AB considered relevant in this regard that Article 2.2 separately identified low volume sales and sales not in the ordinary course of trade while the Article 2.2.2 chapeau explicitly excluded only the latter.[69]

Where the first method is impossible to use, typically because a producer does not have domestic sales in the ordinary course of trade of any exported PCNs, Article 2.2.2 ADA offers three alternative allocation methods. It is important to note that Article 2.2.2 does not establish a hierarchy between the three second-best methods in sub-paragraphs (i) to (iii), thereby leaving full discretion to the investigating authorities as to which method to use.[70]

The method in sub-paragraph (i) sticks with the producer under investigation, but authorizes use of his SGA incurred and profits realized with respect to production and sales in the domestic market of the *same general category of products*. The method in sub-paragraph (ii) departs from the data pertaining to the producer under investigation, but sticks with the like product in authorizing the use of SGA incurred and profits realized on the like product in the domestic market by *other* producers or exporters. It is noted here that use of this method raises a major due process issue because such data are typically confidential and

---

[68] *EC–Malleable cast iron tube or pipe fittings from Brazil*, AB, para 101.

[69] *EC–Malleable cast iron tube or pipe fittings from Brazil*, AB, para 98.

[70] Compare *Thailand–H-Beams from Poland*, Panel, para 7.123; *EC–Bed linen from India*, Panel, para 6.62; Koulen, 'The New Anti-Dumping Code Through its Negotiating History' in Bourgeois, Berrod and Gippini Fournier (eds), *The Uruguay Round Results* (1995) 151, 208.

consequently cannot be checked by the producer for which the method is used. Last, the sub-paragraph (iii) method authorizes any other reasonable method, provided that the amount for profit so established shall not exceed the profit normally realized by other exporters or producers on sales of products of the same general category in the domestic market of the country of origin.

General and administrative costs   General and administrative (G&A) costs tend to be costs that are incurred for the company as a whole. As a result, such costs are often allocated company-wide on the basis of a company's turnover. However, it may happen that companies take the position that certain general and/or administrative costs do not relate to domestic sales of the product concerned, as a result of which they should be excluded from the calculation. Investigating authorities may not always agree with such exclusion.

This happened, for example, in *United States–Softwood lumber II*. The panel started out by noting that general costs are costs affecting all or nearly all products manufactured by a company while administrative costs are costs concerning the management of the company's affairs and considered that both types of costs can only have a bearing on all the products manufactured by a company, although in varying degrees. Thus, the panel found that by their *nature*, G&A costs are costs that will normally affect all products produced or sold by a company.[71] Unless a producer/exporter can therefore demonstrate that the product under investigation does not benefit from a particular G&A cost item, an investigating authority is not precluded from attributing at least a portion of that cost to the product under investigation.[72]

On this basis, the panel reached the conclusion that an unbiased and objective investigating authority could treat legal settlement costs related to hardboard siding that was produced and sold between 1 and 18 years before the period of investigation and not related to the production process as such of hardboard siding, as a general expense.[73]

Same general category of products   Sub-paragraphs 2.2.2(i) and 2.2.2(iii) introduce the concept of *the same general category of products*, but do not define it. In many cases, this will not necessarily present a problem because the answer can often be found in the accounting records of the producer. If, for example, a company produces audio and video apparatus in two separate divisions and maintains divisional accounting records, the same general category of products in an investigation involving DVD players will be the

---

[71] *United States–Softwood lumber from Canada II*, Panel, para 7.263.
[72] *United States–Softwood lumber from Canada II*, Panel, para 7.267.
[73] *United States–Softwood lumber from Canada II*, Panel, para 7.267.

video apparatus division and not the audio apparatus division nor the company-wide range of products.

In *Thailand–H-Beams*, the panel considered that the intention of the sub-paragraphs is to obtain results that approximate as closely as possible the price of the like product in the ordinary course of trade in the domestic market of the exporting country.[74] It therefore rejected Polish arguments that a broader rather than a narrower definition is *required*[75] and hinted that in fact the opposite approach might be more appropriate:

. . . the use under subparagraph (i) of a narrower rather than a broader 'same general category of products' certainly is permitted. Indeed, the narrower the category, the fewer products other than the like product will be included in the category, and this would seem to be fully consistent with the goal of obtaining results that approximate as closely as possible the price of the like product in the ordinary course of trade in the domestic market of the exporting country.[76]

Given that nothing in the text of the ADA or anywhere else mandates the use of HS categories in the context of Article 2.2.2 (i), we do not find that Thailand was 'obligated' to use the HS category proposed by Poland.[77]

Ordinary course of trade   It is important to note that methods (i)–(iii) do not contain the *ordinary course of trade* limitation, contained in the primary method. In *EC–Bed linen from India*, the panel had ruled that while an authority is not obligated to exclude sales not in the ordinary course of trade for purposes of determining the profit rate under the subparagraphs of Article 2.2.2, neither is such exclusion prohibited. The panel based this finding on what it saw as a general principle in Article 2 that authorities may base their calculations of normal value only on sales made in the ordinary course of trade.[78] The panel therefore considered the exclusion by the EC of sales not in the ordinary course of trade from the determination of the profit amount to be used in the calculation of a constructed normal value to be a permissible interpretation of the ADA.[79]

On appeal by India, however, the AB overruled the panel on the basis of a textual interpretation of Article 2.2.2(ii). The AB first noted that Article 2.2.2(ii) refers to the weighted average of the actual amounts incurred and realized by other exporters or producers and did not make any exceptions or qualifications. Thus, there was no basis in Article 2.2.2(ii) for excluding some

---

[74] *Thailand–H-Beams from Poland*, Panel, para 7.112.
[75] *Thailand–H-Beams from Poland*, Panel, para 7.111.
[76] *Thailand–H-Beams from Poland*, Panel, para 7.113.
[77] *Thailand–H-Beams from Poland*, Panel, para 7.116.
[78] *EC–Bed linen from India*, Panel, para 6.85.
[79] *EC–Bed linen from India*, Panel, para 6.87.

amounts that were actually incurred or realized from the actual amounts incurred or realized and, as a result, an investigating authority is not allowed to exclude sales not made in the ordinary course of trade from the calculation of the weighted average under Article 2.2.2(ii).

The AB found support for this interpretation in the context of Article 2.2.2(ii), in particular, in the first sentence of the chapeau of Article 2.2.2. In contrast to Article 2.2.2(ii), the first sentence of the chapeau of Article 2.2.2 refers to actual data pertaining to production and sales in the ordinary course of trade. Thus, it was clear that sales not in the ordinary course of trade are to be excluded when calculating amounts for SGA and profits using the method set out in the chapeau of Article 2.2.2.

The exclusion in the chapeau led the AB to believe that, where there is no such explicit exclusion elsewhere in the same Article of the ADA, no exclusion should be implied. Reading into the text of Article 2.2.2(ii) a requirement provided for in the chapeau of Article 2.2.2 was not justified either by the text or by the context of Article 2.2.2(ii). The AB therefore reversed the panel finding that, in calculating the amount for profits under Article 2.2.2(ii) of the ADA, an investigating authority may exclude sales by other exporters or producers that are not made in the ordinary course of trade.[80]

Other exporters or producers/weighted average   Sub-paragraphs 2.2.2(ii) and 2.2.2(iii) authorize investigating authorities to use data of *other exporters or producers* for, respectively, the like product or the same general category of products. The question may therefore arise whether investigating authorities can resort to these methods where there is *only one* producer or exporter with such domestic sales, particularly in the case of option 2.2.2(ii) which not only uses the plural form, but also refers to weighted average amounts.

This situation arose in *EC–Bed linen* where only the Indian producer Bombay Dyeing had viable sales of the like product in India in the ordinary course of trade. The panel considered that the phrase 'other exporters or producers' as a general matter admits an understanding where the plural form includes the singular case and that in both common speech and legal texts, the ordinary meaning of the plural form may include the singular case. Thus, the plural form did not necessarily preclude resort to option (ii) where there is only one other producer or exporter of the like product.[81] The panel also found that the phrases 'weighted average' and 'other producers and exporters' did not constitute two separate requirements, but rather that the concept of weighted averaging came into play only when there is information from more than one

---

[80] *EC–Bed linen from India*, AB, paras 80–84.   [81] *EC–Bed linen from India*, Panel, para 6.70.

other producer or exporter available and that this was the reason why it had been put there.

On appeal, the AB rejected both points and considered the term 'weighted average' the key:

... First of all, and obviously, an 'average' of amounts for SG&A and profits cannot be calculated on the basis of data on SG&A and profits relating to only one exporter or producer. Moreover, the textual directive to 'weight' the average further supports this view because the 'average' which results from combining the data from different exporters or producers must reflect the relative importance of these different exporters or producers in the overall mean. In short, it is simply not possible to calculate the 'weighted average' relating to only one exporter or producer...

The requirement to calculate a 'weighted average' in Article 2.2.2(ii) is... the key to interpreting that provision. It is indispensable to the calculation method set forth in this provision, and, thus, it is indispensable to the entire provision – which deals only with the mechanics of that calculation. We disagree with the Panel that 'the concept of weighted averaging is relevant only when there is information from more than one other producer or exporter available to be considered'. We see no justification, textual or otherwise, for concluding that amounts for SG&A and profits are to be determined on the basis of the weighted average some of the time but not all of the time...

... the use of the phrase 'weighted average', combined with the use of the words 'amounts' and 'exporters or producers' in the plural in the text of Article 2.2.2(ii), clearly anticipates the use of data from more than one exporter or producer. We conclude that the method for calculating amounts for SG&A and profits set out in this provision can only be used if data relating to more than one other exporter or producer is available.[82]

Amounts for profits   The application of various calculation methods on a type-by-type basis may lead to findings of high profit margins. Thus, as we have seen above,[83] in *Thailand–H-Beams*, the Thai authorities used a profit margin of 36.3 per cent and in *EC–Bed linen*, the EC authorities a profit margin of 18.6 per cent. Use of such high profit margins will often lead to findings of dumping. Not surprisingly, therefore, in both cases the argument was made that such high profit margins were not reasonable. However, both panels rejected this argument by juxtaposing the texts and the methods of sub-paragraphs 2.2.2(i) and 2.2.2(ii) on the one hand and sub-paragraph 2.2.2(iii) on the other hand.[84]

Whatever the argument about the 'reasonability' of a particular result – a 50% profit rate, for instance – if it is based on actual data and properly calculated, then that is the

---

[82] *EC–Bed linen from India*, AB, paras 72–77.   [83] See section 1.3.2.2, above.
[84] *Thailand–H-Beams from Poland*, Panel, paras 7.124–7.125; *EC–Bed linen from India*, Panel, paras 6.96–6.98.

reality. An important object and purpose of Article 2.2.2 is to base the calculation of the profit amount on actual data. Similarly, while the methods set out in paragraphs (i) and (ii) are derivatives of the chapeau methodology, where actual data are used as required and the calculation is correct, the results obtained themselves reflect objective reality. Thus, the use of actual data itself ensures that subjective judgments about the reasonability of the results do not affect the calculation of constructed normal value. No purpose would be served by testing the results obtained under the chapeau and sub-paragraphs (i) and (ii) against some arbitrary or subjective standard of reasonability.[85]

1.3.3 Normal Value: Country of Origin of Export?

It may happen that the country of origin and the country of export of an exported product are not the same. The question then arises whether normal value should be based on the domestic sales in the country of origin or in the country of export. Article 2.5 ADA sets out the principle that in such situations the export price shall *normally* be compared with the comparable price in the country of export.

2.5 In the case where products are not imported directly from the country of origin but are exported to the importing Member from an intermediate country, the price at which the products are sold from the country of export to the importing Member shall normally be compared with the comparable price in the country of export. However, comparison may be made with the price in the country of origin, if, for example, the products are merely trans-shipped through the country of export, or such products are not produced in the country of export, or there is no comparable price for them in the country of export.

This preference for country of export over country of origin is surprising because reliance on the price in the country of origin at first sight seems more appropriate in that this is the country where the last substantial process or transformation of the exported product took place. The country of export (in cases where it differs from the country of origin), on the other hand, will tend to depend mostly on logistical reasons. Typical examples of this might be shipments from Hong Kong of Chinese origin merchandise and shipments from Singapore of Malaysian or Indonesian origin merchandise.

However, Article 2.5 provides that the export price may be compared with the price in the country of origin if, for example, the exported products are merely trans-shipped through or not produced in the country of export or if there is no comparable price for them in the country of export. Thus, these

---

[85] *EC–Bed Linen*, Panel, para 6.99.

exceptions will take care of the most problematic situations. Furthermore, the use of the words 'normally' in the main rule and 'for example' in the exceptions indicates that even in other situations, the authorities may resort to prices in the country of origin. Suppose, for example, that some finishing operations take place in the country of export which are insufficient to confer origin and that the product concerned is produced and sold by others in the country of export. None of the three exceptions is then applicable and normal value could therefore be established on the basis of the prices in the country of export, even though this might not be the most appropriate basis. Arguably, however, the authorities even then could still decide to use prices in the country of origin because the exceptions given are merely illustrative.

It is noted that both the main rule and the exceptions only refer to the 'price' concept. Presumably, however, Article 2.5 also authorizes resort to constructed normal value in cases where there are no sales in the ordinary course of trade. Indeed, an unduly literal reading of the word 'price' might lead to situations where a normal value could not be established, for example in cases where the exported product is sold neither in the country of origin nor in the country of export.

1.3.4 Normal Value: Non-market Economies

Article 2.7 ADA provides that Article 2 is without prejudice to the second Supplementary Provision to paragraph 1 of Article VI in Annex I to GATT 1994. The second Supplementary Provision to Article VI:1 states that it is recognized that, in the case of imports from a country which has a complete or substantially complete monopoly of its trade and where all domestic prices are fixed by the State, special difficulties may exist in determining price comparability for the purposes of paragraph 1, and in such cases importing contracting parties may find it necessary to take into account the possibility that a strict comparison with domestic prices in such a country may not always be appropriate.

The second Supplementary Provision traditionally has been used by various authorities to ignore prices and costs in 'non-market economies' on the ground that they are unreliable because they are not set by market forces but by the State. Rather, therefore, these authorities would then use prices or costs in a market economy country as the basis for normal value in cases involving non-market economies (the so-called surrogate or analogue country concept).[86] A further consequence would be that producers in a

---

[86] Compare Czako, Human and Miranda, *A Handbook on Anti-Dumping Investigations* (2003) 35.

non-market economy might all be subjected to the same duty rate to avoid circumvention.

This blunt approach has been criticized on two basic grounds. First, it has been argued that there are very few countries which have a complete or substantially complete monopoly of their trade and where all domestic prices are fixed by the State; thus, the second Supplementary Provision should not be used against countries such as China, Vietnam, Ukraine and other economies in transition which have a vibrant and ever-increasing private sector. Second, the use of the surrogate country concept as such has often been criticized because it tends to lead to high dumping margins, among others, because the surrogate countries chosen may be at a different stage of economic development and because the only reason that producers in the surrogate countries have typically cooperated is to ensure that their non-market economy competitors receive a high anti-dumping duty.

In recognition of the fast changes occurring in many non-market economies, many WTO members have loosened their treatment of non-market economy producers in recent years. Countries that were long treated as non-market economies, such as Russia, are now treated as market economies by many WTO members for anti-dumping purposes. In addition, many WTO members acknowledge the existence of 'bubbles of capitalism' in non-market economies which may lead them to grant non-market economy producers individual duty rates or even to accept their domestic prices and/or costs for the determination of normal value.

1.4 Fair Comparison

Once export price and normal value have been determined on the basis of the rules described in the preceding sections, they must be compared with each other. It is recalled here that normally, as an intermediate step, these comparisons are made on a PCN-per-PCN basis.

Article 2.4, first sentence, sets out the overarching principle or 'generic rule'[87] that a *fair comparison* shall be made between the export price and the normal value. It has been observed that the pre-eminence of the explicit fair comparison requirement in the ADA was one of the major accomplishments of

---

[87] Koulen, 'The New Anti-Dumping Code Through its Negotiating History' in Bourgeois, Berrod and Gippini Fournier (eds), *The Uruguay Round Results* (1995) 151, 210.

the negotiations.[88] The AB has held that this sentence constitutes an obligation for the administering authorities:[89]

2.4 A fair comparison shall be made between the export price and the normal value. This comparison shall be made at the same level of trade, normally at the ex-factory level, and in respect of sales made at as nearly as possible the same time. Due allowance shall be made in each case, on its merits, for differences which affect price comparability, including differences in conditions and terms of sale, taxation, levels of trade, quantities, physical characteristics, and any other differences which are also demonstrated to affect price comparability.[90] In the cases referred to in paragraph 3, allowances for costs, including duties and taxes, incurred between importation and resale, and for profits accruing, should also be made. If in these cases price comparability has been affected, the authorities shall establish the normal value at a level of trade equivalent to the level of trade of the constructed export price, or shall make due allowance as warranted under this paragraph. The authorities shall indicate to the parties in question what information is necessary to ensure a fair comparison and shall not impose an unreasonable burden of proof on those parties.

1.4.1 Adjustments

Article 2.4, second sentence, concretizes the general fair comparison obligation by providing that the comparison must be made at the same level of trade, normally at the ex-factory level, and in respect of sales made at, as nearly as possible, the same time.

The export price and the normal value are essentially the gross prices that are found in the market, as evidenced by invoices and other relevant sales documents. However, these prices may be prices to distributors, wholesalers or end-users. In addition, various cost items may be included in the price. Thus, to give a simple example, a delivered price will normally be higher than an ex-warehouse price because the freight costs from the factory to the customer are borne by the producer and therefore included in the price. Such costs should therefore be deducted. In practice, most administering authorities will deduct all expenses included in the price from the moment the product leaves the factory in order to calculate the ex-factory price. Some authorities will also deduct packing costs. This process is sometimes called *netting back*.

---

[88] Holmer, Horlick and Stewart, 'Enacted and Rejected Amendments to the Anti-Dumping Law: In Implementation or Contravention of the Anti-Dumping Agreement' (1995) 29 The International Lawyer 483–511, at 497 (comment by Horlick).

[89] *United States–Hot Rolled Steel from Japan*, AB, para 180.

[90] Fn 7 in ADA: It is understood that some of the above factors may overlap, and authorities shall ensure that they do not duplicate adjustments that have been already made under this provision.

On the other hand, the requirement that the comparison must be made in respect of sales made at, as nearly as possible, the same time is often ignored as it is the practice of most authorities to calculate weighted averages during the investigation period, particularly where the volume of transactions is high. Thus, only in cases where the volume of export transactions is low, will administering authorities try to locate domestic sales made on or around the same date and use those as the basis or normal value, rather than an average of all domestic sales during the investigation period. In relatively small importing markets, such as New Zealand, such method may be more administratively convenient.

Article 2.4, third sentence, then requires due allowance to be made for all differences which affect price comparability. These include differences in conditions and terms of sale, taxation, levels of trade, quantities and physical characteristics.

1.4.1.1 Conditions and Terms of Sale

In *United States–Stainless steel plate in coils and stainless steel sheet and strip*, the panel held that the bad debt expense resulting from the failure of a customer to pay because of bankruptcy is not a condition or term of sale within the meaning of Article 2.4 for which adjustment may be made. The panel considered that the term 'conditions and terms of sale' refers to differences in the bundle of contractual rights and obligations arising from a sales agreement. Failure of a customer to pay constituted a breach of such conditions, rather than a condition as such.[91]

In *Argentina–Poultry*, Argentina claimed to have rejected an adjustment for *freight* costs claimed by one exporter on the ground that this exporter had reported its freight costs on an annualized basis, without supporting evidence. The panel considered, *inter alia*, that the questionnaire did not exclude reporting freight costs on such basis and that this was therefore insufficient reason to reject the adjustment.[92]

1.4.1.2 Physical Differences

In *Argentina–Ceramic floor tiles*, the question arose to what extent the authorities should proactively make an allowance for differences in physical characteristics. The panel in that case adopted a fairly high standard by considering that at a minimum the authorities have to *evaluate identified differences* in physical characteristics to see whether an adjustment is required to maintain price

---

[91] *United States–Stainless steel plate in coils and stainless steel sheet and strip from Korea*, Panel, para 6.75. [92] *Argentina–Poultry from Brazil*, Panel, para 7.236.

comparability and to ensure a fair comparison, and to adjust where necessary. The case record indicated that ceramic tiles can be distinguished on the basis of a number of characteristics, such as dimensions (length and width), colour, degree of processing (polished/unpolished), and quality, and that the price of the products differs as a function of these differences in physical characteristics. The authority had made an allowance for three types of physical differences, either directly (differences in size) or indirectly (by collecting data only for first-quality, unpolished tiles), but not for other important differences. The panel decided that an objective and unbiased evaluation of the facts of the case would have required the authority to make additional adjustments and, as a result, the authority acted inconsistently with Article 2.4 by failing to make adjustments for physical differences affecting price comparability.[93]

In *Argentina–Poultry*, the panel considered that a 9.09 per cent upward adjustment to the normal value to take into account physical differences between poultry sold in Brazil and poultry exported to Argentina was not justified by the information on the record.[94]

In *United States–Softwood lumber II*, the panel, faced with a claim for an allowance based on differences in dimension, seemed to shift the burden of proof from the authority to the party claiming the allowance. The panel agreed with previous panels that the authority must at least evaluate identified differences. However, it considered that Article 2.4 does *not* require that an adjustment be made automatically in all cases where a difference is found to exist, but only where – based on the merits of the case – that difference is *demonstrated* to affect price comparability. In the view of this panel, an interpretation that an adjustment would have to be made automatically where a difference in physical characteristics is found to exist would render the term 'which affect price comparability' nugatory.[95]

1.4.1.3 Any other Differences

Under Article 2.4, third sentence, due allowance must also be made for *any other* differences which are demonstrated to affect price comparability. The *Argentina–Ceramic floor tiles* panel ruled that this is an open-ended provision which places an obligation upon the administering authorities:[96]

. . . Article 2.4 expressly requires that 'allowances' be made for 'any other differences which are also demonstrated to affect price comparability'. There are, therefore, no

---

[93] *Argentina–Ceramic floor tiles from Italy*, Panel, paras 6.113–6.117.
[94] *Argentina–Poultry from Brazil*, Panel, para 7.260.
[95] *United States–Softwood lumber from Canada II*, Panel, para 7.165.
[96] *Argentina–Ceramic floor tiles from Italy*, Panel, para 6.113.

differences 'affect[ing] price comparability' which are precluded, as such, from being the object of an 'allowance'.

We would also emphasize that, under Article 2.4, the obligation to ensure a 'fair comparison' lies on the investigating authorities, and not the exporters. It is those authorities which, as part of their investigation, are charged with comparing normal value and export price and determining whether there is dumping of imports . . . [97]

1.4.1.4 Constructed Export Price

This has been discussed in section 1.2.2 above.

1.4.1.5 Burden of Proof

As regards the requirement in the last sentence of Article 2.4 that the authorities shall not impose an unreasonable burden of proof on interested parties, the *United States–Softwood lumber II* panel ruled that this requirement does not remove the burden from interested parties to constructively substantiate their claimed adjustments:

. . . the requirement in the last sentence of Article 2.4 that the authorities 'shall not impose an unreasonable burden of proof' on interested parties does not remove the burden from interested parties to substantiate their assertions concerning claimed adjustments.[98]

The panel further considered that the provision does not impose on investigating authorities any particular method for examining whether any given difference affects price comparability.[99]

1.4.2 Currency Conversions

Export prices are often expressed in currencies such as US dollars or euros while normal value is typically expressed in the local currency of the exporters. Thus, one of the two has to be converted in order to compare the export price with the normal value. Many authorities will convert the currency of export into the local currency of the exporting country.

Article 2.4.1 of the ADA contains rules on currency conversions,[100] but does not address this specific issue, thereby leaving discretion to the authorities.

Some authorities will provide a list of average exchange rates during the investigation period in (an annex to) the questionnaire which interested parties are then requested to use. While this may facilitate the workload, Article 2.4.1

---

[97] *United States–Hot Rolled Steel from Japan*, AB, paras 177–180.
[98] *United States–Softwood lumber from Canada II*, Panel, para 7.167.
[99] *United States–Softwood lumber from Canada II*, Panel, para 7.167.
[100] See Czako, Human and Miranda, *A Handbook on Anti-Dumping Investigations* (2003) 146–148 for more detail.

does require currency conversions to be made on the basis of the exchange rate prevailing on the date of sale. Interested parties therefore have the right to use such exchange rates rather than the average exchange rate provided in the questionnaire, if they so prefer:

2.4.1 When the comparison under paragraph 4 requires a conversion of currencies, such conversion should be made using the rate of exchange on the date of sale,[101] provided that when a sale of foreign currency on forward markets is directly linked to the export sale involved, the rate of exchange in the forward sale shall be used. Fluctuations in exchange rates shall be ignored and in an investigation the authorities shall allow exporters at least 60 days to have adjusted their export prices to reflect sustained movements in exchange rates during the period of investigation.

Article 2.4.1 provides rules for two special situations:

- First, if a sale in a foreign currency on forward markets (hedging) is shown to be directly rated to the export sale involved, then the exchange rate in the forward sale must be used; and
- Second, exchange rates fluctuations are to be ignored and exporters must be given 60 days in which to adjust their export prices to reflect sustained currency movements.[102]

1.4.2.1 Local L/C Sales

In anti-dumping cases involving Korea, authorities may encounter the phenomenon of so-called local L/C sales. These are domestic sales of the like product, made by letter of credit and expressed in US dollars. The like product thus sold will be processed into another product which will eventually be exported. The reason why this special sales channel exists is related to the Korean duty drawback system. In *United States–Stainless steel plate in coils and stainless steel sheet and strip*, the USDOC had converted the local L/C sales first into Korean Won and then back again into US dollars. The panel ruled that the United States thereby had acted inconsistently with Article 2.4.1 by performing a currency conversion that was not *required*.[103]

1.4.2.2 Date of Sale

Footnote 8 to Article 2.4.1 ADA provides that the date of sale would normally be the date of contract, purchase order, order confirmation, or invoice,

---

[101] Fn 8 in ADA: Normally, the date of sale would be the date of contract, purchase order, order confirmation, or invoice, whichever establishes the material terms of sale.

[102] Horlick and Shea, 'The World Trade Organization Anti-Dumping Agreement' (1995) 29 Journal of World Trade, 5, 25.

[103] *United States–Stainless steel plate in coils and stainless steel sheet and strip from Korea*, Panel, para 7.1.

whichever establishes the material terms of sale. While technically relevant only for determining the date of sales for currency conversion purposes, the footnote effectively provides a definition of what constitutes a sale.

This definition is sometimes also used by authorities in order to determine whether specific sales transactions fall inside or outside the investigation period. Suppose, for example, that the investigation period is the calendar year 2005 and that an export sale is invoiced 23 December 2005. Although this sale would probably arrive in the importing country market only in the course of 2006, arguably it should nevertheless be reported in the questionnaire response and used in the calculation because it was invoiced and thus sold during the investigation period.

1.4.3 Comparison Methods: Zeroing

Once all costs included in the price and incurred from the moment the product left the factory are deducted from both export price and normal value and various other adjustments, such as level of trade and physical differences, have been made, two sets of ex-factory prices remain: a set of export prices and a set of domestic prices. At first sight, these sets of prices can be compared in two obvious ways. The following simplified example may clarify this:

Weighted average to weighted average and transaction to transaction comparisons

Suppose four transactions of equal weight are sold in the domestic and the export market as follows:

	Domestic	Export
(1) 1 June	50	50
(2) 10 June	100	100
(3) 15 June	150	150
(4) 20 June	200	200

Under the first method, one can calculate a weighted average domestic price and a weighted average export price and then compare these weighted averages with each other. This is called the *weighted average to weighted average* method. In the example above, both the weighted average domestic price (normal value) and the weighted average export price are

(Continued)

125 [(50 + 100 + 150 + 200)/4 = 125]. As a result, again *no dumping* would be found.

Under the second method, one can compare domestic prices and export prices sold on or around the same date. This is called the *transaction-to-transaction* method. Use of this method will lead to a finding of *no dumping* in the example because the domestic prices are identical to the export prices on the four dates that the sales take place.

Conceptually, however, a third – less obvious – comparison is possible: one in which one calculates a weighted average domestic price and then compares this price with prices of export transactions on a transaction by transaction basis. The following example shows the result of this third calculation method:

Comparison of weighted average normal value with export prices on a transaction-by-transaction basis

Suppose four transactions of equal weight are sold in the domestic and the export market as follows:

	Domestic	Export
(1) 1 June	50	50
(2) 10 June	100	100
(3) 15 June	150	150
(4) 20 June	200	200
WANV	125	

When the weighted average normal value of 125 is compared with the export prices on a transaction-by-transaction basis, the result becomes as follows:

	Domestic	Export	Dumping amount
(1) 1 June	125	50	+ 75
(2) 10 June	125	100	+ 25
(3) 15 June	125	150	− 25
(4) 20 June	125	200	− 75

(Continued)

Thus, as a result of this comparison, the dumping amount on the first transaction is 75 and the dumping amount on the second transaction is 25. On the other hand, the dumping amount on the third transaction is −25 (because the export price of 150 is 25 *higher* than the weighted average normal value of 125) and the dumping amount on the fourth transaction is −75 (because the export price of 200 is 75 *higher* than the weighted average normal value of 125). In the case of the third and the fourth transaction, there is therefore a *negative* dumping amount.

Under the third method, we now have found two transactions which are dumped and two transactions which are not, or negatively, dumped. The total dumping amount is 100 and the total non-dumped amount is also 100.

Prior to the entry into force of the Uruguay Round Anti-Dumping Agreement, some authorities would routinely use this third method to compare export prices with normal value and calculate dumping margins. They would then take the position that the third and the fourth transaction are not dumped and therefore attribute a zero dumping amount to these third and fourth transactions. This became known as the practice of *zeroing*.[104] The result of this was that non-dumped prices could not be used to offset dumped prices.

Comparison of weighted average normal value with export prices on a transaction-by-transaction basis: the magic of zeroing

	Domestic	Export	Dumping amount
(1) 1 June	125	50	75
(2) 10 June	125	100	25
(3) 15 June	125	150	− 25 = 0
(4) 20 June	125	200	− 75 = 0

The total dumping amount in the example above is 100 (25 on the first transaction and 75 on the second transaction). Assuming that the total CIF price of the four export transactions is 525, this will give a dumping margin of 100 / 525 × 100 = **19.05%**.

---

[104] For a well-written overview of GATT and the first WTO panel reports on zeroing (*EC–Bed linen from India* and *United States–Stainless steel plate in coils and stainless steel sheet and strip from Korea*), see Kim, 'Fair Price Comparison in the WTO Anti-Dumping Agreement: Recent WTO Panel Decisions Against the "Zeroing" Method' (2002) 36 Journal of World Trade 39–56.

Thus, in the example above, the first and the second obvious comparison methods will lead to a finding of no dumping, while the use of the third – less obvious – method, coupled to the practice of zeroing, will result in a dumping margin of over 19 per cent. The logic often presented for using such an asymmetrical comparison method is that it allows the authorities to focus on *targeted* dumping.[105] The analogy often invoked is that of getting a ticket for speeding: if you drive too fast and are ticketed for speeding, you cannot claim credit for the times that you drove within the speed limit.

It does not require much imagination to understand that use of this third method will make it easier to find dumping in most cases, particularly when compared with the first, weighted average to weighted average, method. In fact, if just one export transaction is lower-priced than the weighted average normal value, a finding of dumping will result from the use of the third method, even if all other export transactions are *higher-priced* than the weighted average normal value (if all export transactions are dumped, on the other hand, the first and the third method will yield the same result).

Admittedly, the above example is of a symmetrical perfection that will seldom be found in practice. In less symmetrically perfect 'real life' factual situations, the result of the third method will not always be worse than the use of the transaction-to-transaction method because the latter can lead to extremely arbitrary results. However, it will virtually always be worse than the use of the weighted average to weighted average method and, at best, will lead to an equal result in the rare cases where *all* export transactions are dumped. This is of course because the use of a weighted average to weighted average method automatically offsets positive and negative dumping.

A first GATT challenge to the practice of zeroing, brought in 1992 by Norway in *United States–Fresh and chilled Atlantic salmon*,[106] failed because the panel found that the weighted average normal value (NV) to transaction-by-transaction export price (EP) comparison was not inherently biased. In support, the panel noted that where all export transactions were priced below the average normal value, the bias would not occur.[107] While Norway had provided an example showing the bias, the panel found that there was no evidence that the example reflected the factual situation in the *Salmon* case.[108]

---

[105] Compare *United States–Fresh and chilled Atlantic salmon from Norway*, para 476, ADP/87, 30 November 1992.

[106] *United States–Fresh and chilled Atlantic salmon from Norway*, ADP/87, 30 November 1992.

[107] Compare *United States–Fresh and chilled Atlantic salmon from Norway*, para 482, ADP/87, 30 November 1992.

[108] Compare *United States–Fresh and chilled Atlantic salmon from Norway*, para 484, ADP/87, 30 November 1992.

Similarly, a second challenge brought by Japan against the EC in 1994, *EC–Audio tapes in cassettes*,[109] failed because Japan had argued that the weighted average NV to transaction-by-transaction EP comparison would *always* inflate dumping margins.[110] The GATT panel decided to take the transaction-to-transaction method as a benchmark and correctly concluded that the claim was mathematically incorrect because either method might lead to worse results than the other method, depending on the facts of the case:[111]

. . . the average to average benchmark proposed by Japan also failed in some instances accurately to reflect the results that would be obtained if the existence and extent of dumping were determined on a transaction-to-transaction basis. In fact, the Panel was aware of no averaging methodology that would not in some cases produce results that differed from those obtained through the determination of the extent of dumping on a transaction-to-transaction basis.

In light of this fact, and taking into account that Japan did not contend that the use of averaging was inconsistent with the Agreement per se, the Panel could not conclude that the EC's methodology as applied in this case was unfair on the grounds of arbitrariness.[112]

While Japan had submitted dumping margin calculations pertaining to the largest exporter, which showed that the use of a weighted average NV to a weighted average EP comparison would have led to a better result than the method used by the EC, the panel again considered that the transaction to transaction method was the appropriate benchmark, as Article 2 of the Tokyo Round Code did not require the averaging method.[113] Observers have pointed out that the panel's insistence on using the transaction-to-transaction method as the benchmark resulted in the panel effectively imposing an impossible burden of proof on the applicant as it will be impossible for any applicant to predict how the authorities would apply such method in a particular case.[114]

In a third GATT case, *EC–Cotton yarn*,[115] the panel rejected Brazil's claim that the EC should have made an adjustment[116] for distortions caused by zeroing in hyper-inflationary economies. The panel considered that zeroing took place

[109] *EC–Audio tapes in cassettes from Japan*, ADP/136, 28 April 1995.
[110] *EC–Audio tapes in cassettes from Japan*, paras 125–126, ADP/136, 28 April 1995.
[111] *EC–Audio tapes in cassettes from Japan*, para 354, ADP/136, 28 April 1995.
[112] *EC–Audio tapes in cassettes from Japan*, para 357, ADP/136, 28 April 1995.
[113] *EC–Audio tapes in cassettes from Japan*, para 358, ADP/136, 28 April 1995.
[114] Horlick and Clarke, 'Standards for Panels Reviewing Anti-Dumping Determinations under the GATT and WTO' in Petersman (ed), *International Trade Law and the GATT/WTO Dispute Settlement System* (1997) 313, 321–322.
[115] *EC–Imposition of anti-dumping duties on imports of cotton yarn from Brazil*, ADP/137, 485–486, 4 July 1995.   [116] See section 1.4.1, above.

only *after* adjustments had already been made.[117] However, the battle between
users of the anti-dumping instrument and its victims did not end there. In the
then-ongoing Uruguay Round negotiations, a push to limit the use of the third
method resulted in the following compromise Article 2.4.2:

2.4.2 Subject to the provisions governing fair comparison in paragraph 4, the existence
of margins of dumping during the investigation phase shall normally be established on
the basis of a comparison of a weighted average normal value with a weighted average
of prices of all comparable export transactions or by a comparison of normal value and
export prices on a transaction-to-transaction basis. A normal value established on a
weighted average basis may be compared to prices of individual export transactions if
the authorities find a pattern of export prices which differ significantly among different purchasers, regions or time periods, and if an explanation is provided as to why
such differences cannot be taken into account appropriately by the use of a weighted
average-to-weighted average or transaction-to-transaction comparison.

Thus, the weighted average to weighted average or transaction-to-transaction
methods became the preferred methods. The third method may be resorted to
only if the authority finds a pattern of export prices, which differs significantly
among different purchasers, regions or time periods and if the authority
provides an explanation as to why such differences cannot be taken into
account appropriately by the use of one of the preferred methods. This
compromise solution therefore allows the authorities to counter three forms of
hidden[118] or *targeted dumping* (purchaser; region; time period).[119]

It is emphasized that Article 2.4.2 contains the phrase 'during the investigation phase'. It is therefore possible that the obligation does not apply in the
context of reviews, including the duty assessment reviews that the USDOC
conducts annually. This issue is currently pending in the case *United States–Laws,
regulations and methodology for calculating dumping margins* ("*zeroing*"),
brought by the EC.[120]

---

[117] *EC–Imposition of anti-dumping duties on imports of cotton yarn from Brazil*, para 501, ADP/137,
4 July 1995.

[118] Horlick and Shea, 'The World Trade Organization Anti-Dumping Agreement' (1995) 29
Journal of World Trade, 5.

[119] Compare Croome, *Reshaping the World Trading System* (1995) 305:

Curbs were imposed on comparing isolated export selling prices with average prices in the home market, unless evidence could be produced that the sellers were targeting particular regions, purchasers or
periods for dumping.

See also *EC–Bed linen from India*, AB, para 62.

[120] *United States–Laws, regulations and methodology for calculating dumping margins* ("*zeroing*"),
WT/DS294/8, 2 November 2004, Constitution of the Panel Established at the Request of the
European Communities.

1.4.3.1 Inter-model Zeroing

Virtually as soon as the Uruguay Round Anti-Dumping Agreement entered into force on 1 January 2005, some authorities started using a new type of zeroing, the so-called *inter-model zeroing* (as opposed to the *intra-model zeroing* that was used previously and which is arguably still allowed under the exceptional third method of Article 2.4.2).

It is recalled that when comparing export price and normal value, such comparisons are typically first made on a PCN-by-PCN basis, before the results of these PCN-based calculations are weighted to come up with a dumping margin for each cooperating exporter. Thus, in this intermediate step, a positive or negative dumping amount will have been calculated for each PCN. Using the inter-model zeroing concept, some authorities will then zero negatively dumped PCNs, thereby not allowing such non-dumped PCNs to offset positively dumped PCNs.

New kid on the block: inter-model zeroing

	Domestic	Export	Dumping amount
(1) Model A	1,250	500	750
(2) Model B	1,250	1,000	250
(3) Model C	1,250	1,500	− 250 = 0
(4) Model D	1,250	2,000	− 750 = 0

The total dumping amount in the example above is 1,000 (250 on model A and 750 on model B). The negatively dumped models C and D are zeroed. Assuming that the total CIF price of the four models is 5,250, this will give a dumping margin of 1,000 / 5,250 × 100 = **19.05%**.

As a result of inter-model zeroing, dumping will be found as soon as one model is dumped even if all other models are not dumped. Again, therefore, inter-model zeroing facilitates dumping findings.[121]

In 1999, India challenged the EC on inter-model zeroing in *EC–Bed linen*. The panel agreed with India that inter-model zeroing was not allowed under Article 2.4.2.[122] The panel started out by noting that in light of Article 2.1 of

---

[121] Compare Durling, 'Deference, But Only When Due: WTO Review of Anti-Dumping Measures' (2003) 6 Journal of International Economic Law 125, 136.

[122] See for a good discussion of the panel report, Kim, 'Fair Price Comparison in the WTO Anti-Dumping Agreement: Recent WTO Panel Decisions Against the "Zeroing" Method' (2002) 36

the ADA, the 'margins of dumping' established under Article 2.4.2 must relate to the product at issue. Thus, a margin of dumping can only be established for the product at issue, and not for individual transactions concerning that product, or discrete models of that product.[123]

The panel attached importance to the fact that Article 2.4.2 specifies that the weighted average normal value shall be compared with a weighted average of prices of *all* comparable export transactions. By counting as zero the results of comparisons showing a negative margin, the EC, in effect, changed the prices of the export transactions in those comparisons. The panel considered it impermissible to zero such negative margins in establishing the existence of dumping for the product under investigation, since this had the effect of changing the results of an otherwise proper comparison.[124]

The panel took pains to point out that it did not mean to suggest that Article 2.4.2 prohibits an investigating authority from undertaking multiple comparisons as such, ie the intermediate step.[125] (This view was echoed by subsequent panels in *United States–Stainless Steel*, *Argentina–Ceramic Tiles* and *United States-Softwood lumber II*.)

On appeal, the AB agreed with the findings of the panel:

By 'zeroing' the 'negative dumping margins', the European Communities . . . did not take fully into account the entirety of the prices of some export transactions, namely, those export transactions involving models of cotton-type bed linen where 'negative dumping margins' were found. Instead, the European Communities treated those export prices as if they were less than what they were. This, in turn, inflated the result from the calculation of the margin of dumping . . . Furthermore, we are also of the view that a comparison between export price and normal value that does not take fully into account the prices of all comparable export transactions – such as the practice of 'zeroing' at issue in this dispute – is not a 'fair comparison' between export price and normal value, as required by Article 2.4 and by Article 2.4.2.[126]

The AB also rejected the argument that inter-model zeroing should be allowed to offset *targeted model dumping*. In the view of the AB, Article 2.4.2, second sentence, ie the exceptional method, only allowed members to

Journal of World Trade 39–56. For criticism, see Greenwald, 'WTO Dispute Settlement: An Exercise in Trade Law Legislation' (2003) 6 Journal of International Economic Law 113, 118–120. But see Durling, 'Deference, But Only When Due: WTO Review of Anti-Dumping Measures' (2003) 6 Journal of International Economic Law 125, 136.

123 *EC–Bed linen from India*, Panel, para 6.114.
124 *EC–Bed linen from India*, Panel, para 6.115.
125 *EC–Bed linen from India*, Panel, para 6.117.
126 *EC–Bed linen from India*, AB, para 55.

address three kinds of targeted dumping: dumping that targets certain purchasers, certain regions or certain periods. Neither Article 2.4.2, second sentence, nor any other provision of the ADA referred to dumping targeted to certain models or types of the same product under investigation: had the drafters of the ADA intended to authorize members to respond to such kind of dumping, they would have done so explicitly in Article 2.4.2, second sentence.[127]

Last, the AB summarily rejected the argument of the EC that the panel had violated Article 17.6(ii) ADA by not considering inter-model zeroing a permissible interpretation:[128]

It appears clear to us from the emphatic and unqualified nature of this finding of inconsistency that the Panel did not view the interpretation given by the European Communities of Article 2.4.2 of the ADA as a 'permissible interpretation' within the meaning of Article 17.6(ii) of the ADA. Thus, the Panel was not faced with a choice among multiple 'permissible' interpretations which would have required it, under Article 17.6(ii), to give deference to the interpretation relied upon by the European Communities. Rather, the Panel was faced with a situation in which the interpretation relied upon by the European Communities was, to borrow a word from the European Communities, 'impermissible'. We do not share the view of the European Communities that the Panel failed to apply the standard of review set out in Article 17.6(ii) of the ADA.[129]

In rejecting the practice of inter-model zeroing, the AB had put much emphasis on the fact that dumping margins are established for the product under investigation. This had led some to conclude that the AB had prohibited the concept of multiple averaging as such. In *United States–Softwood lumber II*, the AB corrected this misperception:

We agree with the participants in this dispute that multiple averaging is permitted under Article 2.4.2 to establish the existence of margins of dumping for the product under investigation. We disagree with those who suggest that the Appellate Body Report in EC – Bed Linen is premised on an assumption that multiple averaging is prohibited. The issue of multiple averaging was not before the Appellate Body in EC – Bed Linen and the reasoning of the Appellate Body in that case should therefore not be read as prohibiting that practice. This is not to say that EC – Bed Linen is not relevant in this appeal. Indeed, there are a number of relevant findings to which we refer to

---

[127] *EC-Bed linen from India*, AB, para 62. [128] *EC–Bed linen from India*, AB, para 65.
[129] *EC–Bed linen from India*, AB, para 65. For criticism of the AB report on this point, see Tarullo, 'Paved with Good Intentions: The Dynamic Effects of WTO Review of Anti-Dumping Action' (2003) 2 World Trade Review 373, 377–378; Tarullo, 'The Hidden Costs of International Dispute Settlement: WTO Review of Domestic Anti-Dumping Decisions' (2002) Law and Policy in International Business 109, 132–136.

below. However, the Appellate Body did not rule on multiple averaging in that case and therefore it is incorrect to argue, as the United States does, that '[t]he agreement of both parties to this dispute and a unanimous Panel that Article 2.4.2 permits multiple comparisons is a fundamental departure from the premise' of the Appellate Body Report in EC – Bed Linen.[130]

In *EC–Malleable cast iron tube or pipe fittings*, the panel again rejected inter-model zeroing and considered irrelevant the EC assertion that the zeroing had had limited impact on the dumping margin (2.73 per cent).[131]

In *United States–Softwood lumber II*, Canada attacked inter-model zeroing applied by the USDOC. While two of the three panellists firmly rejected the practice, one panel member strongly disagreed in a dissenting opinion. On appeal, however, the AB summarily confirmed its findings in *EC–Bed linen* and paid no attention to the dissenting opinion:

Zeroing means, in effect, that at least in the case of some export transactions, the export prices are treated as if they were less than what they actually are. Zeroing, therefore, does not take into account the entirety of the prices of some export transactions, namely, the prices of export transactions in those sub-groups in which the weighted average normal value is less than the weighted average export price. Zeroing thus inflates the margin of dumping for the product as a whole.[132]

As the treatment of zeroing in WTO dispute settlement has created some controversy, [133] it is important to emphasize that thus far the AB has only ruled on the illegality of *inter-model* zeroing under the weighted average method in original investigations.[134] Although the AB used relatively broad language to condemn the zeroing practice in these three cases, it remains to be seen which position the AB will take with respect to:

- inter-model zeroing under the transaction-to-transaction method;
- (*intra*-model) zeroing under the exceptional weighted average normal value to transaction-by-transaction export price method;[135]

[130] *United States–Softwood lumber from Canada II*, AB, para 81.

[131] *EC–Malleable cast iron tube or pipe fittings from Brazil*, Panel, paras 7.216–7.219.

[132] *United States–Softwood lumber from Canada II*, AB, para 98.

[133] Compare WorldTradeLaw.net, *Dispute Settlement Commentary on United States–Final lumber AD determination*, p 13, checked on 13 April 2005.

[134] But see Kim, 'Fair Price Comparison in the WTO Anti-Dumping Agreement: Recent WTO Panel Decisions Against the "Zeroing" Method' (2002) 36 Journal of World Trade 39, 56:

If the reasoning applied by the Bed linen panel is broadly upheld, then the practice of forming sub-groups of transactions and assigning zero values to the margins for the sub-groups for which dumping margins were negative would also be found inconsistent with the WTO Anti-Dumping Agreement.

[135] If the AB were to reject zeroing under this third, exceptional method, the outcome of the third method would be identical to that of the weighted average to weighted average method.

- (inter-model) zeroing in interim and sunset reviews;[136] and
- (inter-model) zeroing US duty assessment reviews.

1.4.3.2 Multiple Averaging Periods

In *United States–Stainless steel plate in coils and stainless steel sheet and strip*, the USDOC had cut the investigation period which fell in the middle of the Asian financial crisis into two parts: a pre- and a post-Korean Won devaluation phase, based on a finding that the normal value in the latter phase, expressed in dollars, differed significantly from the normal value in the earlier phase of the investigation period and initially calculated separate dumping margins for the two periods.[137] The USDOC had then calculated one average dumping margin for the whole period, but in that process it had applied *zeroing* for the sub-periods where the average export price was higher than the average normal value. Korea had not attacked the zeroing[138] as such,[139] but rather had contested the appropriateness of sub-dividing the investigation period.

The panel considered that this sub-division was inconsistent with the requirement of Article 2.4.2 to compare a weighted average normal value with a weighted average of all comparable export transactions.[140] In light of the requirement that a comparison be made between sales made at as nearly as possible the same time, the panel considered that as a general matter the periods on the basis of which the weighted average normal value and the weighted average export price are calculated must be the same.[141]

The panel did not preclude that there might be factual circumstances where the use of multiple averaging periods could be appropriate in order to insure that comparability is not affected by differences in the timing of sales within the averaging periods in the home and export markets. This might be the case, for

---

The exceptional method then would have no meaning. Compare Durling and Nicely, *Understanding the WTO Anti-Dumping Agreement: Negotiating History and Subsequent Interpretation* (2002) 109:

. . . it was resolved [during the Uruguay Round negotiations] that the ability to make weighted average-to-transaction comparisons when export prices vary significantly would permit authorities to address the issue of targeted dumping – the practice meant to be avoided by zeroing.

[136] Compare Durling and Nicely, *Understanding the WTO Anti-Dumping Agreement: Negotiating History and Subsequent Interpretation* (2002) 109.

[137] *United States–Stainless steel plate in coils and stainless steel sheet and strip from Korea*, Panel, para 6.124.   [138] See section 1.4.3.1, above.

[139] Compare Kim, 'Fair Price Comparison in the WTO Anti-Dumping Agreement: Recent WTO Panel Decisions Against the "Zeroing" Method' (2002) 36 Journal of World Trade 39, 52–53.

[140] *United States–Stainless steel plate in coils and stainless steel sheet and strip from Korea*, Panel, para 7.3.

[141] *United States–Stainless steel plate in coils and stainless steel sheet and strip from Korea*, Panel, para 6.121.

example, where changes in normal value or export price during the course of the investigation period are combined with differences in the relative weights by volume within the investigation period of sales in the home market as compared to the export market. The use of weighted averages for the entire investigation period might then indicate the existence of a margin of dumping that did not reflect the situation at any given moment within the investigation period.[142] However, such considerations had not been an element in the decision of the USDOC.[143]

As we have seen above, the AB also ruled in the later *United States–Softwood lumber II* case that there is nothing wrong with multiple averaging as such, albeit in the context of inter-model zeroing.[144]

1.4.3.3 Sampling

In *Argentina–Poultry*, Argentina had compared the weighted average export price with a weighted average allegedly *statistical sample* of domestic sales transactions, even though the Brazilian exporters had reported all domestic sales transactions.[145] The panel considered Article 2.2.1 which contains the conditions under which domestic sales may be excluded (may be disregarded in determining normal value *only if . . .*) as relevant context and concluded that Argentina had violated Article 2.4.2 by failing to compare the weighted average export price with a proper weighted average normal value.[146]

---

[142] *United States–Stainless steel plate in coils and stainless steel sheet and strip from Korea*, Panel, para 6.123.

[143] For criticism, see Tarullo, 'The Hidden Costs of International Dispute Settlement: WTO Review of Domestic Anti-Dumping Decisions' (2002) 34 Law and Policy in International Business 109, 142–143.   [144] *United States–Softwood lumber from Canada II*, AB, para 81.

[145] *Argentina–Poultry from Brazil*, Panel, para 7.268.

[146] *Argentina–Poultry from Brazil*, Panel, paras 7.272; 7.276.

Chapter 2

INJURY

Introduction

Article 3 and, indirectly, Articles 2.6 and 4 ADA cover the determination whether material injury has been caused to the domestic industry of the importing country producing the like product as a result of the dumped imports.

Conceptually, there are four – interrelated – steps that need to be performed in a proper injury determination:

- the definition of the like product;
- the definition of the domestic industry;

- the determination of material injury; and
- the establishment of a causal link between dumped imports and the material injury caused.

These topics are discussed in this chapter.

In addition, the authorities which apply the lesser duty rule will have to calculate injury margins.[1]

2.1 The Like Product

The like product is defined in Article 2.6 ADA and has been discussed in section 1.1 above. It is recalled here that, for injury purposes, the term like product refers to the product produced by the domestic industry and allegedly being injured by the dumped product. The like product definition is a key parameter in the injury determination and is closely linked to the definition of the domestic industry. It is with respect to the like product that the authorities have to find material injury as a result of dumped imports.

2.1.1 Narrowest Group or Range of Products

It may happen that separate economic data with respect to the like product are not available in all respects. This is more likely to occur in cases where the like product is narrowly defined. Suppose, for example, that the product under investigation is polyester film with a thickness of less than 6 microns. It is possible that the domestic producers do not distinguish between polyester film of less than and more than 6 microns in terms of the production process because all types of polyester film are manufactured on the same production lines.

Article 3.6 ADA allows the authorities to assess the effects of the dumped imports on the basis of an examination of the production of the narrowest group or range of products, including the like product, in cases where available data do not permit the separate identification of the production of the like product on the basis of such criteria as the production process, producers' sales and profits:

3.6 The effect of the dumped imports shall be assessed in relation to the domestic production of the like product when available data permit the separate identification of that production on the basis of such criteria as the production process, producers' sales and profits. If such separate identification of that production is not possible, the

---

[1] See section 3.2.8.1, below.

effects of the dumped imports shall be assessed by the examination of the production of the narrowest group or range of products, which includes the like product, for which the necessary information can be provided.

As Article 3.6 is a limited exception to the like product definition, it must be applied restrictively. Thus, in the example above, the authorities presumably could examine the narrowest group or range of polyester film with respect to the injury factors pertaining to the production process; however, if the producers do in fact have separate like product data with respect to other injury factors, presumably the authorities would have to limit their assessment with respect to such other injury factors to the like product data.

A decision to use the narrowest 'group or range of products' provision may have repercussions also for the definition of the domestic industry. Presumably for that reason, Article 4.4 notes that the provisions of Article 3.6 apply to Article 4 too.

In *Mexico–HFCS*, the question arose whether Article 3.6 could be used to base an injury determination on a portion of the domestic production, sold in a particular sector of the market (the industrial sector as opposed to the household sector). The panel ruled that nothing in Article 3.6 allows the authority to consider information concerning production of a product sub-group that is *narrower* than the like product produced by the domestic industry, even if the competition with the dumped imports in the particular market sector is most direct.[2] Therefore, this Article could not be invoked.[3]

2.2 The Domestic Industry

Article 4 ADA covers the substantive definition of the domestic industry. Its procedural counterpart is the standing determination of Article 5.4 ADA, discussed in more detail in section 3.1.3, below. As standing is determined in the pre-initiation phase, an interesting question is whether authorities which have determined that the applicants have standing, may subsequently limit the injury investigation to those applicants, for example, by only sending questionnaires to those applicants. Presumably this would not be allowed because an unbiased and objective injury analysis presupposes that the entire domestic industry is canvassed.[4] Limiting the investigation only to the complaining

---

[2] *Mexico–HFCS from the United States*, Panel, para 7.157.
[3] Compare Durling and Nicely, *Understanding the WTO Anti-Dumping Agreement: Negotiating History and Subsequent Interpretation* (2002) 209.
[4] Compare Czako, Human and Miranda, *A Handbook on Anti-Dumping Investigations* (2003) 49.

producers would make the injury assessment biased from the outset by restricting the pool of examined data:

Article 4: Definition of Domestic Industry

4.1 For the purposes of this Agreement, the term 'domestic industry' shall be interpreted as referring to the domestic producers as a whole of the like products or to those of them whose collective output of the products constitutes a major proportion of the total domestic production of those products, except that:

(i) when producers are related[5] to the exporters or importers or are themselves importers of the allegedly dumped product, the term 'domestic industry' may be interpreted as referring to the rest of the producers;

(ii) in exceptional circumstances the territory of a Member may, for the production in question, be divided into two or more competitive markets and the producers within each market may be regarded as a separate industry if (a) the producers within such market sell all or almost all of their production of the product in question in that market, and (b) the demand in that market is not to any substantial degree supplied by producers of the product in question located elsewhere in the territory. In such circumstances, injury may be found to exist even where a major portion of the total domestic industry is not injured, provided there is a concentration of dumped imports into such an isolated market and provided further that the dumped imports are causing injury to the producers of all or almost all of the production within such market.

4.2 When the domestic industry has been interpreted as referring to the producers in a certain area, i.e. a market as defined in paragraph 1 (ii), anti-dumping duties shall be levied[6] only on the products in question consigned for final consumption to that area. When the constitutional law of the importing Member does not permit the levying of anti-dumping duties on such a basis, the importing Member may levy the anti-dumping duties without limitation only if (a) the exporters shall have been given an opportunity to cease exporting at dumped prices to the area concerned or otherwise give assurances pursuant to Article 8 and adequate assurances in this regard have not been promptly given, and (b) such duties cannot be levied only on products of specific producers which supply the area in question.

4.3 Where two or more countries have reached under the provisions of paragraph 8(a) of Article XXIV of GATT 1994 such a level of integration that they have the

---

[5] Fn 11 in ADA: For the purpose of this paragraph, producers shall be deemed to be related to exporters or importers only if (a) one of them directly or indirectly controls the other; or (b) both of them are directly or indirectly controlled by a third person; or (c) together they directly or indirectly control a third person, provided that there are grounds for believing or suspecting that the effect of the relationship is such as to cause the producer concerned to behave differently from non-related producers. For the purpose of this paragraph, one shall be deemed to control another when the former is legally or operationally in a position to exercise restraint or direction over the latter.

[6] As used in this Agreement 'levy' shall mean the definitive or final legal assessment or collection of a duty or tax.

characteristics of a single, unified market, the industry in the entire area of integration shall be taken to be the domestic industry referred to in paragraph 1.

4.4 The provisions of paragraph 6 of Article 3 shall be applicable to this Article.

Article 4.1 lays down the principal rule that the domestic industry refers to *all* domestic producers of the like product or those of them accounting for *a major proportion* of its total domestic production. It is often pointed out that use of the term 'a major proportion' rather than 'the major proportion' signifies that the domestic industry does not have to represent more than 50 per cent of domestic production and, in fact, some authorities take the position that 25 per cent or more is sufficient to constitute a major proportion.

In *Argentina–Poultry*, the United States had argued as a third party that Article 4.1 merely provides a definition and does not impose a direct obligation on members. The panel brushed aside this argument by pointing out that the term 'shall' imposes an express obligation on members to interpret the term domestic industry in the specified manner.[7]

In *Argentina–Poultry*, the panel also ruled that by defining the 'domestic industry' as the poultry producers of 46 per cent of total domestic production, Argentina had not violated Article 4.1 ADA:

. . . the reference to *a* major proportion suggests that there may be more than one 'major proportion' for the purpose of defining 'domestic industry'. In the event of multiple 'major proportions', it is inconceivable that each individual 'major proportion' could – or must – exceed 50 per cent.[8]

The panel held that an interpretation that defines the domestic industry in terms of domestic producers of an important, serious or significant proportion of total domestic production is permissible and found support for its interpretation in the Spanish version of Article 4.1, which refers to producers representing 'una proporción importante' of domestic production. The panel also pointed out that Article 4.1 does not define the domestic industry in terms of producers of *the* major proportion of total domestic production, but rather refers to producers of *a* major proportion of total domestic production. If Article 4.1 had referred to *the* major proportion, the requirement would clearly have been to define the domestic industry as producers constituting more than 50 per cent of total domestic production.[9] However, this was not the case. In challenges brought by the EC[10] and Japan[11] against the *United States–1916*

---

[7] *Argentina–Poultry from Brazil*, Panel, paras 7.331, 7.338.
[8] *Argentina–Poultry from Brazil*, Panel, para 7.341.
[9] *Argentina–Poultry from Brazil*, Panel, para 7.341.
[10] *United States–1916 Act–EC*, Panel, para 6.214.
[11] *United States–1916 Act–Japan*, Panel, para 6.261.

Act, the panels found, among others, that the 1916 Act had violated Article 4.1 ADA because it did not require a minimum representation of a United States industry.

It is important to note that, as is the case for the like product definition, the definition of the domestic industry is a key variable that has consequences for the rest of the injury determination. In other words, once the domestic industry has been defined, that definition must be applied consistently throughout the rest of the injury determination, particularly when material injury and causation are assessed.

In *Mexico–HFCS*, for example, the panel found that the Mexican authority SECOFI had defined the domestic industry as the manufacturers of cane sugar. As a result, SECOFI was required to consider and determine the question of threat of material injury with respect to that industry.[12] As SECOFI's analysis and findings concerning market share and prices had based on information accounting for only 53 per cent of the production of the domestic industry (the industrial sector), and not on information regarding the domestic industry as a whole, it had acted inconsistently with Articles 3.1, 3.2 and 3.7 ADA.[13]

2.2.1 Sampling

In cases where the number of domestic producers is high, the authority may decide to resort to sampling. It is noteworthy that there is no explicit authorization for sampling of domestic producers in the ADA. Assuming that a representative sample is selected, however, there would not appear to be a problem with such domestic producers' sampling. The results found with respect to the sample may then be extrapolated to the non-sampled producers.

In *EC–Bed linen*, India had argued that in cases where a sample has been selected, the authority then should base its findings on the sample. However, the panel disagreed and considered that the situation of companies outside the *sample* may be taken into account:

. . . it would be anomalous to conclude that, because the European Communities chose to consider a sample of the domestic industry, it was required to close its eyes to and ignore other information available to it concerning the domestic industry it had defined. Such a conclusion would be inconsistent with the fundamental underlying principle that anti-dumping investigations should be fair and that investigating authorities should base their conclusions on an objective evaluation of the evidence. It is not possible to have an objective evaluation of the evidence if some of the evidence is

---

[12] *Mexico–HFCS from the United States*, Panel, para 7.148.
[13] *Mexico–HFCS from the United States*, Panel, para 7.153.

required to be ignored, even though it relates precisely to the issues to be resolved. Thus, the European Communities did not act inconsistently with Articles 3.1, 3.4, and 3.5 of the ADA by taking into account in its analysis information regarding the Community industry as a whole, including information pertaining to companies that were not included in the sample.[14]

2.2.2 Companies outside the Domestic Industry

In the same *EC–Bed linen*, case on the other hand, the panel held that once the domestic industry has been defined in a certain manner, the condition of producers outside the domestic industry definition is no longer relevant and may not be used to support an injury finding:

... information concerning companies that are not within the domestic industry is irrelevant to the evaluation of the 'relevant economic factors and indices having a bearing on the state of the industry' required under Article 3.4. This is true even though those companies may presently produce, or may have in the past produced, the like product, bed linen. Information concerning the Article 3.4 factors for companies outside the domestic industry provides no basis for conclusions about the impact of dumped imports on the domestic industry itself. If other present or former bed linen producers had been considered part of the domestic industry, the fact that some of them went out of business would be relevant to the evaluation of the impact of dumped imports on the domestic industry. But given that the European Communities defined the domestic industry as 35 producers of bed linen, information concerning other companies does not inform the evaluation of 'factors and indices having a bearing on the state of the industry' under Article 3.4 of the ADA, and thus cannot serve as the basis of findings regarding the impact of dumped imports on the domestic industry.[15]

2.2.3 Captive Production

In the steel sector, it often happens that intermediate products are both used internally for further processing and for sale on the open market. If, for example, the like product is hot-rolled coils, a portion of the hot-rolled coils is likely to be used internally for the production of cold-rolled products while the rest is sold to independent customers. The former is sometimes called the captive market as opposed to the open or merchant market. For injury purposes, the question then may arise whether the authorities should consider total production or only the portion of the production sold on the open market.

---

14 *EC–Bed linen from India*, Panel, para 6.181.
15 *EC–Bed linen from India*, Panel, para 6.182.

United States anti-dumping law contains a special provision on captive production which requires the US International Trade Commission (hereinafter: USITC) to *focus primarily* on the merchant market for the domestic like product in determining market share and factors affecting financial performance. In *United States–Hot-rolled steel*, Japan challenged both the legality of the captive production provision as such and the legality of the application of that provision by the USITC in the *Hot-rolled steel* case. The panel had found that both the provision and its application in the case were not inconsistent with the ADA. However, on appeal, the AB overruled the panel on the latter point.[16]

As it had done in other cases,[17] the AB started out by emphasizing the general obligation for authorities laid down in Article 3.1 ADA to conduct an *objective examination* on the basis of positive evidence:

The word 'objective'...indicates that the 'examination' process must conform to the dictates of good faith and fundamental fairness. In short, an objective examination requires that the domestic industry, and the effects of the dumped imports, be investigated in an unbiased manner, without favouring the interests of any interested party...in the investigation.[18]

...If an examination is to be 'objective', the identification, investigation and evaluation of the relevant factors must be even-handed.[19]

As long as this obligation is respected, however, a member might well require its investigating authorities to undertake an evaluation of particular parts, sectors or segments within a domestic industry. Indeed, such a sectoral analysis could be highly pertinent, from an economic perspective, in assessing the state of an industry as a whole:

...nothing in the ADA prevents the United States from directing its investigating authorities to evaluate the potential relevance of the structure of a domestic industry, and, in particular, the importance to that industry, as a whole, of the fact that the production of certain domestic producers is captively consumed, while the production of other domestic producers competes directly with imports in the merchant market. Indeed, we believe that it may be highly pertinent for investigating authorities to evaluate the relevance of the fact that a significant proportion of the domestic production of the like product is shielded from direct competition with imports, and that the part of the domestic industry that is most likely to be affected by the imports is limited to the merchant market.[20]

---

[16] Compare Durling, 'Deference, But Only When Due: WTO Review of Anti-Dumping Measures' (2003) 6 Journal of International Economic Law 125, 139.

[17] See section 2.3, below.   [18] *United States–Hot Rolled Steel from Japan*, AB, para 193.

[19] *United States–Hot Rolled Steel from Japan*, AB, para 196.

[20] *United States–Hot Rolled Steel from Japan*, AB, para 198.

The AB then noted that, under United States law, the required focus on the merchant market is not per se exclusive, and does not, by itself, exclude consideration of either the captive portion of the domestic industry or the domestic industry as a whole and that the same law also directs the USITC to examine the domestic industry as a whole, and make a final determination about the industry as a whole:[21]

...in an industry with significant captive production, a 'comparative' examination of each part of the domestic market – which 'juxtaposes' the merchant market and captive market – 'enhances' the ability of the investigating authorities...to make an appropriate determination about the state of the domestic industry as a whole.[22]

...

The captive production provision allows investigating authorities to take account of the need to ensure an 'objective examination', and of the need to evaluate, and make a determination concerning, the domestic industry as a whole. Accordingly, if and to the extent that it is interpreted in a manner consistent with our reasoning, we see no necessary inconsistency between the captive production provision, on its face, and the ADA.[23]

Thus, the AB concluded that there was nothing wrong with the law as such.

However, the objective examination requirement of Article 3.1 ADA requires that, if the authorities separately examine one part of the domestic industry (ie the merchant market), they must also separately examine, in a like or comparable manner, the other part of the industry (ie the captive market), or, in the alternative, provide a satisfactory explanation as to why it is not necessary to examine directly or specifically the other parts.[24]

While the ITC determination contained data and analysis thereof for the merchant market separately as well as for the overall market, it did not contain separate data and analysis thereof for the captive market, nor did it contain an explanation for the ITC's failure to do so.[25] As a result, the United States had acted inconsistently with Articles 3.1 and 3.4 ADA in the application of the captive production provision in the *United States–Hot-rolled steel* case.[26]

---

[21] *United States–Hot Rolled Steel from Japan*, AB, para 203
[22] *United States–Hot Rolled Steel from Japan*, AB, para 207
[23] *United States–Hot Rolled Steel from Japan*, AB, para 208
[24] *United States–Hot Rolled Steel from Japan*, AB, paras 204–205.
[25] Thus, the USITC analysis *was 'too one-sided'*, see Durling, 'Deference, But Only When Due: WTO Review of Anti-Dumping Measures' (2003) 6 Journal of International Economic Law 125, 139. [26] *United States–Hot Rolled Steel from Japan*, AB, para 215.

2.2.4 Related Parties

Article 4.1(i) authorizes the authorities to exclude domestic producers from the definition of the domestic industry if they are *related* to the exporters or importers or are themselves importers of the allegedly dumped product.

Footnote 11 ADA offers an effective definition of 'related parties' that, although technically applicable only for domestic industry definition purposes, is often used by authorities for dumping purposes as well,[27] including for the definition of related importers,[28] related traders[29] and related domestic distributors.[30]

Footnote 11 ADA

For the purpose of this paragraph, producers shall be deemed to be related to exporters or importers only if (a) one of them directly or indirectly controls the other; or (b) both of them are directly or indirectly controlled by a third person; or (c) together they directly or indirectly control a third person, provided that there are grounds for believing or suspecting that the effect of the relationship is such as to cause the producer concerned to behave differently from non-related producers. For the purpose of this paragraph, one shall be deemed to control another when the former is legally or operationally in a position to exercise restraint or direction over the latter.

Article 4.1(i) essentially offers the authorities complete discretion in deciding whether to include or exclude related domestic producers (or producers which are themselves importers).[31] Many authorities base their decision on analysis as to where the main economic interests of the related domestic producers lie. If, for example, the domestic producer is a subsidiary of a foreign-owned exporter under investigation for dumping which produces a few models in the importing country market, it will typically be excluded. If, on the other hand, the domestic producer imports a few models from the exporting country to complement its domestically-produced product gamma, it will normally be included.

It may be noted that in many cases the decision of the authorities will follow a decision as regards its composition by the domestic industry when it files the anti-dumping complaint. If, for example, colour television producers A, B and C bring a dumping complaint against imports of colour televisions from countries X, Y and Z, their complaint may well state that they have not included domestic producers x, y and z because these are related to producers located in the exporting countries.

---

[27] Compare Durling and Nicely, *Understanding the WTO Anti-Dumping Agreement: Negotiating History and Subsequent Interpretation* (2002) 246.   [28] See section 1.2.2, above.
[29] See section 1.2.1, above.   [30] See section 1.3.1.2, above.
[31] Compare Czako, Human and Miranda, *A Handbook on Anti-Dumping Investigations* (2003) 234.

2.2.5 Regional Industry

Article 4.1(ii) provides a second exception to the basic definition of the domestic industry in Article 4.1 by providing that the territory of a member may be divided into two or more competitive markets and the producers within each market may be regarded as a separate industry if (a) the producers within such market sell all or almost all of their production of the product in question in that market; and (b) the demand in that market is not to any substantial degree supplied by producers of the product in question located elsewhere in the territory.

In such circumstances, injury may be found to exist even where a major portion of the total domestic industry is not injured, provided there is a concentration of dumped imports into such an isolated market and provided further that the dumped imports are causing injury to the producers of all or almost all of the production within such market. This is often called the regional industry exception.

In terms of remedies, Article 4.2 provides that, when a regional industry has been found to exist, anti-dumping duties shall be levied[32] only on the products in question consigned for final consumption to that area. When the constitutional law of the importing member does not permit the levying of anti-dumping duties on such a basis (as will normally be the case), the importing member may levy the anti-dumping duties without limitation only if (a) the exporters shall have been given an opportunity to cease exporting at dumped prices to the area concerned or otherwise give assurances pursuant to Article 8 and adequate assurances in this regard have not been promptly given; and (b) such duties cannot be levied only on products of specific producers which supply the area in question.

The conditions for finding a regional industry are strict. As a result, such findings are relatively rare and tend to be confined to large importing countries markets and products such as cement which incur relatively high transportation costs.

2.3 Material Injury

Article 3 ADA is titled 'determination of injury' and provides the basic framework for making the injury determination. However, as discussed above, it is closely linked with the definition of the like product in Article 2.6 and the definition of the domestic industry, covered by Article 4.

---

[32] As used in this Agreement 'levy' shall mean the definitive or final legal assessment or collection of a duty or tax.

Footnote 9 ADA provides that the term 'injury' shall be taken to mean material injury to a domestic industry, threat of material injury to a domestic industry or material retardation of the establishment of such an industry and shall be interpreted in accordance with the provisions of this Article, unless otherwise specified. Threat of material injury is discussed separately in Article 3.7 ADA.[33] The notion of material retardation is not further discussed in the ADA and, in fact, findings of material retardation have been extremely rare in anti-dumping history.

Article 3.1 is a general introductory provision that has assumed much importance because of the AB's emphasizing time and again that an injury determination must be based on positive evidence and involve an objective examination:

3.1 A determination of injury for purposes of Article VI of GATT 1994 shall be based on positive evidence and involve an objective examination of both (a) the volume of the dumped imports and the effect of the dumped imports on prices in the domestic market for like products, and (b) the consequent impact of these imports on domestic producers of such products.

3.2 With regard to the volume of the dumped imports, the investigating authorities shall consider whether there has been a significant increase in dumped imports, either in absolute terms or relative to production or consumption in the importing Member. With regard to the effect of the dumped imports on prices, the investigating authorities shall consider whether there has been a significant price undercutting by the dumped imports as compared with the price of a like product of the importing Member, or whether the effect of such imports is otherwise to depress prices to a significant degree or prevent price increases, which otherwise would have occurred, to a significant degree. No one or several of these factors can necessarily give decisive guidance.

Particularly the *objective examination* requirement has often been used by the AB as an overarching benchmark for determining whether the authorities have conducted their investigation and/or reached their findings and conclusions in an even-handed manner. We have seen this above already when discussing the issue of captive production[34] and will encounter several other examples below:[35]

Article 3.1 is an overarching provision that sets forth a Member's fundamental, substantive obligation in this respect. Article 3.1 informs the more detailed obligations in succeeding paragraphs.[36]

---

[33] See section 2.5, below.   [34] See section 2.2.1, above.
[35] See sections 2.3.2 and 2.3.3, below.   [36] *Thailand–H-Beams from Poland*, AB, para 106.

These obligations are absolute. They provide for no exceptions, and they include no qualifications. They must be met by every investigating authority in every injury determination.[37]

In *Thailand–H-Beams*, the AB considered that the term *positive evidence* relates to the quality of the evidence that the authorities rely upon. The word *positive* indicates that the evidence must be of an '*affirmative, objective and verifiable character and that it must be credible*'.[38]

The requirement in Article 3.1(a) that the injury determination must involve an objective examination of the *volume* of the dumped imports and the effect of the dumped imports on *prices* in the domestic market is further elaborated in Article 3.2. With regard to the volume of dumped imports, Article 3.2 requires the authorities to *consider* whether there has been a *significant* increase in dumped imports. In *Thailand–H-Beams*, the panel held that the textual term 'consider' in Article 3.2 does not require an explicit finding or determination by the investigating authority as to whether the increase in dumped imports is significant. Thus, the word significant does not necessarily need to appear in the text of the relevant document in order for the requirements of this provision to be fulfilled. Nevertheless, the panel considered that it must be apparent in the relevant documents in the record that the investigating authority has given attention to and taken into account whether there has been a significant increase in dumped imports, in absolute or relative terms.[39] In *EC–Malleable cast iron tube or pipe fittings*, the AB considered that Article 3.2 does not require the authorities to analyse volume and price effects on a country-specific basis in multi-country proceedings.[40]

The Article 3.1(b) requirement that the injury determination must involve an objective examination of the consequent impact of the dumped imports on the domestic industry, in turn, is elaborated in Article 3.4. The *Argentina–Poultry* panel considered that Article 3.1(b) and Article 3.4 are so closely interrelated that a finding of violation of Article 3.4 also entails a finding of violation of Article 3.1(b).[41]

In *Mexico–Rice*, the panel considered that the use of a 'stale' investigation period[42] violated the Article 3.1 'positive evidence' obligation.[43] In the same

[37] *EC–Bed linen from India*, 21.5 AB, para 109.
[38] *Thailand–H-Beams from Poland*, AB, para 111. Compare *United States–Hot rolled steel*, AB, para 191. [39] *Thailand–H-Beams from Poland*, Panel, para 7.161.
[40] *EC–Malleable cast iron tube or pipe fittings from Brazil*, AB, para 111.
[41] *Argentina–Poultry from Brazil*, Panel, para 7.325.
[42] See section 2.3.3, below, for more detail.
[43] *Mexico–Rice from the United States*, Panel, paras 7.64–7.65.

case, the panel considered that Mexico's decision to limit the injury investigation period (IIP) to six-month periods of the years 1997–1999, despite having collected data for the full three years, violated the objective examination requirement of Article 3.1.[44]

Again in *Mexico–Rice*, the panel considered that the authorities violated Articles 3.1 and 3.2 by basing their analysis of the volume of dumped imports on biased assumptions:

... the volume analysis is not based on facts, but on assumption after assumption. The methodology of the applicant which the authority decided to use is based on the unsubstantiated assumption that rice sold below a certain price level must be long-grain white rice. Although the authority itself concludes that this was a flawed assumption, it decided to use this methodology. However, because the assumption apparently held true only for the investigated period of the year 1999, the authority had to make another unsubstantiated assumption, which was that in fact during the previous years the subject imports kept the same share in the total amount of imports of all types of rice from the United States. We recall that these assumptions were used in order to establish the trends in the volume of the imports of the subject product, long-grain white rice from the United States, without any distinction between the dumped and the non-dumped imports.

In parallel with the applicant's methodology for the determination of the volume trends of subject imports, the authority determined the trends in the volume of imports from the examined exporters. The authority first rejected the information provided by two of the three exporters examined, among which the Rice Company, the only company of these three for which a positive margin of dumping was established, and again based its conclusion as to their volume of subject imports on an unsubstantiated assumption, i.e. the assumption that all examined firms' export volumes showed a similar trend to that of the exporter which provided full three year volume information, Farmers Rice. We note that no margin of dumping was established with regard of exports from this company, Farmers Rice. On the basis of all these assumptions, the authority then determined the volume of dumped imports by subtracting all imports from the three examined exporters from the total amount of assumed subject imports, and adding the imports from the one examined company for which a margin for dumping was found, the Rice Company. It is clear that the authority did not base itself on positive evidence, but on, in our view unjustified, assumptions, and the authority has therefore failed to properly establish the facts. We do not wish to imply by this that an authority is never allowed to complete its analysis by drawing certain inferences, provided it offers a well reasoned explanation. However, we are of the view that the investigating authority did not do this in this case. Actually, it appears that in making

---

[44] *Mexico–Rice from the United States*, Panel, paras 7.81–7.82. See section 2.3.3, below, for more detail.

its assumptions, the investigating authority consistently chose to make assumptions which negatively affected the exporters' interests. In our view, the authority could just as readily have concluded the exact opposite from the facts on which it based its assumptions. For that reason as well, we consider that the Mexican authority failed to conduct an objective examination of the volume of the dumped imports.[45]

With regard to the Article 3.2 price effects of the dumped imports, the panel reached a similar conclusion.[46]

2.3.1 The Record

Injury determinations by their nature are largely based on confidential information that is pulled from the questionnaire responses of domestic producers, exporters and importers. Because of the confidentiality provisions in the ADA,[47] interested parties throughout the investigation will typically[48] be able to access only information classified as non-confidential by the interested parties and/or the importing country authorities. In most jurisdictions, this excludes all confidential submissions by interested parties as well as internal memoranda prepared by the authorities. The published provisional and definitive determinations then often provide summaries of the findings and conclusions of the authorities.

When members bring a WTO complaint against a measure, it may happen that the defending WTO member in the course of the dispute settlement proceeding before the panel invokes documentary evidence to defend the measure that was not seen by the interested parties during the administrative proceeding, but that supposedly was part of the administrative record.[49] The panel then will have to consider what weight to give to this evidence. In *Thailand–H-Beams*, the panel effectively decided that it could not take into account such type of evidence.

The panel ruled that the textual reference to 'positive evidence' and the requirement of an 'objective examination' in Article 3.1 require that the reasoning supporting the determination be formally or explicitly stated in documents in the record of the investigation to which interested parties (and/or their legal counsel) have access at least from the time of the final determination and that the factual basis relied upon by the authorities must be discernible from those documents.[50]

---

[45] *Mexico–Rice from the United States*, Panel, paras 7.111–7.112.

[46] *Mexico–Rice from the United States*, Panel, para 7.113.   [47] See section 3.2.5.6, below.

[48] The exceptions would appear to be the United States and Canada where a system of disclosure of confidential information under administrative protective order exists.

[49] See, for example, *Mexico–High-fructose corn syrup from the United States; Thailand–H-Beams from Poland*.   [50] *Thailand–H-Beams from Poland*, Panel, para 7.143.

The panel considered that Article 12 provides important context for Article 3 in indicating the significance attached by Members to allowing interested parties access to information on fact and law relevant to the final determination.[51] In the panel's view, the disclosed facts could not be considered to be 'properly established' if they are inaccurate.[52] This was particularly important in cases where virtually all of the data of record are confidential and may not be disclosed by the administering authority, and therefore are not capable of independent verification by interested parties. In such cases, the responsibility of the authorities to ensure the accuracy and clarity of the public summaries of data and statements of reasoning made available to the interested parties in the investigation is particularly significant.[53] As a result, the panel based its findings only on the documents in the record to which interested parties (could have) had access.

On appeal, however, the AB rejected the panel's approach and characterized the problem as one of due process instead. The AB held that the ordinary meaning of the terms positive evidence and objective examination does not require an authority to base an injury determination only upon evidence disclosed to, or discernible by, the parties to the investigation. An anti-dumping investigation involves the collection and assessment of both confidential and non-confidential information; an injury determination conducted pursuant to the provisions of Article 3 of the ADA must be based on the totality of that evidence. The AB saw nothing in Article 3.1 which limits the authorities to base an injury determination only upon non-confidential information.

The AB found contextual support for its interpretation of Article 3.1 in Articles 6 and 12 ADA, both of which in its view established important procedural and due process obligations. However, there was no justification for reading these obligations into the substantive provisions of Article 3.1. The AB took pains to point out that it did not mean to imply that the injury determination by the Thai authorities in this case necessarily met the requirements of Articles 6 and 12.[54]

On the basis of the AB ruling in this case, it is therefore clear that, while an injury determination may be based on confidential information that was not disclosed to interested parties in the course of the administrative proceeding, such a determination almost certainly would violate the procedural and due process requirements of Articles 6.2, 6.9 and 12.2.2.

[51] *Thailand–H-Beams from Poland*, Panel, para 7.151.
[52] *Thailand–H-Beams from Poland*, Panel, para 7.188.
[53] *Thailand–H-Beams from Poland*, Panel, para 7.189.
[54] *Thailand–H-Beams from Poland*, AB, paras 106–112.

2.3.2 Dumped Imports

Article 3.1 and the rest of Article 3 contain many references to the term 'dumped imports.' Thus, it seems evident that the basic requirement in Article 3 is that injury must be caused by *dumped* imports:

It is clear from the text of Article 3.1 that investigating authorities must ensure that a 'determination of injury' is made on the basis of 'positive evidence' and an 'objective examination' of the volume and effect of imports that are dumped – and to the exclusion of the volume and effect of imports that are not dumped.[55]

Many authorities took the position that this requirement is satisfied if they find that the imports from a country under investigation on average are dumped. In *EC–Bed linen*, India argued before the panel that it considered this interpretation incorrect. Rather, in India's view, only dumped *transactions* should be taken into account. The panel rejected this argument,[56] but in *obiter dictum* stated that, in its view, imports from producers which were found not to have dumped should be excluded from the 'dumped imports.'[57] The following example may clarify the significance of the panel's interpretation:

Dumped imports

Producer	Volume	Dumping margin
A	250	20%
B	250	0
C	250	10%
D	250	0

In the example above, the total volume of imports is 1,000, but producers B and D, each accounting for 250, were found not to have dumped. Therefore, the volume of dumped imports is 500 (and not 1,000).

On the basis of the view of the panel in the initial dispute settlement proceeding, the European authorities issued a new determination in which they excluded

[55] *EC–Bed linen from India*, 21.5 AB, para 111.
[56] *EC–Bed linen from India*, Panel, paras 6.136, 6.139–6.140.
[57] *EC–Bed linen from India*, Panel, para 6.138:

It is possible that a calculation conducted consistently with the ADA would lead to the conclusion that one or another Indian producer should be attributed a zero or de minimis margin of dumping. In such a case, the imports attributable to such a producer/exporter may not be considered as 'dumped' for purposes of injury analysis.

the imports from the producers which they had found not to have dumped. However, the authorities had resorted to *sampling* in the original administrative determination and took the position in the re-determination that they needed to deduct only the *absolute* amount of non-dumped imports from total Indian imports. In the view of India, on the other hand, the sample was a substitute for the whole and the result of the sample should therefore be *extrapolated* to the entire pool from which the sample had been constituted. The following example shows the difference between the two positions:

Dumped imports in case of sampling

Total volume of imports from the country concerned: 3,000

Sampled producer	Volume	Dumping margin
A	250	20%
B	250	0
C	250	10%
D	250	0

In the example above, the total volume of sampled imports is 1,000, but producers B and D, each accounting for 250, were found not to have dumped. Therefore, the volume of sampled dumped imports is 500.

Absolute approach: The non-dumped imports of 500 are to be deducted from the total imports of 3,000; as a result, dumped imports amount to 2,500.

Relative approach: The non-dumped imports of 500 represent 50% of the total sampled imports of 1,000; as a result 50% of the total imports of 3,000 is not dumped and only 1,500 is dumped.

India, among others for this reason, considered that the EC had failed to properly implement the panel report and brought an Article 21.5 case. The panel held that the absolute approach of the EC in the re-determination constituted a permissible interpretation of the ADA within the meaning of Article 17.6(ii) ADA. On appeal, however, the AB disagreed:

... neither paragraph 1 nor paragraph 2 of Article 3 – nor any other provision of the Anti-Dumping Agreement – sets forth a specific methodology that must be followed by investigating authorities when calculating the volume of dumped imports for purposes of determining injury. Still, whatever methodology investigating authorities choose for calculating the volume of 'dumped imports', that calculation and, ultimately, the determination of injury under Article 3, clearly must be made on the basis of 'positive evidence' and involve an 'objective examination'. These requirements are not ambiguous, and they do not 'admit of more than one permissible interpretation' within the meaning of the second sentence of Article 17.6(ii).[58]

The AB accepted that the EC's *absolute* approach was based on *positive evidence*,[59] but ruled that it did not constitute an *objective examination* because 'its result was predetermined by the methodology itself'. The AB found that under the EC approach, whenever the investigating authority decides to resort to sampling, all imports from all non-sampled producers will necessarily always be included in the volume of dumped imports, as long as any of the sampled producers is found to be dumping. This approach makes it more likely that the investigating authorities will determine that the domestic industry is injured, and, therefore, it could not be objective:[60]

… the European Communities' determination that all imports attributable to non-examined producers were dumped – even though the evidence from examined producers showed that producers accounting for 53 percent of imports attributed to examined producers were not dumping – did not lead to a result that was unbiased, even-handed, and fair. Therefore, the European Communities did not satisfy the requirements of paragraphs 1 and 2 of Article 3 to determine the volume of dumped imports on the basis of an examination that is 'objective'.[61]

In the circumstances of the case, the AB found it difficult to conceive of a determination based on positive evidence and objective examination that is made other than through some form of extrapolation of the evidence. This could be done, for example, by extrapolating from the import volumes attributed to sampled producers found to be dumping to the import volumes attributed to non-sampled producers. India's proposed *relative* approach might be one way of doing so, especially if the sampled producers constitute a *statistically valid sample* representative of all producers. Even if the sampled producers accounted instead for the *largest percentage of exports that could reasonably be investigated*, the evidence from the sampled producers could, nonetheless, qualify as part of the positive evidence that might serve as a basis for an objective examination of import volumes that can be attributed to the remaining non-sampled producers. However, there might also be other ways of making these calculations that satisfy the requirements of paragraphs 1 and 2 of Article 3.[62]

---

[58] *EC–Bed linen from India*, 21.5 AB, para 118.
[59] *EC–Bed linen from India*, 21.5 AB, para 130.
[60] *EC–Bed linen from India*, 21.5 AB, para 132.
[61] *EC–Bed linen from India*, 21.5 AB, para 133.
[62] *EC–Bed linen from India*, 21.5 AB, paras 137–139.

It has been noted[63] that the AB statements on the issue of the volume of *dumped imports* have two important implications for investigating authorities. First, where sampling has taken place, the authorities may no longer assume that all imports from non-sampled producers are dumped for injury purposes. Second, on a broader level, the implicit AB's finding that members may not include in the volume of dumped imports, imports from producers that are not found to be dumping,[64] strongly suggests that the imports from producers found not to have dumped must be excluded from the volume of dumped imports for injury purposes.

Indeed, in the *Argentina–Poultry* case, decided soon after the AB report came out, the panel explicitly ruled that non-dumped imports may not be included in the volume of dumped imports for injury purposes:[65]

On the basis of the ordinary meaning of the text, we find that the term 'dumped imports' refers to all imports attributable to producers or exporters for which a margin of dumping greater than de minimis has been calculated. The term 'dumped imports' excludes imports from producers/exporters found in the course of the investigation not to have dumped.[66]

2.3.3 Injury Investigation Period

A determination whether material injury has been caused by dumped imports requires an analysis over time. The choice of this time period is a crucial element of the injury determination as it determines the data that will form the basis for the assessment of the impact of dumping.[67] The ADA contains no rules on this important aspect. However, the Committee on Anti-Dumping Practices has adopted a recommendation[68] which calls on members to use a data collection period of at least three years and to include the dumping investigation period.[69] This period is normally called the injury investigation period or IIP.

In *Guatemala–Cement II*, the panel acknowledged that this adopted recommendation reflects the common practice of members, but had to conclude that it had no binding effect in the absence of rules in the ADA.

---

[63] WorldTradeLaw.net, *Dispute Settlement Commentary on EC–Bed linen*, 21.5 AB, pp 10–11, checked on 23 April 2005.   [64] *EC–Bed linen from India*, 21.5 AB, paras 111–113.

[65] WorldTradeLaw.net, *Dispute Settlement Commentary on EC–Bed linen*, 21.5 AB, p 11, checked on 23 April 2005.   [66] *Argentina–Poultry from Brazil*, Panel, para 7.303.

[67] Compare *Mexico–Rice from the United States*, Panel, para 7.79.

[68] Committee on Anti-Dumping Practices, *Recommendation concerning the periods of data collection for anti-dumping investigations*, G/ADP/6 (16 May 2000), reproduced in Annex 3.

[69] See chapter 1, Introduction, above.

As a result, the use of a one year period in that case did not as such violate the ADA:

it cannot be said a priori that the use of a one-year period of data collection would not be consistent with the requirement of Article 3.2 to consider whether there has been a significant increase in the volume of dumped imports in the circumstances of a particular case.[70]

In *Argentina–Poultry*, on the other hand, Argentina had examined the various Article 3.4 injury factors during different time periods. The panel considered that where the authorities examine different injury factors using different periods, there is a *prima facie* case that the authorities have failed to conduct an *objective examination* within the meaning of Article 3.1 ADA. While the *prima facie* case may be rebuttable if the authorities can show that they have objective grounds for using different periods (eg, because data for more recent periods is not available for certain injury factors), Argentina was unable to show any such grounds.[71] As a result, Argentina was found to have violated Article 3.1 by only examining 1999 data for certain injury factors.[72]

In the same case, Brazil had also claimed that Argentina had violated Article 3.5 ADA because the dumping IP ended in January 1999, while the IIP ended in June 1999. On this point, however, the panel found that neither the ADA itself nor the recommendation of the ADP prohibited the use of an IIP that exceeded the IP (as long as it included the IP).[73]

In *Mexico–Rice*, Mexico had used an IP covering the period from March to August 1999 and an IIP covering the period from March to August in the three years 1997 to 1999, despite the fact that the investigation was initiated on 11 December 2000. There was, then, a gap of 15 months between the end of the IP/IIP and the start of the investigation. The panel considered that the use of such a 'stale' investigation period violated the Article 3.1 'positive evidence' obligation and referred, among others, to the ADP recommendation in support of is finding.[74]

In the same case, the panel considered that Mexico's limitation of the IIP to cover only six-month periods for the years 1997–1999, despite having collected data for the full three years, violated the objective examination requirement of Article 3.1 ADA:

...in its examination of that data, it decided not to use half of the information gathered. The authority thus based its determination on data relating to six months of each of the

---

[70] *Guatemala–Cement from Mexico II*, Panel, para 8.266.
[71] *Argentina–Poultry from Brazil*, Panel, para 7.283.
[72] *Argentina–Poultry from Brazil*, Panel, para 7.285.
[73] *Argentina–Poultry from Brazil*, Panel, paras 7.287–7.288.
[74] *Mexico–Rice from the United States*, Panel, paras 7.64–7.65.

three years of the period of investigation, the months of March to August. In our view, and absent any proper justification for doing so, such an examination on the basis of an incomplete set of data cannot be objective, nor does the selective use of certain data for the injury analysis constitute a proper establishment of the facts on which to base the determination.

We wish to note in this respect that our ruling should not be read as to imply that there could never be any convincing and valid reasons for examining only parts of years. Mexico has not however presented any convincing arguments to this effect, whether in its investigation or in its arguments before us. Mexico's only argument is that it was necessary to examine only data relating to the six months from March to August because this was also the six month period chosen for the analysis of the existence of dumping. We see no a priori reason why a period of investigation on the injury analysis should be chosen to fit the period of investigation for the dumping analysis in case the latter period of investigation covers a period of less than 12 months. In our view, there is nothing in the ADA that would require such an approach, quite to the contrary. Mexico submits that in order to avoid distortions due to the differences in volume of imports, sales or production during the other six months, it used for its injury analysis a similar six month period. We do not find this to constitute a proper justification for ignoring half of the data concerning the domestic industry. In fact, it seems that what Mexico refers to as distortions are certain developments which occur in the remaining six months which perhaps undo part of the effect of the imports that entered the country during the six months that were examined. This is precisely the kind of information we consider it is necessary to examine in order for the determination to be that of an objective and unbiased investigating authority.[75]

2.3.4 Cumulation

Anti-dumping investigations often cover several exporting countries at the same time. A benchmark question for injury purposes then is whether injury should be assessed on a country-by-country basis or whether imports from the countries under investigation may be *cumulated*.

While the Tokyo Round Anti-Dumping Code did not contain any rules on this, the developed country users routinely cumulated in practice. The Uruguay Round ADA now authorizes cumulation where the authorities determine that the dumping margins are more than *de minimis*[76] and the volumes of imports from each country are not *negligible*[77] and the imported products compete with each other and with the like domestic product. Most authorities routinely cumulate where these conditions are fulfilled:

3.3 Where imports of a product from more than one country are simultaneously subject to anti-dumping investigations, the investigating authorities may cumulatively

---

[75] *Mexico–Rice from the United States*, Panel, paras 7.81–7.82.
[76] See section 3.2.2.1, below.   [77] See section 3.2.2.2, below.

assess the effects of such imports only if they determine that (a) the margin of dumping established in relation to the imports from each country is more than de minimis as defined in paragraph 8 of Article 5 and the volume of imports from each country is not negligible and (b) a cumulative assessment of the effects of the imports is appropriate in light of the conditions of competition between the imported products and the conditions of competition between the imported products and the like domestic product.

In *EC–Malleable cast iron tube or pipe fittings*, the AB rejected Brazilian claims challenging the EC cumulation of various countries in that case:

...by expressly providing for cumulation...the negotiators appear to have recognized that a domestic industry confronted with dumped imports originating from various countries may be injured by the cumulated effects of those imports and that those effects may not be adequately taken into account in a country-specific analysis...Consistent with the rationale behind cumulation, we consider that changes in import volumes from individual countries...are of little significance in determining whether injury is being caused to the domestic industry by the dumped imports as a whole.[78]

Thus, the AB implicitly recognized that even declining imports from one or more specific countries may still cause injury if cumulated in accordance with the provisions of Article 3.3.

In *United States–Corrosion-resistant carbon steel flat products*, the panel concluded that these conditions do not have to be satisfied separately in sunset reviews on the basis of the reference to 'investigations' in Article 3.3 as well as the cross-reference to Article 5.8. The panel found support for its view in the fact that, by contrast, nowhere else in Article 3 is the word 'investigation' mentioned.[79] In *United States–Oil country tubular goods*, the AB confirmed this interpretation.[80]

It may happen that authorities conduct anti-dumping and countervailing duty investigations against various countries at the same time. The question then arises whether the authorities may cumulate the dumped imports with the subsidized imports for injury assessment purposes. This is called cross-cumulation. As neither the ADA nor the ASCM contains provisions on cross-cumulation, it seems doubtful that this practice would be allowed.[81]

Cross-cumulation is to be distinguished from the situation where authorities initiate both anti-dumping *and* countervailing duty investigations against one or more specific countries at the same time. Although Article VI:5 GATT 1994

---

[78] *EC–Malleable cast iron tube or pipe fittings from Brazil*, AB, para 116.
[79] *United States–Corrosion-resistant carbon steel flat products from Japan*, Panel, paras 7.97–7.98.
[80] *United States–Oil country tubular goods from Argentina*, AB, para 285.
[81] Compare Lowenfeld, *International Economic Law* (2002) 268.

provides that no product of the territory of any contracting party imported into the territory of any other contracting party shall be subject to both anti-dumping and countervailing duties to compensate for the same situation of dumping or export subsidization, a similar provision designed to avoid overlap of material injury findings in such cases is lacking. Conceptually, however, authorities supposedly would need to establish material injury separately for the dumping and the countervailing duty investigation.

Similarly, the question may arise whether a product may be subjected to both anti-dumping or countervailing measures, on the one hand, and safeguard measures, on the other hand. Practice among WTO members is not uniform on this point, with some members taking the position that a serious injury finding in a safeguard case tends to be quantity-based while material injury in an anti-dumping/countervailing duty case tends to be price-based, as a result of which both types of measures may co-exist. Other members recognize that there may be overlap and will make an adjustment to take it into account.

2.3.5 The Article 3.4 Injury Factors

Articles 3.1(b) and 3.4 require the investigating authority to objectively examine the impact of the dumped imports on the domestic industry:

3.4 The examination of the impact of the dumped imports on the domestic industry concerned shall include an evaluation of all relevant economic factors and indices having a bearing on the state of the industry, including actual and potential decline in sales, profits, output, market share, productivity, return on investments, or utilization of capacity; factors affecting domestic prices; the magnitude of the margin of dumping; actual and potential negative effects on cash flow, inventories, employment, wages, growth, ability to raise capital or investments. This list is not exhaustive, nor can one or several of these factors necessarily give decisive guidance.

Article 3.4 requires this examination to include an evaluation of all relevant economic factors and indices having a bearing on the state of the industry, *including*[82] the following 15 factors:

- actual and potential decline in sales;
- actual and potential decline in profits;
- actual and potential decline in output;

---

[82] The panel in *EC–Bed linen from India*, Panel, para 6.156, pointed out that, in the Tokyo Round Anti-Dumping Code, the same list of factors was preceded by the phrase 'such as,' which was changed to the word 'including' that now appears in Article 3.4 of the ADA. In the view of the panel the change in the wording that was introduced in the Uruguay Round supports an interpretation of the current text of Article 3.4 as setting forth a list that is mandatory, and not merely indicative or illustrative.

- actual and potential decline in market share;
- actual and potential decline in productivity;
- actual and potential decline in return on investments; or
- actual and potential decline in utilization of capacity; and
- factors affecting domestic prices;
- the magnitude of the margin of dumping;[83]
- actual and potential negative effects on cash flow;
- actual and potential negative effects on inventories;
- actual and potential negative effects on employment;
- actual and potential negative effects on wages;
- actual and potential negative effects on growth;
- actual and potential negative effects on the ability to raise capital or investments.

Article 3.4, last sentence, provides that this list is not exhaustive, nor can one or several of these factors necessarily give decisive guidance.

It has been the practice of various authorities to focus on the injury factors that actual point to injury in the case before them and to ignore or, at least, not discuss, other factors that do not indicate injury. As a result, an issue that has come up repeatedly in WTO dispute settlement proceedings is whether the 15 listed injury factors must be evaluated in each and every case and whether the evaluation must be apparent in the final determination. The answers of panels[84] and the AB[85] have been affirmative on both counts.[86] In *Thailand–H-Beams*, the AB also ruled that Article 3.4 left no room for a permissible interpretation that all 15 factors need not be considered:[87]

In determining whether all the factors mentioned in Article 3.4 have to be considered in each case, the Panel began its interpretation in accordance with the customary rules of interpretation of public international law as required by Article 17.6(ii), first sentence, by examining at length the meaning and context of the wording of Article 3.4, and by contrasting it with the wording of Article 3.5. The Panel also

---

[83] This injury factor was added during the Uruguay Round negotiations, see Koulen, 'The New Anti-Dumping Code Through its Negotiating History' in Bourgeois, Berrod and Gippini Fournier (eds), *The Uruguay Round Results* (1995) 151, 213.

[84] *Mexico–HFCS from the United States*, Panel, para 7.128; *Thailand–H-Beams from Poland*, Panel, para 7.229; *Guatemala–Cement from Mexico II*, Panel, para 8.283; *EC–Bed linen from India*, Panel, para 6.154; *United States–Hot Rolled Steel from Japan*, Panel, paras 7.231–7.236; *Egypt–Steel rebar from Turkey*, Panel, para 7.51; *Argentina–Poultry from Brazil*, Panel, para 7.327.

[85] *Thailand–H-Beams from Poland*, AB, para 125; *EC–Malleable cast iron tube or pipe fittings from Brazil*, AB, para 131.

[86] Compare Durling and Nicely, *Understanding the WTO Anti-Dumping Agreement: Negotiating History and Subsequent Interpretation* (2002) 182.

[87] *Thailand–H-Beams from Poland*, AB, para 125.

examined, with respect to this issue, the interpretation by a previous panel of Article 3.4, and an earlier interpretation given by us of an analogous provision, Article 4.2(a) of the SA. The Panel concluded its comprehensive analysis by stating that 'each of the fifteen individual factors listed in the mandatory list of factors in Article 3.4 must be evaluated by the investigating authorities . . .' We agree with the Panel's analysis in its entirety, and with the Panel's interpretation of the mandatory nature of the factors mentioned in Article 3.4 of the ADA.[88]

Several panels have explicitly stated that one reason why it is so important that the evaluation of the Article 3.4 injury factors is reflected in the final determination is to enable the panel to assess whether the authority acted in accordance with Article 3.4 at the time of the investigation:[89]

We believe it would not be sufficient if the investigating authority merely mentioned data for certain of the Article 3.4 factors without undertaking an evaluation of that factor. An evaluation of a factor implies putting data in context and assessing such data both in their internal evolution and vis-à-vis other factors examined. Only on the basis of the evaluation of data in the determination would a reviewing panel be able to assess whether the conclusions drawn from the examination are those of an unbiased and objective authority.[90]

Needless to say, an 'evaluation' of data presupposes that the authorities in fact *collect* data regarding all 15 factors in the course of its investigation:

It appears that data was not even collected for all the factors listed in Article 3.4, let alone evaluated by the EC investigating authorities. Surely a factor cannot be evaluated without the collection of relevant data.[91]

These rulings do not mean that all injury factors will be *relevant* in each and every case:

. . . consideration of the Article 3.4 factors is required in every case, even though such consideration may lead the investigating authority to conclude that a particular factor is not probative in the circumstances of a particular industry or a particular case, and therefore is not relevant to the actual determination. Moreover, the consideration of each of the Article 3.4 factors must be apparent in the final determination of the investigating authority.[92]

To give an example: in a case involving highly perishable products such as fresh tomatoes, actual and potential negative effects on inventories probably will not

---

[88] *Thailand–H-Beams from Poland*, AB, paras 125.

[89] *EC–Bed linen from India*, Panel, para 6.163; *Guatemala–Cement from Mexico II*, Panel, para 8.283; *United States–Hot Rolled Steel from Japan*, Panel, paras 7.231–7.236.

[90] *United States–Hot Rolled Steel from Japan*, Panel, para 7.232.

[91] *EC–Bed linen from India*, Panel, para 6.167.

[92] *Mexico–HFCS from the United States*, Panel, para 7.128.

be a relevant factor. Nevertheless, the authorities will have to evaluate the factor and explain why it is not relevant in the case at hand rather than simply ignore it.

Similarly, the requirement to evaluate does not mean that all injury factors have to show a *negative* trend. In fact, it happens often that some of the factors show injury and others do not:

While we do not consider that positive trends in a number of factors during the IP would necessarily preclude the investigating authorities from making an affirmative determination of injury, we are of the view that such positive movements in a number of factors would require a compelling explanation of why and how, in light of such apparent positive trends, the domestic industry was, or remained, injured within the meaning of the ADA. In particular, such a situation would require a thorough and persuasive explanation as to whether and how such positive movements were outweighed by any other factors and indices which might be moving in a negative direction during the IP. [93]

The panel in *Thailand–H-Beams* emphasized that the mandatory evaluation of the 15 injury factors is more than a 'checklist'[94] approach: indeed, not only must the 15 factors be mentioned in the record, but they must be analysed in an economically and factually correct manner.

. . . in determining that Article 3.4 contains a mandatory list of fifteen factors to be looked at, this does not establish a mere 'checklist approach' that would consist of a mechanical exercise of merely ensuring that each listed factor is in some way referred to by the investigating authority. It may well be in the circumstances of a particular case that certain factors enumerated in Article 3.4 are not relevant, that their relative importance or weight can vary significantly from case to case, or that some other non-listed factors could be deemed relevant. Rather, we are of the view that Article 3.4 requires the authorities properly to establish whether a factual basis exists to support a well-reasoned and meaningful analysis of the state of the industry and a finding of injury. This analysis does not derive from a mere characterization of the degree of 'relevance or irrelevance' of each and every individual factor, but rather must be based on a thorough evaluation of the state of the industry and, in light of the last sentence of Article 3.4, must contain a persuasive explanation as to how the evaluation of relevant factors led to the determination of injury.

We are of the view that the evaluation of the mandatory factors must be apparent in the documents forming the basis of our review. [95]

In *Egypt–Steel rebar*, the panel found that while the injury analysis contained data on all 15 injury factors, it contained no narrative, but rather consisted only

---

[93] *Thailand–H-Beams from Poland*, Panel, para 7.249.
[94] See also *EC–Bed linen from India*, Panel, para 6.163.
[95] *Thailand–H-Beams from Poland*, Panel, paras 7.236–7.237.

of tables of data concerning the various factors, for the domestic industry as a whole, and individually, for the two domestic producers. In the view of the panel, the mere presentation of tables of data, without more, in respect of productivity, actual and potential negative effects on cash flow, employment, wages, and ability to raise capital or investments did not constitute an evaluation in the sense of Article 3.4.[96]

In *EC–Malleable cast iron tube or pipe fittings*, the AB accepted that some of the 15 injury factors are interrelated and that an evaluation of certain factors might therefore implicitly include an evaluation of another factor. Particularly with respect to evaluation of the factor *growth*, the AB considered that it might form part of the evaluation of other factors.[97] As the EC had found negative trends with respect to several other factors, this pointed to a lack of growth and supported the EC's contention that it had in fact considered it.[98] Commentators have observed that the AB's acceptance of an *implicit* evaluation in this case may be contrasted with the AB's insistence in other areas that findings must be *explicit*.[99]

2.4 Causation

The causal link between dumping and injury is discussed in Article 3.5 ADA. Article 3.5 requires a demonstration that the dumped imports are, through the effects of dumping, causing injury. The demonstration must be based on an examination of all relevant evidence:

3.5 It must be demonstrated that the dumped imports are, through the effects of dumping, as set forth in paragraphs 2 and 4, causing injury within the meaning of this Agreement. The demonstration of a causal relationship between the dumped imports and the injury to the domestic industry shall be based on an examination of all relevant evidence before the authorities. The authorities shall also examine any known factors other than the dumped imports which at the same time are injuring the domestic industry, and the injuries caused by these other factors must not be attributed to the dumped imports. Factors which may be relevant in this respect include inter alia the volume and prices of imports not sold at dumping prices, contraction in demand or changes in the patterns of consumption, trade restrictive practices of and competition

---

[96] *Egypt–Steel rebar from Turkey*, Panel, paras 7.41–7.51.
[97] *EC–Malleable cast iron tube or pipe fittings from Brazil*, AB, para 162.
[98] *EC–Malleable cast iron tube or pipe fittings from Brazil*, AB, para 165.
[99] WorldTradeLaw.net, *Dispute Settlement Commentary on EC–Pipe fittings*, p 13, checked on 23 April 2005.

between the foreign and domestic producers, developments in technology and the export performance and productivity of the domestic industry.

In addition, the authorities must examine any *known* factors other than the dumped imports which also cause injury to the domestic industry. The injuries caused by these other factors must not be attributed to the dumped imports. This last condition is known as the *non-attribution* requirement.

Last, Article 3.5 specifies that, among others, the following 'other factors' *may* be relevant:

- the volume and prices of imports not sold at dumping prices;
- contraction in demand or changes in the patterns of consumption;
- trade restrictive practices of and competition between the foreign and domestic producers;
- developments in technology; and
- the export performance and productivity of the domestic industry.

2.4.1 Known Factors

In *EC–Malleable cast iron tube or pipe fittings*, the AB ruled that the requirement to examine other known factors kicks in if three conditions are fulfilled:

- the factor must be known;
- it must be a factor other than dumped imports; and
- it must be injuring the domestic industry at the same time as the dumped imports.[100]

In the same case, the AB ruled that Article 3.5 does not require the authorities to examine the *collective* effects of other known factors, in addition to their individual effects, provided that the authorities do not attribute injury caused by other known factors to the dumped imports.[101]

In *United States–Hot-rolled steel*, Japan had argued that the USITC had failed to examine the *prices* of non-dumped imports and only collected information on the *volume* of non-dumped imports. The panel disagreed with Japan that Article 3.5 of the ADA *requires* that the investigating authority explicitly examine the volume and price effects of non-dumped imports, in the absence of a *prima facie* case by Japan that the prices of the non-dumped imports were a known factor injuring the industry or that they were otherwise relevant to the USITC's examination of the effects of other known factors that might be causing injury.[102]

---

[100] *EC–Malleable cast iron tube or pipe fittings from Brazil*, AB, para 175.
[101] *EC–Malleable cast iron tube or pipe fittings from Brazil*, AB, paras 190–192.
[102] *United States–Hot Rolled Steel from Japan*, Panel, para 7.247.

There may be additional factors which are causing injury, in addition to those expressly listed in Article 3.5.[103] While authorities are under no obligation to proactively find such factors, if they are clearly raised by interested parties, the authorities are required to examine such claims:

The text of Article 3.5 refers to 'known' factors other than the dumped imports which at the same time are injuring the domestic industry but does not make clear how factors are 'known' or are to become 'known' to the investigating authorities. We consider that other 'known' factors would include those causal factors that are clearly raised before the investigating authorities by interested parties in the course of an AD investigation. We are of the view that there is no express requirement in Article 3.5 that investigating authorities seek out and examine in each case on their own initiative the effects of all possible factors other than imports that may be causing injury to the domestic industry under investigation.[104]

2.4.2 Other Factors

Panels have held repeatedly[105] that – contrary to the mandatory evaluation of the 15 Article 3.4 injury factors – authorities are not obliged to examine the other factors listed in Article 3.5:[106]

We do not agree with the apparent view of Poland that the factors enumerated in Article 3.5 ADA constitute a mandatory list of factors that must necessarily be examined by the investigating authorities in every case. Consequently, it is not necessary for the relevant documents to reflect that each and every factor enumerated in Article 3.5 was examined . . . The text of Article 3.5 indicates that the list of other possible causal factors enumerated in that provision is illustrative. Thus, while the listed factors in Article 3.5 might be relevant in many cases, and the list contains useful guidance as to the kinds of factors other than imports that might cause injury to the domestic industry, the specific list in Article 3.5 is not itself mandatory.[107]

In *EC–Malleable cast iron tube or pipe fittings*, the AB held that, if the authorities reject the factual accuracy of a claim made with respect to any other factor, they obviously do not need to analyse it any further.[108]

---

[103] Compare Czako, Human and Miranda, *A Handbook on Anti-Dumping Investigations* (2003) 298.   [104] *Thailand–H-Beams from Poland*, Panel, para 7.273.

[105] *Thailand–H-Beams from Poland*, Panel, para 7.274; *United States-Hot Rolled Steel from Japan*, Panel, para 7.247.

[106] Compare Durling and, Nicely, *Understanding the WTO Anti-Dumping Agreement: Negotiating History and Subsequent Interpretation* (2002) 205.

[107] *Thailand–H-Beams from Poland*, Panel, para 7.274.

[108] *EC–Malleable cast iron tube or pipe fittings from Brazil*, AB, para 177.

2.4.3 Non-attribution

The non-attribution language in Article 3.5 ADA is quite similar to the non-attribution requirement found in Article 4.2(b) of the Safeguards Agreement. This observation is important because, in its interpretation of Article 4.2(b), the Appellate Body has laid out two important principles.[109] First of all, it is not necessary that the imports by themselves cause the injury, as long as they are a contributory cause. Second, in order to satisfy the non-attribution requirement, the authorities must separate the injury caused by the imports, on the one hand, and the injury caused by other factors, on the other hand:

Article 3.5 . . . seems to warn against quick and overly simplistic conclusions by requiring the investigating authorities to consider and examine other known factors that are at the same time injuring the domestic industry before determining that dumped imports are causing material injury within the meaning of Articles 3.2 and 3.4.[110]

The non-attribution requirement and the links between the ADA and the Safeguards Agreement in this respect were discussed at length by the panel and the AB in *United States–Hot rolled steel*.

The AB clearly established that a similar separation is necessitated by Article 3.5 ADA:

The non-attribution language in Article 3.5 of the ADA applies solely in situations where dumped imports and other known factors are causing injury to the domestic industry at the same time. In order that investigating authorities, applying Article 3.5, are able to ensure that the injurious effects of the other known factors are not 'attributed' to dumped imports, they must appropriately assess the injurious effects of those other factors. Logically, such an assessment must involve separating and distinguishing the injurious effects of the other factors from the injurious effects of the dumped imports. If the injurious effects of the dumped imports are not appropriately separated and distinguished from the injurious effects of the other factors, the authorities will be unable to conclude that the injury they ascribe to dumped imports is actually caused by those imports, rather than by the other factors. Thus, in the absence of such separation and distinction of the different injurious effects, the investigating authorities would have no rational basis to conclude that the dumped imports are indeed causing the injury which, under the ADA, justifies the imposition of anti-dumping duties.[111]

---

[109] See, eg, *United States–Wheat Gluten from the EC*, AB, paras 67 and 68; *United States–Lamb meat from New Zealand and Australia*, AB, paras 167 and 170.

[110] *United States–Hot Rolled Steel from Japan*, Panel, para 7.251.

[111] *United States–Hot Rolled Steel from Japan*, AB, para 223. Compare *EC–Malleable cast iron tube or pipe fittings from Brazil*, AB, para 188.

The AB overruled the conclusion of the panel, which had relied in part on the GATT report *United States–Fresh and chilled Atlantic salmon*,[112] that it was *not* necessary to isolate the injury caused by other factors from the injury caused by the dumped imports. The AB agreed with the position of the United States that the different causal factors operating on a domestic industry may interact, and their effects may well be inter-related, such that they produce a combined effect on the domestic industry. However, although it might therefore not be easy, as a practical matter, to separate and distinguish the injurious effects of different causal factors, nevertheless this was precisely what is envisaged by the non-attribution language.[113]

The AB felt *fortified* by the interpretation it had given to Article 4.2(b) Safeguards Agreement and agreed with the panel that adopted panel and AB reports relating to the non-attribution language in the Safeguards Agreement can *provide guidance* in interpreting the non-attribution language in Article 3.5 of the ADA.[114]

Japan had argued that the USITC had attributed to dumped imports injury that was, in reality, caused by four other factors, ie an increase in capacity in mini-mills, the effects of a strike at General Motors in 1998, declining demand for hot-rolled steel from the United States' pipe and tube industry, and the effects of prices of non-dumped imports. However, the AB found that, in the absence of an adequate factual record, there was no basis for it to complete the analysis of Japan's claim under Article 3.5 of the ADA.[115]

2.5 Threat of Material Injury

It is possible that dumped imports have not yet caused material injury, but may cause such injury in the future unless anti-dumping measures are taken. Thus, the dumped imports may threaten to cause material injury. A determination of threat of material injury is, by its nature, speculative and for that reason Article 3.7 contains four extra conditions that need to be satisfied for a threat of injury finding.

First, the threat determination must be based on facts and not merely on allegation, conjecture or speculation. Second, the change in circumstances

---

[112] *United States–Fresh and chilled Atlantic salmon from Norway*, ADP/87, 30 November 1992, adopted on 27 April 2004.   [113] *United States–Hot Rolled Steel from Japan*, AB, para 227.
[114] Compare the discussion in Durling, 'Deference, But Only When Due: WTO Review of Anti-Dumping Measures' (2003) 6 Journal of International Economic Law 125, 138–139.
[115] *United States–Hot Rolled Steel from Japan*, AB, paras 222–236.

which would create actual injurious dumping must be clearly foreseen and imminent.

In *United States–Softwood lumber*, the panel observed that the second condition of Article 3.7 is 'not a model of clarity'. Faced with a Canadian challenge that the USITC had not adequately addressed that the change in circumstances which would create actual injurious dumping must be clearly foreseen and imminent, the panel seemed to wonder whether it actually constituted a separate condition, which needed to be addressed separately. In support, the panel noted that the example of a change in circumstances provided in footnote 10 ADA comes back again in Article 3.7(i) as one of the four threat factors.[116] The panel further noted that there need not be one single event triggering the change in circumstances, but that it might well be possible that the change in circumstances is caused by a series of events or developments relating to the domestic industry and/or the dumped imports.[117] Nevertheless, the panel then considered how it would examine the condition:

What is critical . . . is that it be clear from the determination that the investigating authority has evaluated how the future will be different from the immediate past, such that the situation of no present material injury will change in the imminent future to a situation of material injury, in the absence of measures.[118]

. . .

In this case, the facts the United States points to as demonstrating the 'progression' of circumstances which would create a situation in which injury would occur in the near future are thoroughly intertwined with the USITC's discussion of the present condition of the domestic industry, the present impact of imports, and the facts asserted in support of the conclusion that imports will increase substantially. Thus, in our view, the USITC considered these various elements in concluding that the continuation of the trends in the situation of the domestic industry, coupled with predicted substantially increased imports, would result in an imminent change in circumstances such that injury would occur.[119]

In the *Mexico–HFCS 21.5* case, the AB also considered that in a threat case, the establishment of the facts by the authorities includes both affirmative findings of events that took place during the investigation period as well as *assumptions* relating to such events made by the authorities in the course of their analysis. These are necessarily assumptions because they relate to the possible occurrence of future events. Nevertheless, a proper establishment of

---

[116] *United States–Softwood lumber from Canada*, Panel, para 7.53.
[117] *United States–Softwood lumber from Canada*, Panel, para 7.57.
[118] *United States–Softwood lumber from Canada*, Panel, para 7.58.
[119] *United States–Softwood lumber from Canada*, Panel, para 7.60.

the facts in a threat case should be based on events that are clearly foreseen and imminent.[120]

Third, a threat determination must include consideration of four specific factors:

(i) a significant rate of increase of dumped imports into the domestic market indicating the likelihood of substantially increased importation;

(ii) sufficient freely disposable, or an imminent, substantial increase in, capacity of the exporter indicating the likelihood of substantially increased dumped exports to the importing member's market, taking into account the availability of other export markets to absorb any additional exports;

(iii) whether imports are entering at prices that will have a significant depressing or suppressing effect on domestic prices, and would likely increase demand for further imports; and

(iv) inventories of the product being investigated.

Fourth, the totality of the factors considered must lead to the conclusion that further dumped exports are imminent and that, unless protective action is taken, material injury would occur.

3.7 A determination of a threat of material injury shall be based on facts and not merely on allegation, conjecture or remote possibility. The change in circumstances which would create a situation in which the dumping would cause injury must be clearly foreseen and imminent.[121] In making a determination regarding the existence of a threat of material injury, the authorities should consider inter alia such factors as:

(i) a significant rate of increase of dumped imports into the domestic market indicating the likelihood of substantially increased importation;

(ii) sufficient freely disposable, or an imminent, substantial increase in, capacity of the exporter indicating the likelihood of substantially increased dumped exports to the importing Member's market, taking into account the availability of other export markets to absorb any additional exports;

(iii) whether imports are entering at prices that will have a significant depressing or suppressing effect on domestic prices, and would likely increase demand for further imports; and

(iv) inventories of the product being investigated.

No one of these factors by itself can necessarily give decisive guidance but the totality of the factors considered must lead to the conclusion that further dumped exports are imminent and that, unless protective action is taken, material injury would occur.

---

[120] *Mexico–HFCS from the United States*, 21.5 AB, para 85.

[121] Fn 10 in ADA: One example, though not an exclusive one, is that there is convincing reason to believe that there will be, in the near future, substantially increased importation of the product at dumped prices.

3.8 With respect to cases where injury is threatened by dumped imports, the application of anti-dumping measures shall be considered and decided with special care.

In *Mexico–HFCS*, the panel advocated a strict interpretation of Article 3.7 by holding that, *in addition* to consideration of the four specific threat factors mentioned in Article 3.7, a threat determination must also cover the regular 15 Article 3.4 injury factors:

While an examination of the Article 3.7 factors is required in a threat of injury case, that analysis alone is not a sufficient basis for a determination of threat of injury, because the Article 3.7 factors do not relate to the consideration of the impact of the dumped imports on the domestic industry . . . They are not, in themselves, relevant to a decision concerning what the 'consequent impact' of continued dumped imports on the domestic industry is likely to be. However, it is precisely this latter question – whether the 'consequent impact' of continued dumped imports is likely to be material injury to the domestic industry – which must be answered in a threat of material injury analysis. Thus, an analysis of the consequent impact of imports is required in a threat of material injury determination. Therefore, the Article 3.4 evaluation is also relevant in a threat case.[122]

This approach was implicitly upheld by the AB in *Mexico–HFCS 21.5*.[123]

In *United States–Softwood lumber I*, the panel interpreted Article 3.7 more leniently by focusing on the words 'should' and 'consider'. Thus, the panel deduced from the use of the word *consider* that it must be apparent from the final determination that the investigating authorities have given attention to and taken into account the four factors. While that consideration must go beyond a mere recitation of the facts in question, and put them into context, Article 3.7 in the view of the panel did not require the authorities to make an explicit 'finding' or 'determination' with respect to the four factors.[124] The panel also concluded from the use of the word *should* that failure to consider one or more of the Article 3.7 factors would not as such constitute a violation of Article 3.7:

In this context we note that the parties agreed that the use of the word 'should' in Article 3.7 of the ADA . . . indicated that, unlike the situation under Article 3.4 of the ADA, consideration of each of the factors listed in Articles 3.7 . . . is not mandatory. Consequently, a failure to consider a factor at all, or a failure to adequately consider, a particular factor would not necessarily demonstrate a violation of the provisions.

---

[122] *Mexico–HFCS from the United States*, Panel, paras 7.126–7.127.
[123] *Mexico–HFCS from the United States*, 21.5 AB, paras 112–118.
[124] *United States–Softwood lumber from Canada I*, Panel, para 7.67.

Whether a violation existed would depend on the particular facts of the case, in light of the totality of the factors considered and the explanations given. In this case, it is clear from the face of the determination that the USITC in fact addressed the facts concerning each of the factors set out in Articles 3.7 and 15.7 of the Agreements. Indeed, Canada does not argue that any relevant factor was ignored by the USITC, or not addressed in the determination. Thus, we cannot conclude that the USITC failed to consider the factors set forth in Articles 3.7 and 15.7, in the sense of not taking them into account at all.[125]

Although the panel set a low standard, it nevertheless found that the United States had violated Article 3.7 because the USITC's conclusion that dumped imports from Canada would increase substantially was not supported by the evidence relied upon by the United States in support of the determination. In the view of the panel, that evidence at most could support a conclusion that imports of softwood lumber would continue at the historical levels, and might increase somewhat, in keeping with increased demand, and consistent with historical patterns.[126]

In *Mexico–HFCS*, the American producers had argued in the course of the administrative proceeding that a restraint agreement existed between the soft-drink bottlers and the Mexican sugar producers,[127] as a result of which increased imports of high-fructose corn syrup were unlikely. The Mexican authorities had rejected this argument on the ground that the restraint agreement was not proven to exist. The panel considered this rejection inadequate:

... the question for purposes of an anti-dumping investigation is not whether an alleged restraint agreement in violation of Mexican law existed, an issue which might well be beyond the jurisdiction of an anti-dumping authority to resolve, but whether there was evidence of and arguments concerning the effect of the alleged restraint agreement, which, if it existed, would be relevant to the analysis of the likelihood of increased dumped imports in the near future. If the latter is the case, the investigating authority is obliged to consider the effects of such an alleged agreement, assuming it exists.[128]

In the subsequent 21.5 proceeding, the panel found that the re-determination issued by the Mexican authorities (SECOFI) following the original panel report remained inadequate. The re-determination provided in relevant part that the alleged restraint agreement would not eliminate the threat of injury to

---

[125] *United States–Softwood lumber from Canada I*, Panel, para 7.68.
[126] *United States–Softwood lumber from Canada*, Panel, para 7.89.
[127] *Mexico–HFCS from the United States*, Panel, para 2.4.
[128] *Mexico–HFCS from the United States*, Panel, para 7.174.

the domestic sugar industry because it does not eliminate the likelihood that both soft-drink bottlers and other users would continue to acquire dumped imports. In the view of the panel, a conclusion that the likelihood of further dumped imports is not eliminated does not demonstrate that there is a likelihood of substantially increased importation and consequent threat of material injury.[129] On appeal, the AB upheld the panel's findings:

SECOFI chose to assume the existence and effectiveness of the alleged restraint agreement for purposes of its analysis of the likelihood of increased imports. We further note that none of the parties to this dispute challenged, before the panel, SECOFI's decision to make such assumptions. In these circumstances, it was logical for the panel to examine SECOFI's conclusions using the same premises. Indeed, we consider that it would have been improper for the panel to have sought, on its own initiative, to go behind the assumptions made by SECOFI.[130]

Last, it may be noted that it is unclear to what extent Article 3.8 adds independent obligations:

It is not clear to us what the parameters of such 'special care' in the context of an objective evaluation based on positive evidence would be. In these circumstances, we consider it appropriate to consider alleged violations of Article 3.8 . . . only after consideration of the alleged violations of specific provisions. While we do not consider that a violation of the special care obligation could not be demonstrated in the absence of a violation of the more specific provision of the ADA governing injury determinations, we believe such a demonstration would require additional or independent arguments concerning the asserted violation of the special care requirement beyond the arguments in support of the specific violations.[131]

In the *Softwood lumber* case, the panel decided not to make any findings with respect to this claim as Canada had not raised Article 3.8 – specific arguments.[132]

---

[129] *Mexico–HFCS from the United States*, 21.5 Panel, para 6.22.
[130] *Mexico–HFCS from the United States*, 21.5 AB, para 90.
[131] *United States–Softwood lumber from Canada*, Panel, para 7.34.
[132] *United States–Softwood lumber from Canada*, Panel, para 7.36.

Chapter 3

PROCEDURES

Introduction

This chapter will discuss the many procedural requirements that the ADA imposes.

Article 1 lays down the principle that anti-dumping measures may be applied only under the circumstances provided for in Article VI GATT 1994 and pursuant to investigations initiated and conducted in accordance with the ADA provisions:

Article 1: Principles
An anti-dumping measure shall be applied only under the circumstances provided for in Article VI of GATT 1994 and pursuant to investigations initiated[1] and conducted in accordance with the provisions of this Agreement. The following provisions govern the application of Article VI of GATT 1994 in so far as action is taken under anti-dumping legislation or regulations.

In *United States–1916 Act*, the panel considered that that the provisions of Articles 1 and 18.1 limit the anti-dumping instruments that may be used by Members to those expressly contained in Article VI and the ADA, ie provisional measures, price undertakings and the imposition of anti-dumping duties.[2]

3.1 Initiation

Article 5 is titled initiation and subsequent investigation. However, it deals mostly with the requirements that must be met before an investigation is initiated.

The panel in *Thailand–H-Beams* ruled that Article 5 is one of the articles of the ADA which contains multiple obligations. As a result, a WTO member claiming a violation of Article 5 provisions will have to specify which paragraphs of Article 5 are violated and why in its request for establishment of the panel; the mere listing of Article 5 may be insufficient as it would not specify with sufficient clarity what the member is complaining about.[3]

Article 5.1 provides the general rule that an anti-dumping investigation shall be initiated upon a written application by or on behalf of the domestic industry. Article 5.6 provides that, in special circumstances, the authorities

---

[1] Fn 1 in ADA: The term 'initiated' as used in this Agreement means the procedural action by which a member formally commences an investigation as provided in Article 5.

[2] *United States–1916 Act–EC*, Panel, para 6.196.

[3] *Thailand–H-Beams from Poland*, Panel, para 7.18.

may self-initiate an anti-dumping investigation, but only if they have sufficient evidence of dumping, injury and a causal link, as described in Article 5.2. Such self-initiation is very rare:

5.1 Except as provided for in paragraph 6, an investigation to determine the existence, degree and effect of any alleged dumping shall be initiated upon a written application by or on behalf of the domestic industry.

. . .

5.6 If, in special circumstances, the authorities concerned decide to initiate an investigation without having received a written application by or on behalf of a domestic industry for the initiation of such investigation, they shall proceed only if they have sufficient evidence of dumping, injury and a causal link, as described in paragraph 2, to justify the initiation of an investigation.

The panel in *United States–1916 Act* found that the American 1916 Act violated Articles 4.1, 5.1, 5.2 and 5.4 of the ADA because it does not require a minimum representation of a US industry in applications for the initiation of proceedings under the Act.[4]

3.1.1 The Application

Article 5.2 contains the requirements for the application (sometimes also called the complaint or the petition) and starts out by requiring evidence of dumping, injury and a causal link between the dumped imports and the alleged injury. This general obligation is then concretized by requiring four types of information, but only to the extent *reasonably available to the applicant.* Clearly, at this pre-initiation stage, the quantity and quality of the information provided by the applicant need not be such as would be required in order to make a preliminary or final determination of injury:[5]

5.2 An application under paragraph 1 shall include evidence of (a) dumping, (b) injury within the meaning of Article VI of GATT 1994 as interpreted by this Agreement and (c) a causal link between the dumped imports and the alleged injury. Simple assertion, unsubstantiated by relevant evidence, cannot be considered sufficient to meet the requirements of this paragraph. The application shall contain such information as is reasonably available to the applicant on the following:

(i) the identity of the applicant and a description of the volume and value of the domestic production of the like product by the applicant. Where a written

---

[4] *United States–1916 Act–Japan*, Panel, para 6.261.

[5] *Guatemala–Cement from Mexico I*, Panel, para 7.64; *Mexico–HFCS from the United States*, Panel, para 7.74.

application is made on behalf of the domestic industry, the application shall identify the industry on behalf of which the application is made by a list of all known domestic producers of the like product (or associations of domestic producers of the like product) and, to the extent possible, a description of the volume and value of domestic production of the like product accounted for by such producers;

(ii) a complete description of the allegedly dumped product, the names of the country or countries of origin or export in question, the identity of each known exporter or foreign producer and a list of known persons importing the product in question;

(iii) information on prices at which the product in question is sold when destined for consumption in the domestic markets of the country or countries of origin or export (or, where appropriate, information on the prices at which the product is sold from the country or countries of origin or export to a third country or countries, or on the constructed value of the product) and information on export prices or, where appropriate, on the prices at which the product is first resold to an independent buyer in the territory of the importing Member.

(iv) information on the evolution of the volume of the allegedly dumped imports, the effect of these imports on prices of the like product in the domestic market and the consequent impact of the imports on the domestic industry, as demonstrated by relevant factors and indices having a bearing on the state of the domestic industry, such as those listed in paragraphs 2 and 4 of Article 3.

The panel in *United States–Softwood lumber* opined that the 'reasonably available' language was intended to avoid putting an undue burden on the applicant to submit information which is not reasonably available to it. It further considered that the phrase was not intended to require an applicant to submit *all* information reasonably available to it, but rather such reasonably available information on the relevant matters as the applicant deems necessary to substantiate its allegations of dumping, injury and causality.[6]

Within the context of the Article 5.2 (iv) obligation that an application shall contain such information as is reasonably available to the applicant on the effect of the allegedly dumped imports on prices of the like product in the domestic market and the consequent impact of the allegedly dumped imports on the domestic industry, the *Guatemala–Cement II* panel observed that such information would normally be in the hands of the domestic industry filing the application for anti-dumping relief, even more so when the company bringing the application is the sole producer of the domestic product, as was the case there.[7] As a result, a relatively high standard might be appropriate.

---

[6] *United States–Softwood lumber from Canada II*, Panel, para 7.54.
[7] *Guatemala–Cement from Mexico II*, Panel, para 8.61.

On the other hand, the panel in *Mexico–HFCS* pointed out that the words 'relevant' and 'such as' in Article 5.2 (iv) make it clear that an application is not required to contain information on *all* the factors and indices set forth in Articles 3.2 and 3.4. Rather, Article 5.2 (iv) requires that the application contain information on factors and indices relating to the impact of imports on the domestic industry, and refers to Articles 3.2 and 3.4 as illustrative of factors which may be relevant. The relevance of the various factors would depend on the nature of the allegations made by the industry, and the nature of the industry itself. If the industry provides information reasonably available to it concerning factors which are relevant to the allegation of injury it makes in the application, and the information concerning those factors demonstrates the impact of the dumped imports on the domestic industry, Article 5.2 (iv) would be satisfied.[8]

Panels have also repeatedly[9] held that it is sufficient that the application contains the necessary information. *Analysis* of such information in the application is therefore not required:

Article 5.2 does not require an application to contain analysis, but rather to contain information, in the sense of evidence, in support of allegations. While some analysis linking the information and the allegations would be helpful in assessing the merits of an application, the text of Article 5.2 does not require such an analysis in the application itself.[10]

Similarly, the panel in *Thailand–H-Beams* considered that while the chapeau of Article 5.2 provides that simple assertion, unsubstantiated by relevant evidence, cannot be considered sufficient to meet the requirements of this paragraph, raw numerical data constitutes relevant evidence rather than merely a simple assertion within the meaning of the provision. While Article 5.2 (iv) requires the application to contain information, in the sense of evidence, on certain identified factors, this did not impose an additional requirement that the application contain *analysis* of the data submitted in support of the application.[11]

In *Argentina–Poultry*, the panel seems to have gone very far in stating that it did not exclude the possibility that Article 5.2 could oblige members to *verify* that an application contain evidence, and not mere assertion, of dumping, injury and causal link. In particular, in cases where applicants propose adjustments to normal value, Article 5.2 could oblige members to verify that such

---

[8] *Mexico–HFCS from the United States*, Panel, para 7.73.
[9] *Mexico–HFCS from the United States*, Panel, para 7.76; *Thailand–H-Beams from Poland*, Panel, paras 7.76–7.77. [10] *Mexico–HFCS from the United States*, Panel, para 7.76.
[11] *Thailand–H-Beams from Poland*, Panel, para 7.77.

adjustments are supported by evidence, rather than mere assertion. A consequence of this obligation might be that applications not meeting the requirements of Article 5.2 are rejected.[12] It seems to us that any such obligation would be covered by Article 5.3, rather than Article 5.2.

In *United States–1916 Act*, the panel concluded that there is no obligation for a complainant under the 1916 Act to respect the obligations of Article 5.2 of the ADA in terms of the type of evidence to be included in an application.[13] As a result, the 1916 Act violated Article 5.2 ADA.

3.1.2 Pre-initiation Examination of the Evidence

Article 5.3 ADA requires the authority to examine the accuracy and the adequacy of the evidence in the application *prior to initiation*:

5.3 The authorities shall examine the accuracy and adequacy of the evidence provided in the application to determine whether there is sufficient evidence to justify the initiation of an investigation.

We have seen above[14] that the quantity and the quality of the evidence required for an application may be less than that required for a preliminary or final determination of dumping, injury and causation. In other words, evidence which would be insufficient to justify a preliminary or final determination of dumping, injury or causal link, may well be sufficient to justify initiation of the investigation.[15]

For similar reasons, the obligation incumbent upon the authority to examine the evidence in the application has its limits too: there is no investigation before the investigation.[16] This also means that the authority at this pre-initiation stage does not have to resolve or explain how it has resolved all legal or factual issues.

... Article 5.3 does not impose an obligation on the investigating authority to set out its resolution of **all** underlying issues considered in making that determination.[17]

    . . .

... Article 5.3 cannot be interpreted to require the investigating authority to issue an explanation of how it has resolved **all** underlying questions of fact at initiation. That is a requirement that arises at later stages of the proceeding, and is explicitly set forth in Article 12.2.[18]

---

[12] *Argentina–Poultry from Brazil*, Panel, para 7.98.
[13] *United States–1916 Act–Japan*, Panel, para 6.258.   [14] See section 3.1.1, above.
[15] *Mexico–HFCS from the United States*, Panel, para 7.94, quoting panel report in *Guatemala-Cement I*, which in turn relied on the GATT panel report in *United States-Softwood lumber*.
[16] Compare Czako, Human and Miranda, *A Handbook on Anti-Dumping Investigations* (2003) 30.
[17] *Mexico–HFCS from the United States*, Panel, para 7.102.
[18] *Mexico–HFCS from the United States*, Panel, para 7.110.

In *Mexico–HFCS*, for example, an issue arose concerning the exclusion of certain Mexican producers related to the exporters under investigation in defining the relevant domestic industry.[19] The panel ruled that the authorities did not necessarily have to resolve this issue prior to initiation.

The pre-initiation examination obligation has been discussed in great detail in the *Guatemala–Cement* cases. The panel first noted that while the authority must examine the accuracy and the adequacy of the evidence in the application, the relevant legal standard is the *sufficiency* of the evidence.

Article 5.3 requires the authority to examine, in making this determination, the accuracy and adequacy of the evidence in the application. Clearly, the accuracy and adequacy of the evidence is relevant to the investigating authorities' determination whether there is sufficient evidence to justify the initiation of an investigation. It is however the sufficiency of the evidence, and not its adequacy and accuracy per se, which represents the legal standard to be applied in the case of a determination whether to initiate an investigation.[20]

By linking back Article 5.3 to Article 5.2, the panel then considered that the evidence would need to pertain to dumping, injury and the causal link between the two. Dumping, on the one hand, and injury and causation, on the other hand, were then linked back to Articles 2 and 3 respectively:

We do not of course mean that an investigating authority must have before it at the time it initiates an investigation evidence of dumping within the meaning of Article 2 of the quantity and quality that would be necessary to support a preliminary or final determination. An anti-dumping investigation is a process where certainty on the existence of all the elements necessary in order to adopt a measure is reached gradually as the investigation moves forward. However, the evidence must be such that an unbiased and objective investigating authority could determine that there was sufficient evidence of dumping within the meaning of Article 2 to justify initiation of an investigation.[21]

With respect to dumping, the panel considered that if, for example, it is obvious on the face of the application that the normal value and export price alleged in the application will require adjustments in order to effectuate a fair comparison, at a minimum, there should be some recognition that a fair comparison will require such adjustments.[22] The fact that the sales in the Mexican and Guatemalan

---

[19] *Mexico–HFCS from the United States*, Panel, para 7.105.
[20] *Guatemala–Cement from Mexico II*, Panel, para 8.31.
[21] *Guatemala–Cement from Mexico II*, Panel, para 8.35.
[22] *Guatemala–Cement from Mexico I*, Panel, para 7.64. Compare *Argentina–Poultry from Brazil*, Panel, para 7.72, where the panel found that the authority could *not* have simply accepted an – unsupported – 9.09% adjustment for yield rate made in the application.

markets were at different levels of trade was apparent from the application itself, and an unbiased and objective authority should have recognized this fact.[23]

Similarly, in a threat of injury case, the authority should have before it evidence of threat of material injury, as defined in Article 3, sufficient to justify the initiation of an investigation.[24] The panel found that Guatemala had failed to demonstrate that, at the time of initiation, there was:

- any evidence on the volume of imports other than two import certificates for 7,035 and 4,221 bags of cement respectively.[25] (The panel considered Guatemala's argument that any increase in imports from a level of zero would be 'massive' as *ex post* rationalization and therefore irrelevant);[26]
- any evidence that imports had increased relative to domestic consumption;[27]
- any evidence to suggest that the authority had considered any of the Article 3.2 elements concerning the effect of the relevant imports on Guatemalan cement prices;[28]
- any evidence to suggest that the authority considered the Article 3.4 injury factors. (The panel noted that while the application contained statements which may be relevant to some of the factors enumerated in Article 3.4 such as employment and investments, it contained no quantifiable information except for some data on the expansion plan and the number of workers to be laid off in case of a shutdown of the Guatemalan cement industry.);[29]
- information concerning any of the four factors listed in Article 3.7.[30]

The panel considered that the authority need not content itself with the information provided in the application but may gather information on its own in order to meet the standard of sufficient evidence for initiation in Article 5.3.[31] However, the authority had not done so in that case.

In *Argentina–Poultry*, the panel again applied Article 5.3 rigorously in finding that Argentina had violated its Article 5.3 obligations by:

- accepting at face value the quantification in the application of an adjustment for physical differences between poultry sold in Argentina and poultry sold in Brazil;[32]

---

[23] *Guatemala–Cement from Mexico II*, Panel, para 8.38. Compare *Argentina–Poultry from Brazil*, Panel, para 7.78, where the panel found that the authority cannot ignore non-dumped export prices, a practice it called 'more egregious than zeroing'.   [24] *Guatemala–Cement from Mexico II*, Panel, para 8.45.

[25] *Guatemala–Cement from Mexico II*, Panel, para 8.47.

[26] *Guatemala–Cement from Mexico II*, Panel, para 8.48.

[27] *Guatemala–Cement from Mexico II*, Panel, para 8.49.

[28] *Guatemala–Cement from Mexico II*, Panel, para 8.50.

[29] *Guatemala–Cement from Mexico II*, Panel, para 8.51.

[30] *Guatemala–Cement from Mexico II*, Panel, para 8.52.

[31] *Guatemala–Cement from Mexico II*, Panel, para 8.62.

[32] *Argentina–Poultry from Brazil*, Panel, para 7.73.

- accepting an application which only considered dumped transactions and excluded non-dumped transactions;[33] and
- accepting a comparison in the application of normal value, based on sales for one day, with export prices covering a period of seven months.[34]

In *United States–Softwood lumber*, on the other hand, the panel found that the Article 5.3 standard is satisfied if an unbiased and objective authority can find that the evidence in the application is sufficient, even though more probative evidence might reasonably be available to the authority.[35]

3.1.3 Pre-initiation Standing Determination

Article 5.4 ADA requires the authorities to determine, prior to initiating an anti-dumping proceeding, that the complainants have sufficient standing to make the application on behalf of the domestic industry:

By their terms, Articles 5.4 . . . do not permit investigating authorities to 'presume' that industry support for an application exists. For the thresholds set out in Articles 5.4 . . . to be met, a sufficient number of domestic producers must have 'expressed support' for an application. The CDSOA does not change the fact that investigating authorities are required to examine the 'degree of support' that exists for an application and that an application shall be considered to have been made 'by or on behalf of the domestic industry' only if sufficient support has been 'expressed'.[36]

This is an important requirement because GATT panels previously ruled that failure to properly determine standing prior to initiation constitutes a fatal error which cannot be repaired later in the proceeding. The two panel reports were blocked by the United States and, as a result, were never adopted.

In *United States–Seamless stainless steel hollow products*,[37] the panel considered that then-Article 5:1 of the Anti-Dumping Code was an essential procedural requirement, an infringement of which could not be cured retroactively. The panel was of the view that it followed from Article 1 of the Agreement that any anti-dumping duty imposed as a result of an investigation initiated in a manner inconsistent with Article 5:1 was thereby also inconsistent with Article 1.

As the panel had found that the investigation which had resulted in the imposition of definitive anti-dumping duties had been initiated in a manner inconsistent with Article 5:1, the panel concluded that the imposition of the

---

[33] *Argentina–Poultry from Brazil*, Panel, para 7.81.
[34] *Argentina–Poultry from Brazil*, Panel, para 7.86.
[35] *United States–Softwood lumber from Canada II*, Panel, para 7.87.
[36] *United States–CDSOA (Byrd amendment)*, AB, para 289.
[37] *United States–Imposition of anti-dumping duties on imports of seamless stainless steel hollow products from Sweden*, paras 521–524, ADP/47, 20 August 1990, unadopted.

anti-dumping duties was inconsistent with the obligations of the United States under Article 1 of the Agreement and that the United States therefore was obliged under Article 15 of the Agreement to revoke the anti-dumping duties in question, and, in accordance with past GATT practice,[38] to reimburse the anti-dumping duties paid.

Similarly, in *United States–Grey Portland cement and cement clinker*[39] the panel recommended that the Anti-Dumping Committee request the United States to revoke the anti-dumping duty order on grey Portland cement and cement clinker from Mexico and to reimburse any anti-dumping duties paid or deposited under the order.

In making this recommendation, the panel considered that a failure to observe the requirements in Article 5 (illegal initiation) could not be remedied by action subsequent to the initiation of the investigation because the very purpose of these requirements was to ensure that certain conditions be met before the initiation was decided upon. The panel was therefore of the view that the United States could not now bring itself into conformity with the requirements of Article 5:1 through a re-examination of the case; a re-examination could only take place in the context of a new initiation in accordance with the requirements of the Agreement. The panel concluded therefore that no action was available to the United States through which the imposition of the duties could now be rendered consistent and therefore recommended the revocation.

With respect to the reimbursement of the duties, the panel recognized that there might be situations in which such reimbursement would be excessively onerous for the importing country and should therefore not be requested of it. In the view of the panel, such situations might include those where the measure had not been challenged for an extended period of time and where the reimbursement would therefore cause particular difficulties.

However, the panel considered that no such difficulties existed in the present case: Mexico had promptly initiated the dispute settlement procedures under the Anti-Dumping Code and the United States had therefore been advised in a timely fashion that Mexico was challenging the consistency of the measures with the Agreement.[40]

---

[38] The panel referred here to *New Zealand–Imports of electrical transformers from Finland*, BISD, 32d Supp., 55 at 70 (1986).

[39] *United States–Anti-dumping duties on grey Portland cement and cement clinker from Mexico*, paras 5.35–6.2, ADP/82, 7 September 1992, unadopted.

[40] See for a detailed overview of GATT AD dispute settlement, Komuro and Vermulst, 'Anti-Dumping Disputes in the GATT/WTO: Navigating Dire Straits' (1997) 31 Journal of World Trade, 5.

The WTO DSU no longer allows such recommendations by panels or the AB. Indeed, the only possible recommendation now is that members bring the measures into conformity with the provisions of the agreement. However, suggestions to that effect might still be possible. Since the entry into force of the WTO, WTO panels and the AB have refrained from suggesting refunds of anti-dumping duties paid, although the panel in *Guatemala–Cement II* suggested revocation of the anti-dumping duties.

The new Article 5.4 now provides that the authorities must determine that the application has been made by or on behalf of the domestic industry, on the basis of an examination of the degree of support for, or opposition to, the application expressed by domestic producers of the like product. In order to reach this determination, two tests must be met:

- The application is supported by those domestic producers whose collective output constitutes more than 50 per cent of the total production of the like product produced by that portion of the domestic industry expressing either support for or opposition to the application.
- Domestic producers expressly supporting the application account for 25 per cent or more of total production of the like product produced by the domestic industry.

5.4 An investigation shall not be initiated pursuant to paragraph 1 unless the authorities have determined, on the basis of an examination of the degree of support for, or opposition to, the application expressed[41] by domestic producers of the like product, that the application has been made by or on behalf of the domestic industry.[42] The application shall be considered to have been made 'by or on behalf of the domestic industry' if it is supported by those domestic producers whose collective output constitutes more than 50 per cent of the total production of the like product produced by that portion of the domestic industry expressing either support for or opposition to the application. However, no investigation shall be initiated when domestic producers expressly supporting the application account for less than 25 per cent of total production of the like product produced by the domestic industry.

---

[41] Fn 13 in ADA: In the case of fragmented industries involving an exceptionally large number of producers, authorities may determine support and opposition by using statistically valid sampling techniques.

[42] Fn 14 in ADA: Members are aware that in the territory of certain Members employees of domestic producers of the like product or representatives of those employees may make or support an application for an investigation under paragraph 1. [This footnote was added at the request of the United States; see Koulen, 'The New Anti-Dumping Code Through its Negotiating History', in Bourgeois, Berrod and Gippini Fournier (eds), *The Uruguay Round Results* (1995) 151, 199.]

Thus, while the numerator for both tests appears the same,[43] the denominator is different, as the following example[44] may clarify:

Suppose that there are two domestic producers A and B of the like product. A represents 35 per cent of domestic production while B represents 65 per cent of domestic production. The application is brought by A.

Scenario 1: B stays neutral:

- 50% test: Satisfied because A represents 100% of those expressing support for or opposition to the application.
- 25% test: Satisfied because A represents 35% of total domestic production.

Scenario 2: B opposes the application:

- 50% test: Not satisfied because A represents 35% of those expressing support for or opposition to the application.
- 25% test: Satisfied because A represents 35% of total domestic production.

In both cases, however, the 'total production' includes all production, whether destined for the domestic market or for the export market.

It may further be noted that Article 5.4 refers back to the notion of the 'domestic industry', as defined in Article 4. This is important because it implies, for example, that producers which are related to exporters presumably may be excluded from the application of the test.

Standing issues have been raised only in a few cases since the WTO ADA entered into force. In *United States–1916 Act*, the panel had little trouble with finding that the 1916 Act violated Article 5.4 (as well as Articles 4.1, 5.1 and 5.2) ADA because it did not require a minimum representation of a US industry in applications for the initiation of proceedings under the 1916 Act.[45]

In *United States–Continued Dumping and Subsidy Offset Act*, the Appellate Body ruled that the authorities need not determine *why* domestic producers support an application:

A textual examination of Article 5.4 of the Anti-Dumping Agreement . . . reveals that those provisions contain no requirement that an investigating authority examine the

---

[43] Unless there is a distinction between 'supporting' and 'expressly supporting'.

[44] Compare the examples in Czako, Human and Miranda, *A Handbook on Anti-Dumping Investigations* (2003) 32–34.   [45] *United States–1916 Act–Japan*, Panel, para 6.261.

motives of domestic producers that elect to support an investigation. Nor do they contain any explicit requirement that support be based on certain motives, rather than on others. The use of the terms 'expressing support' and 'expressly supporting' clarify that Articles 5.4 ... require only that authorities 'determine' that support has been 'expressed' by a sufficient number of domestic producers. Thus, in our view, an 'examination' of the 'degree' of support, and not the 'nature' of support is required. In other words, it is the 'quantity', rather than the 'quality', of support that is the issue.[46]

In *EC–Bed linen*, the standing determination made by the European Commission was bitterly contested by India during the panel proceeding. However, the panel essentially ruled that India had failed to make a *prima facie* case:

We presume that Members act in good faith in the context of dispute settlement proceedings, and are unwilling to assume possible malfeasance in the absence of evidence to that effect. We consider that the 'doubts' which India has as to the European Communities' actions in this regard do not establish the necessary prima facie case in this context – the 'evidence' of the fax headers relied on by India does not constitute evidence of fraud sufficient to overcome the presumption of good faith. Moreover, we believe that it is more probable that these inconsistencies in the photocopies are attributable to the photocopying itself, rather than to the perpetration of a massive fabrication of fax headers and footers by the EC investigating authority to hide a failure to make a determination of standing prior to initiation.[47]

It is to be noted that the panel ruling makes it difficult to challenge standing determinations made in systems which do not disclose confidential information under administrative protective orders. Much of the information on which a standing determination is based is typically confidential and exporting countries challenging a standing determination invariably will be shooting in the dark to some extent. The ruling of the panel places a high burden of proof on their shoulders.[48]

3.1.4 Pre-initiation Notification/Publicizing of the Application

5.5 The authorities shall avoid, unless a decision has been made to initiate an investigation, any publicizing of the application for the initiation of an investigation.

---

[46] *United States–CDSOA (Byrd amendment)*, AB, para 283.

[47] *EC–Bed linen from India*, Panel, para 6.216.

[48] Compare Horlick and Clarke, 'Standards for Panels Reviewing Anti-Dumping Determinations under the GATT and the WTO', in Petersman (ed), *International Trade Law and the GATT/WTO Dispute Settlement System* (1997) 315, 321–322, who make the same point with respect to the zeroing issue, as decided by the GATT panels in *EC–Audio tapes in cassettes from Japan* and *United States–Salmon from Norway*.

However, after receipt of a properly documented application and before proceeding to initiate an investigation, the authorities shall notify the government of the exporting Member concerned.

3.1.4.1 Pre-initiation Notification

Article 5.5 obliges the authorities to 'notify' the government of the exporting member after receipt of the application, but before proceeding to initiate an investigation. In most cases, it will be relatively easy to establish whether the authorities have complied with this obligation.

Thus, for example, in *Guatemala–Cement I*, the panel determined that Guatemala had violated the provisions of the ADA by failing to notify the Government of Mexico before proceeding to initiate, as required by Article 5.5.[49] The argument by Guatemala that its failure to notify Mexico constituted a 'harmless error', was squarely rejected by the panel:

> ...while arguments regarding the existence and extent of the possible harm suffered by Mexico may be relevant to the issue of nullification or impairment, an argument of harmless error does not represent a defence in itself to an alleged infringement of a provision of the WTO Agreement.[50]

Similarly, in *United States–1916 Act*, the panel ruled that the 1916 Act violated Article 5.5 because the text of the 1916 Act as such did not provide for the notification required by Article 5.5, neither under the 'civil track' nor under the 'criminal track'.[51]

In *Thailand–H-Beams*, the panel had to determine whether an oral notification met the requirements of Article 5.5:

> Article 5.5 ADA does not specify the form that the notification must take. The Concise Oxford Dictionary defines the term 'notify' as: 'inform or give notice to (a person)'; 'make known, announce or report (a thing).' The form of the notification under Article 5.5 must be sufficient for the importing Member to 'inform' or 'make known' to the exporting Member certain facts. While a written notification might arguably best serve this goal and the promotion of transparency and certainty among Members, and might also provide a written record upon which an importing Member could rely in the event of a subsequent claim of inconsistency with Article 5.5 of the ADA, the text of Article 5.5 does not expressly require that the notification be in writing.

---

[49] *Guatemala–Cement from Mexico I*, Panel, para 8.4
[50] *Guatemala–Cement from Mexico II*, Panel, para 8.22.
[51] *United States–1916 Act–EC*, Panel, para 6.216.

We consider that a formal meeting between government officials could satisfy the notification requirement of Article 5.5, provided that the meeting is sufficiently documented to support meaningful review by a panel. For these reasons, the fact that Thailand notified Poland under Article 5.5 orally in the course of a meeting between government officials, rather than in written form, does not render the notification inconsistent with Article 5.5.[52]

While the panel conceded that the oral notification provided in that case did not violate Article 5.5, it is obviously preferable to notify in writing, as the panel also noted.

3.1.4.2 Pre-initiation Publicizing of the Application

There is normally a certain time period between the lodging of an application and the subsequent initiation of a proceeding. Such a period is necessary for the authorities to comply with the various pre-initiation obligations. The ADA does not prescribe any rules for the length of such period and therefore leaves it up to the WTO members to establish their own rules. In the EC, for example, this period is 45 days. Similarly, in the United States, the period is 20–40 days.[53]

Article 5.5 requires the authorities to avoid the publicizing of the application during this period. As a result, many countries will treat an application as confidential until the moment that the proceeding is officially initiated. The major exception to this is the United States where – for transparency reasons – the application is accessible from the moment that it is lodged.[54]

It is sometimes suggested that the rationale of this Article 5.5 obligation is to avoid that early publicity of the receipt of an application has a negative – and unwarranted[55] – impact on trade flows. In practice, the effect is often the opposite because it happens frequently that the receipt of a complaint is leaked and the resulting uncertainty concerning the details is then worse than transparent publication would be. The alternative rationale that has been advanced is that pre-initiation publicity might cause the exporters to modify their export sales strategies, for example by increasing their export prices, to minimize findings of dumping. In reality, however, prices tend to be dictated by the market and are often fixed in advance.

---

[52] *Thailand–H-Beams from Poland*, Panel, paras 7.89–7.90.

[53] Title VII of the Tariff Act of 1930, s 732(c)(1)(A) and (B.)

[54] Durling and Nicely, *Understanding the WTO Anti-Dumping Agreement: Negotiating History and Subsequent Interpretation* (2002) 290.

[55] Indeed, the authorities might well decide that the application does not contain sufficient evidence to warrant the initiation of a proceeding.

3.2 The Investigation

The remainder of Article 5 deals with provisions that either apply to both the pre-initiation phase and the investigation or only to the investigation. Articles 5.7 and 5.8 cover both stages and are discussed in sections 3.2.1 and 3.2.2, below, respectively. We will then discuss the remainder of Article 5 and move to Article 6.

3.2.1 Simultaneous Consideration of Dumping and Injury

Article 5.7 requires the authorities to consider the evidence of both dumping and injury simultaneously, both in the pre-initiation phase (the decision whether or not to initiate) and afterwards during the investigation. This seems a logical requirement as dumping and injury are two distinct conditions that need to be fulfilled. If either condition is not satisfied, the application should be rejected or the investigation terminated without the unnecessary delays which might result from a sequential approach:

5.7 The evidence of both dumping and injury shall be considered simultaneously *(a)* in the decision whether or not to initiate an investigation, and *(b)* thereafter, during the course of the investigation, starting on a date not later than the earliest date on which in accordance with the provisions of this Agreement provisional measures may be applied.

Article 5.7 as such deals only with the temporal aspect of the consideration of the evidence of dumping and injury and not with the substance of that evidence:[56]

... Article 5.7 imposes a procedural obligation on the investigating authority to examine the evidence before it of dumping and injury simultaneously, rather than sequentially, inter alia in the decision whether or not to initiate an investigation. We are of the view that Article 5.7 is not concerned wit the substance of the decision to initiate an investigation, which is dealt with in Article 5.3 ADA.[57]

The *Argentina–Poultry* panel also emphasized that the pre-initiation element of the obligation applies *only* to the decision whether or not to initiate an investigation:

At the outset, we consider that 'the decision whether or not to initiate an investigation' must be a decision that occurs before, or at the same time as, the moment of initiation of an investigation, because the purpose of the decision is to determine whether or not to initiate an investigation. We further note that Article 5.7 uses the term 'decision' in

---

[56] *Guatemala–Cement from Mexico II*, Panel, para 8.67.
[57] *Argentina–Poultry from Brazil*, Panel, para 7.118.

singular form rather than plural. We believe that this means that there is normally one decision in which the relevant authority of the importing Member determines whether or not to initiate an investigation. We consider that it is only in this decision, and not in other decisions, that the relevant investigating authority must simultaneously consider the evidence of dumping and injury.[58]

As a result, the panel rejected Brazil's Article 5.7 claim.[59]

It is important to note that the ADA does not require dumping and injury to be investigated by different agencies, as is the practice in many countries, including, for example, Argentina, Australia, Canada and the United States. Thus, it is perfectly possible for a country to have dumping and injury investigated by different teams within the same agency or even by the same team of case handlers. While a bifurcated system would appear to enhance objectivity, it is more difficult to administer as there are certain borderline issues in an anti-dumping case, such as the exact scope of the investigation and the definition of PCNs,[60] which would normally require coordination between the agencies.

3.2.2 De Minimis Dumping; Negligible Injury

Article 5.8 starts out by requiring that an application shall be rejected and an investigation terminated promptly as soon as the authorities are satisfied that the evidence of either dumping or injury is insufficient. While this first obligation of Article 5.8 seems obvious enough, surprisingly it has given rise to a fair amount of dispute settlement.

First, and similarly to the panel ruling with respect to Article 5.7 in *Argentina–Poultry*,[61] the panel in *United States–HFCS* ruled that Article 5.8 ADA does not impose additional substantive requirements on the authorities beyond the ones set out in Article 5.3 relating to the initiation of an investigation. Thus, if there is sufficient evidence to justify initiation under Article 5.3, there is no violation of Article 5.8 in not rejecting the application.[62]

In *Guatemala–Cement I*, the panel did not hide its incredulity at the defence advanced by Guatemala that Article 5.8 applied only to investigations that had already been initiated:

We note Guatemala's argument that Article 5.8 applies only to investigations that have already been initiated. This argument is in stark contradiction to the text of Article 5.8 itself, which refers to the 'rejection of an application' as soon as authorities conclude that there is not sufficient evidence of dumping or injury to justify a proceeding. In our

---

[58] *Argentina–Poultry from Brazil*, Panel, para 7.121.
[59] *Argentina–Poultry from Brazil*, Panel, para 7.124.   [60] See section 1.1.1, above.
[61] See section 3.2.1, above.   [62] *Mexico–HFCS from the United States*, Panel, para 7.99.

view, there is no way to interpret this language other than as a statement of the requirement that an investigation may only be initiated if the application contains sufficient
evidence of dumping and injury.[63]

Perhaps less clear-cut was the situation in *Argentina–Poultry*:

Argentina operates a bifurcated anti-dumping system . . . Thus, while the DCD . . .
investigates issues of dumping, the CNCE investigates issues of injury. This division of
labour applies both at the time of the (pre-initiation) review of the application, and
during any subsequent investigation. Although only the Secretary has the authority to
decide whether or not to initiate an investigation, the Secretary cannot decide to initiate an investigation if either the CNCE or the DCD/APCDS have found that there is
insufficient evidence of injury or dumping, respectively, to justify the initiation of an
investigation. In the case at hand, the CNCE issued Record No. 405 on 7 January 1998
to the effect that the application did not contain sufficient evidence of injury to justify
the initiation of an investigation. The CNCE's determination was received by the
Secretary on 9 January 1998. We recall that, faced with a negative assessment of the
application by the CNCE, the Secretary is precluded from initiating an investigation.
Accordingly, from the time that the Secretary received the CNCE's negative assessment
of the application, the Secretary should have been satisfied that there was not sufficient
evidence on injury to justify proceeding with the case. Thus, in accordance with
Article 5.8, the Secretary should have rejected the application 'as soon as' it received
CNCE Record No. 405 dated 7 January 1998. Rather than doing so, however, the
Secretary kept the file open, subsequently deciding to initiate the investigation
following the submission of additional information by the applicant. The Secretary
therefore failed to meet the requirements of Article 5.8 of the ADA.[64]

In *United States–Softwood lumber II*, the panel ruled that once an investigation
is initiated on the basis of sufficient evidence of dumping, the Article 5.8
standard shifts to the investigation part. In other words, the authorities are not
obliged to re-assess the sufficiency of the evidence in the application during the
investigation.

We can . . . find no basis to conclude that Article 5.8 imposes upon an investigating
authority a continuing obligation after initiation to continue to assess the sufficiency
of the evidence in the application and to terminate the investigation on the grounds
that other information undermines the sufficiency of that evidence. Once an investigation has been initiated on the basis of sufficient evidence of dumping, the application has served its purpose. Logically, the continuing obligation to terminate an
investigation where an investigating authority is satisfied that there is not sufficient
evidence to justify proceeding must be based on an assessment of the overall state of the

---

[63] *Guatemala–Cement from Mexico I*, Panel, para 7.5. Compare *Guatemala–Cement from Mexico II*,
Panel, para 8.74.   [64] *Argentina–Poultry from Brazil*, Panel, para 7.107.

evidence deduced before it in the investigation, not on an assessment of the continuing sufficiency of the information in the application. We are of the view that it could not have been the intention of the drafters of Article 5.8 that its interpretation could result in that an investigation could have been initiated on the basis of sufficient evidence, but that the very same investigation had to be terminated if additional evidence was made available by the respondents at a later stage, while the evidence being gathered during the course of the investigation, indicates dumping.[65]

Article 5.8 then goes on to introduce the innovative concepts of *de minimis* dumping and *negligible* injury:

5.8 An application under paragraph 1 shall be rejected and an investigation shall be terminated promptly as soon as the authorities concerned are satisfied that there is not sufficient evidence of either dumping or of injury to justify proceeding with the case. There shall be immediate termination in cases where the authorities determine that the margin of dumping is *de minimis*, or that the volume of dumped imports, actual or potential, or the injury, is negligible. The margin of dumping shall be considered to be *de minimis* if this margin is less than 2 per cent, expressed as a percentage of the export price. The volume of dumped imports shall normally be regarded as negligible if the volume of dumped imports from a particular country is found to account for less than 3 per cent of imports of the like product in the importing Member, unless countries which individually account for less than 3 per cent of the imports of the like product in the importing Member collectively account for more than 7 per cent of imports of the like product in the importing Member.

3.2.2.1 De Minimis Dumping

De minimis dumping occurs if the dumping margin is less than 2 per cent, expressed as a percentage of the export price. This determination seems by nature producer-specific. It might possibly be extended to a country-wide basis in cases where all investigated exporters are found to have *de minimis* dumping margins.

As we will see below in more detail,[66] the ADA acknowledges in Article 9.3 that there are different systems of collecting anti-dumping duties. Under the so-called *prospective* system, anti-dumping duties are collected on the basis of the findings and conclusions reached during the original investigation. Under the *retrospective* system, on the other hand, the original investigation leads only to an estimate of the future liability of the importers for the payment of anti-dumping duties. The actual payment will then depend on the results of annual review or duty assessment investigations that cover the preceding 12 month

---

[65] *United States–Softwood lumber from Canada II*, Panel, para 7.137.
[66] See section 3.3.3.3, below.

period. The only major user of anti-dumping that uses the retrospective system is the United States. The *United States–DRAMS* panel ruled that the Article 5.8 *de minimis* rule applies only to original investigations and notably not to these US duty assessment investigations:

We conclude that Article 5.8, second sentence, does not apply in the context of Article 9.3 duty assessment procedures. As Article 5.8, second sentence, does not require Members to apply a de minimis test in Article 9.3 duty assessment procedures, it certainly cannot require Members to apply a particular de minimis standard in such procedures.[67]

Similarly, in *United States–Corrosion-resistant carbon steel flat products*, the panel ruled that the *de minimis* rule did not apply to Article 11.3 sunset reviews:[68]

Article 5.8 does not suggest that the de minimis standard set out for investigations also applies to sunset reviews. In particular, the text of paragraph 8 of Article 5 refers expressly to the termination of an investigation in the event of de minimis dumping margins. There is, therefore, no textual indication in Article 5.8 that would suggest or require that the obligation in Article 5.8 also applies to sunset reviews. Nor is there any such suggestion or requirement in the other provisions of Article 5.[69]

In *Mexico–Rice*, the authorities had found that two American exporters had not dumped during the investigation period. Although it had applied a zero duty to them, it had not excluded them altogether.[70] The panel first of all considered that the term 'margin of dumping' in the ADA refers to the individual margin of dumping of an exporter or producer rather than to a country-wide margin of dumping.[71] The panel also considered it relevant that Article 5.8, second sentence, requires the immediate termination of the investigation in case the margin of dumping is *de minimis* or the *volume of dumped imports is negligible* and that negligibility is to be determined in respect of the volume of dumped imports '*from a particular country*'. Thus, while the ADA expressly stipulates that the negligibility test is to be examined on a country-wide basis, no such stipulation is made with regard to the margin of dumping.[72] The panel therefore concluded that the authorities' failure to terminate the investigation with respect to the two non-dumping producers violated Article 5.8 ADA.[73]

---

[67] *United States–DRAMS from Korea*, Panel, para 6.89.   [68] See section 3.5.2.5, below.
[69] *United States–Corrosion-resistant carbon steel flat products from Japan*, Panel, para 7.70.
[70] *Mexico–Rice from the United States*, Panel, para 7.135.
[71] *Mexico–Rice from the United States*, Panel, para 7.137.
[72] *Mexico–Rice from the United States*, Panel, para 7.141.
[73] *Mexico–Rice from the United States*, Panel, para 7.145.

This panel finding is more important than it may seem at first sight because it is the practice of several WTO members[74] to apply a zero duty to non-dumping producers, but to keep them in the investigation. This entails that if the authorities initiate an interim review while the measure is in force, the non-dumping producers will need to cooperate in that review again.

Last, it is noteworthy that, contrary to a similar provision in the ASCM,[75] the ADA does not distinguish between developing and developed countries as far as the level of *de minimis* dumping is concerned.

3.2.2.2 *Negligible Injury*

Article 5.8 provides that the volume of dumped imports shall normally be regarded as negligible if the volume of dumped imports from a particular country is found to account for less than 3 per cent of imports of the like product in the importing member, unless countries which individually account for less than 3 per cent of the imports of the like product in the importing member collectively account for more than 7 per cent of imports of the like product in the importing member. Thus, under the WTO rule the negligibility test is expressed as a percentage of total imports (import share test).

In contrast, a draft version of the ADA, which did not make it into law,[76] had expressed negligible injury as a percentage of the total market for the like product in the importing country (market share test).[77] It has been noted that the import share test, even set at 1 per cent, in many cases will be more strict than the market share test because imports often represent a small percentage of the total market.[78]

A version of this market share test has been retained by the EC which provides in Article 5(7) of its basic Anti-Dumping Regulation that proceedings shall not be initiated against countries whose imports represent a market share of below

---

[74] See, for example, the EC third party intervention, summarized in fn 144 of the panel report *Mexico–Rice from the United States*.

[75] Thus, Articles 11.9, 27.10 *jo*. 27.11 ASCM provide that the *de minimis* subsidy rate is 1% in case of developed countries and 2% in case of developing countries.

[76] Art 5:8 of the Dunkel draft Agreement originally provided that the volume of dumped imports shall normally be regarded as negligible if the volume of dumped imports from a particular country is found to account for less than 1% of the domestic market for the like product in the importing country unless countries which individually account for less than 1% of the domestic market for the like product in the importing country collectively account for more than 2.5% of that market. Compare Koulen, 'The New Anti-Dumping Code Through its Negotiating History', in Bourgeois, Berrod and Gippini Fournier (eds), *The Uruguay Round Results* (1995) 151, 191.

[77] It has been argued that the market share test makes more sense than the current import share test, see Lima-Campos, 'Nineteen Proposals to Curb Abuse in Anti-Dumping and Countervailing Duty Proceedings' (2005) 39 Journal of World Trade 239, 247–248.

[78] Durling and Nicely, *Understanding the WTO Anti-Dumping Agreement: Negotiating History and Subsequent Interpretation* (2002) 301–302.

1 per cent, unless such countries collectively account for 3 per cent or more of Community consumption. The obvious question is whether the EC's market share test violates Article 5.8 ADA. The following example clarifies that this will depend on the facts of the case:

Suppose that the EC market for a particular product is 1000. The following table will then compare the results of the two tests in four examples.

Total imports	Country X	3% import test	1% market share test
100	9	not met (9%)	*de minimis* (0.9%)
290	9	not met (3.1%)	*de minimis* (0.9%)
340	10	*de minimis* (2.94%)	not met (1%)
700	20	*de minimis* (2.85%)	not met (2%)

Thus, in cases where imports are comparatively low, ie where the EC producers have a high market share, the EC test will be more liberal than the WTO test. However, where imports are comparatively high, ie where the EC industry has a low market share, the WTO test will be more liberal. It will therefore depend on the specifics of each case whether the WTO or the EC test is more liberal. However, in order to avoid WTO inconsistencies, the EC will apply the test which leads to the most liberal result.

This example illustrates an important aspect of WTO members' implementation of the ADA that sometimes is not sufficiently realized: members may always decide to be more liberal than the ADA regime. However, they can never be more restrictive than the ADA allows.[79]

As is the case for the *de minimis* dumping rule, the negligibility test does not distinguish between developing and developed countries, contrary to similar provisions in the ASCM[80] and the ASG.[81]

---

[79] Another example of this relates to verifications. Under the ADA, the authorities arguably are not required to verify the questionnaire responses of exporters (because they may decide to accept the questionnaire responses of the exporters at face value, a liberal approach). However, they are obliged to verify the questionnaire responses of the domestic producers for purposes of the injury determination (because pure reliance on the questionnaire responses would be more restrictive than the ADA).

[80] Thus, Art 27.10(b) ASCM provides that for developing countries the negligibility level is 4%, unless countries which individually represent less than 4% together represent more than 9% of total imports of the like product. For developed countries, Art 11.9 does not define the negligibility level.

[81] Thus, Art 9.1 ASG provides that safeguard measures shall not be applied to those imports from developing countries which do not exceed 3%, provided that the developing countries with less than

Different from the operation of the *de minimis* dumping criterion, which typically necessitates a calculation exercise which can only be performed at a relatively advanced stage of the anti-dumping investigation, the authorities should normally be able to determine early on whether countries under investigation meet the negligibility test because the test relies on country-wide data. Although Article 5.8 provides no guidance with respect to the period to be used for making this determination, a 2002 recommendation of the Committee on Anti-Dumping Practices[82] provides that this should be:

(a) the period of data collection for the dumping investigation; or
(b) the most recent 12 consecutive months prior to initiation for which data are available; or
(c) the most recent 12 consecutive months prior to the date on which the application was filed, for which data are available, provided that the lapse of time between the filing of the application and the initiation of the investigation is no longer than 90 days.

3.2.3 Customs Clearance

Article 5.9 provides that an anti-dumping proceeding shall not hinder customs clearance procedures:

5.9 An anti-dumping proceeding shall not hinder the procedures of customs clearance.

Thus far, this provision has not given rise to problems.

3.2.4 Time Limit Investigations

Article 5.10 provides that investigations shall normally be concluded within one year and in no case more than 18 months after initiation:

5.10 Investigations shall, except in special circumstances, be concluded within one year, and in no case more than 18 months, after their initiation.

While the one year 'normal' deadline is met by virtually no WTO member, the 18 months' deadline is an absolute one and must be adhered to strictly.

Although some WTO members seem to argue that the conclusion of the investigation as such must be distinguished from the decision to impose

---

3% together do not account for more than 9% of total imports of the like or directly competitive product.

[82] See Annex III, G/ADP/10, below.

anti-dumping measures following the conclusion of the investigation, such an artificial distinction is unlikely to be upheld by WTO panels in light of the clear underlying rationale of the time limit to avoid uncertainty. It is therefore advisable for the authorities to complete the whole process within 18 months.

Needless to say, authorities are always free to decide within the 18 month deadline that imposition of anti-dumping measures is justified by the facts of the case, but to simultaneously suspend the application of the measures. This would be another example of a more liberal interpretation than the ADA regime allows.

3.2.5 Investigation Techniques and Due Process Rights

Article 6 is entitled evidence but also contains a number of due process rights:[83]

At the outset, we wish to underscore the importance of the obligations contained in Article 6 of the ADA. This Article 'establishes a framework of procedural and due process obligations'. Its provisions 'set out evidentiary rules that apply throughout the course of the anti-dumping investigation, and provide also for due process rights that are enjoyed by "interested parties" throughout such an investigation'.[84]

Article 6 is an article that contains *multiple obligations* with respect to the procedural and evidentiary requirements in an anti-dumping investigation.[85] As we have seen above,[86] this entails that any WTO challenges on the basis of alleged Article 6 violations will need to be further specified.

3.2.5.1 Ample Opportunity to Present Evidence

6.1 All interested parties in an anti-dumping investigation shall be given notice of the information which the authorities require and ample opportunity to present in writing all evidence which they consider relevant in respect of the investigation in question.

Article 6.1 imposes the twin obligations upon authorities to give notice of the information they require and to provide *ample* opportunity to interested parties to present all relevant evidence. Article 6.1 therefore also introduces the concept of *interested parties*.[87]

With respect to the first obligation, the panel in *Mexico–Rice* found that where there is *prima facie* evidence that the information in the application

---

[83] In *United States–Oil country tubular goods from Argentina*, AB, para 241, for example, the AB noted that Articles 6.1 and 6.2 set out 'fundamental due process rights'.

[84] *EC–Malleable cast iron tube or pipe fittings from Brazil*, AB, para 138.

[85] *Thailand–H-Beams from Poland*, Panel, para 7.27.   [86] Chapter 1, Introduction.

[87] See section 3.2.5.11, below, for more detail.

concerning exporters of the product concerned is incomplete, the authorities must actively undertake efforts to identify the exporters:

> . . . we consider that an objective and unbiased investigating authority conducting an investigation in a reasonable manner should have made more of an effort to obtain knowledge of other US exporters. The authority knew that the listing in the application was far from complete, and it had sufficient information before it that would have enabled the authority to identify other US producers and exporters. It is, in our view, the task of the investigating authority and not of the interested parties to inform all interested parties of the information that is required and to conduct a proper investigation. We are of the view that the investigating authority is not allowed to rely on the initiative of the interested parties for the fulfilment of obligations which are really its own.[88]

The panel in *Argentina–Ceramic floor tiles* ruled that an investigating authority may not fault an interested party for not providing information it was not clearly requested to submit.[89]

The panel in *Guatemala–Cement II* considered that Article 6.1 does not explicitly require the authorities to set time limits for the submission of arguments and evidence during the final stage of an investigation. Thus, Article 6.1 imposes substantive obligations without requiring them to be met in a particular way. The failure to set time limits for the submission of arguments and evidence during the final stage of the investigation did not therefore in itself constitute a violation of Article 6.1.[90]

In *United States–Oil country tubular goods*, Argentina challenged certain aspects of US law which require the USDOC to reach an affirmative likelihood determination in cases where exporters do not or do not fully cooperate in a sunset review. Under US statutory provisions, participation by an exporter is deemed to be waived if it files either an incomplete submission or no submission at all (*deemed waiver*).

The AB considered that Article 6.1 also applied to sunset reviews and that the deemed waiver provisions violated Article 6.1 as far as exporters were concerned with respect to which the USDOC had found insufficient cooperation. On the other hand, regarding exporters which did not cooperate at all, the deemed waiver provisions were found not to violate Article 6.1.[91]

---

[88] *Mexico–Rice from the United States*, Panel, para 7.199.
[89] *Argentina–Ceramic floor tiles from Italy*, Panel, para 6.54.
[90] *Guatemala–Cement from Mexico II*, Panel, para 8.119. Compare WorldTradeLaw.net, *Dispute Settlement Commentary on Egypt–Steel rebar from Turkey*, at p 28, checked on 23 April 2005, where it is noted that the ADA provides only limited guidance on the time frame to be followed by authorities in the conduct of their investigations.   [91] *United States–Oil country tubular goods*, AB, para 253.

In our view, the rights to present evidence and request a hearing cannot be said to be 'denied' to a respondent that is given an opportunity to submit an initial response to the notice of initiation simply because it must do so by a deadline that is conceded to be reasonable. We do not see it as an unreasonable burden on respondents to require them to file a timely submission in order to preserve their rights for the remainder of the sunset review. Indeed, even an incomplete submission will serve to preserve those rights. Accordingly, we are of the view that, if a respondent decides not to undertake the necessary initial steps to avail itself of the 'ample' and 'full' opportunities available for the defence of its interests, the fault lies with the respondent, and not with the deemed waiver provision.[92]

3.2.5.2 Questionnaires

Anti-dumping investigations are typically initiated with the publication of a notice of initiation in the member's official gazette.[93] In most cases, the authorities will then send out *questionnaires* on the same day as or shortly after the notice of initiation is published. The questionnaires contain detailed requests for information focusing on the investigation period[94] for the dumping determination and the injury investigation period[95] for the injury determination. It will then be in these questionnaires that the authorities indicate to the interested parties the information that they require within the meaning of Article 6.1. It is noted that each member is free to conduct the investigation in its own language.[96]

Most WTO members will send out three types[97] of questionnaires:

- questionnaire for exporters;
- questionnaire for (unrelated) importers; and
- questionnaire for domestic producers.

The questionnaires for exporters will be designed in such a manner that duly completed questionnaire responses will enable the authorities to calculate their dumping margins and to compare their prices charged on the importing country market with the prices charged by the domestic producers.

The questionnaires for unrelated importers tend to request information on purchases and resales of the product concerned from the countries under investigation.

---

[92] *United States–Oil country tubular goods*, AB, para 252.
[93] See Article 12 ADA, discussed in more detail in section 3.6.1, below.
[94] See chapter 1, Introduction, above.   [95] See section 2.3.3, above.
[96] Compare Czako, Human and Miranda, *A Handbook on Anti-Dumping Investigations* (2003) 51.
[97] Sample questionnaires are provided as Annexes in Czako, Human and Miranda, *A Handbook on Anti-Dumping Investigations* (2003).

The questionnaires for domestic producers will solicit the information necessary to determine whether they have suffered injury as a result of the dumped imports. These questionnaires would normally be sent not only to the complaining domestic producers, but to *all* domestic producers.[98]

Some WTO members have a fourth type of questionnaire intended for importers which are related to exporters. Others use a special portion in the exporters' questionnaire, which then will have to be completed by the related importers. To facilitate comparison of information, contained in the various questionnaire responses, most WTO members will use a system of product control numbers, with which all interested parties will need to comply.[99]

Article 6.1.1 provides that exporters of foreign producers should be given at least *30 days* to reply. While a similar rule for domestic producers and importers is lacking, presumably they should *ceteris paribus* never receive a longer time period than the exporters because the exporters' questionnaires of necessity are the most complicated and therefore require most time to complete:

6.1.1 Exporters or foreign producers receiving questionnaires used in an anti-dumping investigation shall be given at least 30 days for reply.[100] Due consideration should be given to any request for an extension of the 30-day period and, upon cause shown, such an extension should be granted whenever practicable.

In *Argentina–Poultry*, the panel ruled that Argentina had violated the 30 days' requirement by granting the Brazilian exporters only 20 days to respond to the questionnaires sent by the Argentine authority DCD.[101] However, Argentina had not violated Article 6.1.1 by not sending the exporters injury questionnaires as Article 6.1.1 did not require the authorities to send the exporters such questionnaires.[102]

In *Mexico–Rice*, the United States argued that Article 53 of Mexico's Foreign Trade Act violates Article 6.1.1. Article 53 provides a deadline of 28 working days counting from the date of publication of the notice of initiation. The US and Mexico agreed that this statutory deadline is not necessarily in violation of Article 6.1.1 as far as exporters are concerned which are listed in the application

---

[98] Compare Czako, Human and Miranda, *A Handbook on Anti-Dumping Investigations* (2003) 49.

[99] See section 1.1.1, above.

[100] Fn 15 in ADA: As a general rule, the time-limit for exporters shall be counted from the date of receipt of the questionnaire, which for this purpose shall be deemed to have been received one week from the date on which it was sent to the respondent or transmitted to the appropriate diplomatic representative of the exporting Member or, in the case of a separate customs territory Member of the WTO, an official representative of the exporting territory.

[101] *Argentina–Poultry from Brazil*, Panel, para 7.144.

[102] *Argentina–Poultry from Brazil*, Panel, para 7.145.

and to which questionnaires will be sent on the day following the publication of the notice of initiation. However, non-listed exporters which will not receive a questionnaire at initiation will have less than 30 days to reply. In the view of Mexico, Article 6.1.1 did not apply to non-listed exporters.[103] The panel agreed with the United States:

> We consider that Article 6.1.1 of the ADA clearly provides that any exporter or foreign producer receiving a questionnaire shall be given 30 days for reply. This 30-day rule does not make a distinction between those exporters that received a questionnaire at the time of initiation because they happened to be known to the applicant and were thus informed of the initiation, and those that make themselves known or the existence of which becomes known to the authorities and to which questionnaires are sent following initiation. In our view, by using the date of publication of the initiation notice as the starting point for the time period for questionnaire responses, Article 53 of the Act effectively prevents Mexico from giving each exporter or foreign producer receiving a questionnaire 30 days to respond. For that reason we consider Article 53 of the Act to be inconsistent with the unequivocal requirement in Article 6.1.1 of the ADA to provide for 30 days to respond to questionnaires.[104]

In *United States–Hot rolled steel*, the AB agreed with the United States that Article 6.1.1 clearly contemplated that the authorities may impose *deadlines* for the response to the questionnaires, even though Article 6.1.1 did not explicitly use that word. However, the AB also found that any deadlines imposed by the authorities are *not necessarily absolute and immutable* because the second sentence of Article 6.1.1 expressly provides that the authorities must extend the time limit for responses to questionnaires upon cause shown, where granting such an extension is practicable:[105]

> In sum, Article 6.1.1 establishes that investigating authorities may impose time-limits for questionnaire responses, and that in appropriate circumstances these time-limits must be extended. However, Article 6.1.1 does not, on its own, resolve the issue of when investigating authorities are entitled to reject information submitted, and instead resort to facts available, as USDOC did in this case. We consider that this issue is to be resolved by reading Article 6.1.1 together with Article 6.8 of the ADA, and Annex II of that Agreement, which is incorporated by reference into Article 6.8.[106]

---

[103] *Mexico–Rice from the United States*, Panel, para 7.219.
[104] *Mexico–Rice from the United States*, Panel, para 7.220.
[105] *United States–Hot Rolled Steel from Japan*, AB, paras 73–75.
[106] *United States–Hot Rolled Steel from Japan*, AB, paras 73–75.

A 2001 recommendation of the Committee on Anti-Dumping Practices[107] provides the following – non-exhaustive – list of elements that authorities may consider in deciding whether or not to grant extensions of deadlines, including that for responding to the questionnaires:

- the time available for the conduct of the investigation and making the necessary determinations, including the time periods established in national legislation, regulations and schedules governing the conduct of the investigation at hand, and whether the information can be considered in a subsequent phase of the investigation;
- previous extension(s) of time granted to the same party in the same investigation;
- the ability of the party from whom information is sought to respond to the request, in light of the nature and extent of the information requested, including the party's available resources, personnel and technological capability;
- any unusual burdens that will be incurred by the party being asked for information in searching for, identifying and/or compiling the information requested;
- whether the party requesting the extension has provided a partial response to the request, or has previously provided information requested in the same investigation, although the absence of a partial response alone is not an appropriate basis for denial of a request;
- any unforeseen circumstances affecting the ability of the party to provide the information requested within the time limit established;
- whether other parties have been granted extensions of time for similar reasons during the same phase of the same investigation.

3.2.5.3 *Access to Information*

Article 6.1.2 requires the authorities to ensure that written evidence by interested parties shall be made available promptly to other interested parties participating in the investigation:

6.1.2 Subject to the requirement to protect confidential information, evidence presented in writing by one interested party shall be made available promptly to other interested parties participating in the investigation.

As the panel in *Guatemala–Cement II* pointed out, it is up to the authorities to establish a system that satisfies this requirement. The most obvious way of

---

[107] See Annex 3, below.

doing so might be for the authorities to maintain a (non-confidential) case file to which other interested parties participating in the investigation can have access upon request. However, one can envisage other systems which might satisfy the requirement equally well:

For example, if an investigating authority required each interested party to serve its submissions on all other interested parties, or if the investigating authority itself undertook to provide copies of each interested party's submission to other interested parties, there may be no need for interested parties to have access to the file.[108]

The same panel considered that access to the file need not necessarily be unlimited nor would the file have to be made available on demand, as long as the access is regular and routine.[109] Clearly, this may require judgment calls in concrete cases:

In the factual circumstances set forth ... a denial of access on 4 November 1996 because the relevant official is overseas, followed by a denial of access during the following week because the investigating authority is working on the file, and in the absence of any indication as to when access to the file would be granted, would not be consistent with the need to ensure routine and regular access to the file. We are of the view that these circumstances are indicative of a pattern of behaviour which would prevent regular and routine access to the file, and which would fail to ensure that evidence presented by one interested party would be 'made available promptly' to other interested parties (consistent with Article 6.1.2), and which would fail to ensure that interested parties have 'timely opportunities' to see information relevant to the presentation of their cases (consistent with Article 6.4).[110]

Similarly, the requirement to protect confidential information cannot be used as an excuse to delay making available evidence submitted by one interested party to another interested party (for 20 days) because of the possibility that the evidence contains confidential information.[111]

In *Argentina–Poultry*, the panel ruled that the right of access to the file may be limited to interested parties actively taking part in the investigation:

We note that Article 6.1.2 does not refer to 'interested parties' but to 'interested parties participating in the investigation.' Thus, the term 'interested parties' is qualified by the term 'participating'. . . The ordinary meaning of the term 'participate' is 'share or take part (in)'. This definition of the term 'participating' suggests to us that, in order to participate in an investigation, a party must undertake some action. In our view, the

---

[108] *Guatemala–Cement from Mexico II*, Panel, para 8.133.
[109] *Guatemala–Cement from Mexico II*, Panel, para 8.133.
[110] *Guatemala–Cement from Mexico II*, Panel, para 8.135.
[111] *Guatemala–Cement from Mexico II*, Panel, para 8.143.

mere knowledge by an interested party of an ongoing investigation does not make that party an interested party 'participating in the investigation' within the meaning of Article 6.1.2 unless it actively takes part in the investigation.[112]

Closely related to Article 6.1.2 is Article 6.4. Article 6.4 extends the right of interested parties of access to information to all information that is:

- relevant to the presentation of their case;
- not confidential as defined in Article 6.5; and
- used by the authorities in the anti-dumping investigation.

6.4 The authorities shall whenever practicable provide timely opportunities for all interested parties to see all information that is relevant to the presentation of their cases, that is not confidential as defined in paragraph 5, and that is used by the authorities in an anti-dumping investigation, and to prepare presentations on the basis of this information.

In addition, the authorities must provide timely opportunities for all interested parties to prepare presentations on the basis of such information.

In *Guatemala–Cement II*, the panel again considered that there may be various ways in which the authorities can satisfy the requirement to provide access to information, as it had done with respect to Article 6.1.2, one of these being access to the file maintained by the authorities. The panel report offers a useful illustration of the extent to which panels may check whether the fundamental right of access to the file in reality is exercisable:

In the present case, the Ministry chose to offer interested parties copies of the file, against payment of a fee.[113] An investigating authority cannot 'provide timely opportunities for all interested parties to see all information that is relevant to the presentation of their cases' if it conditions the provision of copies on the payment of a fee without at least informing the requesting party how much the fee would be, or without at least providing the requesting party with the information it would need (e.g., the number of pages in the file) to calculate the fee for itself.[114]

In *EC–Malleable cast iron tube or pipe fittings*, the AB was called upon to determine whether the EC's refusal to grant Brazilian exporters access to an internal Commission working document containing information on some of the Article 3.4 injury factors violated Articles 6.2[115] and 6.4. The working document had been submitted by the EC to the panel as Exhibit EC-12 in support of the EC's claim that it had in fact considered all Article 3.4 injury factors.

---

[112] *Argentina–Poultry from Brazil*, Panel, para 7.153.
[113] *Guatemala–Cement from Mexico II*, Panel, para 8.151.
[114] *Guatemala–Cement from Mexico II*, Panel, para 8.153.   [115] See section 3.2.5.5, below.

The AB first of all ruled that the term *relevant* (first condition) meant relevant to the interested parties (rather than relevant to the authorities):

We turn first to the requirement that the information be 'relevant'. From the Panel's reasoning, it is apparent that it read this requirement to mean 'relevant' from the perspective of the investigating authority. We disagree. Article 6.4 refers to 'provid[ing] timely opportunities for all interested parties to see all information that is relevant to the presentation of their cases' ... The possessive pronoun 'their' clearly refers to the earlier reference in that sentence to 'interested parties'. The investigating authorities are not mentioned in Article 6.4 until later in the sentence, when the provision refers to the additional requirement that the information be 'used by the authorities'. Thus, whether or not the investigating authorities regarded the information in Exhibit EC-12 to be relevant does not determine whether the information would in fact have been 'relevant' for the purposes of Article 6.4.[116]

This ruling is more important than it may seem at first sight because it would appear to entail that it is for interested parties to determine what is relevant, and not for the authorities. The AB did not explicitly go that far, however, but rather determined that as the document contained information on some of the Article 3.4 factors and it had previously held that the Article 3.4 factors are relevant in every investigation, the information in Exhibit EC-12 was necessarily relevant.[117]

The AB also disagreed with the panel's reasoning as to whether the EC had actually *used* (third condition) the information in Exhibit EC-12:

The Panel did not expressly determine that the European Commission did not 'use' the information in Exhibit EC-12 as contemplated under Article 6.4. Instead, the Panel stated that the information in Exhibit EC-12 'was not specifically relied upon by the EC in reaching the anti-dumping determination'. It appears that the Panel arrived at this conclusion because, in its view, the European Commission had 'essentially concluded that this data was "in line" with other data (that was disclosed) and that there was no "value added" to the substance of their investigation in the analysis of these factors.' In our view, however, the Panel's reasoning overlooks the fact that the European Commission was required to evaluate all the injury factors listed in Article 3.4, and the evaluation of some of these factors is set out exclusively in Exhibit EC-12. In other words, Exhibit EC-12 relates to a required step in the anti-dumping investigation. The European Communities relies on Exhibit EC-12 as the sole evidence that it performed this required step. As we see it, this necessarily leads to the conclusion that the information in Exhibit EC-12 was in fact 'used' by the European Commission in the anti-dumping investigation and that, therefore, Exhibit EC-12 also satisfies this

---

[116] *EC–Malleable cast iron tube or pipe fittings from Brazil*, AB, para 145.
[117] *EC–Malleable cast iron tube or pipe fittings from Brazil*, AB, para 146.

criterion of Article 6.4. Thus, the European Communities was not entitled to exclude this information on the basis that it did not consider that it provided 'value added' to the investigation.[118]

3.2.5.4 *Access to the Application*

Article 6.1.3 requires the authorities to provide the full text of the application to known exporters and the authorities of the exporting member as soon as the case is initiated. Because of the need to protect confidential information, acknowledged by the second sentence of Article 6.1.3, the authorities will normally require the domestic industry to submit both a confidential and a non-confidential version of the application. The non-confidential version of the application will then be provided to other interested parties. Some members will send a copy of the application together with the questionnaires:

6.1.3 As soon as an investigation has been initiated, the authorities shall provide the full text of the written application received under paragraph 1 of Article 5 to the known exporters[119] and to the authorities of the exporting Member and shall make it available, upon request, to other interested parties involved. Due regard shall be paid to the requirement for the protection of confidential information, as provided for in paragraph 5.

In *Guatemala–Cement II*, the panel ruled that the application must be provided *immediately*. A delay of eight days will not be acceptable:

We note that Article 6.1.3 does not specify the number of days within which the text of the application shall be provided. What it does specify is that the text of the application be provided 'as soon as' the investigation has been initiated. In this regard, the term 'as soon as' conveys a sense of substantial urgency. In fact, the terms 'immediately' and 'as soon as' are considered to be interchangeable. Providing the text of the application 24 or even 18 days after the date of initiation does not fulfil the requirement of Article 6.1.3 that the text be provided 'as soon as an investigation has been initiated.'[120]

We are of the view that given the nature of the obligation in Article 6.1.3 sending the application even 8 days after the initiation of investigation is not adequate to fulfil the requirement that it be done 'as soon as an investigation has been initiated.'[121]

---

[118] *EC–Malleable cast iron tube or pipe fittings from Brazil*, AB, para 147.

[119] Fn 16 in ADA: It being understood that, where the number of exporters involved is particularly high, the full text of the written application should instead be provided only to the authorities of the exporting Member or to the relevant trade association.

[120] *Guatemala–Cement from Mexico II*, Panel, para 8.101.

[121] *Guatemala–Cement from Mexico II*, Panel, para 8.104.

Article 6.1.3 makes a distinction between the obligation of the authorities to *provide* the application to exporters and the exporting country member and the obligation of the authorities to *make* it *available*, upon request, to other interested parties involved. The panel in *Argentina–Poultry* considered that the former obligation requires positive action on the part of the authorities: simply granting exporters access to the application will not meet the requirement:[122]

In our view, with the use of different verbs in the first sentence of Article 6.1.3, 'provide' on the one hand and 'make available' on the other, the drafters intended to impose different obligations on investigating authorities depending on the party concerned. The first obligation requires a positive action on the part of the investigating authority, while the second envisages only a passive act.[123]

The panel noted in *obiter dicta* that an application sent to known exporters more than 15 days from the publication of the notice of initiation would violate the Article 6.1.3 obligation.[124]

3.2.5.5 *Right of Defence; Hearings*

Article 6.2, first sentence, establishes the fundamental due process right[125] of all interested parties to have a full opportunity to defend their interests:

6.2 Throughout the anti-dumping investigation all interested parties shall have a full opportunity for the defence of their interests. To this end, the authorities shall, on request, provide opportunities for all interested parties to meet those parties with adverse interests, so that opposing views may be presented and rebuttal arguments offered. Provision of such opportunities must take account of the need to preserve confidentiality and of the convenience to the parties. There shall be no obligation on any party to attend a meeting, and failure to do so shall not be prejudicial to that party's case. Interested parties shall also have the right, on justification, to present other information orally.

Article 6.2 then obliges the authorities to grant interested parties:

- on request, opportunities to meet parties with adverse interests, so that opposing views may be presented and rebuttal arguments offered (this could be done, for example, in the form of public hearings or in the form of private confrontation meetings);
- the right, on justification, to present information orally (*ex parte* hearings).

---

[122] *Argentina–Poultry from Brazil*, Panel, paras 7.169–7.170.
[123] *Argentina–Poultry from Brazil*, Panel, paras 7.169–7.170.
[124] *Argentina–Poultry from Brazil*, Panel, para 7.173, fn 143.
[125] *Guatemala–Cement from Mexico II*, Panel, para 8.179. Compare Durling and Nicely, *Understanding the WTO Anti-Dumping Agreement: Negotiating History and Subsequent Interpretation*, (2002) 331.

Article 6.2 does not provide procedural requirements as to how the authorities should structure hearings. As a result, practice among WTO members varies widely. Some members will organize public hearings, of which detailed transcripts are made. Others will grant more informal hearings in which the officials assigned to the case (the case handlers) will simply take notes. However, it must be borne in mind that whatever system the authorities use, they should always ensure that it meets the fundamental due process right of Article 6.2, first sentence.

The right to have a full opportunity to defend one's interests is closely linked to other provisions of Article 6. In *Thailand–H-Beams*, for example, the panel considered that it is predicated on having timely access to relevant information.[126] This view was later echoed by the AB in *EC–Malleable cast iron tube or pipe fittings*, discussed below.[127]

In *Guatemala–Cement II*, the panel relied on this right to rule that the authorities, when faced with a request from one interested party to extend the investigation period, are obliged to solicit the views of other interested parties before deciding on such a request:

We interpret the first sentence of Article 6.2 of the ADA is a fundamental due process provision. When a request for an extension of the POI comes from one interested party, due process requires that the investigating authority seeks the views of other interested parties before acting on that request. Failure to respect the requirements of due process would conflict with the requirement to provide interested parties with 'a full opportunity for the defence of their interests,' consistent with Article 6.2. Clearly, an interested party is not able to defend *its* interests if it is prevented from commenting on requests made by other interested parties in pursuit of *their* interests.[128]

In *EC–Malleable cast iron tube or pipe fittings*, the AB ruled that the EC's failure to disclose to the Brazilian exporters an internal working document in which it had discussed certain of the Article 3.4 injury factors and which it had submitted to the panel as Exhibit EC-12 constituted a violation of Article 6.2:[129]

The European Communities recognized during the oral hearing that a finding of violation in this case under Article 6.4 would necessarily entail a violation of Article 6.2. We are also of the view that, by failing to meet its legal obligation to disclose Exhibit EC-12, the European Communities did not afford the Brazilian exporter 'a full

---

[126] *Thailand–H-Beams from Poland*, Panel, para 7.150.
[127] *EC–Malleable cast iron tube or pipe fittings from Brazil*, AB, para 149.
[128] *Guatemala–Cement from Mexico II*, Panel, para 8.179.
[129] See also section 3.2.5.3, above.

opportunity for the defence of [its] interests' as required under Article 6.2 of the ADA. One of the stated objectives of the disclosure of information required under Article 6.4 is to allow interested parties 'to prepare presentations on the basis of this information'. The 'presentations' referred to in Article 6.4, whether written or oral, logically are the principal mechanisms through which an exporter subject to an anti-dumping investigation can defend its interests. Thus, by failing to disclose Exhibit EC-12 and thereby depriving the Brazilian exporter of an opportunity to present its defence, the European Communities did not act consistently with Article 6.2.[130]

In *United States–Oil country tubular goods*, the panel ruled that Article 6.2 also applies in sunset reviews. The fact that certain exporters did not or insufficiently cooperate in a sunset review did not provide a justification for depriving cooperating exporters of their right to have a hearing.[131] On appeal, the AB upheld the panel's finding as regards exporters that did not cooperate sufficiently. However, as regards exporters that did not cooperate at all, the AB reversed the panel's finding.[132]

6.3 Oral information provided under paragraph 2 shall be taken into account by the authorities only in so far as it is subsequently reproduced in writing and made available to other interested parties, as provided for in subparagraph 1.2.

Article 6.3 essentially requires interested parties to submit a written version of information provided orally and the authorities to make the written version available to other interested parties. The most obvious way for authorities to meet this obligation would be to put the (non-confidential version of the) document in the case file that is accessible to the other interested parties.

3.2.5.6 *Confidentiality of Information*

Article 6.5 lays down the principle that confidential information submitted by interested parties in the course of an anti-dumping investigation is to be kept confidential by the authorities, upon good cause shown. Confidential information may not be disclosed by the authorities without specific permission of the party that submitted the information.

Article 6.5 appears to distinguish between two types of confidential information:

- information which is by nature confidential, for example, because its disclosure would be of significant competitive advantage to a competitor or because its disclosure would have a significantly adverse impact upon a

---

[130] *EC–Malleable cast iron tube or pipe fittings from Brazil*, AB, para 149.

[131] *United States–Oil country tubular goods from Argentina*, Panel, para 7.219.

[132] *United States–Oil country tubular goods from Argentina*, Panel, para 253, discussed in more detail in section 3.2.5.1, above.

person supplying the information or upon a person from whom that
person acquired the information; and

• information which is provided on a confidential basis by parties to an
investigation.

6.5 Any information which is by nature confidential (for example, because its
disclosure would be of significant competitive advantage to a competitor or because its
disclosure would have a significantly adverse effect upon a person supplying the information or upon a person from whom that person acquired the information), or which
is provided on a confidential basis by parties to an investigation shall, upon good cause
shown, be treated as such by the authorities. Such information shall not be disclosed
without specific permission of the party submitting it.[133]

However, as interpreted by the panel in *Guatemala–Cement II*, the provision
treats both types of confidential information on a par:

The requirement to show 'good cause' appears to apply for both types of confidential
information, such that even information 'which is by nature confidential' cannot be
afforded confidential treatment unless 'good cause' has been shown.[134]

In our view, the requisite 'good cause' must be shown by the interested party
submitting the confidential information at issue. The panel does not consider that
Article 6.5 envisages 'good cause' being shown by the investigating authority itself,
since – with respect to information that is not 'by nature confidential' in particular –
the investigating authority may not even know whether or why there is cause to provide
confidential treatment.[135]

However, it is important to note that the panel clearly established that the good
cause showing is a burden for the interested party concerned and that it may
not be used by the authorities to hide inconvenient facts.[136]

In *Argentina–Ceramic floor tiles*, the issue was raised whether authorities
could rely on confidential information which had not been disclosed to
other interested parties. Not surprisingly, the panel answered this question
affirmatively: any other interpretation would have made the application of the
ADA unworkable as anti-dumping investigations are full of confidential
information.

In our view, the presence in the ADA of a requirement to protect confidential
information indicates that investigating authorities might need to rely on such

---

[133] Fn 17 in ADA: Members are aware that in the territory of certain Members disclosure pursuant
to a narrowly-drawn protective order may be required.

[134] *Guatemala–Cement from Mexico II*, Panel, para 8.219.

[135] *Guatemala–Cement from Mexico II*, Panel, para 8.220.

[136] Durling and Nicely, *Understanding the WTO Anti-Dumping Agreement: Negotiating History
and Subsequent Interpretation* (2002) 336.

information in making the determinations required under the ADA. The ADA therefore contains a mechanism that allows parties to provide investigating authorities with such information for the purposes of making their determinations, while ensuring that the information is not used for other purposes. In accordance with the accepted principles of treaty interpretation, we are to give meaning to all the terms of the Agreement. It would be contradictory to suggest that the ADA creates a mechanism for the protection of confidential information, but precludes investigating authorities from relying on such information in making its determinations. If that were the case, then there would be no reason for the investigating authority to seek such information in the first place.[137]

While the decision of the WTO members to choose a system of confidentiality of information is understandable in light of the commercial sensitivity of virtually all data involved, it requires a high level of integrity and professionalism on the part of the authorities. The system also impinges on elementary due process rights of interested parties because findings will be reached and decisions made partially based upon information to which they will not have had access.

This is less of a problem on the dumping side (where the parties submitting the information are also the parties to whom the results of the data will be applied) than on the injury side. A crucial component of any injury determination will be a comparison of the prices charged by the exporters and their importers, on the one hand, and by the domestic producers, on the other hand. As the various data necessary for making this comparison emanate from different interested parties, none of the interested parties will be in a position to assess the accuracy of the analysis of such data by the authorities.

The domestic legislation of some WTO members, including the United States and Canada, offers a solution for this problem by authorizing disclosure of confidential information under an administrative protective order. Although the details vary, the principle is that the legal representatives of the interested parties may be granted access to (parts of) the confidential information submitted by the other parties. Footnote 17 ADA explicitly authorizes the use of this solution.

6.5.1 The authorities shall require interested parties providing confidential information to furnish non-confidential summaries thereof. These summaries shall be in sufficient detail to permit a reasonable understanding of the substance of the

---

[137] *Argentina–Ceramic floor tiles from Italy*, Panel, para 6.34.

information submitted in confidence. In exceptional circumstances, such parties may indicate that such information is not susceptible of summary. In such exceptional circumstances, a statement of the reasons why summarization is not possible must be provided.

Article 6.5.1 obliges the authorities to require interested parties to provide non-confidential summaries of confidential information. Such summaries should be sufficiently detailed to permit a reasonable understanding of the substance of the confidential information. This would appear to necessitate a proactive check on the part of the authorities as it will be the natural inclination of interested parties to disclose as little as possible.

The *ratio legis* of this requirement is to enable the other interested parties to defend their interests. While the authorities have an independent duty to ensure that the non-confidential summaries are meaningful from that perspective, the panel in *Argentina–Ceramic floor tiles* ruled that the authorities were not authorized to disregard confidential information on the basis that the non-confidential summary thereof was not sufficiently detailed to calculate the dumping margin. In other words, there is no linkage between the non-confidential summaries submitted in a case and the published (non-confidential) findings and conclusions by the authorities:

...we see nothing in Article 6.5.1, nor elsewhere in Article 6.5, that authorizes a Member to disregard confidential information solely on the basis that the non-confidential summary of that information contains insufficient detail to permit authorities to calculate normal value, export price and the margin of dumping.

Consistent with our view that authorities may rely on confidential information in making their determination, the purpose of the non-confidential summaries provided for in Article 6.5.1 is to inform the *interested parties* so as to enable them to defend their interests. We do not consider that the purpose of the non-confidential summaries is to enable the *authorities* to arrive at public conclusions, as Argentina contends. Thus, an authority would not in our view be justified in rejecting the exporters' responses simply because the information in the non-confidential summaries was not sufficient to allow the calculation of normal value, export price, and the margin of dumping.[138]

In exceptional circumstances, parties may indicate that non-confidential summarization is not possible, provided that they motivate why this is the case. The panel in *Guatemala–Cement II* ruled that the authorities must enforce this

---

[138] *Argentina–Ceramic floor tiles from Italy*, Panel, paras 6.38–6.39.

obligation incumbent upon the interested parties and that, in other words, Article 6.5.1 imposes an obligation upon the authorities:[139]

Although Article 6.5.1 does not explicitly provide that 'the authorities shall require' interested parties to provide a statement of the reasons why summarization is not possible, any meaningful interpretation of Article 6.5.1 must impose such an obligation on the investigating authorities. It is certainly not possible to conclude that the obligation concerning the need to provide a statement of reasons is an obligation imposed exclusively on the interested party submitting the information, and not the investigating authority, since the ADA is not addressed at interested parties ... Accordingly, Article 6.5.1 imposes an obligation on investigating authorities to require parties that indicate that information is not susceptible of summary to provide a statement of the reasons why summarization is not possible.[140]

In *Guatemala–Cement II*, the panel found that Guatemala had failed to abide by this requirement.

It is for the authorities to decide whether requests for confidentiality are warranted. However, even if the authorities disagree, they cannot compel any party to disclose such information. At most, they can *disregard* the information, after having giving the party concerned the opportunity to either make the information public or to authorize its disclosure in generalized or summary form and the party has declined. Even then, the authorities may not disregard the information if the party can demonstrate to their satisfaction from appropriate sources that the information is in fact correct.

6.5.2 If the authorities find that a request for confidentiality is not warranted and if the supplier of the information is either unwilling to make the information public or to authorize its disclosure in generalized or summary form, the authorities may disregard such information unless it can be demonstrated to their satisfaction from appropriate sources that the information is correct.[141]

3.2.5.7 Verifications

Accuracy check   The information submitted by interested parties in an anti-dumping proceeding is mostly contained in the questionnaire responses[142] and the responses to subsequent requests by the authorities for clarification or additional information (often called *deficiency letters*). While evidence provided orally may support the written documentation, it is seldom

[139] Compare Durling and Nicely, *Understanding the WTO Anti-Dumping Agreement: Negotiating History and Subsequent Interpretation* (2002) 343.

[140] *Guatemala–Cement from Mexico II*, Panel, para 8.213.

[141] Fn 18 in ADA: Members agree that requests for confidentiality should not be arbitrarily rejected.   [142] See section 3.2.5.2, above.

dispositive. Instead, findings and conclusions will almost always be based on the written documentation provided by the interested parties. Such evidence tends to be voluminous and must be compiled within the relatively short time period of 30 days. Clerical errors may therefore occur. Furthermore, interested parties obviously have an interest to present their case in the best possible light.

It is therefore logical for authorities to check the correctness of the written information. Article 6.6 in fact requires authorities to satisfy themselves as to the accuracy of the information supplied by interested parties upon which their findings are based:

6.6 Except in circumstances provided for in paragraph 8, the authorities shall during the course of an investigation satisfy themselves as to the accuracy of the information supplied by interested parties upon which their findings are based.

This check is normally done through on-the-spot visits, called *verifications* in the ADA and in AD parlance. Technically, however, the term verifications appears only in Article 6.7 in the context of visits of exporters.[143] This was an important reason for the panel in *United States–DRAMS* to hold that the accuracy check of Article 6.6 does not require verifications:

The text of Article 6.6 does not explicitly require verification of all information to be relied on. Indeed, the term 'verify' only arises in Article 6.7 of the ADA. Article 6.6 simply requires Members to 'satisfy themselves as to the accuracy of the information.' In our view, Members could 'satisfy themselves as to the accuracy of the information' in a number of ways without proceeding to some type of formal verification, including for example reliance on the reputation of the original source of the information. Indeed, we consider that anti-dumping investigations would become totally unmanageable if investigating authorities were required to actually verify the accuracy of all information relied on.[144]

It is hard to envisage how authorities can effectively check the accuracy of written information in this fact-specific area without conducting verifications. The possible reliance on the 'reputation of the original source of the information' suggested by the panel seems a risky invitation for authorities to use administrative short-cuts. It is recalled that while the ADA allows authorities to skip exporters' verifications.[145] (for example, if they elect to

---

[143] Compare Czako, Human and Miranda, *A Handbook on Anti-Dumping Investigations* (2003) 19.   [144] *United States–DRAMS from Korea*, Panel, para 6.78.
[145] Compare *Egypt–Steel rebar from Turkey*, Panel, para 7.326. See also Czako, Human and Miranda, *A Handbook on Anti-Dumping Investigations* (2003) 18.

accept the exporters' questionnaire responses at face value), they arguably have no such choice regarding domestic producers' questionnaire responses as the information contained therein will in large part form the basis for the injury finding. If the authorities rely on that information to find affirmatively, they are obliged to check its veracity.

However, it is not apparent that the panel in *United States–DRAMS* went that far. The information in question concerned independent market analysts' and business reports. Korea had not attacked the reliability of the reports as such, but rather had taken the position that *all* information should be verified.

In *Guatemala–Cement II*, the panel noted that the accuracy check applies only to information used by the authorities to base their findings on. In the view of the panel, this necessitates a two-step approach on the part of the authorities:

- determine which information is substantively relevant;
- check the accuracy of that information.

In our view, it is important to distinguish between the accuracy of information, and the substantive relevance of such information. Once an investigating authority has determined what information is of substantive relevance to its investigation, Article 6.6 requires the investigating authority to satisfy itself (except when 'best information available' is used) that the substantively relevant information is accurate. Thus, Article 6.6 applies once an initial determination has been made that the information is of substantive relevance to the investigation. Article 6.6 provides no guidance in respect of the initial determination of whether information is, or is not, of substantive relevance to the investigation.[146]

Exporters' verifications   Article 6.7 jo. Annex I contain rules for the conduct of exporters' verifications. Article 6.7 lays out the basic framework while Annex 1 contains more detailed procedures:

6.7 In order to verify information provided or to obtain further details, the authorities may carry out investigations in the territory of other Members as required, provided they obtain the agreement of the firms concerned and notify the representatives of the government of the Member in question, and unless that Member objects to the investigation. The procedures described in Annex I shall apply to investigations carried out in the territory of other Members. Subject to the requirement to protect confidential information, the authorities shall make the results of any such investigations available, or shall provide disclosure thereof pursuant to paragraph 9, to the firms to which they pertain and may make such results available to the applicants.

---

[146] *Guatemala–Cement from Mexico II*, Panel, para 8.172.

Article 6.7 first of all provides that the authorities *may* carry out verifications in third countries, provided that they obtain the agreement of the firms concerned and notify the exporting country government representatives, and unless the exporting country government objects. As far as this author is aware, only the Swiss government objects to verifications being conducted in its territory, and this for constitutional reasons. Although the exporters under investigation technically must agree to the verifications, in reality they have little choice as their refusal to cooperate in a planned verification will lead the authorities to use facts available.[147]

On the other hand, authorities are not obliged to verify the information provided by the exporters.[148]

... we find determinative the use of the word 'may' ... This language makes clear that on-the-spot verifications in the territory of other Members are permitted, but not required, by Article 6.7.[149]

Turkish objections against Egypt having carried out 'mail order' verifications[150] of costs were therefore overruled.

Most members will assign a team of at least two so-called case handlers to conduct the dumping investigation. These case handlers will prepare the questionnaires, analyse the questionnaire responses, send out deficiency letters, conduct the verifications and make the calculations.

Nevertheless, verifications tend to be very system- and case-specific. Broadly speaking, some systems painstakingly verify virtually all information contained in the questionnaire responses while other systems will check the overall consistency and accuracy of the information through spot-checks. In the former case, a verification may sometimes take weeks while in the latter case it tends to take two to three days. Some systems also conduct separate verifications of prices and costs, while others routinely verify both.

Verifications are relatively costly and some WTO members therefore rely on local staff (for example from the member's embassy in the exporting country). Other members sometimes rely on external experts to conduct verifications. This tends to happen particularly in WTO members with relatively little experience, such as new users of the anti-dumping instrument.

In *Guatemala–Cement II*, Mexico alleged that Guatemala had used non-governmental experts with a conflict of interest (two non-governmental

---

[147] See section 3.2.5.8, below
[148] Compare Czako, Human and Miranda, *A Handbook on Anti-Dumping Investigations* (2003) 18.　　　　　[149] *Egypt–Steel rebar from Turkey*, Panel, para 7.326.
[150] *Egypt–Steel rebar from Turkey*, Panel, para 7.316.

experts had represented US cement producers against Mexican cement producers in US anti-dumping proceedings). The panel ruled that this practice did not as such violate the provisions of Article 6.7 and Annex I:

> Although we are of the view that an impartial and objective investigating authority would not include non-governmental experts with a conflict of interest in its verification team, none of the provisions cited by Mexico explicitly prohibit such conduct. Accordingly, we are unable to find that the Ministry violated Article 6.7 and Annex I (2), (3), (7) and (8) of the ADA by including non-governmental experts with a conflict of interest in its verification team.[151]

From the wording of the panel report, one may possibly infer that Mexico invoked the wrong provision.

Article 6.7 *in fine* provides that, subject to the requirement to protect confidential information, the authorities shall make the results of any such investigations available, or shall provide disclosure thereof pursuant to Article 6.9, to the firms to which they pertain and may make such results available to the applicants. The authorities therefore have two options to comply.

The authorities of some members will prepare a detailed verification report, a copy of which will be provided to the party that was verified. Other interested parties will then have access to the non-confidential version of this verification report.[152] Other members will treat the detailed verification reports as internal working documents, which will not be provided to any of the interested parties, including the party that was verified. The latter will then be apprised of the results of the verification in the disclosure, provided under Article 6.9. In countries using this system, other interested parties normally will not get access to the results.

ANNEX I: *Procedures for on-the-spot verifications pursuant to paragraph 7 of Article 6*

1. Upon initiation of an investigation, the authorities of the exporting Member and the firms known to be concerned should be informed of the intention to carry out on-the-sport investigations.

2. If in exceptional circumstances it is intended to include non-governmental experts in the investigating team, the firms and the authorities of the exporting Member should be so informed. Such non-governmental experts should be subject to effective sanctions for breach of confidentiality requirements.

3. It should be standard practice to obtain explicit agreement of the firms concerned in the exporting Member before the visit is finally scheduled.

---

[151] *Guatemala–Cement from Mexico II*, Panel, para 8.189.
[152] Compare Czako, Human and Miranda, *A Handbook on Anti-Dumping Investigations* (2003) 21.

4. As soon as the agreement of the firms concerned has been obtained, the investigating authorities should notify the authorities of the exporting Member of the names and addresses of the firms to be visited and the dates agreed.

5. Sufficient advance notice should be given to the firms in question before the visit is made.

6. Visits to explain the questionnaire should only be made at the request of an exporting firm. Such a visit may only be made if (a) the authorities of the importing Member notify the representatives of the Member in question and (b) the latter do not object to the visit.

7. As the main purpose of the on-the-spot investigation is to verify information provided or to obtain further details, it should be carried out after the response to the questionnaire has been received unless the firm agrees to the contrary and the government of the exporting Member is informed by the investigating authorities of the anticipated visit and does not object to it; further, it should be standard practice prior to the visit to advise the firms concerned of the general nature of the information to be verified and of any further information which needs to be provided, though this should not preclude requests to be made on the spot for further details to be provided in the light of information obtained.

8. Enquiries or questions put by the authorities or firms of the exporting Members and essential to a successful on-the-spot investigation should, whenever possible, be answered before the visit is made.

In *Guatemala–Cement II*, the panel found that Guatemala had violated the Annex I, paragraph 2, obligation to inform the exporting country authorities about its inclusion of non-governmental experts on the verification team:

Although an investigating authority should normally be able to demonstrate that it complied with a formal requirement to inform the authorities of another Member, Guatemala has failed to rebut the strong suggestion that it failed to do so. In fact, Guatemala has simply referred to the very letter which suggests strongly that Mexico was *not* notified by Guatemala. In these circumstances, the evidence and arguments of the parties do not 'remain in equipoise.' Accordingly, we find that the Ministry violated paragraph 2 of Annex I of the ADA by failing to inform the Government of Mexico of the inclusion of non-governmental experts in the Ministry's verification team.[153]

In the same case, the panel rejected Mexico's argument ex Annex I, paragraph 7, that the authorities may only verify information submitted prior to the verification visit:

Although Annex I(7) provides that the 'main purpose' of the verification visit is to verify information already provided, or to obtain further details in respect of that

---

[153] *Guatemala–Cement from Mexico II*, Panel, para 8.196.

information, it also provides that an investigating authority may 'prior to the visit . . . advise the firms concerned . . . of any further information which needs to be provided.' Since there would be little point in advising a firm of 'further information . . . to be provided' in advance of the verification visit if the investigating authority were precluded from examining that 'further information' during the visit, we consider that the phrase 'further information . . . to be provided' refers to information to be provided during the course of the verification. Mexico's view that an investigating authority may only verify information submitted prior to the verification visit is not consistent with this interpretation of Annex I(7).[154]

This makes perfect sense as verifications are unpredictable and may need to go in all kinds of directions. Documentary evidence provided during the verification to back up information submitted prior to the verification may need to be verified itself against yet further documentation. Understandably therefore, the same panel also held that the authorities may request further details during the course of the investigation in light of the information obtained.[155]

3.2.5.8 Facts Available

Anti-dumping cases rely on voluntary cooperation of all interested parties: under the WTO rules, the authorities have no power to force anyone to cooperate. However, Article 6.8 authorizes the authorities to make determinations on the basis of the *facts available* or the *best information available* (BIA) if any interested party refuses access to, or otherwise does not provide, necessary information within a reasonable period or significantly impedes the results of the investigation. Thus, Article 6.8 ensures that the authorities will be able to complete an investigation and make determinations under the ADA on the basis of facts even in the event that an interested party is unable or unwilling to provide necessary information within a reasonable period:[156]

6.8 In cases in which any interested party refuses access to, or otherwise does not provide, necessary information within a reasonable period or significantly impedes the investigation, preliminary and final determinations, affirmative or negative, may be made on the basis of the facts available. The provisions of Annex II shall be observed in the application of this paragraph.

Put in very simple terms: if a domestic industry does not cooperate, for example by not filing questionnaire responses, the authorities would normally conclude that it has not suffered material injury. Similarly, if exporters do not

---

[154] *Guatemala–Cement from Mexico II*, Panel, para 8.203.
[155] *Guatemala–Cement from Mexico II*, Panel, para 8.205.
[156] *United States–Hot Rolled Steel from Japan*, Panel, para 7.51.

cooperate, the authorities will often conclude that their dumping margins are at least as high as those alleged by the domestic industry in the application.[157] These are examples of full non-cooperation.

In reality, the situation will seldom be as clear-cut as the examples above. In grey situations the facts available may then become a powerful weapon for the authorities which can easily be abused: if you want to beat a dog, it is easy to find a stick. As parties in an anti-dumping investigation must submit massive amounts of information within a relatively short period of time, it is very likely that parties will not be able to submit *all* requested information within the time limit or that they may make inadvertent clerical errors. The authorities might then decide to treat this as partial – or even full – non-cooperation.

To some extent, the drafters of the ADA seem to have been aware of the possibilities for abuse that Article 6.8 offers. Annex II of the ADA provides fairly detailed obligations for the authorities to comply with in the use of the best information available (BIA). Despite that, Article 6.8 and Annex II have given rise to extensive WTO litigation. In most of these cases, panels and the AB were called upon to determine whether the BIA 'punishment' meted out fitted the imperfect cooperation 'crime'. In other words, the issue in these cases was what one might call the proportionality between the use of the BIA and the degree of cooperation provided by the interested party concerned in a specific case. Because of what has been called the 'drive for perfection'[158] of the US Department of Commerce, many of these have involved the United States as a defendant.

In *Guatemala–Cement II*, the panel ruled that failure to cooperate does not necessarily constitute a significant impediment of the investigation:

> ... we do not consider that an objective and impartial investigating authority could properly have found that Cruz Azul significantly impeded its investigation by objecting to the inclusion of non-governmental experts with a conflict of interest in its verification team. We do not consider that a failure to cooperate necessarily constitutes significant impediment of an investigation, since, in our view, the ADA does not require cooperation by interested parties at any cost. Although there are certain consequences (under Article 6.8) for interested parties if they fail to cooperate with an investigating authority, such consequences only arise if the investigating authority itself has acted in a reasonable, objective and impartial manner. In light of the facts of this case, we find that the Ministry did not act in such a manner.[159]

---

[157] Compare Czako, Human and Miranda, *A Handbook on Anti-Dumping Investigations* (2003) 17.

[158] Horlick, 'The 10 Major Problems with the Anti-Dumping Instrument in the United States', (2005) 39 Journal of World Trade, 169, 169.

[159] *Guatemala–Cement from Mexico II*, Panel, paras 8.250–8.251.

In the same case, the panel also ruled that application of facts available for the entire investigation period is inappropriate when data is missing only for part of the period.[160]

Probably more typical of the problems that may arise in this area have been the cases *United States–Hot rolled steel*[161] and *United States–Steel plate*. In *United States–Hot rolled steel*, the two Japanese exporters NSC and NKK had submitted the requested information concerning a weight conversion factor for their theoretical weight sales after the regulatory deadlines for the questionnaire responses, but before verification. This had led the US Department of Commerce (USDOC) to reject such information and use facts available instead. The question therefore was whether the USDOC had correctly interpreted the *reasonable period* provision. Both the panel and later the AB agreed that this had not been the case.

The panel ruled that rigid adherence to regulatory deadlines did not in all cases suffice as the basis for a conclusion that information was not submitted within a reasonable period and, consequently, that facts available may be applied. The panel referred to Annex II, paragraph 2, and considered that where information is actually submitted in time to be verified, and actually could be verified, it should generally be accepted, unless to do so would impede the ability of the authorities to complete the investigation within the time limits established by the ADA. The latter might have been the case if more substantial portions of the requested information would not have been provided in time, but that had not been the case here.[162]

On appeal, the AB essentially agreed with the conclusion of the panel, but provided more principled guidance for future interpretation of the *reasonable period* criterion:

In considering whether information is submitted within a reasonable period of time, investigating authorities should consider, in the context of a particular case, factors such as: (i) the nature and quantity of the information submitted; (ii) the difficulties encountered by an investigated exporter in obtaining the information; (iii) the verifiability of the information and the ease with which it can be used by the investigating authorities in making their determination; (iv) whether other interested parties are

---

[160] *Guatemala–Cement from Mexico II*, Panel, paras 8.254–8.255. Compare Durling and Nicely, *Understanding the WTO Anti-Dumping Agreement: Negotiating History and Subsequent Interpretation* (2002) 386.

[161] The AB ruling on Art 6.8 in *United States–Hot rolled steel* has been extensively criticized in Tarullo, 'The Hidden Costs of International Dispute Settlement: WTO Review of Domestic Anti-Dumping Decisions' (2002) 34 Law and Policy in International Business 109, 120–125.

[162] *United States–Hot Rolled Steel from Japan*, Panel, paras 7.53–7.55.

likely to be prejudiced if the information is used; (v) whether acceptance of the information would compromise the ability of the investigating authorities to conduct the investigation expeditiously; and (vi) the numbers of days by which the investigated exporter missed the applicable time-limit.[163]

. . .

USDOC relied exclusively on the fact that the deadline had expired, even though NSC and NKK had requested that USDOC accept the information as a correction to the information submitted in the questionnaire. USDOC did not consider any other facts and circumstances – even though several were raised – which indicated that the information might have been submitted within a reasonable period of time. Moreover, in the case of NKK, USDOC in fact verified the information, before subsequently rejecting it as out of time.

The approach taken by the United States in this case excludes the very possibility, recognized by Articles 6.1.1 and 6.8 and Annex II of the ADA, that USDOC might be required, by these provisions, to extend the time-limits and accept the information submitted, as requested by NSC and NKK.

We are, therefore, of the view that USDOC acted inconsistently with Article 6.8 of the ADA through its failure to consider whether, in the light of all the facts and circumstances, the weight conversion factors submitted by NSC and NKK were submitted within a reasonable period of time. In reaching this conclusion, we are not finding that USDOC could not, consistently with the ADA, have rejected the weight conversion factors submitted by NSC and NKK. Rather, we conclude simply that, under Article 6.8, USDOC was not entitled to reject this information for the sole reason that it was submitted beyond the deadlines for responses to the questionnaires. Accordingly, we find that USDOC's action does not rest upon a permissible interpretation of Article 6.8 of the ADA.[164]

In the same case, the Japanese exporter KSC had not provided the requested information regarding resale prices and further manufacturing costs with respect to its sales through its affiliate CSI. On this point, the panel had ruled that that the USDOC had been justified in deciding to apply facts available with respect to the information not provided by KSC concerning CSI's further manufacturing costs.[165]

On appeal, the AB ruled that facts available may be used even where only a small portion of required information has not been appropriately submitted (but then in an appropriate manner):

There is . . . no requirement in Article 6.8 that resort to facts available be limited to situations where there is no information whatsoever which can be used to calculate a

[163] *United States–Hot Rolled Steel from Japan*, AB, para 85.
[164] *United States–Hot Rolled Steel from Japan*, AB, paras 86–89.
[165] *United States–Hot Rolled Steel from Japan*, Panel, para 7.69.

margin. Thus, the application of Article 6.8, authorizing the use of facts available, is not confined to cases where the entire margin is established using only facts available. Rather, under Article 6.8, investigating authorities are entitled to have recourse to facts available whenever an interested party does not provide some necessary information within a reasonable period, or significantly impedes the investigation. Whenever such a situation exists, investigating authorities may remedy the lack of any necessary information by drawing appropriately from the 'facts available'. As the United States acknowledges, Article 6.8 may apply in situations where recourse to facts available is needed to cure the lack of even a very small amount of information.

In consequence, we are of the view that the 'circumstances referred to' in Article 6.8 are the circumstances in which the investigating authorities properly have recourse to 'facts available' to overcome a lack of necessary information in the record, and that these 'circumstances' may, in fact, involve only a small amount of information to be used in the calculation of the individual margin of dumping for an exporter or producer.[166]

In *United States–Steel plate*, the panel considered that while Article 6.8 did not explicitly answer the question of the degree to which facts available may be used in a case in which some necessary information is submitted and some is not,[167] Annex II, read together with Article 6.8, did:

... the failure to provide necessary information ... triggers the authority granted by Article 6.8 to make determinations on the basis of facts available. The provisions of Annex II, which set out conditions on the use of facts available, inform the question of whether necessary information has not been provided, by establishing considerations for when information submitted must be used by the investigating authority. Thus, the provisions of Annex II inform an investigating authority's evaluation whether necessary information, in the sense of Article 6.8, has been provided, and whether resort to facts available with respect to that element of information is justified. If, after considering the provisions of Annex II, and in particular the criteria of paragraph 3, the conclusion is that information provided satisfies the conditions therein, the investigating authority must use that information in its determinations, and may not resort to facts available with respect to that element of information. That is, the investigating authority may not conclude, with respect to that information, that 'necessary information' has not been provided.

We note that there is disagreement between the parties as to whether the provisions of Annex II, which are largely phrased in the conditional tense ('should') are mandatory. We consider that Article 6.8 itself answers this question. Article 6.8.explicitly provides that 'The provisions of Annex II *shall* be observed in the application of this paragraph'

---

[166] *United States–Hot Rolled Steel from Japan*, AB, paras 119–120.
[167] *United States–Steel plate from India*, Panel, para 7.53.

(emphasis added). In our view, the use of the word 'shall' in this context establishes that the provisions of Annex II are mandatory. Indeed, this would seem a necessary conclusion. The alternative reading would mean that investigating authorities are required ('shall') to apply provisions which are not themselves required, an interpretation that makes no sense. Moreover, the provisions of Annex II, while worded in the conditional, give specific guidance to investigating authorities regarding certain aspects of their determinations which, without more, clearly establish the operational requirements.[168]

In *Argentina–Ceramic floor tiles*[169] and *Egypt–Steel rebar*,[170] the panels once again concluded that the authorities had resorted to use of BIA too easily. Arguably, these cases were more straightforward.[171]

In *Mexico–Rice*, the panel found that use of facts available, based on the information provided by the applicant, with respect to a cooperating producer which did not export during the investigation period, violated Article 6.8 and Annex II, paragraph 7 ADA.[172] In the same case, the panel also considered that where the authorities do not properly notify and inform the interested parties, they are not permitted to apply facts available to make determinations with regard to these interested parties.[173]

ANNEX II: *Best information available in terms of paragraph 8 of Article 6*
1. As soon as possible after the initiation of the investigation, the investigating authorities should specify in detail the information required from any interested party, and the manner in which that information should be structured by the interested party in its response. The authorities should also ensure that the party is aware that if information is not supplied within a reasonable time, the authorities will be free to make determinations on the basis of the facts available, including those contained in the application for the initiation of the investigation by the domestic industry.

In *Guatemala–Cement II*, the panel rejected a Mexican argument that Annex II, paragraph 1, or any other provision of the ADA prevents the authorities from extending the investigation period[174] during the course of an investigation:

We agree with Guatemala that there may be a number of circumstances in which the investigating authority will need updated information during the course of its

---

[168] *United States–Steel plate from India*, Panel, paras 7.55–7.56.
[169] *Argentina–Ceramic floor tiles from the EC*, Panel, para 6.78.
[170] *Egypt–Steel rebar from Turkey*, Panel, paras 7.265–7.266.
[171] Compare WorldTradeLaw.net, *Dispute Settlement Commentary on Argentina–Ceramic floor tiles*, p 10, checked on 23 April 2005.   [172] *Mexico–Rice from the United States*, Panel, para 7.168.
[173] *Mexico–Rice from the United States*, Panel, para 7.200.
[174] See chapter 1, Introduction, above.

investigation ... The fact that the POI may be extended after the imposition of provisional measures is not necessarily problematic, since even without any extension of the POI there is no guarantee that the factual basis for the preliminary determination will be the same as that of the final determination ... Although Annex II(1) provides that interested parties should be informed of the information required by the investigating authority 'as soon as possible after the initiation of the investigation,' this does not mean that information concerning a particular period of time may only be required if the request for that information is made immediately after initiation. We interpret the first sentence of paragraph 1 of Annex II to mean that any request for specific information should be communicated to interested parties as soon as possible.[175]

In *Argentina–Ceramic floor tiles*, the panel considered that the inclusion of the requirement to specify in detail the information required strongly implied that the authorities are not entitled to resort to BIA in a situation where a party does not provide certain information if the authorities failed to specify in detail the information which was required.[176]

Annex II

2. The authorities may also request that an interested party provide its response in a particular medium (e.g. computer tape) or computer language. Where such a request is made, the authorities should consider the reasonable ability of the interested party to respond in the preferred medium or computer language, and should not request the party to use for its response a computer system other than that used by the party. The authority should not maintain a request for a computerized response if the interested party does not maintain computerized accounts and if presenting the response as requested would result in an unreasonable extra burden on the interested party, e.g. it would entail unreasonable additional cost and trouble. The authorities should not maintain a request for a response in a particular medium or computer language if the interested party does not maintain its computerized accounts in such medium or computer language and if presenting the response as requested would result in an unreasonable extra burden on the interested party, e.g. it would entail unreasonable additional cost and trouble.

3. All information which is verifiable, which is appropriately submitted so that it can be used in the investigation without undue difficulties, which is supplied in a timely fashion, and, where applicable, which is supplied in a medium or computer language requested by the authorities, should be taken into account when determinations are made. If a party does not respond in the preferred medium or computer language but the authorities find that the circumstances set out in paragraph 2 have been

---

[175] *Guatemala–Cement from Mexico II*, Panel, para 8.177.
[176] *Argentina–Ceramic floor tiles from Italy*, Panel, para 6.55.

satisfied, the failure to respond in the preferred medium or computer language should not be considered to significantly impede the investigation.

While Annex II, paragraph 2, has not given rise to litigation thus far, violations of Annex II, paragraph 3, have been found repeatedly, often in conjunction with violations of Article 6.8 itself. In *United States–Hot rolled steel*, the AB explored the link between these two provisions, as well as Article 6.1.1:

Neither Article 6.8 nor paragraph 1 of Annex II expressly addresses the question of when the investigating authorities are entitled to reject information submitted by interested parties, as USDOC did in this case. In our view, paragraph 3 of Annex II of the ADA bears on this issue . . .

. . . according to paragraph 3 of Annex II, investigating authorities are directed to use information if three, and, in some circumstances, four, conditions are satisfied. In our view, it follows that if these conditions are met, investigating authorities are not entitled to reject information submitted, when making a determination. One of these conditions is that information must be submitted 'in a timely fashion'.

The text of paragraph 3 of Annex II of the ADA is silent as to the appropriate measure of 'timeliness' under that provision. In our view, 'timeliness' under paragraph 3 of Annex II must be read in light of the collective requirements, in Articles 6.1.1 and 6.8, and in Annex II, relating to the submission of information by interested parties. Taken together, these provisions establish a coherent framework for the treatment, by investigating authorities, of information submitted by interested parties. Article 6.1.1 establishes that investigating authorities may fix time-limits for responses to questionnaires, but indicates that, 'upon cause shown', and if 'practicable', these time-limits are to be extended. Article 6.8 and paragraph 1 of Annex II provide that investigating authorities may use facts available only if information is not submitted within a reasonable period of time, which, in turn, indicates that information which is submitted in a reasonable period of time should be used by the investigating authorities.

That being so, we consider that, under paragraph 3 of Annex II, investigating authorities should not be entitled to reject information as untimely if the information is submitted within a reasonable period of time. In other words, we see, 'in a timely fashion', in paragraph 3 of Annex II as a reference to a 'reasonable period' or a 'reasonable time'. This reading of 'timely' contributes to, and becomes part of, the coherent framework for fact-finding by investigating authorities. Investigating authorities may reject information under paragraph 3 of Annex II only in the same circumstances in which they are entitled to overcome the lack of this information through recourse to facts available, under Article 6.8 and paragraph 1 of Annex II of the ADA.[177]

In *United States–Steel plate*, the panel convincingly interpreted Annex II, paragraph 3, to require the authorities to use the information properly submitted

---

[177] *United States–Hot Rolled Steel from Japan*, AB, paras 80–83.

within the meaning of that provision. The absence of *some* information does not therefore give the authorities the right to ignore *all* information:[178]

> . . . a straightforward reading of paragraph 3 leads to the understanding that it requires that every element of information submitted which satisfies the criteria set out therein must be considered by the investigating authority when making its determinations. If information must be considered under paragraph 3, an investigating authority may not conclude, with respect to that information, that necessary information has not been provided, in the sense of Article 6.8. Consequently, we do not accept the United States' position that 'information' in Article 6.8 means all information, such that Members have an unlimited right to reject all information submitted in a case where some necessary information is not provided.
>
> Of course, we do not mean to suggest that the investigating authority must, in every case, scrutinize each item of information submitted in order explicitly to determine whether it satisfies the criteria of paragraph 3 of Annex II before it uses it in its determination. Clearly, if the authority is satisfied with the information submitted, and concludes that an interested party has fully complied with the requests for information, there is no need to undertake any separate analysis under paragraph 3 of Annex II. However, to the extent the authority is not satisfied with the information submitted, it must examine those elements of information with which it is **not** satisfied, in light of the criteria of paragraph 3.[179]

On the other hand, the panel acknowledged that the various categories of information necessary to calculate dumping margins are often interconnected. As a result, the failure to provide certain information may have repercussions for the treatment by the authorities of other – related – categories of information:

> For instance, a failure to provide cost of production information would leave the investigating authority unable to determine whether sales were in the ordinary course of trade, and further unable to calculate a constructed normal value. Thus, a failure to provide cost of production information might justify resort to facts available with respect to elements of the determination beyond just the calculation of cost of production . . .
>
> . . . when there is a question whether necessary information has been submitted, the investigating authority must . . . consider whether the information that has been submitted satisfies the criteria therein. If yes, it must be taken into account in making determinations. If not, it may be rejected and facts available used instead. In a case in which some information is rejected and facts available used instead, the further question may arise whether the fact that some information submitted was rejected

---

[178] Compare Czako, Human and Miranda, *A Handbook on Anti-Dumping Investigations* (2003) 16.   [179] *United States–Steel plate from India*, Panel, paras 7.57–7.58.

has consequences for the remainder of the information submitted. In particular, the investigating authority may need to consider whether the fact that some information is rejected results in other information failing to satisfy the criteria of paragraph 3. In this context, we consider to be critical the question of whether information which itself may satisfy the criteria of paragraph 3 can be used without undue difficulties in light of its relationship to rejected information.[180]

The panel found no information in the USDOC's determination, or the other information from the record submitted to the panel, that indicated how the problems with other data submitted, which led to their rejection, had affected the US sales price information.[181] In other words, it found no linkage between the two categories of information in that case.

Annex II
4. Where the authorities do not have the ability to process information if provided in a particular medium (e.g. computer tape), the information should be supplied in the form of written material or any other form acceptable to the authorities.

5. Even though the information provided may not be ideal in all respects, this should not justify the authorities from disregarding it, provided the interested party has acted to the best of its ability.

In the *United States–Steel plate* case, the panel was also called upon to interpret the relationship between Annex II, paragraphs 3 and 5. India had essentially argued that information which did not meet the requirements of paragraph 3 should nevertheless be taken into account if the party that submitted the information had acted to the best of its ability within the meaning of paragraph 5. In the view of the panel, this position would undermine the recognition in paragraph 3 that the authorities must be able to complete the investigation and make determinations based on facts, the accuracy of which has been established to the authorities' satisfaction:

. . . if we understand paragraph 5 to emphasize the obligation on the investigating authority to cooperate with interested parties, and particularly to actively make efforts to use information submitted if the interested party has acted to the best of its ability, we believe that it does not undo the framework for use of information submitted and resort to facts available set out in the ADA overall. Similarly, paragraph 5 can be understood to highlight that information that satisfies the requirements of paragraph 3, but which is not perfect, must nonetheless not be disregarded.[182]

---

[180] *United States–Steel plate from India*, Panel, paras 7.60–7.61.
[181] *United States–Steel plate from India*, Panel, para 7.67.
[182] *United States–Steel plate from India*, Panel, paras 7.64–7.65.

Thus, information need not be perfect in order to be accepted.[183]

Annex II, paragraph 6, requires the authorities to inform interested parties of the proposed rejection of evidence or information and to give them the possibility to provide further information; in other words, the authorities must give them a second chance to submit satisfactory information. If the authorities consider the explanations unsatisfactory and therefore reject the information, this must be motivated in the published determinations.

Annex II

6. If evidence or information is not accepted, the supplying party should be informed forthwith of the reasons therefore, and should have an opportunity to provide further explanations within a reasonable period, due account being taken of the time-limits of the investigation. If the explanations are considered by the authorities as not being satisfactory, the reasons for the rejection of such evidence or information should be given in any published determinations.

In *Argentina–Ceramic floor tiles*, the panel found that Argentina had never informed the Italian exporters that their information was going to be rejected, let alone given them an opportunity to provide further explanations.[184] Nor had Argentina explained its evaluation of the information that led it to disregard the exporters' information and resort to the use of BIA in the final determination or any other document on the record.[185] These failures constituted violations of Article 6.8 and Annex II, paragraph 6.

In the same case, the panel refused to consider arguments and reasons that did not form part of the evaluation process of the investigating authority, but instead were *ex post facto* justifications which were not provided at the time the determination was made.[186]

Annex II

7. If the authorities have to base their findings, including those with respect to normal value, on information from a secondary source, including the information supplied in the application for the initiation of the investigation, they should do so with special circumspection. In such cases, the authorities should, where practicable, check the information from other independent sources at their disposal, such as published price lists, official import statistics and customs returns, and from the information obtained from other interested parties during the investigation. It is clear, however, that if an

---

[183] *United States-Steel plate from India*, Panel, para 7.71.

[184] *Argentina–Ceramic floor tiles from Italy*, Panel, para 6.80.

[185] *Argentina–Ceramic floor tiles from Italy*, Panel, para 6.24.

[186] *Argentina–Ceramic floor tiles from Italy*, Panel, paras 6.27–6.28. Compare *United States–Steel plate from India*, Panel, para 7.67; *Argentina–Poultry from Brazil*, Panel, para 7.188.

interested party does not cooperate and thus relevant information is being withheld from the authorities, this situation could lead to a result which is less favourable to the party than if the party did cooperate.

In *United States–Hot rolled steel*, an issue was whether the USDOC had had the right to use adverse facts available *ex* Annex II, paragraph 7, against the Japanese exporter KSC because it had failed to convince its related party CSI to cooperate in the investigation. CSI was a joint venture between KSC and another company CVRD, but CSI had been a petitioner in the case and the joint venture partner CVRD was a competitor of KSC in the US market. In the view of the USDOC, KSC had not made utmost efforts to convince CSI to cooperate, notably because KSC had not instructed its members of the CSI board to address the issue, had not invoked the Shareholder's Agreement, and had not discussed this issue with its joint venture partner.

On appeal, the AB essentially upheld the panel's findings:

> . . . cooperation is a process, involving joint effort, whereby parties work together towards a common goal. In that respect, we note that parties may very well 'cooperate' to a high degree, even though the requested information is, ultimately, not obtained. This is because the fact of 'cooperating' is in itself not determinative of the end result of the cooperation. Thus, investigating authorities should not arrive at a 'less favourable' outcome simply because an interested party fails to furnish requested information if, in fact, the interested party has 'cooperated' with the investigating authorities, within the meaning of paragraph 7 of Annex II of the ADA.
>
> . . .
>
> We observe . . . that . . . KSC made several attempts to obtain the requested information from CSI . . . KSC also repeatedly reported to USDOC its difficulties in obtaining information from CSI. However, USDOC took no steps to assist KSC to overcome these difficulties, or to make allowances for the resulting deficiencies in the information supplied. USDOC declined to allow KSC to attend a meeting with petitioners' counsel to discuss the issue. Although USDOC met with KSC to discuss the issue, it appears that USDOC did not provide any specific guidance or assistance to KSC – USDOC simply repeated that KSC should obtain the requested information from CSI. USDOC did not take any steps to secure the necessary information by requesting it directly from CSI. We find nothing in the ADA which would have prevented USDOC from asking CSI directly for the information. To the contrary, Articles 6.1 and 6.11 of the ADA contemplate precisely such an approach.
>
> We also note that, in its initial responses to KSC, CSI indicated that it would provide KSC with certain assistance, and that it was only as the deadline for questionnaire responses approached that CSI unequivocally refused to provide the requested information. Furthermore, following KSC's letter to USDOC explaining the difficulties it was experiencing, the petitioners, of which CSI was one, submitted comments to

USDOC urging USDOC not to excuse KSC from providing any information relating to CSI.

According to USDOC's final determination, 'it cannot be said that KSC was fully cooperative and made every effort to obtain and provide the information requested' . . . The United States, and USDOC, seem, therefore, to have expected KSC to have gone to very considerable lengths in pursuit of the necessary information. In particular, in contrast to USDOC's reluctance to take any available step, pursuant to Article 6.13 of the ADA, to assist KSC in obtaining the information from CSI, USDOC seems to have expected KSC to have exhausted all legal means at its disposal to compel CSI to divulge the requested information, within the short time-limits of the investigation.

Against this background, the Panel found that the interpretation of 'cooperate' applied by USDOC 'went far beyond any reasonable understanding of any obligation to cooperate implied by paragraph 7 of Annex II.' The Panel stated that, in 'the absence of a justified conclusion that there was a lack of cooperation', there was no basis, pursuant to that provision, for a result 'less favourable' than would have been the case had KSC cooperated. In effect, the Panel held that USDOC's conclusion that KSC failed to 'cooperate' in the investigation did not rest on a permissible interpretation of that word. In the light of our own interpretation of the word 'cooperate', and taking account of the circumstances of this case, we agree with the Panel's finding on this issue.[187]

In *Mexico–Rice*, the panel considered that Mexico's use of facts available, based on information provided by the applicant, to impose an anti-dumping duty of 10.18 per cent on a cooperating American producer that had not exported during the investigation period,[188] violated Annex II, paragraph 7, because the authorities did not check the information obtained from other interested parties during the investigation (two of which had not been dumping while the dumping margin for the third was only 3.93 per cent),[189] nor use the information provided by the applicant with special circumspection.[190]

3.2.5.9 Disclosure

In a typical anti-dumping investigation, the authorities will first issue a provisional determination. The provisional determination will later be followed by a final determination. Some authorities conduct the verifications before the provisional determination, while other authorities will do so between the provisional and the final determinations. In the former case, the final determination often closely mirrors the provisional determination

---

[187] *United States–Hot Rolled Steel from Japan*, AB, paras 99–110.
[188] A so-called newcomer, see section 3.5.4, below.
[189] *Mexico–Rice from the United States*, Panel, fn 164.
[190] *Mexico–Rice from the United States*, Panel, paras 7.167–7.168.

because the provisional determination itself is already based on verified information. In the latter case, the final determination may be substantially different from the provisional determination, notably if one or more of the exporters 'fail' the verification.

Although there are therefore two – clearly distinct – phases in an anti-dumping investigation, Article 6.9 only requires the authorities to inform all interested parties of the essential facts under consideration which form the basis for the decision whether to apply *definitive* measures, before a final determination is made and in sufficient time for the parties to defend their interests. The latter condition entails that parties must be given sufficient time to submit comments on the essential facts.[191] This information requirement incumbent upon the authorities is often called the disclosure requirement. The Article 6.9 disclosure provision has been called 'probably the most significant new provision' in its category.[192]

The ADA therefore contemplates only *one* disclosure, although members obviously are free to grant more disclosures if they wish to do so. Indeed, some members will provide disclosure both after having imposed provisional measures and before taking definitive action.

In *Argentina–Ceramic floor tiles*, Argentina took the position that it had met Article 6.9 by inviting the Italian exporters to view the complete public record of the investigation. The panel agreed with Argentina that Article 6.9 left the authorities discretion as to how to meet its disclosure obligation, but considered that, whatever form the disclosure takes, it must be done in such a way that parties can defend their interests, for example by commenting on the completeness of the essential facts under consideration.[193]

As the Argentine authorities had relied mostly on evidence submitted by the domestic industry for their final determination, the panel checked whether exporters could have known this from checking the public record.[194] It found this not to be the case, as a result of which Argentina had not complied with Article 6.9:[195]

6.9 The authorities shall, before a final determination is made, inform all interested parties of the essential facts under consideration which form the basis for the decision

[191] Compare Czako, Human and Miranda, *A Handbook on Anti-Dumping Investigations* (2003) 773, where one or two weeks are mentioned as not being uncommon.

[192] Koulen, 'The New Anti-Dumping Code Through its Negotiating History' in Bourgeois, Berrod and Gippini Fournier (eds), *The Uruguay Round Results* (1995) 151, 202.

[193] *Argentina–Ceramic floor tiles from Italy*, Panel, para 6.125.

[194] *Argentina–Ceramic floor tiles from Italy*, Panel, para 6.127.

[195] *Argentina–Ceramic floor tiles from Italy*, Panel, para 6.129. For a critical commentary, see WorldTradeLaw.net, *Dispute Settlement Commentary on Argentina–Ceramic floor tiles*, pp 11–13, checked on 23 April 2005.

whether to apply definitive measures. Such disclosure should take place in sufficient time for the parties to defend their interests.

Article 6.9 leaves the authorities substantial discretion as to *when* to grant the disclosure, but the linkage of the disclosure to the definitive measures makes it clear that the essential facts which form the basis for the *definitive* measures are to be disclosed. If, for example, the authorities grant disclosure of essential facts underlying the provisional measures, but the definitive measures are significantly different from the provisional measures, the authorities will have to grant an additional disclosure to explain the differences:

Disclosure of the 'essential facts' forming the basis of a preliminary determination is clearly inadequate in circumstances where the factual basis of the provisional measure is significantly different from the factual basis of the definitive measure. In the present case, the preliminary measure was based on a preliminary determination of *threat* of material injury, whereas the final determination was based on *actual* material injury. Furthermore, the Ministry's preliminary determination was based on a POI different from that used for its final determination, since the POI was extended on 4 October 1996.[196]

In the same case, the panel also ruled that an offer by the authorities to provide interested parties with copies of all information in the file would not meet the Article 6.9 requirements.[197] In such a case, an interested party would not know whether a particular fact was essential or not.[198]

In *Argentina–Ceramic floor tiles*, the authorities had again invited the exporters to check the entire file. The panel agreed with Argentina that there were various forms that disclosure might take:

Article 6.9 of the ADA does not prescribe the manner in which the authority is to comply with this disclosure obligation. The requirement to disclose the 'essential facts under consideration' may well be met, for example, by disclosing a specially prepared document summarizing the essential facts under consideration by the investigating authority or through the inclusion in the record of documents – such as verification reports, a preliminary determination, or correspondence exchanged between the investigating authorities and individual exporters – which actually disclose to the interested parties the essential facts which, being under consideration, are anticipated by the authorities as being those which will form the basis for the decision whether to apply definitive measures.[199]

---

[196] *Guatemala–Cement from Mexico II*, Panel, para 8.228.

[197] *Guatemala–Cement from Mexico II*, Panel, para 8.230.

[198] *Guatemala–Cement from Mexico II*, Panel, para 8.229. Compare Durling and Nicely, *Understanding the WTO Anti-Dumping Agreement: Negotiating History and Subsequent Interpretation* (2002) 394.   [199] *Argentina–Ceramic floor tiles from Italy*, Panel, para 6.125.

The panel found that in the factual circumstances of the case, petitioners' and secondary source – rather than exporters' – information, had constituted the essential facts for the dumping determination. However, it would have been impossible for the exporters to discern this from the information on the record. As a result, the exporters had been unable to defend their interests within the meaning of Article 6.9, for example, by giving reasons why their responses should not be rejected or by suggesting alternative sources for facts available if their responses were nonetheless disregarded. Therefore, the authorities had not met their Article 6.9 obligations.[200]

In *Argentina–Poultry*, the panel considered that facts which did not form the basis for the decision whether to apply definitive measures cannot be considered to be essential facts within the meaning of Article 6.9.[201]

Some members will provide the opportunity to interested parties to have disclosure meetings during which the parties may comment on the findings of the authorities. However, such meetings are not required under Article 6.9.

3.2.5.10 Individual Dumping Margins/Sampling

Article 6.10, first sentence, lays down the principle that the authorities shall, as a rule, determine an individual margin of dumping for each known exporter or producer concerned of the product under investigation.

In *Mexico–Rice*, the application had mentioned two US rice producers to whom the Mexican authorities had sent questionnaires. Following the initiation, two more US producers came forward and cooperated in the investigation. These four participating producers received individual dumping margins, while the authorities imposed a residual duty on all others, based on facts available. The US argued that the authorities had undertaken no efforts to identify other exporters and that, because of that failure coupled to the imposition of the residual duty based on facts available, Mexico had violated Article 6.8.[202] The panel first found that the terms of Article 6.8, particularly the term 'known' exporter, were inconclusive.[203] However, on the basis of other provisions of the ADA, including Articles 1, 5, 6 and 12, the panel considered that the authorities must play an active role in the search of the information it requires in order to make their determination:[204]

. . . we are of the view that the term 'known exporter or producer' in Article 6.10 of the ADA refers to the exporters or producers that an unbiased and objective investigating

---

[200] *Argentina–Ceramic floor tiles from Italy*, Panel, paras 6.125–6.129.
[201] *Argentina–Poultry from Brazil*, Panel, para 7.223.
[202] *Mexico–Rice from the United States*, Panel, para 7.180.
[203] *Mexico–Rice from the United States*, Panel, para 7.183.
[204] *Mexico–Rice from the United States*, Panel, para 7.185.

authority properly establishing the facts would be reasonably expected to have become conversant with. Article 6.10 of the ADA is a general requirement that the authority has to comply with, at the latest, at the end of the investigation when making the determinations. This implies that the exporters that are known to the authorities at that point are those that an objective and unbiased investigating authority properly establishing the facts and conducting an active investigation could have and should have reasonably been considered to have knowledge of.[205]

The panel found that Mexico had violated Article 6.10 by remaining entirely passive in the identification of exporters or producers interested in the investigation, and by not calculating an individual margin for dumping for each exporter or producer that was known or should reasonably have been known to the investigating authority.[206]

In cases where the number of exporters, producers, importers or types of products is so large as to make the determination of individual dumping margins for each known exporter impracticable, the authorities may select a sample. Articles 6.10 and 9.4[207] ADA provide important rules for sampling. Under Article 6.10, the authorities may limit their investigation:

- to a reasonable number of interested parties or products by using samples which are statistically valid on the basis of information available to the authorities at the time of the selection; or
- to the largest percentage of the volume of exports from the country concerned which can reasonably be investigated.

The concept of a 'statistically valid sample' is hard to apply in practice. As a result, samples tend to be constituted in such a manner as to cover the largest percentage of exports which can reasonably be investigated. In order to decide how to properly constitute the sample, the authorities will then often announce their intention to sample in the notice of initiation or shortly afterwards and request all interested parties to provide the necessary information.

6.10 The authorities shall, as a rule, determine an individual margin of dumping for each known exporter or producer concerned of the product under investigation. In cases where the number of exporters, producers, importers or types of products involved is so large as to make such a determination impracticable, the authorities may limit their examination either to a reasonable number of interested parties or products by using samples which are statistically valid on the basis of information available to the authorities at the time of the selection, or to the largest percentage of the volume of the exports from the country in question which can reasonably be investigated.

[205] *Mexico–Rice from the United States*, Panel, para 7.187.
[206] *Mexico–Rice from the United States*, Panel, para 7.201.   [207] See section 3.3.3.4, below.

6.10.1 Any selection of exporters, producers, importers or types of products made under this paragraph shall preferably be chosen in consultation with and with the consent of the exporters, producers or importers concerned.

6.10.2 In cases where the authorities have limited their examination, as provided for in this paragraph, they shall nevertheless determine an individual margin of dumping for any exporter or producer not initially selected who submits the necessary information in time for that information to be considered during the course of the investigation, except where the number of exporters or producers is so large that individual examinations would be unduly burdensome to the authorities and prevent the timely completion of the investigation. Voluntary responses shall not be discouraged.

Article 6.10 envisages two types of sampling:

- sampling of the interested parties; and
- sampling of product types (PCNs).

While the latter is very rare, authorities often resort to sampling of interested parties. Although not explicitly foreseen by Article 6.10, authorities sometimes also resort to sampling of the domestic industry. It is an open question whether such sampling of domestic producers is authorized under the ADA.

In *Argentina–Ceramic floor tiles*, the authorities had established separate dumping margins for three groups of tiles, irrespective of the exporters.[208] The panel considered this practice to violate Article 6.10 because sampled producers should always get their individual margins.[209] In the same case, Argentina had further argued that it could not calculate individual dumping margins for the sampled exporters because the information submitted by these exporters did not contain reliable and useful information with regard to *each* of the size categories of the product subject of the investigation. The panel did not consider this excuse valid, even assuming *arguendo* that it was correct:

. . . it is important not to confuse the usefulness of grouping (by size, model, type) for the purpose of making a fair comparison under Article 2.4 and the requirement under Article 6.10 to determine an individual margin of dumping for the product as a whole. We consider that the use of types or models is a valid method of ensuring a fair comparison between normal value and export price under Article 2.4. We see nothing in the Appellate Body Report in the EC – Bed Linen case that suggests otherwise so long as the investigating authority goes on to determine a margin of dumping for the product *as a whole*. The product under investigation in the case before us is ceramic tiles of any size, and the authority was thus required to establish an individual dumping margin for each exporter for this product as a whole and not for each size category.

---

[208] *Argentina–Ceramic floor tiles from Italy*, Panel, para 6.86.
[209] *Argentina–Ceramic floor tiles from Italy*, Panel, para 6.90.

Nor was the DCD entitled to invoke any problems it encountered with regard to the use of such models, such as lack of information concerning a certain size category, as a reason for not determining an individual margin of dumping for the product as a whole, in this case ceramic floor tiles of any size from Italy. Therefore, even if the DCD was entitled to disregard data concerning certain size categories for one reason or another, this should not have stopped the DCD from determining an individual margin of dumping for each of the exporters included in the sample for the product subject to the investigation.[210]

In *Argentina–Poultry*, the panel ruled that failure of an exporter to cooperate, in whole or in part, does not give the authorities the right not to calculate an individual dumping margin for that exporter:

The fact that an investigating authority does not receive any information from an exporter, or only receives partial information, or information that is not usable or is unreliable, should not prevent the calculation of an individual margin of dumping for that exporter, since the substantive provisions in the ADA expressly allow investigating authorities to complete the data with regard to a particular exporter in order to determine a dumping margin in case the information provided is unreliable or necessary information is simply not provided.[211]

Thus, insufficient cooperation by sampled producers in the investigation does not deprive them of the right to obtain an individual dumping margin, although the margin may then well be based, in whole or in part, on facts available.[212]

Article 6.10.1 provides that a sample shall preferably be chosen in consultation with and with the consent of the parties concerned. Use of the word 'preferably' makes clear that if such agreement is not possible, the authorities may go ahead and impose the sample unilaterally.

Article 6.10.2 requires that the authorities in sampling cases nevertheless determine individual dumping margins for non-sampled producers which submit the necessary information in time for that information to be considered during the course of the investigation (so-called voluntary respondents).[213] However, where the number of exporters or producers is so large that individual examinations would be unduly burdensome to the authorities and prevent the timely completion of the investigation, such requests for individual treatment may be rejected. Although Article 6.10.2 provides *in fine* that voluntary

---

[210] *Argentina–Ceramic floor tiles from Italy*, Panel, paras 6.95–6.100.
[211] *Argentina–Poultry from Brazil*, Panel, para 7.216.   [212] See section 3.2.5.8, above.
[213] Compare Czako, Human and Miranda, *A Handbook on Anti-Dumping Investigations* (2003) 48.

responses shall not be discouraged, some authorities as a matter of practice make it difficult for non-sampled producers to cooperate, for example, by subjecting them to shorter deadlines than those granted to sampled producers.

3.2.5.11 Interested Parties

The typical interested parties in an anti-dumping proceeding are the foreign exporters, their importers and the domestic producers of the product concerned. These three groups have a direct stake in the investigation because the outcome is likely to influence their future business prospects.

6.11 For the purposes of this Agreement, 'interested parties' shall include:

(i) an exporter or foreign producer or the importer of a product subject to investigation, or a trade or business association a majority of the members of which are producers, exporters or importers of such product;

(ii) the government of the exporting Member; and

(iii) a producer of the like product in the importing Member or a trade and business association a majority of the members of which produce the like product in the territory of the importing Member.

This list shall not preclude Members from allowing domestic or foreign parties other than those mentioned above to be included as interested parties.

In addition to these three groups, Article 6.11 explicitly recognizes the exporting country government as well as representative trade associations in the exporting and the importing country as interested parties. Article 6.11 furthermore authorizes members to allow other domestic or foreign parties as interested parties. Article 6.11 therefore takes an open-ended approach. Some members allow trade unions as interested parties while others allow consumer associations.

In cases where members were not to allow industrial users or consumers associations as interested parties, Article 6.12 nevertheless obliges them to provide these groups with opportunities to provide relevant information:

6.12 The authorities shall provide opportunities for industrial users of the product under investigation, and for representative consumer organizations in cases where the product is commonly sold at the retail level, to provide information which is relevant to the investigation regarding dumping, injury and causality.

3.2.5.12 Small Companies

Article 6.13 requires the authorities to take due account of any difficulties experienced by interested parties, particularly small companies, in supplying the requested information and to provide any assistance practicable:

6.13 The authorities shall take due account of any difficulties experienced by interested parties, in particular small companies, in supplying information requested, and shall provide any assistance practicable.

This soft obligation has not given rise to problems thus far. In practice, authorities may sometimes grant longer deadlines for small companies.

In *United States–Hot rolled steel*, the AB distilled a two-way cooperation process from Article 6.13:

Article 6.13 thus underscores that 'cooperation' is ... a two-way process involving joint effort. If the ... authorities fail to 'take due account' of genuine 'difficulties' experienced by interested parties, they cannot, in our view, fault the interested parties concerned for a lack of cooperation.[214]

3.2.5.13 Final Provision

Article 6.14 notes that the procedures discussed above are not intended to prevent the authorities from proceeding expeditiously with regard to initiating an investigation, reaching preliminary or final determinations or from applying provisional or final measures, in accordance with the provisions of the ADA:

6.14 The procedures set out above are not intended to prevent the authorities of a Member from proceeding expeditiously with regard to initiating an investigation, reaching preliminary or final determinations, whether affirmative or negative, or from applying provisional or final measures, in accordance with relevant provisions of this Agreement.

It would appear that this provision does not add anything to the provisions discussed elsewhere.

3.3 Measures

3.3.1 Provisional Measures

Article 7 covers the imposition of provisional measures. Article 7.1 *jo.* 7.3 lay down the following conditions for the application of provisional measures:

- the investigation must have been properly initiated, public notice of initiation must have been provided and interested parties must have been given adequate opportunities to submit information and make comments;

---

[214] *United States–Hot rolled steel from Japan*, AB, para 104.

- a preliminary affirmative determination of dumping and resulting injury must have been reached;
- the authorities consider provisional measures necessary to prevent injury being caused during the investigation; and
- 60 days must have lapsed from the date of initiation of the investigation.

These conditions would appear to be designed to ensure that provisional measures are not imposed lightly.

Article 7: Provisional measures

7.1 Provisional measures may be applied only if:

(i) an investigation has been initiated in accordance with the provisions of Article 5, a public notice has been given to that effect and interested parties have been given adequate opportunities to submit information and make comments;

(ii) a preliminary affirmative determination has been made of dumping and consequent injury to a domestic industry; and

(iii) the authorities concerned judge such measures necessary to prevent injury being caused during the investigation.

7.2 Provisional measures may take the form of a provisional duty or, preferably, a security – by cash deposit or bond – equal to the amount of the anti-dumping duty provisionally estimated, being not greater than the provisionally estimated margin of dumping. Withholding of appraisement is an appropriate provisional measure, provided that the normal duty and the estimated amount of the anti-dumping duty be indicated and as long as the withholding of appraisement is subject to the same conditions as other provisional measures.

7.3 Provisional measures shall not be applied sooner than 60 days from the date of initiation of the investigation.

7.4 The application of provisional measures shall be limited to as short a period as possible, not exceeding four months or, on decision of the authorities concerned, upon request by exporters representing a significant percentage of the trade involved, to a period not exceeding six months. When authorities, in the course of an investigation, examine whether a duty lower than the margin of dumping would be sufficient to remove injury, these periods may be six and nine months, respectively.

7.5 The relevant provisions of Article 9 shall be followed in the application of provisional measures.

As regards the duration of provisional measures, Article 7.4 establishes that such measures should be as short as possible and in no event should exceed four months, unless exporters representing a significant percentage of the trade involved request a two month extension and the authorities decide to grant such request. The total maximum duration of the provisional measures may then be six months.

Where the authorities apply the lesser duty rule,[215] these time periods for imposing provisional duties periods may be extended from four and six to six and nine months respectively.

Provisional measures preferably should take the form of a security, in the form of a bond or a cash deposit.

In *Mexico–HFCS*, the panel ruled that the deadlines of Article 7 are absolute:

The language of Article 7.4 is clear and explicit on the question of the allowable duration of a provisional measure. Unless exporters representing a significant percentage of the trade involved request an extension of the period of application, a situation which undisputedly did not arise in this case, Article 7.4 limits the period of application of a provisional measure to a period no longer than six months, and provides no basis for extension of that period.[216]

3.3.2 Undertakings

Article 8 contains provisions on undertakings. Undertakings are an alternative to the imposition of anti-dumping duties and typically consist of a written agreement between individual exporters and the importing country authorities. Article 8.1 envisages two types of undertaking:

- undertaking whereby an exporter agrees to revise its export prices to non-dumped or non-injurious levels; or
- undertaking whereby an exporter agrees to cease exports to the importing country at dumped prices.

The first type is a price undertaking. The second type would appear to be an agreement to stop exports. It has sometimes been suggested that as the ADA authorizes an import stop, it also authorizes a quantity undertaking. Indeed, quantity undertakings have been accepted by some members. However, there is no consensus on this.[217]

---

[215] See section 3.3.3.1, below.   [216] *Mexico–HFCS from the United States*, Panel, para 7.182.

[217] Koulen, 'The New Anti-Dumping Code Through its Negotiating History' Bourgeois, Berrod and Gippini Fournier (eds), in *The Uruguay Round Results* (1995) 151, 216. Compare Durling and Nicely, *Understanding the WTO Anti-Dumping Agreement: Negotiating History and Subsequent Interpretation* (2002) 424:

... there is nothing ... that prohibits authorities from incorporating quantitative restrictions as part of an undertaking. Although such a restriction was proposed in the Carlisle I text, it was later removed, thus indicating that quota-based undertakings would be permitted ...

Article 8: Price undertakings

8.1 Proceedings may[218] be suspended or terminated without the imposition of provisional measures or anti-dumping duties upon receipt of satisfactory voluntary undertakings from any exporter to revise its prices or to cease exports to the area in question at dumped prices so that the authorities are satisfied that the injurious effect of the dumping is eliminated. Price increases under such undertakings shall not be higher than necessary to eliminate the margin of dumping. It is desirable that the price increases be less than the margin of dumping if such increases would be adequate to remove the injury to the domestic industry.

8.2 Price undertakings shall not be sought or accepted from exporters unless the authorities of the importing Member have made a preliminary affirmative determination of dumping and injury caused by such dumping.

8.3 Undertakings offered need not be accepted if the authorities consider their acceptance impractical, for example, if the number of actual or potential exporters is too great, or for other reasons, including reasons of general policy. Should the case arise and where practicable, the authorities shall provide to the exporter the reasons which have led them to consider acceptance of an undertaking as inappropriate, and shall, to the extent possible, give the exporter an opportunity to make comments thereon.

8.4 If an undertaking is accepted, the investigation of dumping and injury shall nevertheless be completed if the exporter so desires or the authorities so decide. In such a case, if a negative determination of dumping or injury is made, the undertaking shall automatically lapse, except in cases where such a determination is due in large part to the existence of a price undertaking. In such cases, the authorities may require that an undertaking be maintained for a reasonable period consistent with the provisions of this Agreement. In the event that an affirmative determination of dumping and injury is made, the undertaking shall continue consistent with its terms and the provisions of this Agreement.

8.5 Price undertakings may be suggested by the authorities of the importing Member, but no exporter shall be forced to enter into such undertakings. The fact that exporters do not offer such undertakings, or do not accept an invitation to do so, shall in no way prejudice the consideration of the case. However, the authorities are free to determine that a threat of injury is more likely to be realized if the dumped imports continue.

8.6 Authorities of an importing Member may require any exporter from whom an undertaking has been accepted to provide periodically information relevant to the fulfilment of such an undertaking and to permit verification of pertinent data. In case of violation of an undertaking, the authorities of the importing Member may take, under this Agreement in conformity with its provisions, expeditious actions which may constitute immediate application of provisional measures using the best information available. In such cases, definitive duties may be levied in accordance with

---

[218] Fn 19 in ADA: The word 'may' shall not be interpreted to allow the simultaneous continuation of proceedings with the implementation of price undertakings except as provided in paragraph 4.

this Agreement on products entered for consumption not more than 90 days before the application of such provisional measures, except that any such retroactive assessment shall not apply to imports entered before the violation of the undertaking.

In order for undertakings to be effective, they need to be detailed (normally PCN-based), well structured and regularly checked. Article 8.6 understandably authorizes the authorities to require exporters to provide regular reports and to allow verifications. In practice, the authorities will often require quarterly or bi-yearly reports of all export sales transactions – together with all costs involved – to the country concerned and verify these on a regular basis. It will be apparent that this is a time-consuming and a costly exercise for the authorities (and for the exporters).

Possibly for that reason, the authorities often view their acceptance of price undertakings as a favour to the exporters and consider that they have wide discretion as to whether or not to accept undertakings. This is now reflected in Article 8.3 which provides that authorities need not accept undertakings if they consider such acceptance impractical, for example, if the number of actual or potential exporters is too great, or for other reasons, *including reasons of general policy*.[219]

In fact, from the perspective of the exporters, the advantages of an undertaking may not always be so clear. While the extra profit generated from increased export prices will go to them (rather than to the customs authorities of the importing country), the volume of their sales is likely to go down. In addition, they will have to comply with burdensome reporting and verification requirements.

3.3.3 Anti-dumping Duties

Article 9 is entitled 'imposition and collection of anti-dumping duties'. Thus, it provides rules both for imposing anti-dumping duties and for collecting them. Anti-dumping duties theoretically can take three forms, as is the case for regular customs duties:

* *ad valorem* (percentage) duties;
* specific duties, eg a fixed amount per unit or per weight; or
* variable duties, ie the difference between a fixed minimum price (typically the non-dumped or the non-injurious price) and the actual import price, if it is lower.

---

[219] According to Koulen, 'The New Anti-Dumping Code Through Its Negotiating History' in Bourgeois, Berrod and Gippini Fournier (eds), *The Uruguay Round Results* (1995) 151, 217, the italicized portion of this sentence was added as a result of pressure from the United States.

In *Argentina–Poultry*, the panel considered that the ADA did not contain explicit rules on the form of anti-dumping duties and upheld Argentina's decision to impose anti-dumping duties in the form of variable duties:

In addressing this claim, we note that nothing in the ADA explicitly identifies the form that anti-dumping duties must take. In particular, nothing in the ADA explicitly prohibits the use of variable anti-dumping duties.[220]

Article 9.1 ADA lays down two important, albeit soft, principles:

9.1 The decision whether or not to impose an anti-dumping duty in cases where all requirements for the imposition have been fulfilled, and the decision whether the amount of the anti-dumping duty to be imposed shall be the full margin of dumping or less, are decisions to be made by the authorities of the importing Member. It is desirable that the imposition be permissive in the territory of all Members, and that the duty be less than the margin if such lesser duty would be adequate to remove the injury to the domestic industry.

First, it is desirable that the imposition of anti-dumping duties in cases where all conditions have been fulfilled should be permissive. A variety of WTO members have implemented this desire through the adoption of a *public interest test*. This means that, even if dumping and resulting injury have been found, they will then determine whether the imposition of anti-dumping duties is in the public interest of the importing country. Perhaps not surprisingly, in most cases, the answer tends to be affirmative.[221]

3.3.3.1 *Lesser Duty Rule*

Second, it is desirable that the anti-dumping duty be less than the dumping margin if such lesser duty would be adequate to remove the injury to the domestic industry. This is often called the *lesser duty rule*.

Although the details vary, WTO members that apply a lesser duty rule will typically compare the prices charged by the exporters in the importing country market with the prices charged by the domestic producers there, and this on a PCN-by-PCN basis.[222] In its simplest form, the *price undercutting* method will calculate to what extent the exporters' prices undercut those of the domestic producers. Expressed as a percentage of the CIF export price, this will give the injury margin, based on the price undercutting method.

However, other methods can also be used, particularly because the ADA does not give any guidance on how the lesser duty rule is to be applied. One

---

[220] *Argentina–Poultry from Brazil*, Panel para 7.355.

[221] See for the EC experience, Didier, 'The WTO Anti-Dumping Code and EC practice' (2001) 35 Journal of World Trade 33, 54. But see Wenig, 'The European Community's Anti-Dumping System: Salient Features' (2005) 39 Journal of World Trade 787, 791.   [222] See section 1.1.1, above.

method which is often used also is sometimes called the *price underselling* method. Authorities may resort to this method where they find, typically as a result of allegations of the domestic industry, that the domestic prices were forced downwards by the dumped imports to such an extent that the domestic producers sold at a loss or at less than a 'reasonable' profit. In such cases, the authorities may decide to construct target prices for the domestic producers, consisting of their full costs of production plus a 'reasonable' profit; they will then determine to what extent the exporters' prices were lower than the target prices. As the target prices are by definition higher than the actual market prices charged by the domestic producers, this entails that price underselling margins will be higher than price undercutting margins.[223]

The following simplified examples show the operation of the two methods:

Price undercutting method

	Producer A	Exporter X	Exporter Y	Exporter Z
Dumping margin	–	14%	35%	13%
Price	100	90	110	80
Undercutting	–	100 − 90	100 − 110	100 − 80
		= 10	= − 10	= 20
Injury margin	–	11.11%	0	25%
Duty	–	11.11% [IM]	0 [IM]	13% [DM]

Suppose that the full cost of production of Producer A is 100 and that the authorities determine that 12 per cent constitutes a reasonable profit. The target price (TP) then becomes: $100 + 12 = 112$.

Price underselling method

	Producer A	Exporter X	Exporter Y	Exporter Z
Dumping margin	–	14%	35%	13%
Price	112	90	110	80
Undercutting	–	112 − 90	112 − 110	112 − 80
		= 22	= 2	= 32
Injury margin	–	24.44%	1.82%	40%
Duty	–	14% [DM]	1.82% [IM]	13% [DM]

[223] In the calculation of injury margins, both under the undercutting and the underselling method, some authorities will *zero* negative injury margins.

The above examples will result in individual injury margins for exporters. However, some authorities have sometimes also calculated global injury margins.

Thus far, the calculation of injury margins has not given rise to WTO litigation. This is probably not surprising as Article 9.1 leaves the authorities complete discretion. Nevertheless, a patently incorrect or arbitrary application of the lesser duty rule might lead a panel to conclude that the authorities' establishment of the facts was improper or that their evaluation thereof was biased or not objective within the meaning of Article 17.6(i) ADA.

3.3.3.2 Non-discrimination

Article 9.2 requires that, when an anti-dumping duty is *imposed*, it shall be *collected* on a non-discriminatory basis, except with respect to exporters from which price undertakings have been accepted. Although this non-discrimination principle technically only applies to the collection of anti-dumping duties, supposedly it also applies to the imposition. Indeed, some authorities have invoked this non-discrimination principle to refrain from imposing anti-dumping duties when they found convincing evidence that the domestic industry had filed a selective application against certain countries, while excluding other countries with respect to which a *prima facie* case of injurious dumping appeared to exist:

9.2 When an anti-dumping duty is imposed in respect of any product, such anti-dumping duty shall be collected in the appropriate amounts in each case, on a non-discriminatory basis on imports of such product from all sources found to be dumped and causing injury, except as to imports from those sources from which price undertakings under the terms of this Agreement have been accepted. The authorities shall name the supplier or suppliers of the product concerned. If, however, several suppliers from the same country are involved, and it is impracticable to name all these suppliers, the authorities may name the supplying country concerned. If several suppliers from more than one country are involved, the authorities may name either all the suppliers involved, or, if this is impracticable, all the supplying countries involved.

Article 9.2 furthermore provides that the authorities should normally name the suppliers. Where this is impracticable, however, the authorities may name the supplying country. In practice, most authorities will name the exporters that were investigated as well as the cooperating, non-sampled exporters. Non-cooperating producers will normally not be identified by name and will be subjected to a *residual* or *all others* duty.

However, the ADA does not contain any rules on the level of this duty, as a result of which different countries apply different methods.[224] Thus, some members may set the all others rate at the level of the weighted average duty imposed with respect to any cooperating exporter while other members will set the level of the residual duty at the level of the highest duty imposed with respect to any cooperating exporter because the application of a lower rate would constitute a bonus for non-cooperation.[225]

In *United States–Corrosion-resistant carbon steel flat products*, the AB invoked Article 9.2 in support of its finding that the Article 11.3 likelihood determination[226] does not require the authorities to make company-specific findings.[227]

3.3.3.3 Collection Systems

Article 9.3 covers the collection of anti-dumping duties. The principle laid down in Article 9.3 is that the amount of the anti-dumping duty shall not exceed the dumping margin, as established per Article 2:

9.3 The amount of the anti-dumping duty shall not exceed the margin of dumping as established under Article 2.

In *Argentina–Poultry*, the panel found nothing in Article 9.3 that would prohibit the imposition of a variable anti-dumping duty:

Neither the ordinary meaning of Article 9.3, nor its context (i.e., sub-paragraphs 1–3), supports that view. If Article 9.3 were designed to prohibit the use of variable customs duties, presumably that prohibition would have been clearly spelled out.[228]

Articles 9.3.1 and 9.3.2 acknowledge the existence of two different systems of duty collection:

- the *retrospective system*, used by the United States[229] and covered by Article 9.3.1; and
- the *prospective system*, used by most other AD users and covered by article 9.3.2.

---

[224] Compare Czako, Human and Miranda, *A Handbook on Anti-Dumping Investigations* (2003) 61.

[225] In cases where the level of non-cooperation from a country is very high, some members will even impose a residual duty at a level *higher* than the duty imposed with respect to any cooperating producer to prevent exporters trying to manipulate the results of the investigation by having only exporters with expected low duties cooperate.   [226] See section 3.5.2.3, below.

[227] *United States–Corrosion-resistant carbon steel flat products from Japan*, AB, para 150.

[228] *Argentina–Poultry from Brazil*, Panel, para 7.355.

[229] See, for example, WorldTradeLaw.net, *Dispute settlement Commentary on United States–Section 129(c)(1) of the Uruguay Round Agreements Act*, 2, checked on 23 April 2005.

Under the retrospective system, the original investigation leads only to an estimate of future liability: the amount of anti-dumping duties payable will then be determined retrospectively in the course of annual reviews (duty assessment reviews) covering the previous one year period. The advantage of the retrospective system is that it is very accurate and rewards exporters that increase their export prices to non-dumped levels; the disadvantage is that it is time-consuming and costly.

Under the prospective system, the anti-dumping duties are imposed on the basis of the findings reached during the investigation period and will be collected at the rates determined during the original investigation for the next five years. The advantage of the prospective system is that it is very simple, both for the authorities and for the exporters. The disadvantage is that the system is very imprecise: indeed at the moment that the duties are imposed, the underlying facts are already between one-and-a-half and two-and-a-half years out of date. Furthermore, the prospective system, particularly where *ad valorem* duties are imposed, implies that the same percentage duty will be applied to all subsequent imports, no matter their price levels. If, therefore, an exporter were to raise his export prices to non-dumped levels, the importer in fact will have to pay a higher amount of anti-dumping duties.

9.3.1 When the amount of the anti-dumping duty is assessed on a retrospective basis, the determination of the final liability for payment of anti-dumping duties shall take place as soon as possible, normally within 12 months, and in no case more than 18 months, after the date on which a request for a final assessment of the amount of the anti-dumping duty has been made.[230] Any refund shall be made promptly and normally in not more than 90 days following the determination of final liability made pursuant to this sub-paragraph. In any case, where a refund is not made within 90 days, the authorities shall provide an explanation if so requested.

Under Article 9.3.1 the authorities in the retrospective system must determine the final liability for payment of anti-dumping duties within 12 months, and in no event more than 18 months, from the date on which the request was made. Any refund of anti-dumping duties paid should then normally be made within 90 days from the determination.

It may be noted that the focus of the retrospective system, as used by the United States, is the situation of the importer. If importer A has purchased at non-dumped prices while importer B has continued to purchase at dumped prices, importer A will get a refund, while importer B will not get a refund.

---

[230] Fn 20 in ADA: It is understood that the observance of the time-limits mentioned in this subparagraph and in subparagraph 3.2 may not be possible where the product in question is subject to judicial review proceedings.

In *United States–DRAMS*, the panel ruled that the 2 per cent *de minimis* dumping rule of Article 5.8[231] does not need to be applied in Article 9.3.1 reviews:[232]

9.3.2 When the amount of the anti-dumping duty is assessed on a prospective basis, provision shall be made for a prompt refund, upon request, of any duty paid in excess of the margin of dumping. A refund of any such duty paid in excess of the actual margin of dumping shall normally take place within 12 months, and in no case more than 18 months, after the date on which a request for a refund, duly supported by evidence, has been made by an importer of the product subject to the anti-dumping duty. The refund authorized should normally be made within 90 days of the above-noted decision.

In countries using the prospective system, provision must be made for a prompt refund, upon request, of any duties paid in excess of the dumping margin. As is the case for the retrospective system, the decision to authorize refunds should normally take place within 12 months and in no event after more than 18 months. The actual refund should normally be made within 90 days of the decision.

Some WTO members using the prospective system will, in refund investigations, focus on the situation of the exporter and re-calculate the average dumping margin. Suppose that the original dumping duty was 10 per cent while the re-calculated dumping margin becomes 6 per cent, all importers will then get a 4 per cent reduction.

Refunds in constructed export price situations   One of the most complex provisions of the ADA is Article 9.3.3 which contains special rules for calculating the dumping margin in refund investigations where the export price is constructed.[233] In such cases, the importer which has paid the anti-dumping duties (ADD) is typically a related party to the exporter.

Prior to 1994, it was the practice of some AD users, notably the EC,[234] to treat the ADD paid by the related importer as a cost incurred between importation and resale and therefore to deduct such costs in the process of constructing the export price. This is known as the *duty as a cost* issue. The consequence of this approach is that an exporter, selling through related

[231] See section 3.2.2.1, above.   [232] *United States–DRAMS from Korea*, Panel, para 6.91.
[233] See section 1.2.2, above.
[234] Compare Koulen, 'The New Anti-Dumping Code Through Its Negotiating History' in Bourgeois, Berrod and Gippini Fournier (eds), *The Uruguay Round Results* (1995) 151, 219; Durling and Nicely, *Understanding the WTO Anti-Dumping Agreement: Negotiating History and Subsequent Interpretation* (2002) 447.

importers, has in effect to raise its export prices by twice the amount of the dumping margin originally imposed. The following example may clarify this:

Treatment of ADD as a cost

- Suppose that company X sells in its home market at a price of US$120 and exports to its related importer at a CIF price of US$100,[235] that the SGA and 5% imputed profit of the subsidiary come to 10 and that the subsidiary resells to independent customers at a price of 110. The dumping margin for this company then will be:

$$120 - 100 (110 - 10) = 20 / 100 \times 100 = 20\%$$

- After the imposition of the ADD, company X decides to revise its prices upwards by 20% so that the CIF price becomes US$120 and the resale price of the subsidiary US$132. The company then claims a refund on the basis that it is no longer dumping.
- Some authorities would take the position that the ADD paid, ie $20\% \times 120 = 24$, are a cost incurred by the EC subsidiary and that therefore the dumping margin is still:

$$120 - 98 (132 - 24 - 10) / 120 \times 100 = 18.33\%$$

Thus, the related importer should in fact have revised his prices upwards from US$110 to US$154, an increase of 40%:

$$120 - 120 (154 - 24 - 10) / 120 \times 100 = 0$$

Article 9.3.3 is very much the compromise solution that resulted from the negotiations between users of this practice and its victims, mostly Japanese[236] and, to a lesser extent, Korean exporters:

9.3.3 In determining whether and to what extent a reimbursement should be made when the export price is constructed in accordance with paragraph 3 of Article 2, authorities should take account of any change in normal value, any change in costs incurred between importation and resale, and any movement in the resale price which is duly reflected in subsequent selling prices, and should calculate the export price with no deduction for the amount of anti-dumping duties paid when conclusive evidence of the above is provided.

---

[235] In this simplified example, these prices are not netted back to the *ex factory* level.
[236] Koulen, 'The New Anti-Dumping Code Through Its Negotiating History', in Bourgeois, Berrod and Gippini Fournier (eds), *The Uruguay Round Results* (1995) 151, 219.

Where the exporter and its related importers can prove that the duty has
resulted in a corresponding movement in the resale prices of the related
importers which is duly reflected in subsequent selling prices, then the export
price should be constructed without deducting the anti-dumping duties paid.

Thus, if in the example above, company X and its related importers can
show that the related importers resold at 132 and that their unrelated
customers also increased their prices by 20 per cent, then the authorities would
not be authorized to deduct the anti-dumping duties as a cost for purposes of
calculating refunds. In practice, however, it is virtually impossible for producers
to control the prices that their unrelated customers charge to their customers
and, in fact, any such efforts might well be frowned upon by competition
authorities as a form of resale price maintenance.[237]

Indeed, experience has shown that exporters have typically only been able to
overcome this hurdle (and therefore avoid deduction of anti-dumping duties as
a cost) where they resold to customers which were also end-users. In such cases,
the exercise stops at the point of the resale by the related importers.

3.3.3.4 Sampling

We have seen above that the authorities may under certain conditions resort to
sampling of exporters.[238] Article 9.4 contains special rules for the imposition
of anti-dumping duties on non-sampled exporters in such cases:

9.4 When the authorities have limited their examination in accordance with the
second sentence of paragraph 10 of Article 6, any anti-dumping duty applied to
imports from exporters or producers not included in the examination shall not
exceed:

(i) the weighted average margin of dumping established with respect to the selected
     exporters or producers or
(ii) where the liability for payment of anti-dumping duties is calculated on the basis
     of a prospective normal value, the difference between the weighted average nor-
     mal value of the selected exporters or producers and the export prices of exporters
     or producers not individually examined,

provided that the authorities shall disregard for the purpose of this paragraph any zero
and de minimis margins and margins established under the circumstances referred to
in paragraph 8 of Article 6. The authorities shall apply individual duties or normal
values to imports from any exporter or producer not included in the examination who

---

[237] Compare Horlick and Shea, 'The World Trade Organization Anti-Dumping Agreement'
(1995) 29 Journal of World Trade, 27; Horlick, 'How the GATT Became Protectionist – An Analysis
of the Uruguay Round Draft Final Anti-Dumping Code' (1993) 27 Journal of World Trade 5, 8–9.
[238] See section 3.2.5.10, above.

has provided the necessary information during the course of the investigation, as provided for in subparagraph 10.2 of Article 6.

Thus, in case of sampling, the anti-dumping duty imposed on non-sampled producers may not exceed the weighted average dumping margin established for the sampled producers, with the exception of any *de minimis* dumping margins[239] or dumping margins based on facts available.[240] This is sometimes called the *limited examination* rate.[241]

In practice, some authorities make a distinction between *cooperating* non-sampled producers and *non-cooperating* non-sampled producers and will then impose the highest duty imposed with respect to any cooperating sampled producers to the non-cooperating, non-sampled producers on the ground that non-cooperating producers should not be better off than any cooperating producers. The following example may clarify the operation of the various rules:

Anti-dumping duties in the case of sampling

Sampled companies:[242]

A	5%	D	[1.5%] (*de minimis*)
B	15%	E	10%
C	20%	F	[40%] (facts available)

- Duty applicable to cooperating, non-sampled producers: 12.5%
- Duty applicable to non-cooperating, non-sampled producers: 40%

However, it is not clear whether this distinction between cooperating and non-cooperating producers is authorized by the ADA[243] and some countries will apply the same rate to both groups.[244]

As regards the exclusion of dumping margins based on facts available, the question arose in *United States–Hot rolled steel* whether the mandatory

---

[239] See section 3.2.2.1, above.   [240] See section 3.2.5.8, above.

[241] Compare Czako, Human and Miranda, *A Handbook on Anti-Dumping Investigations* (2003) 61.

[242] It is assumed that all sampled exporters sold the same quantity. Therefore, the weighted average dumping margin is the same as the simple average: 5 + 10 + 15 + 20 = 12.5%.

[243] Indeed, in *United States–Hot rolled steel*, AB, para 116, the AB noted that Art 9.4 identifies a maximum limit, or ceiling, which investigated authorities shall not exceed in establishing an all others rate.

[244] Compare Czako, Human and Miranda, *A Handbook on Anti-Dumping Investigations* (2003) 61.

exclusion applied to all producers with respect to whom resort had been had to facts available or only to those of them whose rates had been based *fully* on facts available. It is recalled here[245] that, depending on the circumstances of the case, the authorities may decide to apply facts available across the board (full facts available), typically vis-à-vis exporters which have failed to cooperate, or only with respect to a portion of the data submitted (partial facts available). Suppose, for example, that authorities were to disagree with an exporter's allocation of ocean freight costs, they then might decide to recalculate such costs based on facts available. This would be an example of partial use of facts available. Partial use of facts available occurs much more frequently than use of full facts available because it happens often that exporters make errors or that disagreements arise between the exporter and the authorities about the calculation or allocation of certain costs.

Under US law, only rates based *entirely* on facts available are excluded from the calculation of the all others rate. In the *United States–Hot rolled steel* case, the USDOC had investigated three Japanese exporters and for each of them had relied on facts available with respect to some elements of the dumping margin calculation. It had then calculated the all others rate applicable to the remaining Japanese producers, by taking the weighted average of the margins calculated for the three investigated respondents.

The panel had found that the US law as such was inconsistent with Article 9.4 ADA and therefore also with Article 18.4 of the ADA and Article XIV:4 of the Marrakesh Agreement.[246] On appeal, the AB agreed with the findings and conclusions of the panel:

Nothing in the text of Article 9.4 supports the United States' argument that the scope of this prohibition should be narrowed so that it would be limited to excluding only margins established 'entirely' on the basis of facts available ... Article 6.8 applies even in situations where only limited use is made of facts available. To read Article 9.4 in the way the United States does is to overlook the many situations where Article 6.8 allows a margin to be calculated, in part, using facts available. Yet, the text of Article 9.4 simply refers, in an open-ended fashion, to 'margins established under the circumstances' in Article 6.8. Accordingly, we see no basis for limiting the scope of this prohibition in Article 9.4, by reading into it the word 'entirely' as suggested by the United States. In our view, a margin does not cease to be 'established under the circumstances referred to' in Article 6.8 simply because not every aspect of the calculation involved the use of 'facts available'.

---

[245] See for more detail section 3.2.5.8, above.
[246] *United States–Hot Rolled Steel from Japan*, Panel, para 7.85–7.90.

...Our reading of Article 9.4 is consistent with the purpose of the provision. Article 6.8 authorizes investigating authorities to make determinations by remedying gaps in the record which are created, in essence, as a result of deficiencies in, or a lack of, information supplied by the investigated exporters. Indeed, in some circumstances, as set forth in paragraph 7 of Annex II of the ADA, 'if an interested party does not cooperate and thus relevant information is being withheld from the authorities, this situation could lead to a result which is less favourable to the party than if the party did cooperate' ... Article 9.4 seeks to prevent the exporters, who were not asked to cooperate in the investigation, from being prejudiced by gaps or shortcomings in the information supplied by the investigated exporters. This objective would be compromised if the ceiling for the rate applied to 'all others' were, as the United States suggests, calculated – due to the failure of investigated parties to supply certain information – using margins 'established' even in part on the basis of the facts available.[247]

The United States had also argued that the panel finding would make it more difficult to calculate an all others rate because there are many cases where dumping margins are partially based on facts available. The AB, while acknowledging a 'lacuna' in Article 9.4, nevertheless did not consider this a reason to change its position. Indeed, even by including such margins, a lacuna could still occur.[248]

The US had further argued that the Panel had failed to apply the standard of review laid down in the second sentence of Article 17.6(ii) ADA (more than one permissible interpretation). However, the AB agreed with the panel that Article 9.4 could not be interpreted in the manner suggested by the US on the basis of the customary rules of treaty interpretation of public international law, as referred to in Article 17.6(ii), first sentence. As a result, the panel had correctly applied Article 17.6(ii) because the second sentence did not come into play.[249]

In the *EC–Bed linen 21.5* case, the AB overruled the panel's finding a linkage between Article 9.4 and Article 3. The EC had argued that Article 9.4 established a methodology for calculating the volume of dumped imports from non-examined producers for purposes of determining injury within the meaning of Articles 3.1 and 3.2.[250]

In the view of the AB, however, the right to impose anti-dumping duties on imports attributable to non-examined producers under Article 9.4 did not permit a derogation from the express and unambiguous requirements of

[247] *United States–Hot Rolled Steel from Japan*, AB, paras 122–123.
[248] *United States–Hot Rolled Steel from Japan*, AB, para 126.
[249] *United States–Hot Rolled Steel from Japan*, AB, para 130.
[250] See for a more detailed description of the issue, section 2.3.2, above.

Articles 3.1 and 3.2 to determine the volume of dumped imports – including dumped import volumes attributable to non-examined producers – on the basis of positive evidence and an objective examination.[251]

... Article 9.4 provides no guidance for determining the volume of dumped imports from producers that were not individually examined on the basis of 'positive evidence' and an 'objective examination' under Article 3. The exception in Article 9.4, which authorizes the imposition of anti-dumping duties on imports from producers for which no individual dumping margin has been calculated, cannot be assumed to extend to Article 3, and, in particular, in this dispute, to paragraphs 1 and 2 of Article 3. For the same reasons, we do not see why the volume of imports that has been found to be dumped by non-examined producers, for purposes of determining injury under paragraphs 1 and 2 of Article 3, must be congruent with the volume of imports from those non-examined producers that is subject to the imposition of anti-dumping duties under Article 9.4, as contended by the European Communities and the Panel.[252]

3.4 Retroactivity

Article 10.1 lays down the principle that provisional measures and anti-dumping duties operate *prospectively*. In other words, they may be applied only to products which enter for consumption in the importing country market from the moment the decision is taken to impose provisional measures *ex* Article 7.1 or to impose anti-dumping duties *ex* Article 9.1.

10.1 Provisional measures and anti-dumping duties shall only be applied to products which enter for consumption after the time when the decision taken under paragraph 1 of Article 7 and paragraph 1 of Article 9, respectively, enters into force, subject to the exceptions set out in this Article.

By way of exception,[253] Article 10 provides for two types of retroactivity:

- imposition of anti-dumping duties for the period for which provisional measures were applied, covered by Articles 10.2–10.5; and
- imposition of a definitive anti-dumping duty on products which entered for consumption during the 90 days prior to the application of provisional measures, but not before initiation, covered by Articles 10.6–10.8.

---

[251] *EC–Bed linen from India*, 21.5 AB, para 125.
[252] *EC–Bed linen from India*, 21.5 AB, para 126.
[253] Compare *Mexico–HFCS from the United States*, Panel, para 7.190.

3.4.1 Provisional Measures

With respect to the first type, Article 10.2 allows anti-dumping duties to be applied retroactively for the period for which provisional measures have been applied where:

- a final determination of material injury is made; or
- a final determination of threat of material injury is made *and* where the effect of the dumped imports would have led to a determination of material injury, in the absence of the provisional measures.

10.2 Where a final determination of injury (but not of a threat thereof or of a material retardation of the establishment of an industry) is made or, in the case of a final determination of a threat of injury, where the effect of the dumped imports would, in the absence of the provisional measures, have led to a determination of injury, anti-dumping duties may be levied retroactively for the period for which provisional measures, if any, have been applied.

In *Mexico–HFCS*, the panel ruled that in the second situation, the authorities should at a minimum address the effect of the dumped imports in the final determination, so as to enable the panel to review whether it was appropriately considered and decided:

While Article 10.2 does not explicitly require a 'determination' that 'the effect of the dumped imports would, in the absence of the provisional measures, have led to a determination of injury', there must be some specific statement in the final determination of the investigating authority from which a reviewing panel can discern that the issue addressed in Article 10.2 was properly considered and decided.[254]

In the same case, the panel also considered that a claim regarding the duration of a provisional measure relates to the definitive anti-dumping duty because the period of time for which a provisional measure is applied is generally determinative of the period for which a definitive anti-dumping duty may be levied retroactively.[255]

Article 10.3 provides that where the definitive anti-dumping duty is higher than the provisional duty or the security, the difference shall not be collected. If, on the other hand, the definitive duty is lower than the provisional duty or the security, the difference shall be refunded:

10.3 If the definitive anti-dumping duty is higher than the provisional duty paid or payable, or the amount estimated for the purpose of the security, the difference shall

---

[254] *Mexico–HFCS from the United States*, Panel, para 7.191.
[255] *Mexico–HFCS from the United States*, Panel, para 7.53.

not be collected. If the definitive duty is lower than the provisional duty paid or payable, or the amount estimated for the purpose of the security, the difference shall be reimbursed or the duty recalculated, as the case may be.

An example may clarify the operation of Article 10.3. Suppose that the provisional duty for producer A is 8 per cent while his definitive duty is 4.5 per cent; he will then be entitled to a refund of 3.5 per cent. If, on the other hand, the provisional duty for producer B is 3.7 per cent while his definitive duty is 8.3 per cent, then he will not have to pay any additional provisional duties. Thus, provisional duties effectively can never be higher than definitive duties.

Article 10.4 is the counterpart of Article 10.2. It provides that, except as provided in Article 10.2, where a determination of threat of material injury or of material retardation is made, but no injury has yet occurred, a definitive anti-dumping duty may be imposed only from the date of the determination of threat or material retardation:

10.4 Except as provided in paragraph 2, where a determination of threat of injury or material retardation is made (but no injury has yet occurred) a definitive anti-dumping duty may be imposed only from the date of the determination of threat of injury or material retardation, and any cash deposit made during the period of the application of provisional measures shall be refunded and any bonds released in an expeditious manner.

In such case, any cash deposits made during the period of application of the provisional measures shall be refunded and bonds released expeditiously. In *Mexico–HFCS*, the panel found that Mexico's failure to expeditiously release the bonds and/or the cash deposits collected under the provisional measure violated Article 10.4 ADA.[256]

Article 10.5 is self-explanatory:

10.5 Where a final determination is negative, any cash deposit made during the period of the application of provisional measures shall be refunded and any bonds released in an expeditious manner.

3.4.2 Critical Circumstances

Article 10.6 provides the opportunity to impose a definitive anti-dumping duty on products which were entered for consumption during the 90 days prior to the date of application of provisional measures, but only if:

- there is a history of injurious dumping which caused injury *or* the importer was, or should have been, aware that the exporter practises injurious dumping; *and*

---

[256] *Mexico–HFCS from the United States*, Panel, para 7.193.

- the injury is caused by massive dumped imports of a product in a relatively short time which in light of the timing and the volume of the dumped imports and other circumstances (eg rapid build-up of inventories) is likely to seriously undermine the remedial effect of the definitive anti-dumping duty. (This is sometimes called *sporadic dumping*.)[257]

This provision is often referred to as the critical circumstances provision, a term taken from the corresponding US implementing provision.

10.6 A definitive anti-dumping duty may be levied on products which were entered for consumption not more than 90 days prior to the date of application of provisional measures, when the authorities determine for the dumped product in question that:

(i) there is a history of dumping which caused injury or that the importer was, or should have been, aware that the exporter practises dumping and that such dumping would cause injury, and

(ii) the injury is caused by massive dumped imports of a product in a relatively short time which in light of the timing and the volume of the dumped imports and other circumstances (such as a rapid build-up of inventories of the imported product) is likely to seriously undermine the remedial effect of the definitive anti-dumping duty to be applied, provided that the importers concerned have been given an opportunity to comment.

As the panel held in *Mexico–HFCS*, Article 10.6 provides the sole basis for a member to retroactively levy a definitive anti-dumping duty for a period during which provisional measures were not applied.[258]

Authorities could presumably find a history of dumping if the exporters concerned have been determined to have dumped previously in the country of importation or in third countries. Establishing awareness on the part of the importer would appear to be much more difficult, but could possibly be inferred from the level of the dumping and the injury margins.

The ADA does not provide any guidance for the establishment of the time period to assess whether massively dumped imports in a relatively short time occurred[259] and therefore leaves the authorities a margin of discretion. Nevertheless, the conditions are cumbersome and the rules difficult to apply, particularly because a determination whether the conditions are fulfilled normally would be made only after the products have already entered the

---

[257] Koulen, 'The New Anti-Dumping Code Through Its Negotiating History' in Bourgeois, Berrod and Gippini Fournier (eds), *The Uruguay Round Results* (1995) 151, 221.

[258] *Mexico–HFCS from the United States*, Panel, para 7.53.

[259] *United States–Hot Rolled Steel from Japan*, Panel, para 7.165.

importing country market. Possibly for these reasons, many WTO members rarely invoke Article 10.6.[260]

Article 10.7 authorizes the authorities, after initiation of the investigation, to take measures such as the withholding of appraisal or assessment necessary to collect anti-dumping duties retroactively as provided in Article 10.6, once they have sufficient evidence that the Article 10.6 conditions are satisfied:

10.7 The authorities may, after initiating an investigation, take such measures as the withholding of appraisement or assessment as may be necessary to collect anti-dumping duties retroactively, as provided for in paragraph 6, once they have sufficient evidence that the conditions set forth in that paragraph are satisfied.

In *United States–Hot rolled steel*, Japan unsuccessfully challenged both the US statute with regard to *critical circumstances* and the application of the statute in the concrete case. The US statute provides that if the petitioner alleges critical circumstances, USDOC shall promptly determine whether there is a reasonable basis to believe or suspect that critical circumstances exist. On the basis of this determination the necessary measures may be taken to collect anti-dumping duties retroactively. The panel considered that this provision neither required the USDOC to take WTO-inconsistent action nor did it preclude the USDOC from acting consistently with the ADA.

First, although the evidentiary standard in the US statute was 'a reasonable basis to believe or suspect', while Article 10.7 of the ADA uses the term 'sufficient evidence', the panel considered that this difference in itself did not constitute a violation. Rather, the panel would have to determine how the standard was applied in practice.

In our view, 'sufficient evidence' refers to the quantum of evidence necessary to make a determination. 'A reasonable basis to believe or suspect' on the other hand, seems to refer to the conclusion reached on the basis of evidence presented, that is, a legal mindset that certain facts exist, based on the evidence presented. It appears that in past cases the US authorities have applied the standard as set out in the statute interchangeably with a standard expressed as 'sufficient evidence' and have made affirmative determinations when sufficient evidence was adduced that the conditions of application were satisfied. We therefore consider that the US statute, as it has been applied is not inconsistent with the requirement of the ADA that the investigating authority must have sufficient evidence of the conditions of Article 10.6 before taking measures necessary to collect the duties retroactively.[261]

---

[260] Compare Czako, Human and Miranda, *A Handbook on Anti-Dumping Investigations* (2003) 82.
[261] *United States–Hot Rolled Steel from Japan*, Panel, para 7.144.

Japan had further argued that the US statute did not require evidence that all the conditions of Article 10.6 of the ADA were satisfied, as required by Article 10.7. Particularly, the statute did not require sufficient evidence of dumping, injury and causation, nor evidence that massive dumped imports were likely to seriously undermine the remedial effect of the duty. Again, the panel ruled that the statute did not necessarily preclude the USDOC from making a WTO-consistent determination. The panel also provided a useful clarification of the awkward reference in Article 10.7 to satisfaction of the Article 10.6 conditions:

We note that Article 10.7 requires that there be sufficient evidence that the conditions of Article 10.6 are satisfied. Article 10.6 of the ADA of course presupposes a final dumping and injury determination, without which no definitive dumping duties may be applied in any case. Rather than being conditions set out in Article 10.6, we consider that findings of dumping and injury are a precondition for any definitive duty to be applied. Article 10.7 of the ADA provides that certain preliminary measures may be taken 'after initiation'. This implies that at the time of the critical circumstances determination, the authority has already determined, under Article 5.3, that the petition contained sufficient information of dumping, injury, and a causal link to justify the initiation of the investigation. For a preliminary critical circumstances determination, Article 10.7 requires, in addition, sufficient evidence of the specific conditions of Article 10.6 as set forth in 10.6 (i) and (ii). It does not, however, in our view necessarily require additional or different evidence of dumping or injury from that on which the decision to initiate was based.[262]

We note that the US statute governing preliminary critical circumstances determinations does not expressly refer to the question whether massive dumped imports seriously undermine the remedial effect of the duty. However, we do not consider that the ADA requires that a separate determination be made with regard to this aspect of Article 10.6 at the preliminary stage of considering whether to take action under Article 10.7. Rather than a 'condition' of Article 10.6 of which there must be sufficient evidence in order to act under Article 10.7, in our view, this requirement establishes the conclusion that must be reached in order to justify retroactive application of the anti-dumping duty under Article 10.6. Consideration of this question at the preliminary stage of deciding whether to apply measures under Article 10.7 would, in our estimation, at best be speculative. Our view is reinforced by the fact that the possible undermining of the remedial effect of a definitive anti-dumping duty is not a question of which evidence would be available at the very early stages of an investigation, after initiation, when the determination under Article 10.7 may be made and authorized precautionary measures taken. The conclusion that the remedial effect of a definitive duty would be undermined by the effect of massive dumped imports can only

---

[262] *United States–Hot Rolled Steel from Japan*, Panel, para 7.147.

meaningfully be addressed at the end of the investigation, when it has been determined that the imposition of a definitive anti-dumping measure is warranted, based on a final determination of dumping, injury, and causal link. To require investigating authorities to undertake what is likely to be an impossible, meaningless task under Article 10.7 is not, in our view, necessary or appropriate.[263]

The panel took pains to emphasize the purely conservatory nature of the Article 10.7 measures:

We read ... [Article 10.7] as allowing the authority to take certain necessary measures of a purely conservatory or precautionary kind which serve the purpose of preserving the possibility of later deciding to collect duties retroactively under Article 10.6. Unlike provisional measures, Article 10.7 measures are not primarily intended to prevent injury being caused during the investigation. They are taken in order to make subsequent retroactive duty collection possible as a practical matter. Measures taken under Article 10.7 are not based on evaluation of the same criteria as final measures that may be imposed at the end of the investigation. They are of a different kind – they preserve the possibility of imposing anti-dumping duties retroactively, on the basis of a determination additional to the ultimate final determination.[264]

Our understanding in this regard is confirmed by the fact that, unlike provisional measures, which can only be imposed after a preliminary affirmative determination of dumping and injury, Article 10.7 measures may be taken at any time 'after initiating an investigation'. In light of the timing and effect of the measures that are taken on the basis of Article 10.7, we consider that the Article 10.7 requirement of 'sufficient evidence that the conditions of Article 10.6 are satisfied' does not require an authority to first make a preliminary affirmative determination within the meaning of Article 7 of the ADA of dumping and consequent injury to a domestic industry. If it were necessary to wait until after such a preliminary determination, there would, in our view, be no purpose served by the Article 10.7 determination. The opportunity to preserve the possibility of applying duties to a period prior to the preliminary determination would be lost, and the provisional measure that could be applied on the basis of the preliminary affirmative determination under Article 7 would prevent further injury during the course of the investigation. Moreover, the requirement in Article 7 that provisional measures may not be applied until 60 days after initiation cannot be reconciled with the right, under Article 10.6, to apply duties retroactively to 90 days prior to the date on which a provisional measure is imposed, if a preliminary affirmative determination is a prerequisite to the Article 10.7 measures which preserve the possibility of retroactive application of duties under Article 10.6.[265]

---

[263] *United States–Hot Rolled Steel from Japan*, Panel, para 7.148.
[264] *United States–Hot Rolled Steel from Japan*, Panel, para 7.155.
[265] *United States–Hot Rolled Steel from Japan*, Panel, para 7.156.

The panel then proceeded to determine whether the statute, as applied in the *Hot rolled steel* case, had violated Article 10.7.

As regards evidence of injurious dumping, the panel considered that, given the precautionary nature of any Article 10.7 measures, sufficient evidence of injurious dumping for Article 5.3 purposes by definition constituted sufficient evidence for Article 10.7 purposes.

With respect to the requirement that the importers knew or should have known that exporters were dumping and that such dumping would cause injury, the panel noted that the USDOC normally considers dumping margins of 25 per cent or more and a USITC preliminary determination of material injury to impute knowledge of dumping and the likelihood of consequent material injury. The panel considered that the evidence in the petition, which indicated dumping margins of over 25 per cent, was sufficient for this purpose. While the USITC in this case had preliminarily found a threat of material injury, the panel considered that injury in Article 10.6 also included threat. Furthermore, the USDOC had not based its finding solely upon the USITC determination, but had also taken into account the injury information in the petition, and considered press reports regarding increasing imports, declining prices, and shifts in purchasing to import sources.[266]

Concerning massively dumped imports in a relatively short period of time, the USDOC had compared the five months before and after April 1988, during which imports had increased over 100 per cent. This period had been selected based on press reports which in the view of the USDOC established that exporters and importers knew or should have known that an anti-dumping investigation was likely. Japan had argued that the authority should have compared the months before and after the *initiation*. However, the panel disagreed:

Article 10.7 allows for certain necessary measures to be taken at any time after initiation of the investigation. In order to be able to make any determination concerning whether there are massive dumped imports, a comparison of data is obviously necessary. However, if a Member were required to wait until information concerning the volume of imports for some period after initiation were available, this right to act at any time after initiation would be vitiated. By the time the necessary information on import volumes for even a brief period after initiation were available, as a practical matter, the possibility to impose final duties retroactively to initiation would be lost, as there would be no Article 10.7 measures in place . . . [267]

---

[266] *United States–Hot Rolled Steel from Japan*, Panel, para 7.161.
[267] *United States–Hot Rolled Steel from Japan*, Panel, para 7.166.

Moreover, in our view, it is not unreasonable to conclude that the remedial effect of the definitive duty could be undermined by massive imports that entered the country before the initiation of the investigation but at a time at which it had become clear that an investigation was imminent. We consider that massive imports that were not made in tempore non suspectu but at a moment in time where it had become public knowledge that an investigation was imminent may be taken into consideration in assessing whether Article 10.7 measures may be imposed. Again, we emphasize that we are not addressing the question whether this would be adequate for purposes of the final determination to apply duties retroactively under Article 10.6.[268]

As we have seen above already, Article 10.8 stipulates that Article 10.6 duties (or any other duties) may never be applied to products that entered into the importing country market prior to initiation:

10.8 No duties shall be levied retroactively pursuant to paragraph 6 on products entered for consumption prior to the date of initiation of the investigation.

3.5 Reviews

Article 11 covers the duration and review of anti-dumping duties and price undertakings. Whereas Article 9.5 also contains a review mechanism, we will discuss in the following sections the three types of review, envisaged by the ADA:

- interim or changed circumstances[269] review, covered by Article 11.2;
- sunset or expiry review, covered by Article 11.3; and
- newcomer review, covered by Article 9.5.

Article 11.1 lays out the principle that an anti-dumping duty shall remain in force only as long as and to the extent necessary to counteract dumping which is causing injury:

11.1 An anti-dumping duty shall remain in force only as long as and to the extent necessary to counteract dumping which is causing injury.

In *United States–DRAMS*, the panel considered that Article 11.1 contained a *general necessity* requirement, the application of which is specified in Article 11.2.[270]

---

[268] *United States–Hot Rolled Steel from Japan*, Panel, para 7.167.
[269] Czako, Human and Miranda, *A Handbook on Anti-Dumping Investigations* (2003) 9.
[270] *United States–DRAMS from Korea*, Panel, para 6.41.

3.5.1 Interim Review

Article 11.2 specifies the general principle laid down in Article 11.1 by providing that the authorities shall review the need for the continued imposition of the duty, where warranted, on their own initiative or, provided that a reasonable period of time has passed since the imposition of the definitive duty, upon duly motivated request by any interested party.

Interested parties may request the authorities to examine whether the continued imposition of the duty is necessary to offset dumping, whether the injury would be likely to continue or recur if the duty were removed or varied or both. It is important to note that the word 'varied' indicates that in an interim review (as opposed to an expiry review), the options on the table are not only whether to maintain the measure or not, but also whether the duty should be imposed at a different rate, as a result of the interim review findings. This observation is particularly important for anti-dumping systems that use the prospective duty collection system[271] because under this system anti-dumping duties normally apply for five years at the rates imposed during the original investigation.

While the authorities may self-initiate an interim review any time and for any reason, interested parties must wait a reasonable period of time (often interpreted as one year) and may advance three bases:

- the duty is no longer necessary to offset dumping (dumping review);
- the injury would not be likely to continue or recur if the duty were removed or varied (injury review);
- both (full-fledged review covering both dumping and injury).

If the results of the review indicate that the duty is no longer warranted, it shall be terminated immediately. Thus, contrary to Article 9.3.2 refunds or Article 9.3.1 annual reviews in the US, Article 11 reviews work prospectively:[272]

11.2 The authorities shall review the need for the continued imposition of the duty, where warranted, on their own initiative or, provided that a reasonable period of time has elapsed since the imposition of the definitive anti-dumping duty, upon request by any interested party which submits positive information substantiating the need for a review.[273] Interested parties shall have the right to request the authorities to examine whether the continued imposition of the duty is necessary to offset dumping, whether the injury would be likely to continue or recur if the duty were removed or varied, or

---

[271] See section 3.3.3.3, above.   [272] See section 3.3.3.3, above.
[273] Fn 21 in original: A determination of final liability for payment of anti-dumping duties, as provided for in paragraph 3 of Article 9, does not by itself constitute a review within the meaning of this Article.

both. If, as a result of the review under this paragraph, the authorities determine that the anti-dumping duty is no longer warranted, it shall be terminated immediately.

Article 11.2 grants the authorities substantial discretion because it involves analysis of future events or, in other words, a prospective analysis. Thus, even if, for example, dumping and injury have stopped during the review investigation period, the authorities could still decide that continued imposition of the duty is necessary to offset dumping or that injury would be likely to recur, ie start again, if the duty were to be lifted.

In *United States–DRAMS*, Korea challenged the USDOC so-called *three zeroes regulation*,[274] under which USDOC could partially revoke anti-dumping duties if it found zero dumping margins for three years in a row for the respondents concerned and found it 'not likely' that the respondents would start dumping again in the future. Korea argued that Article 11.2 required a focus on *present* dumping rather than the possibility of future dumping. The USDOC had found no dumping for two Korean producers for three years in a row, but nevertheless had concluded that it was not 'not likely' that the two companies would dump in the future (one of the conditions under the USDOC regulations) and had therefore refused to revoke the order.

The panel noted that the relevant part of the second sentence of Article 11.2 is expressed in the present tense and that it does not explicitly include any reference to dumping being likely to recur, as is the case with the injury review; on the other hand, the second sentence refers to the *continued* imposition of the duties:

The word 'continued' covers a temporal relationship between past and future. The word 'continued' would be redundant if the investigating authority were restricted to considering only whether the duty was necessary to offset present dumping. Thus, the inclusion of the word 'continued' signifies that the investigating authority is entitled to examine whether imposition of the duty may be applied henceforth to offset dumping.

. . . In conducting an Article 11.2 injury review, an investigating authority may examine the causal link between injury and dumped imports. If, in the context of a review of such a causal link, the only injury under examination is injury that may recur following revocation (i.e., future rather than present injury), an investigating authority must necessarily be examining whether that future injury would be caused by dumping with a commensurately prospective timeframe. To do so, the investigating authority would first need to have established a status regarding the prospects of dumping.

---

[274] See for a more detailed discussion of the case, Cunningham and Cribb, 'Dispute Settlement Through the Lens of "Free Flow of Trade": A Review of WTO Dispute Settlement of US Anti-Dumping and Countervailing Duty Measures' (2003) 6 Journal of International Economic Law 155, 156–157.

For these reasons, Article 11.2 does not preclude a priori the justification of continued imposition of anti-dumping duties when there is no present dumping.[275]

The panel found nothing in Article 11.2 that would foreclose a prospective analysis.[276] Therefore, the absence of present dumping did not in and of itself require the immediate termination of the duty pursuant to Article 11.2 ADA:[277]

. . . the necessity required by Article 11.2 for the continued application of an anti-dumping duty should not be construed in absolute and abstract terms, but as what is appropriate to circumstances of practical reasoning intrinsic to a review process. Mathematical certainty is not required, but the conclusions should be demonstrable on the basis of the evidence adduced.[278]

On the other hand, the panel did find that the regulatory 'not likely' standard violated the Article 11.2 'likely' standard ADA:[279]

We consider that a failure to find that an event is 'not likely' is not equivalent to a finding that the event is 'likely'. We see a clear conceptual difference between establishing something as a positive finding, and failing to establish something as a negative finding. It is perfectly possible that one could not determine that someone was unlikely to dump and find that they were also likely to dump. But the former determination does not, in and of itself, amount to a demonstrable basis for concluding the latter. This is evident from the fact that the former finding is manifestly compatible also with the *reverse* of the latter situation, i.e., it is perfectly logical to find that you cannot determine that someone is unlikely to dump, yet also be unable to determine that they were actually likely to dump. In other words, determining that something is not 'not likely' is entailed by, but does not itself entail, that something is likely.[280]

In the same case, the panel also ruled that three years and six months' findings of no dumping did not require the authorities to self-initiate an injury review.[281]

On the basis of the panel reports in *Korea–DRAMS* and *United States Corrosion-resistant carbon steel flat products*,[282] it also seems clear that the Article 5.8 *de minimis* dumping rule does not apply to interim reviews.

---

[275] *United States–DRAMS from Korea*, Panel, paras 6.26–6.28.
[276] *United States–DRAMS from Korea*, Panel, para 6.29.
[277] *United States–DRAMS from Korea*, Panel, para 6.32.
[278] *United States–DRAMS from Korea*, Panel, para 6.43.
[279] *United States–DRAMS from Korea*, Panel, para 6.54.
[280] *United States–DRAMS from Korea*, Panel, para 6.45.
[281] *United States–DRAMS from Korea*, Panel, para 6.59.
[282] See section 3.2.2.1, above, for a detailed discussion.

In *Mexico–Rice*, the panel effectively ruled that producers which are found not to have dumped during the original investigation may not be subjected later on to interim reviews:

Article 68 of the Act thus requires the review of producers for which during the original investigation it was determined that they had not been engaged in dumping practices or had not received any subsidies . . . [W]e find that Article 5.8 of the ADA requires the termination of the investigation with regard to such exporters found not to have been dumping above de minimis levels, and requires that such exporters be excluded from the measures imposed. The logical consequence of such an exclusion of producers found not to have been dumping is that they can not subsequently be subjected to administrative or changed circumstances reviews. While we agree with Mexico that the specific requirements concerning de minimis do not apply in the case of reviews of the duties imposed, this does not imply that Article 68 of the Act dealing with reviews cannot be inconsistent with Article 5.8 of the ADA insofar as it imposes the review of measures with regard to producers to which such measures should not have been applied in the first place. The possibility of reviewing the zero per cent duty margin imposed on such non-dumping exporters also reveals the important meaning of the imposition of such a zero per cent duty which, in spite of its appearance, does not equal the termination of the investigation as required by Article 5.8 of the ADA. We therefore find that Article 68 of the Act is as such inconsistent with Article 5.8 of the ADA.[283]

3.5.2 Sunset Review

Article 11.3 provides that definitive anti-dumping duties must be terminated within five years from their imposition (or from the most recent full-fledged review), unless the authorities determine in a review *initiated* before the end of the five-year period either at their own initiative or upon a duly motivated request by the domestic industry, that the expiry of the duty would be likely to lead to continuation or recurrence of dumping and injury. It is noteworthy that Article 11.3 therefore contains no evidentiary standard for the authorities to apply when deciding to self-initiate a sunset review.[284]

During the course of the expiry review investigation, the duty may then remain in force.

It has been noted that '[t]he ADA provisions on sunset reviews are quite brief, providing little direct guidance as to the methodology to be followed by

---

[283] *Mexico–Rice from the United States*, Panel, para 7.251.
[284] Compare *United States–Corrosion-resistant carbon steel flat products from Japan*, Panel, paras 7.26–7.27.

investigating authorities in making sunset review determinations.'[285] However, in two cases, *United States–Corrosion-resistant carbon steel flat products* and *United States–Oil country tubular goods*, the Appellate Body has provided important clarifications of Article 11.3:

11.3 Notwithstanding the provisions of paragraphs 1 and 2, any definitive anti-dumping duty shall be terminated on a date not later than five years from its imposition (or from the date of the most recent review under paragraph 2 if that review has covered both dumping and injury, or under this paragraph), unless the authorities determine, in a review initiated before that date on their own initiative or upon a duly substantiated request made by or on behalf of the domestic industry within a reasonable period of time prior to that date, that the expiry of the duty would be likely to lead to continuation or recurrence of dumping and injury.[286] The duty may remain in force pending the outcome of such a review.

Article 11.3 requires members to terminate anti-dumping duties within five years, unless the following three conditions are fulfilled:

- a review is initiated before the end of the five year period;
- in the review the authorities determine that the expiry of the duty would be likely to lead to continuation or recurrence of dumping; and
- in the review the authorities determine that the expiry of the duty would be likely to lead to continuation or recurrence of injury.[287]

3.5.2.1 *The Likelihood Determination*

In *United States–Corrosion-resistant carbon steel flat products*, Japan challenged the American Sunset Policy Bulletin (SPB), both as such and as applied, as being in violation of the Article 11.3 condition that the expiry of the duty would be likely to lead to continuation or recurrence of dumping.[288]

The AB termed this the *likelihood* determination and noted right away that it is *prospective* in nature:[289]

The likelihood determination is a prospective determination. In other words, the authorities must undertake a forward-looking analysis and seek to resolve the issue of what would be likely to occur if the duty were terminated.[290]

---

[285] WorldTradeLaw.net, *Dispute Settlement Commentary on United States–Corrosion-resistant carbon steel flat products from Japan*, p 14, checked on 23 April 2005.

[286] Fn 22 in ADA: When the amount of the anti-dumping duty is assessed on a retrospective basis, a finding in the most recent assessment proceeding under subparagraph 3.1 of Article 9 that no duty is to be levied shall not by itself require the authorities to terminate the definitive duty.

[287] *United States–Corrosion-resistant carbon steel flat products from Japan*, AB, para 104.

[288] *United States–Corrosion-resistant carbon steel flat products from Japan*, Panel, para 3.1.

[289] *United States–Corrosion-resistant carbon steel flat products from Japan*, AB, para 105.

[290] *United States–Corrosion-resistant carbon steel flat products from Japan*, AB, para 105.

However, the AB then emphasized the obligation of the authorities to conduct a rigorous analysis:

This language in Article 11.3 makes clear that it envisages a process combining both investigatory and adjudicatory aspects. In other words, Article 11.3 assigns an active rather than a passive decision-making role to the authorities. The words 'review' and 'determine' in Article 11.3 suggest that authorities conducting a sunset review must act with an appropriate degree of diligence and arrive at a reasoned conclusion on the basis of information gathered as part of a process of reconsideration and examination. In view of the use of the word 'likely' in Article 11.3, an affirmative likelihood determination may be made only if the evidence demonstrates that dumping would be probable if the duty were terminated – and not simply if the evidence suggests that such a result might be possible or plausible.[291]

... the mandatory rule in Article 11.3 applies in addition to, and irrespective of, the obligations set out in the first two paragraphs of Article 11. This also suggests to us that authorities must conduct a rigorous examination in a sunset review before the exception (namely, the continuation of the duty) can apply. In addition, our view of the exacting nature of the obligations imposed on authorities under Article 11.3 is supported by a consideration of the implications of initiating a sunset review. The last sentence of Article 11.3 allows the relevant duty to continue while the review is under-way, and Article 11.4 contemplates that the review process may take up to one year. These provisions create an additional exception to the requirement that anti-dumping duties will be terminated after five years, permitting a Member to maintain the duty for the period during which the review is ongoing, regardless of the outcome of that review. This, too, suggests that the drafters of the ADA saw the sunset review as a rigorous process that can take up to one year, involving a number of procedural steps, and requiring an appropriate degree of diligence on the part of the national authorities.[292]

Japan had argued that Sections II.A.3 and II.A.4 SPB as such were inconsistent with Article 11.3 ADA because they required the USDOC to make specific determinations in specific scenarios.[293] The AB considered that when a measure is challenged as such, the starting point for analysis is the measure on its face. If the meaning and content of the measure are clear on its face, then the consistency of the measure can be assessed solely on that basis. However, where this is not the case, further examination will be necessary.[294]

The AB found that, on its face, under the SPB the USDOC will normally make an affirmative determination under three 'scenarios':

(a) dumping continued at any level above 0.5 per cent after the order was issued;

---

[291] *United States–Corrosion-resistant carbon steel flat products from Japan*, AB, para 111.
[292] *United States–Corrosion-resistant carbon steel flat products from Japan*, AB, para 113.
[293] *United States–Corrosion-resistant carbon steel flat products from Japan*, AB, para 164.
[294] *United States–Corrosion-resistant carbon steel flat products from Japan*, AB, para 168.

(b) imports ceased after the order was issued; or
(c) dumping was eliminated after the order was issued and import volumes declined significantly.

On the other hand, the USDOC will normally make a negative determination if, after the issuance of the order, dumping was eliminated and import volumes remained steady or decreased.[295]

The AB considered that the consistency of these SPB provisions with Article 11.3 depends upon whether they instruct the USDOC to treat dumping margins and/or import volumes as determinative or conclusive, on the one hand, or as merely indicative or probative, on the other hand, of the likelihood of future dumping.[296] The AB found conflicting evidence on this issue and concluded that it was unable to rule on Japan's claim in the absence of relevant factual findings by the panel or uncontested facts on the panel record.[297] In *obiter dicta*, the AB cautioned that the use of presumptions, particularly irrebuttable ones, might be inconsistent with the obligation to make determinations on the basis of positive evidence.[298]

In *United States–Oil country tubular goods*, Argentina again challenged Section II.A.3 of the SPB. As an aside, it may be noted that it would appear that in the original investigation, only one Argentine exporter had cooperated, for which the USDOC had found a dumping margin of 1.36 per cent and that this exporter had stopped shipments to the United States subsequently.

The panel had used the determinative versus. indicative standard, enunciated by the AB in *United States–Corrosion-resistant carbon steel flat products*, and had determined that the text of the SPB did not provide a dispositive reply. The panel had then proceeded to analyse statistics provided by Argentina and had considered that the USDOC applied the contested provisions of the SPB in each sunset review and found likelihood of continuation or recurrence in each one of these sunset reviews on the basis of one of the three scenarios contained in Section II.A.3 of the SPB. As a result, the panel had concluded that the evidence submitted by Argentina demonstrated that the USDOC does in fact perceive the provisions of Section II.A.3 of the SPB as *conclusive* regarding the issue of likelihood of continuation or recurrence of dumping in the case of revocation of an order.[299]

---

[295] *United States–Corrosion-resistant carbon steel flat products from Japan*, AB, paras 172–173.
[296] *United States–Corrosion-resistant carbon steel flat products from Japan*, AB, para 178.
[297] *United States–Corrosion-resistant carbon steel flat products from Japan*, AB, para 178.
[298] *United States–Corrosion-resistant carbon steel flat products from Japan*, AB, para 191.
[299] *United States–Oil country tubular goods from Argentina*, Panel, paras 7.165–7.166.

On appeal, the AB noted that it considered the volume of dumped imports and the dumping margins as *highly important* factors for a likelihood determination. However, it then expressed its concern about the *mechanistic application* of the three scenarios:

In our view, 'volume of dumped imports' and 'dumping margins', before and after the issuance of anti-dumping duty orders, are highly important factors for any determination of likelihood of continuation or recurrence of dumping in sunset reviews, although other factors may also be as important, depending on the circumstances of the case. The three factual scenarios in Section II.A.3 of the SPB, which describe how these two factors will be considered in individual determinations, thus have certain probative value, the degree of which may vary from case to case. For example, if, under scenario (a) of Section II.A.3 of the SPB, dumping continued with substantial margins despite the existence of the anti-dumping duty order, this would be highly probative of the likelihood that dumping would continue if the anti-dumping order were revoked. Conversely, if, under scenarios (b) and (c) of Section II.A.3 of the SPB, imports ceased after issuance of the anti-dumping duty order, or imports continued but without dumping margins, the probative value of the scenarios may be much less, and other relevant factors may have to be examined to determine whether imports with dumping margins would 'recur' if the anti-dumping duty order were revoked. The importance of the two underlying factors (import volumes and dumping margins) for a likelihood-of-dumping determination cannot be questioned; however, our concern here is with the possible mechanistic application of the three scenarios based on these factors, such that other factors that may be of equal importance are disregarded.[300]

The AB agreed with the first two steps of the panel's approach, but considered the analysis by the panel too superficial. In the view of the AB, in order to assess objectively whether the three scenarios are regarded as determinative, it is essential to examine concrete examples of cases where the likelihood determination was based solely on one of the three scenarios, even though the probative value of other factors might have outweighed that of the identified factors. Such examination requires a *qualitative assessment* of individual likelihood determinations,[301] which the panel had not undertaken:

The Panel record does not show that the Panel undertook any such qualitative assessment of at least some of the cases of Exhibit ARG-63 with a view to discerning whether the USDOC regarded the existence of one of the factual scenarios of the SPB as determinative/conclusive for its determinations. The Panel also appears not to have examined in how many cases the foreign respondent parties participated in the proceedings, in how many they introduced other 'good cause' factors, and how the USDOC dealt with

---

300   *United States–Oil country tubular goods from Argentina*, AB, para 208.
301   *United States–Oil country tubular goods from Argentina*, AB, paras 208–209.

those factors when they were introduced. Such an inquiry would have enabled the Panel to identify and undertake a qualitative analysis of at least some of those cases to see whether the affirmative determinations were made solely on the basis of one of the scenarios to the exclusion of other factors. The Panel failed to undertake any such qualitative assessment and relied exclusively on the overall statistics or aggregated results of Exhibit ARG-63. The fact that affirmative determinations were made in reliance on one of the three scenarios in all the sunset reviews of anti-dumping duty orders where domestic interested parties took part strongly suggests that these scenarios are mechanistically applied. However, without a qualitative examination of the reasons leading to such determinations, it is not possible to conclude definitively that these determinations were based exclusively on these scenarios in disregard of other factors.[302]

As a result, the AB found that the panel had not made an objective assessment of the matter, as required by Article 11 DSU.[303]

3.5.2.2 Dumping Margin Calculation

As far as dumping is concerned, the relevant question in a sunset review is whether the expiry of the duty would be likely to lead to continuation or recurrence of dumping. The word *continuation* obviously implies that the dumping is continuing despite the imposition of the duty. The word *recurrence*, on the other hand, would seem to indicate a situation where the dumping has stopped (thus, the measures are 'working'), but may start again if the duty were to be lifted.[304] As an affirmative finding with respect to either of the two is sufficient to maintain the measure, it would not appear absolutely necessary to calculate detailed dumping margins for purposes of an expiry review, although such a calculation would obviously be helpful to determine whether the dumping in fact has continued while the measure was in force and, if so, at what level.

A related question is what the authorities should do if any detailed dumping margin calculation in the sunset review were to show that the margin has gone up or down. Should they then apply the new result or simply maintain the old measure? Most WTO members take the position that the only choice in an

---

[302] *United States–Oil country tubular goods from Argentina*, AB, para 212.

[303] *United States–Oil country tubular goods from Argentina*, AB, para 215. WorldTradeLaw.net, *Dispute Settlement Commentary on United States–Oil country tubular goods*, pp 16–17, checked on 23 April 2005, notes that the AB in this case loosened the Art 11.3 standard a bit by finding an Art 11 DSU violation, although not finding in so many words that the panel had committed an 'egregious error', the standard that the AB has applied in other cases, such as *EC–Bed linen 21.5*. According to WorldTradeLaw.net, '[i]t would be a stretch to argue that the panel's approach constitutes an "egregious error." Indeed, the Appellate Body itself said that the evidence relied upon by the panel provides a strong suggestion of a violation.' Id, at p 17.

[304] Compare *United States–DRAMS from Korea*, Panel, para 6.31, where the Panel rejected the argument advanced by Korea that *present* dumping needed to exist for an affirmative likelihood finding.

expiry review (as opposed to an interim review) is to maintain or to terminate the measure. This position seems supported by the differences in wording between Article 11.2 and 11.3. If, therefore, either the domestic industry or the exporters feel that circumstances have changed to such an extent that the duties originally imposed need to be revised, it might be in their interest to request an interim review instead. In this context, it is noted that some WTO members have sometimes self-initiated an interim review simultaneously with the initiation of an expiry review, so that all options would be on the table. Thus far, these issues have not been challenged in the WTO.

In *United States–Corrosion-resistant carbon steel flat products*, the AB considered that Article 11.3 did not *require* the authorities to calculate dumping margins in an expiry review:

... it is consistent with the different nature and purpose of original investigations, on the one hand, and sunset reviews, on the other hand, to interpret the ADA as requiring investigating authorities to calculate dumping margins in an original investigation, but not in a sunset review. In an original investigation, if investigating authorities of a Member do not determine a positive dumping margin, the Member may not impose anti-dumping measures based on that investigation. In a sunset review, dumping margins may well be relevant to, but they will not necessarily be conclusive of, whether the expiry of the duty would be likely to lead to continuation or recurrence of dumping.[305]

However, if the authorities *do* rely on dumping margins to support an affirmative likelihood determination, as the USDOC had done by relying on dumping margins calculated in two particular administrative reviews, then they must ensure that those dumping margins have been calculated consistently with Article 2.4. Failure to do so (for example, because zeroing[306] has been used), may lead to a violation not only of Article 2.4, also of Article 11.3.[307] As a result, the AB disagreed with the panel's view that the Article 2 dumping margin calculation requirements did not apply to sunset reviews.[308]

As regarded the allegations that the USDOC had applied WTO-inconsistent zeroing in those administrative reviews, the AB found that it was not clear on the basis of the factual record of the case whether the methodology that the USDOC had used was 'equivalent in effect' to the methodology used by the EC and condemned by the AB in the *EC–Bed Linen* case.[309] Commentators

---

[305] *United States–Corrosion-resistant carbon steel flat products from Japan*, AB, para 124.
[306] See section 1.4.3.1, above.
[307] *United States–Corrosion-resistant carbon steel flat products from Japan*, AB, paras 135–136.
[308] *United States–Corrosion-resistant carbon steel flat products from Japan*, AB, paras 127–128.
[309] *United States–Corrosion-resistant carbon steel flat products from Japan*, AB, para 137.

have concluded that the effect of this finding is to impose stronger disciplines on authorities in conducting sunset reviews.[310]

In *United States–Oil country tubular goods*, the question also arose whether the existence of a dumping margin from the *original* investigation can be interpreted to mean that dumping continued over the life of the measure. The panel considered that it could not:

Exporters subject to the measure might have changed their export or home market prices, or, their cost of production might have changed. Thus, if an investigating authority relies upon the existence of dumping over the life of the measure as part of its sunset determination, it has to have an adequate factual basis for so concluding. This can be, inter alia, a determination made as part of a duty assessment process carried out under Article 9 of the ADA, or a review under Article 11.2. In our view however, the original determination of dumping by itself cannot represent a sufficient factual basis for concluding that dumping continued during the life of the measure, let alone representing an adequate factual basis to conclude that dumping is likely to continue or recur after the expiry of the order. The purpose of a sunset review is to examine whether the facts continue to justify the imposition of an anti-dumping measure. The USDOC, however, did not engage in that inquiry because it simply relied on the existence of the dumping margin from the original investigation.[311]

3.5.2.3 *Order-wide Determination*

In *United States–Corrosion-resistant carbon steel flat products*, Japan had claimed that Section II.A.2 of the SPB, both as such and as applied, violated Articles 6.10[312] and 11.3 ADA because it required the USDOC to make the likelihood determination on an order-wide basis. However, the panel,[313] supported by the AB,[314] ruled that neither Article 6.10[315] nor Article 11.3 precluded the authorities from making a likelihood determination on such basis. In other words, the authorities are not *required* in sunset reviews to reach company-specific findings, although they may do so if they wish:

Our conclusions regarding the consistency of this aspect of the SPB 'as such' with Article 11.3 do not imply that Article 11.3 precludes authorities from making separate likelihood determinations for individual exporters or producers in a sunset review and then continuing or terminating the relevant duty for each company according to the

---

[310] WorldTradeLaw.net, *Dispute Settlement Commentary on United States–Corrosion-resistant steel sunset review*, p 14, checked on 23 April 2005.

[311] *United States–Oil country tubular goods from Argentina*, Panel, para 7.219.

[312] See Section 3.2.5.10, above.

[313] *United States–Corrosion-resistant carbon steel flat products from Japan*, Panel, para 7.166.

[314] *United States–Corrosion-resistant carbon steel flat products from Japan*, AB, paras 149 and 156.

[315] See section 3.2.5.10, above.

determination for that company. WTO Members are free to structure their anti-dumping systems as they choose, provided that those systems do not conflict with the provisions of the ADA . . .

In this regard, we observe that the United States indicated in the oral hearing in this appeal that, under the United States' anti-dumping system, an exporter or producer may request that an anti-dumping duty order be revoked in part (that is, with respect to that exporter or producer) in review proceedings separate from a sunset review.[316]

Thus, the AB allowed the authorities discretion on this point.[317]

3.5.2.4 Non-cooperation

In *United States–Oil country tubular goods*, Argentina challenged certain aspects of US law which require the USDOC to reach an affirmative likelihood determination in cases where exporters do not or do not fully cooperate in a sunset review. Under US statutory provisions, participation by an exporter is deemed to be waived if it files either an incomplete submission or no submission at all (*deemed waiver*). If the exporter explicitly states that it will not participate in the sunset review, this is considered to be an *affirmative waiver*. In both cases, the statute directs the USDOC to reach an affirmative likelihood determination.

The AB noted that because the United States makes the likelihood determination on an order-wide basis,[318] the focus of the inquiry must be whether the waiver provisions prevent the USDOC from making an order-wide determination consistently with Article 11.3 ADA.[319] While the panel had taken as its starting point company-specific determinations, it had later examined their impact on the order-wide determination:

. . . The Panel observed that, in the case where the respondent that waives its right to participate is the sole exporter from a country subject to a dumping order, the company-specific determination 'is likely to be conclusive' with respect to the order-wide determination. The Panel also noted that '[t]he United States concedes that company-specific likelihood determinations are "considered" when making an order-wide likelihood determination'. . . The Panel concluded that, '[t]o the extent that' the company-specific determinations were taken into account in the order-wide determination, the order-wide determination could not 'be supported by reasoned and adequate conclusions based on the facts before the investigating authority'.

We agree with the Panel's analysis of the impact of the waiver provisions on order-wide determinations. Because the waiver provisions require the USDOC to arrive at

---

[316] *United States–Corrosion-resistant carbon steel flat products from Japan*, AB, para 158.

[317] Compare WorldTradeLaw.net, *Dispute Settlement Commentary on United States–Corrosion-resistant steel sunset review*, p 14, checked on 23 April 2005.　　[318] See section 3.5.2.3, above.

[319] *United States–Oil country tubular goods from Argentina*, AB, para 231.

affirmative company-specific determinations without regard to any evidence on record, these determinations are merely assumptions made by the agency, rather than findings supported by evidence. The United States contends that respondents waiving the right to participate in a sunset review do so 'intentionally', with full knowledge that, as a result of their failure to submit evidence, the evidence placed on the record by the domestic industry is likely to result in an unfavourable determination on an order-wide basis. In these circumstances, we see no fault in making an unfavourable order-wide determination by taking into account evidence provided by the domestic industry in support thereof. However, the USDOC also takes into account, in such circumstances, statutorily-mandated assumptions. Thus, even assuming that the USDOC takes into account the totality of evidence on the record in making its order-wide determination, it is clear that, as a result of the operation of the waiver provisions, certain order-wide likelihood determinations made by the USDOC will be based, at least in part, on statutorily-mandated assumptions about a company's likelihood of dumping. In our view, this result is inconsistent with the obligation of an investigating authority under Article 11.3 to 'arrive at a reasoned conclusion' on the basis of 'positive evidence'.[320]

It follows from the AB ruling that lack of cooperation by exporters does not give the authorities carte blanche to find affirmatively, even where the authorities apply an order-wide system.

3.5.2.5 De Minimis Dumping and Cumulation

In *United States–Corrosion-resistant carbon steel flat products*, the panel determined that the ADA did not require the authorities to apply the Article 5.8 *de minimis* threshold[321] in sunset reviews.[322]

In *United States–Oil country tubular goods*, the AB upheld a more general panel finding that the Article 3 injury obligations do not apply to likelihood determinations in sunset reviews:[323]

This is not to say, however, that in a sunset review determination, an investigating authority is never required to examine any of the factors listed in the paragraphs of Article 3. Certain of the analyses mandated by Article 3 and necessarily relevant in an original investigation may prove to be probative, or possibly even required, in order for an investigating authority in a sunset review to arrive at a 'reasoned conclusion'. In this respect, we are of the view that the fundamental requirement of Article 3.1 that an injury determination be based on 'positive evidence' and an 'objective examination' would be equally relevant to likelihood determinations under Article 11.3. It seems to

---

[320] *United States–Oil country tubular goods from Argentina*, AB, paras 233–234.
[321] See section 3.2.2.1, above.
[322] *United States–Corrosion-resistant carbon steel flat products from Japan*, Panel, para 7.95.
[323] *United States–Oil country tubular goods from Argentina*, AB, para 285.

us that factors such as the volume, price effects, and the impact on the domestic industry of dumped imports, taking into account the conditions of competition, may be relevant to varying degrees in a given likelihood-of-injury determination. An investigating authority may also, in its own judgement, consider other factors contained in Article 3 when making a likelihood-of-injury determination. But the necessity of conducting such an analysis in a given case results from the requirement imposed by Article 11.3 – not Article 3 – that a likelihood-of-injury determination rest on a 'sufficient factual basis' that allows the agency to draw 'reasoned and adequate conclusions'.[324]

In the same case, the AB also upheld the panel's findings that Article 11.3 does not preclude the authorities from cumulating[325] dumped imports and that the Article 3.3 cumulation conditions do not apply in sunset reviews.[326]

3.5.3 Common Provisions

Article 11.4 requires the authorities to apply the Article 6 due process provisions also in interim and sunset reviews and to carry out such reviews expeditiously, ie normally within 12 months:

11.4 The provisions of Article 6 regarding evidence and procedure shall apply to any review carried out under this Article. Any such review shall be carried out expeditiously and shall normally be concluded within 12 months of the date of initiation of the review.

In *United States–Oil country tubular goods*, the panel found that the US law provisions requiring the USDOC to ignore evidence submitted by parties that did not or did not fully cooperate[327] in a sunset review violated Articles 6.1 and 6.2 ADA:

It follows that the exporter is deprived of its right to submit evidence to the USDOC. This obviously runs foul of Article 6.1 of the ADA, which requires that interested parties be given an ample opportunity to submit information to the investigating authority. We see no provision in the ADA that allows such denial of the procedural rights provided for in Article 6.1 on the grounds that the exporter made an incomplete submission to the notice of initiation.

We also find US law to be inconsistent with Article 6.2 of the ADA in that it denies an exporter that is deemed to have waived its right to participate in a sunset review by submitting an incomplete response to the notice of initiation of a sunset review the right to participate in a hearing or otherwise to confront those parties with adverse

---

[324] *United States–Oil country tubular goods from Argentina*, AB, para 284.
[325] See section 2.3.4, above.
[326] *United States–Oil country tubular goods from Argentina*, AB, para 304.
[327] See also section 3.5.2.2, above.

interests. We find no justification in the ADA that would allow such a departure from the provisions of Article 6.2 on the grounds that that exporter has submitted an incomplete response to the notice of initiation.[328]

With regard to full non-cooperation, the panel reached the same conclusion, although it acknowledged that in such cases, the authorities will generally be entitled to resort to facts available which, in turn, may lead to an unfavourable determination.[329]

Last, Article 11.5 provides that investigations concluded with the acceptance of price undertakings are equally subject to interim and sunset reviews:

11.5 The provisions of this Article shall apply mutatis mutandis to price undertakings accepted under Article 8.

3.5.4 Newcomer Review

Article 9.5 ADA envisages a third type of review. This review is often called a newcomer review because it enables exporters that did not export during the original investigation period to request an accelerated review. Article 9.5 seems inspired by the practice of many countries to apply a *residual* or *all others* duty rate in anti-dumping proceedings. This rate typically applies to all exporters that are not mentioned by name in the definitive determination. It is designed to 'catch' exporters that did not cooperate in the investigation on the ground that not subjecting them to a duty would amount to a bonus for non-cooperation. While this practice makes perfect sense vis-à-vis non-cooperating exporters, it unfairly penalizes newcomers which *could* not cooperate because they did not export. Such newcomers will then also be subject to the residual duty rate.[330]

9.5 If a product is subject to anti-dumping duties in an importing Member, the authorities shall promptly carry out a review for the purpose of determining individual margins of dumping for any exporters or producers in the exporting country in question who have not exported the product to the importing Member during the period of investigation, provided that these exporters or producers can show that they are not related to any of the exporters or producers in the exporting country who are subject to the anti-dumping duties on the product. Such a review shall be initiated and carried out on an accelerated basis, compared to normal duty assessment and review proceedings in the importing Member. No anti-dumping duties shall be levied on imports from such exporters or producers while the review is being carried out. The authorities may, however, withhold appraisement and/or request guarantees to ensure

---

[328] *United States–Oil country tubular goods from Argentina*, Panel, paras 7.121–7.123.
[329] *United States–Oil country tubular goods from Argentina*, Panel, para 7.127.
[330] Compare *Mexico–Rice from the United States*, as discussed in section 3.2.5.8, above.

that, should such a review result in a determination of dumping in respect of such producers or exporters, anti-dumping duties can be levied retroactively to the date of the initiation of the review.

Article 9.5 authorizes newcomers to request a special review at any time and obliges the authorities to carry out the review on an accelerated basis. While the review is being carried out, no anti-dumping duties shall be imposed on their exports, although measures may be taken to ensure that anti-dumping duties can be collected retroactively back to the date of initiation of the review, where warranted. If, for example, the residual duty imposed in the original investigation is 10 per cent and it is found in the course of the newcomer review that the newcomer dumped only 5 per cent, then a 5 per cent anti-dumping duty may be collected retroactively.

In order to qualify for a newcomer review, the newcomer should be able to prove that he:

(i) did not export during the original IP; and
(ii) is not related to any other exporters in the exporting country which *did* export during the original investigation period.[331]

In *Mexico–Rice*, the panel ruled that a third condition that the volume of export sales be representative, imposed by Mexican law, violated Article 9.5.[332]

The weak point of Article 9.5 is that it does not provide explicit rules for the situation where a newcomer is precluded from exporting as a result of the anti-dumping duty, as will often be the case. In such cases, it will not be possible for the authorities to calculate a dumping margin for the newcomer. Theoretically, the authorities could impose an anti-dumping duty, for example in the form of a variable anti-dumping duty, equal to the difference between the newcomer's normal value and his future export prices. However, not all authorities seem prepared to do so, in the absence of a legally binding obligation to that effect.

3.6 Public Notice Requirements

Article 12 ADA is entitled 'public notice and explanation of determinations' and contains rules on what must be notified by the authorities in the various stages of an anti-dumping proceeding and in which form they should be. As such, it is essentially a *transparency* provision:

We ... believe that Article 12 provides important context for Article 3 in indicating the significance attached by Members to allowing interested parties access to information

---

[331] Compare *Mexico–Rice from the United States*, Panel, para 7.266.
[332] *Mexico–Rice from the United States*, Panel, para 7.266.

on fact and law relevant to the final determination. Among other things, such access allows them (through interested Members) to assess the fruitfulness of bringing a WTO dispute settlement complaint.[333]

Article 12.1 covers the initiation stage while Article 12.2 covers preliminary and final determinations. Article 12.3 provides that the Article 12 requirements also apply to interim and expiry reviews[334] and decisions to apply duties retroactively under Article 10.[335]

There is obviously a close linkage between the procedural Article 12 and the substantive articles of the ADA. Indeed, in many cases, a violation of a substantive article will also constitute a violation of Article 12. We will see below in section 3.6.2, however, that panels have not always taken a consistent approach on this issue.

3.6.1 Initiation

Article 12.1 requires the authorities to notify the exporting country member as well as other interested parties known to them when they are satisfied that there is sufficient evidence for the initiation of an anti-dumping investigation *and* to give a public notice. Most WTO members will contact all interested parties known to them in writing and publish a so-called notice of initiation (NOI) in their public gazette.[336]

12.1 When the authorities are satisfied that there is sufficient evidence to justify the initiation of an anti-dumping investigation pursuant to Article 5, the Member or Members the products of which are subject to such investigation and other interested parties known to the investigating authorities to have an interest therein shall be notified and a public notice shall be given.

12.1.1 A public notice of the initiation of an investigation shall contain, or otherwise make available through a separate report,[337] adequate information on the following:

(i) the name of the exporting country or countries and the product involved;
(ii) the date of initiation of the investigation;
(iii) the basis on which dumping is alleged in the application;
(iv) a summary of the factors on which the allegation of injury is based;
(v) the address to which representations by interested parties should be directed;
(vi) the time-limits allowed to interested parties for making their views known.

---

[333] *Thailand–H-Beams from Poland*, Panel, para 7.151.   [334] See section 3.5, above.
[335] See section 3.4, above.
[336] In the EC, for example, notices of initiation will be published in the Official Journal of the EC while in the United States they will be published in the Federal Register.
[337] Fn 23 in ADA: Where authorities provide information and explanations under the provisions of this Article in a separate report, they shall ensure that such report is readily available to the public.

It happens often that some exporters are not identified in the application because the domestic industry was not aware of them. Such exporters will then normally not to be known to the authorities either and, as a result, they will not be contacted directly by the authorities. While such exporters sometimes claim later on that they were not aware of the investigation, such excuses tend to be rejected by the authorities on the ground that the public notice serves as a notice to all.

In *Argentina–Poultry*, however, the panel considered that Article 12.1 obliges the authorities to make reasonable efforts to obtain contact details of exporters in situations where their names, but not their coordinates, are known from the application. In such cases, the mere publication of the public notice will not suffice:

...there may be circumstances in which an investigating authority may not have sufficient information to allow it to notify all interested parties known to have an interest in an investigation. In this sense, the fact that an exporter is 'known' by the investigating authority to have an interest in an investigation does not necessarily mean that sufficient details concerning the exporter are 'known' to the investigating authority such that it may make the Article 12.1 notification. In other words, knowledge of an exporter's interest in an investigation does not necessarily imply knowledge of contact details regarding that exporter. In such circumstances, however, we consider that the nature of the Article 12.1 notification obligation is such that the investigating authority should make all reasonable efforts to obtain the requisite contact details. Sending a letter with only a very general request for assistance, without specifying the exporters for which contact details are required, does not satisfy the need to make all reasonable efforts.[338]

Similarly, in *Mexico–Rice*, the panel considered that, where the information on known exporters in the application is manifestly incomplete, the authorities must actively undertake efforts to identify the exporters.[339]

In *Mexico–HFCS*, the panel considered that Article 12.1 does not require the NOI to contain an explanation of the results of the authorities' Article 5.3 pre-initiation examination:[340]

Article 12.1 does not require that the notice of initiation contain explanation of or reasons for conclusions reached by the investigating authority in the process of satisfying itself that there is sufficient evidence to justify initiation. Thus, while information and explanation concerning all material aspects of an investigating authority's preliminary

---

[338] *Argentina–Poultry from Brazil*, Panel, paras 7.132–7.133.
[339] *Mexico–Rice from the United States*, Panel, para 7.199.
[340] See section 3.1.2, above.

and final determinations are required to be included in the respective notices, this is not the case with respect to notices of initiation.[341]

The panel in *Guatemala–Cement II* ruled that Article 12.1 is a procedural requirement and does not cover the substance of the decision to initiate an investigation, which is dealt with in Article 5.3.[342]

Article 12.1.1 requires the public NOI (or a separate report linked to the notice) to contain adequate information on the following elements:

- the product involved;
- the country/ies involved;
- the date of initiation of the investigation;
- the basis on which dumping is alleged in the application filed by the domestic industry;
- a summary of the factors on which the allegation of injury is based;
- the correspondence address of the authorities; and
- the time limits for interested parties to make their views known.

It seems clear from Article 12.1.1 that the NOI is intended to cover the *key points* of the intended investigation so that all interested parties are in a position to understand whether they are involved and what the allegations are. Use of the words 'the basis' of the dumping allegations and 'a summary' of the injury allegations indicates that a summary of the data contained in the application suffices at this stage. Indeed, in practice notices of initiation seldom run to more than a few printed pages. Clearly panels will rule that Article 12.1.1 is violated where information on one or more of the elements above is missing altogether in the NOI, as was the case in *Guatemala–Cement II* with regard to the dumping allegation.[343]

However, the situation becomes more complicated where panels have to decide to what extent underlying elements of dumping or injury allegations need to be addressed in the NOI:

We do not consider that the phrase 'a summary of the factors on which the allegation of injury is based' can reasonably be read to encompass a requirement that the notice of initiation contain a summary of the allegations pertaining to the specific issue of the definition of the relevant domestic industry. Still less can it reasonably be read to establish a requirement that the notice of initiation contain a summary of the allegations on the even more particular point of exclusion of some producers from consideration as the relevant domestic industry.[344]

---

[341] *Mexico–HFCS from the United States*, Panel, para 7.88. See also para 7.87.
[342] *Guatemala–Cement from Mexico II*, Panel, para 8.89.
[343] *Guatemala–Cement from Mexico II*, Panel, para 8.93.
[344] *Mexico–HFCS from the United States*, Panel, para 7.86.

In *Guatemala–Cement II*, the panel ruled that where the authorities discuss the Article 12.1.1 information in a *separate report*, the NOI must at least refer to the existence of such report:

Under Article 12.1.1, it is the 'public notice', and not the Member, that must 'make available through a separate report', certain information. We take this to mean that the public notice must at a minimum refer to a separate report. This conclusion is logical in that the separate report is a substitute for certain elements of the public notice and thus should perform a notice function comparable to that of the public notice itself. If there were no reference to a separate report in the public notice, how would the public and the interested parties concerned become aware of its existence? If the public and interested parties do not know of the existence of the report, how can it be considered that the required information was properly made available to them?[345]

3.6.2 Preliminary and Final Determinations

Article 12.2 sets out the principles that public notice must be given of all preliminary and final determinations and that the notice must contain, or make available through a separate report, in sufficient detail *the findings and conclusions reached on all issues of fact and law* considered material by the authorities. Clearly, therefore, the public notices of preliminary and final determinations, or the separate report thereof, will need to be much more detailed than the notice of initiation of an anti-dumping proceeding.[346]

12.2 Public notice shall be given of any preliminary or final determination, whether affirmative or negative, of any decision to accept an undertaking pursuant to Article 8, of the termination of such an undertaking, and of the termination of a definitive anti-dumping duty. Each such notice shall set forth, or otherwise make available through a separate report, in sufficient detail the findings and conclusions reached on all issues of fact and law considered material by the investigating authorities. All such notices and reports shall be forwarded to the Member or Members the products of which are subject to such determination or undertaking and to other interested parties known to have an interest therein.

These determinations must include the findings and the conclusions of the authorities pertaining to pre-initiation issues, such as the Article 5.3 examination[347] and the Article 5.4 standing determination,[348] as the panel in *Mexico–HFCS* implicitly ruled.[349]

---

[345] *Guatemala–Cement from Mexico II*, Panel, para 8.95.
[346] Compare, eg, *Mexico–HFCS from the United States*, Panel, para 7.88. See also para 7.87.
[347] See section 3.1.2, above.   [348] See section 3.1.3, above.
[349] *Mexico–HFCS from the United States*, Panel, para 7.110.

In the same case, the panel ruled that Mexico's failure to set forth findings or conclusions on the retroactive[350] application of the final anti-dumping measure violated Article 12.2 (and 12.2.2) ADA.[351] Thus, the panel found that a certain practice may constitute both a substantive and a procedural violation.[352]

Similarly, in *EC–Malleable cast iron tube or pipe fittings*, the panel found Article 12.2 and Article 12.2.2 violations resulting from the EC's failure to address various Article 3.4 factors:

In this case, it is not directly discernible from the published Provisional or Definitive Determination that the EC addressed or explained the lack of significance of the following factors in its injury determination: ability to raise capital; productivity, return on investments; cash flow and wages. The relative significance of these factors is addressed exclusively in the internal 'note to file' Exhibit EC-12 ...

We ... find that the EC acted inconsistently with its obligations under Article 12.2 and Article 12.2.2 of the ADA in that it is not directly discernible from the published Provisional or Definitive Determination that the EC addressed or explained the lack of significance of certain listed Article 3.4 factors.[353]

In the *Mexico–HFCS 21.5* case, on the other hand, the panel declined to rule on the Article 12.2 claims as it had already found that Mexico's re-determination violated the substantive Articles 3.1, 3.4 and 3.7 ADA:

In light of the substantive violations found, the question of whether the notice of the ultimate determination is 'sufficient' under Article 12.2 is immaterial. It is, in our view, meaningless to consider whether the notice of a decision that is substantively inconsistent with the requirements of the ADA is, as a separate matter, insufficient under Article 12.2. We therefore make no findings with respect to the claim of insufficiency of the notice of re-determination.[354]

The same approach was taken by the panels in *Guatemala–Cement II*,[355] *EC–Bed linen*,[356] *United States–Softwood lumber II*[357] and *Argentina–Poultry*.[358]

Article 12.2.1 provides further details on what type of information should be included in provisional determinations. While terms such as 'sufficiently

---

[350] See also section 3.4, above.   [351] *Mexico–HFCS from the United States*, Panel, para 8.2.

[352] See also *Mexico–Rice from the United States*, Panel, para 7.199 where the panel found parallel violations of Arts 6.1 and 12.1.

[353] *EC–Malleable cast iron tube or pipe fittings from Brazil*, Panel, paras 7.433–7.435.

[354] *Mexico–HFCS from the United States*, 21.5 Panel, para 6.40.

[355] *Guatemala–Cement from Mexico II*, Panel, para 8.291.

[356] *EC–Bed linen from India*, Panel, para 6.259.

[357] *United States–Softwood lumber from Canada II*, Panel, para 7.41.

[358] *Argentina–Poultry from Brazil*, Panel, paras 7.199–7.208 (with respect to Art 12.2.2).

detailed explanations' are regrettably vague, the requirement that the determination must refer to *the matters of fact and law which have led to arguments being accepted or rejected* would seem to give sufficient guarantees for effective panel/AB review.

12.2.1 A public notice of the imposition of provisional measures shall set forth, or otherwise make available through a separate report, sufficiently detailed explanations for the preliminary determinations on dumping and injury and shall refer to the matters of fact and law which have led to arguments being accepted or rejected. Such a notice or report shall, due regard being paid to the requirement for the protection of confidential information, contain in particular:

  (i) the names of the suppliers, or when this is impracticable, the supplying countries involved;
 (ii) a description of the product which is sufficient for customs purposes;
(iii) the margins of dumping established and a full explanation of the reasons for the methodology used in the establishment and comparison of the export price and the normal value under Article 2;
(iv) considerations relevant to the injury determination as set out in Article 3;
 (v) the main reasons leading to determination.

In *Guatemala–Cement II*, the panel ruled that the information provided in the public notice in that case was not adequate to fulfil the requirement contained in Article 12.1.1(iii).[359]

Article 12.2.2 is the functional equivalent of Article 12.1.1 for final determinations. It requires the authorities to report *all relevant information on the matters of fact and law and reasons* which have led to the imposition of a definitive anti-dumping duty or the acceptance of a price undertaking:

12.2.2 A public notice of conclusion or suspension of an investigation in the case of an affirmative determination providing for the imposition of a definitive duty or the acceptance of a price undertaking shall contain, or otherwise make available through a separate report, all relevant information on the matters of fact and law and reasons which have led to the imposition of final measures or the acceptance of a price undertaking, due regard being paid to the requirement for the protection of confidential information. In particular, the notice or report shall contain the information described in subparagraph 2.1, as well as the reasons for the acceptance or rejection of relevant arguments or claims made by the exporters and importers, and the basis for any decision made under subparagraph 10.2 of Article 6.

12.2.3 A public notice of the termination or suspension of an investigation following the acceptance of an undertaking pursuant to Article 8 shall include, or

---

[359] *Guatemala–Cement from Mexico II*, Panel, para 8.93.

otherwise make available through a separate report, the non-confidential part of this undertaking.

Article 12.2.3 requires the authorities to make available the non-confidential part of any price undertakings accepted in the course of a proceeding, either in the public notice or through a separate report.

3.6.3 Reviews and Retroactivity Decisions

Article 12.3 requires the above rules to be applied also in interim and expiry reviews and in decisions to apply anti-dumping duties retroactively under Article 10:

12.3 The provisions of this Article shall apply mutatis mutandis to the initiation and completion of reviews pursuant to Article 11 and to decisions under Article 10 to apply duties retroactively.

In *Mexico–HFCS*, the panel found a procedural violation of Article 12.3 because Mexico had failed to address whether the effect of the dumped imports would have led to a finding of injury in the absence of provisional measures:

Thus, it is clear that the investigating authority must set out in sufficient detail its findings and conclusions on the issue of whether 'the effect of the dumped imports would, in the absence of the provisional measures, have led to a determination of injury' before final anti-dumping duties may, consistently with Article 10.2 of the ADA, be levied for the period during which a provisional measure was in place.[360]

3.7 Judicial Review

Article 13 requires WTO members which have adopted anti-dumping legislation to allow for *prompt* judicial review of final, interim and expiry review determinations. Such review may take place through establishment of judicial, arbitral or administrative tribunals or procedures, as long as they are independent from the administering authorities:

Article 13: Judicial review
Each Member whose national legislation contains provisions on anti-dumping measures shall maintain judicial, arbitral or administrative tribunals or procedures for the purpose, inter alia, of the prompt review of administrative actions relating to final determinations and reviews of determinations within the meaning of Article 11. Such

---

[360] *Mexico–HFCS from the United States*, Panel, para 7.191.

tribunals or procedures shall be independent of the authorities responsible for the determination or review in question.

Interestingly, the ADA does not impose an obligation upon WTO members to establish specialized courts to hear anti-dumping and similar trade remedy disputes, thereby leaving this open. While some WTO members, such as the United States, do have specialized courts in place (Court of International Trade and, on appeal, the Court of Appeals for the Federal Circuit), others, such as the EC, let these matters be handled by more general purpose courts (Court of First Instance and, on appeal, the European Court of Justice). While the latter option is clearly the easy way out, it is not necessarily the best solution. General purpose courts tend to be more deferential towards administrative determinations in this area because the determinations are highly technical and fact-specific.

Last, it may be noted that although court proceedings in some WTO members take an embarrassingly long time, thus far this has not been challenged.

3.8 Third Country Dumping

It is possible that country A producers dumping into country B cause injury to producers in country C, for example, by replacing country C exports to country B. Article 14, which goes back all the way to Article VI.6(b) of the GATT,[361] allows the country C authorities in such situations to request the country B authorities to initiate an anti-dumping investigation with regard to country A and to impose anti-dumping duties on country A exporters if they were to find dumping and resulting injury to the domestic industry of country C:

Article 14: Anti-Dumping action on behalf of a Third Country
14.1 An application for anti-dumping action on behalf of a third country shall be made by the authorities of the third country requesting action.

   14.2 Such an application shall be supported by price information to show that the imports are being dumped and by detailed information to show that the alleged dumping is causing injury to the domestic industry concerned in the third country. The government of the third country shall afford all assistance to the authorities of the importing country to obtain any further information which the latter may require.

   14.3 In considering such an application, the authorities of the importing country shall consider the effects of the alleged dumping on the industry concerned as a whole

---

[361] See Annex 2, below.

in the third country; that is to say, the injury shall not be assessed in relation only to the effect of the alleged dumping on the industry's exports to the importing country or even on the industry's total exports.

14.4 The decision whether or not to proceed with a case shall rest with the importing country. If the importing country decides that it is prepared to take action, the initiation of the approach to the Council for Trade in Goods seeking its approval for such action shall rest with the importing country.

Although this type of third country dumping undoubtedly occurs, thus far it has never given rise to the initiation of an anti-dumping investigation by the third country authorities. The reasons for this probably are that the approval of the Council for Trade in Goods (where country A would be likely to block the action) is needed for such anti-dumping action and that the country B authorities in most cases would not find it in their interest to initiate an anti-dumping investigation in such a situation: if country B does not have a domestic industry producing the like product, then it would be in its interest to get the products as cheaply as possible, whether they are dumped or not; if country B *does* have a domestic industry, but the industry is not complaining about injurious dumping, then it will normally have a reason for that.

3.9 Developing Countries

Article 15 recognizes that special regard must be given by *developed* countries to the special situation of *developing* country members when considering the application of anti-dumping measures. It continues by requiring developed countries to *explore* the possibilities of constructive remedies under the ADA before applying anti-dumping duties where they would affect the essential interests of developing country members.

Article 15: Developing Country Members
It is recognized that special regard must be given by developed country Members to the special situation of developing country Members when considering the application of anti-dumping measures under this Agreement. Possibilities of constructive remedies provided for by this Agreement shall be explored before applying anti-dumping duties where they would affect the essential interests of developing country Members.

It may be clear from the soft wording of Article 15 that it does not impose any hard obligations on developed countries wishing to impose anti-dumping measures on imports from developing countries. Indeed, the GATT panel in *Brazil–Cotton yarns* had rejected Brazil's claims under the similar Article 13 of the Tokyo Round Anti-Dumping Code in such a peremptory manner that many considered Article 15 to be a dead letter.[362]

In *EC–Bed linen*, however, the panel gave Article 15 a new lease of life.[363] The panel first considered that imposition of a lesser duty (under the lesser duty rule)[364] or a price undertaking would constitute *constructive remedies*.[365] The panel next found that the term anti-dumping duties in Article 15 referred to the imposition of *definitive* anti-dumping measures,[366] meaning that possibilities of constructive remedies need to be explored only at that stage. However, the panel then gave a remarkably balanced meaning to the term *explore*:

While the exact parameters of the term are difficult to establish, the concept of 'explore' clearly does not imply any particular outcome. Article 15 does not require that 'constructive remedies' must be explored, but rather that the 'possibilities' of such remedies must be explored, which further suggests that the exploration may conclude that no possibilities exist, or that no constructive remedies are possible, in the particular circumstances of a given case. Taken in its context, however, and in light of the object and purpose of Article 15, the 'exploration' of possibilities must be actively undertaken by the developed country authorities with a willingness to reach a positive outcome. Thus, Article 15 imposes no obligation to actually provide or accept any constructive remedy that may be identified and/or offered. It does, however, impose an obligation to actively consider, with an open mind, the possibility of such a remedy prior to imposition of an anti-dumping measure that would affect the essential interests of a developing country.[367]

The rejection expressed in the EC's letter of 22 October 1997 does not, in our view, indicate that the possibility of an undertaking was explored, but rather that the possibility was rejected out of hand. We cannot conclude, based on these facts, that the EC explored the possibilities of constructive remedies prior to imposing anti-dumping duties. In our view, the EC simply did nothing different in this case, than it would have done in any other anti-dumping proceeding – there was no notice or information concerning the opportunities for exploration of possibilities of constructive remedies given to the Indian parties, nothing that would demonstrate that the EC actively undertook the obligation imposed by Article 15 of the ADA. Pure passivity is not sufficient to satisfy the obligation to 'explore' possibilities of constructive remedies, particularly where the possibility of an undertaking has already been broached by the developing country concerned. Thus, we consider that the failure of the EC to respond

---

[362] *EC–Imposition of anti-dumping duties on imports of cotton yarns from Brazil*, Panel, para 595, adopted 30 October 1995, ADP/137, 4 July 1995.

[363] Compare Durling and Nicely, *Understanding the WTO Anti-Dumping Agreement: Negotiating History and Subsequent Interpretation* (2002) 543: 'Any perception that this language had no meaning, however, ended in the EC–Bed linen decision.'　　　　　　[364] See section 3.3.3.1, above.

[365] *EC–Bed linen from India*, Panel, para 6.229.

[366] *EC–Bed linen from India*, Panel, para 6.231.

[367] *EC–Bed linen from India*, Panel, para 6.233.

in some fashion other than bare rejection, particularly once the desire to offer undertakings had been communicated to it, constituted a failure to 'explore possibilities of constructive remedies'.[368]

3.10 Committee on Anti-Dumping Practices

Article 16 ADA establishes the Committee on Anti-Dumping Practices (ADP), consisting of representatives of the WTO members. The ADP is supported by the Rules Division of the WTO and meets twice a year. It has developed its own rules of procedure, which can be found in G/ADP/4.[369]

Article 16: Committee on Anti-Dumping Practices

16.1 There is hereby established a Committee on Anti-Dumping Practices (referred to in this Agreement as the 'Committee') composed of representatives from each of the Members. The Committee shall elect its own Chairman and shall meet not less than twice a year and otherwise as envisaged by relevant provisions of this Agreement at the request of any Member. The Committee shall carry out responsibilities as assigned to it under this Agreement or by the Members and it shall afford Members the opportunity of consulting on any matters relating to the operation of the Agreement or the furtherance of its objectives. The WTO Secretariat shall act as the secretariat to the Committee.

16.2 The Committee may set up subsidiary bodies as appropriate.

16.3 In carrying out their functions, the Committee and any subsidiary bodies may consult with and seek information from any source they deem appropriate. However, before the Committee or a subsidiary body seeks such information from a source within the jurisdiction of a Member, it shall inform the Member involved. It shall obtain the consent of the Member and any firm to be consulted.

16.4 Members shall report without delay to the Committee all preliminary or final anti-dumping actions taken. Such reports shall be available in the Secretariat for inspection by other Members. Members shall also submit, on a semi-annual basis, reports of any anti-dumping actions taken within the preceding six months. The semi-annual reports shall be submitted on an agreed standard form.

16.5 Each Member shall notify the Committee (a) which of its authorities are competent to initiate and conduct investigations referred to in Article 5 and (b) its domestic procedures governing the initiation and conduct of such investigations.

The ADP may set up subsidiary bodies *ex* Article 16.2. Two such bodies are the Ad Hoc Group on Implementation and the Informal Group on Anti-Circumvention. The Ad Hoc Group on Implementation, set up in 1997, has done useful work in discussing various issues under the ADA. The results of some of these

---

[368] *EC–Bed linen from India*, Panel, para 6.238.   [369] See Annex 3, G/ADP/4, below.

discussions were later adopted as recommendations by the ADP (see below). The Informal Group on Anti-Circumvention, on the other hand, has not made much progress to date, presumably because of the controversial nature of the anti-circumvention topic.[370]

Members must report all preliminary and final anti-dumping actions to the ADP. Contrary to similar safeguard determinations, however, these are not put on the WTO website, but are available at the WTO secretariat for inspection by other members. Members must also submit to the ADP, on a semi-annual basis, reports on all anti-dumping actions taken within the preceding six months, according to an agreed standard format.[371] These country reports are then collated by the Rules Division and published on the WTO website. They often receive considerable media attention, for example in the *Financial Times*.

The ADP has issued a number of recommendations that, while not legally binding, provide useful guidance on the interpretation of certain elements of the ADA. These recommendations cover:

- the timing of the notification under Article 5.5;[372]
- the periods of data collection for anti-dumping investigations;[373]
- indicative list of elements relevant to a decision on a request for extension to provide information;[374]
- annual reviews of the ADA;[375] and
- the time period to be considered in making a determination of negligible import volumes for purposes of Article 5.8 of the ADA.[376]

3.11 Dispute Settlement

Article 17 ADA provides special rules for WTO dispute settlement with regard to anti-dumping disputes.

Article 17.1 sets out the principle that the Dispute Settlement Understanding provisions are applicable to consultations and the settlement of disputes under the ADA, except as otherwise provided in Article 17:

17.1 Except as otherwise provided herein, the Dispute Settlement Understanding is applicable to consultations and the settlement of disputes under this Agreement.

---

[370] Compare Durling and Nicely, *Understanding the WTO Anti-Dumping Agreement: Negotiating History and Subsequent Interpretation* (2002) 631–632.   [371] See Annex 3, G/ADP/1–2, below.

[372] See Annex 3, G/ADP/5, below and section 3.1.4.1, above.

[373] See Annex 3, G/ADP/6, below and chapter 1, Introduction and section 2.3.3, above.

[374] See Annex 3, G/ADP/7, below and section 3.2.5.2, above.

[375] See Annex 3, G/ADP/9, below.

[376] See Annex 3, G/ADP/10, below and section 3.2.2.2, above.

Thus, special provisions in Article 17 ADA prevail over more general provisions of the DSU, but Article 17 does not replace the DSU as such:

We conclude that the Panel erred in finding that Article 17 of the ADA 'provides for a coherent set of rules for dispute settlement specific to anti-dumping cases ... that replaces the more general approach of the DSU.'[377]

Article 17.2 requires each member to afford sympathetic consideration to, and afford adequate opportunity for consultation regarding, representations made by another Member concerning any matter affecting the operation of the ADA. It closely tracks Article 4 (2) of the DSU:

17.2 Each Member shall afford sympathetic consideration to, and shall afford adequate opportunity for consultation regarding, representations made by another Member with respect to any matter affecting the operation of this Agreement.

Article 17.3 contains the specific consultation provision for ADA disputes. It authorizes any member which considers that any ADA benefit accruing to it, directly or indirectly, is being nullified or impaired, or that the achievement of any objective is being impeded, by another member or members to request in writing consultations with the member(s):

17.3 If any Member considers that any benefit accruing to it, directly or indirectly, under this Agreement is being nullified or impaired, or that the achievement of any objective is being impeded, by another Member or Members, it may, with a view to reaching a mutually satisfactory resolution of the matter, request in writing consultations with the Member or Members in question. Each Member shall afford sympathetic consideration to any request from another Member for consultation.

This means that Article 17.3 ADA is the legal basis for requesting consultations concerning matters covered by the ADA:

Article 17.3 of the ADA is not listed in Appendix 2 of the DSU as a special or additional rule and procedure. It is not listed precisely because it provides the legal basis for consultations to be requested by a complaining member under the ADA.[378]

On the other hand, Articles 17.4 to 17.7 *are* listed as special or additional rules in Appendix 2 to the DSU.[379] This means that they apply in addition to and, *in case of conflict*, prevail over the DSU rules.

... if there is no 'difference', then the rules and procedures of the DSU apply together with the special or additional provisions of the covered agreement. In our view, it is

---

[377] *Guatemala–Cement from Mexico I*, AB, para 68.
[378] *Guatemala–Cement from Mexico I*, AB, para 64.
[379] *United States–Corrosion-resistant carbon steel flat products from Japan*, AB, fn to para 82.

only where the provisions of the DSU and the special or additional rules and procedures of a covered agreement cannot be read as complementing each other that the special or additional provisions are to prevail. A special or additional provision should only be found to prevail over a provision of the DSU in a situation where adherence to the one provision will lead to a violation of the other provision, that is, in the case of a conflict between them. An interpreter must, therefore, identify an inconsistency or a difference between a provision of the DSU and a special or additional provision of a covered agreement before concluding that the latter prevails and that the provision of the DSU does not apply.[380]

As we will see below, however, the AB has been reluctant to conclude that a conflict in fact exists between the two sets of rules.

Article 17.4 provides that if the member that requested the consultations, considers that the consultations have failed and if final action has been taken by the authorities to levy definitive anti-dumping duties or to accept price undertakings, the member may refer the matter to the DSB. A *provisional* measure may be referred to the DSB only when it has a significant impact:

17.4 If the Member that requested consultations considers that the consultations pursuant to paragraph 3 have failed to achieve a mutually agreed solution, and if final action has been taken by the administering authorities of the importing Member to levy definitive anti-dumping duties or to accept price undertakings, it may refer the matter to the Dispute Settlement Body ('DSB'). When a provisional measure has a significant impact and the Member that requested consultations considers that the measure was taken contrary to the provisions of paragraph 1 of Article 7, that Member may also refer such matter to the DSB.

3.11.1 The Matter

In *Guatemala–Cement*, the AB provided welcome clarification of the term *the matter*:

The matter referred to the DSB for the purposes of Article 7 of the DSU and Article 17.4 ADA must be the 'matter' identified in the request for the establishment of a panel under Article 6.2 of the DSU. The matter referred to the DSB consists of two elements: the specific measures at issue and the legal basis of the complaint (or the claims).[381]

In the same case, the AB also ruled that it followed from Article 17.4 that a member challenging an anti-dumping action must always identify in its

---

[380] *Guatemala–Cement from Mexico I*, AB, para 65. Compare *United States–Hot rolled steel from Japan*, AB, paras 51–53.   [381] *Guatemala–Cement from Mexico I*, AB, para 72.

request for establishment of a panel (REP) one of the three types of measures referred to in Article 17.4:

Article 17.4 specifies the types of 'measure' which may be referred as part of a 'matter' to the DSB. Three types of anti-dumping measure are specified in Article 17.4: definitive anti-dumping duties, the acceptance of price undertakings, and provisional measures. According to Article 17.4, a 'matter' may be referred to the DSB only if one of the relevant three anti-dumping measures is in place. This provision, when read together with Article 6.2 of the DSU, requires a panel request in a dispute brought under the ADA to identify, as the specific measure at issue, either a definitive anti-dumping duty, the acceptance of a price undertaking, or a provisional measure. This requirement to identify a specific anti-dumping measure at issue in a panel request in no way limits the nature of the claims that may be brought concerning alleged nullification or impairment of benefits or the impeding of the achievement of any objective in a dispute under the ADA.[382]

Because Mexico had failed to identify any specific measure and this was a preliminary issue that the panel should have addressed before discussing the merits of Mexico's claims, the AB had no choice but to throw out the entire panel report on the ground that the panel lacked jurisdiction. (As a postscript, it may be noted that Mexico later brought the same case again, this time identifying the measure correctly, as a result of which the panel reaffirmed its substantive findings.)

As the AB later clarified in *United States–1916 Act*, this does not mean that the various steps in an anti-dumping investigation, such as, for example, an initiation decision, cannot be challenged; it merely means that a member must identify one of the three measures in the REP.[383]

3.11.2 Challenging Legislation

Similarly, this does *not* mean that a member is precluded by Article 17.4 from challenging (aspects of) anti-dumping legislation as such, as the AB subsequently ruled in *United States–1916 Act*:[384]

In the same way that Article XXIII of the GATT 1994 allows a WTO Member to challenge legislation as such, Article 17 of the ADA is properly to be regarded as allowing a challenge to legislation as such, unless this possibility is excluded. No such express exclusion is found in Article 17 or elsewhere in the ADA.[385] . . . Nothing in our Report

---

[382] *Guatemala–Cement from Mexico* I, AB, para 79.

[383] *United States–1916 Act*, AB, para 72.

[384] Compare WorldTradeLaw.net, *Dispute Settlement Commentary on Guatemala–Cement AB*, 5, checked on 23 April 2005.   [385] *United States–1916 Act*, AB, para 62.

in Guatemala – Cement suggests that Article 17.4 precludes review of anti-dumping legislation as such. Rather, in that case, we simply found that, for Mexico to challenge Guatemala's initiation and conduct of the anti-dumping investigation, Mexico was required to identify one of the three anti-dumping measures listed in Article 17.4 in its request for establishment of a panel. Since it did not do so, the panel in that case did not have jurisdiction.[386]

In *United States–Section 129(c)(i)*, the panel relied on the GATT distinction between mandatory and discretionary legislation by considering that a member may challenge a statutory provision of another member *as such*, provided that the provision:

- mandates that the other member take action which is inconsistent with its WTO obligations; or
- mandates that the other member not take action which is required by its WTO obligations.[387]

The panel found that Canada could not prove that either was the case.[388] In this context, it is to be noted that the AB in *United States–Corrosion-resistant carbon steel flat products* warned against the application of the mandatory/discretionary distinction in a *mechanistic fashion*.[389] In *United States–Corrosion-resistant flat carbon steel products*, the AB ruled that *administrative regulations* as such are also subject to challenge.[390]

3.11.3 Specificity of Claims

In *Mexico–HFCS*, the panel ruled that Article 17.4 does not contain any additional requirements with respect to the degree of specificity with which claims must be set forth in a REP challenging a final anti-dumping measure. Therefore, a REP that satisfies the requirements of Article 6.2 of the DSU in this regard also satisfies the requirements of Article 17.4 of the ADA.[391]

---

[386] *United States–1916 Act*, AB, para 72. See also paras 74–75.

[387] *United States–Section 129(c)(i) of the Uruguay Round Agreements Act*, Panel, para 6.22.

[388] *United States–Section 129(c)(i) of the Uruguay Round Agreements Act*, Panel, paras 6.122–6.123.

[389] *United States–Corrosion-resistant carbon steel flat products from Japan*, AB, para 93. In *United States–1916 Act*, AB, para 90, on the other hand, the AB had little trouble in finding that the 1916 Act was a mandatory law, brushing aside US arguments that, in the civil action component of the law, courts could interpret the law in a WTO-consistent manner. In the view of the AB, the relevant point was whether the executive branch of the government had discretion. As the executive branch had no role in the civil action (because such an action is brought by private parties and adjudicated by the courts), the Act constituted mandatory legislation as far as the executive branch was concerned.

[390] *United States–Corrosion-resistant carbon steel flat products from Japan*, AB, para 84.

[391] *Mexico–HFCS from the United States*, Panel, para 7.14.

3.11.4 Nullification or Impairment

In *Guatemala–Cement I*, the AB considered that Article 17.5 ADA and Article 6.2 of the DSU are complementary, rather than inconsistent. As a result, a REP claiming ADA violations must comply with both provisions.[392]

17.5 The DSB shall, at the request of the complaining party, establish a panel to examine the matter based upon:

   (i) a written statement of the Member making the request indicating how a benefit accruing to it, directly or indirectly, under this Agreement has been nullified or impaired, or that the achieving of the objectives of the Agreement is being impeded, and
  (ii) the facts made available in conformity with appropriate domestic procedures to the authorities of the importing Member.

Article 17.5(i) requires the member to indicate in its REP how a benefit accruing to it, directly or indirectly, has been nullified or impaired or that the achieving of the objectives of the ADA is being impeded. The *United States–HFCS* panel considered that this did not mean that the REP necessarily had to use these specific terms:

> In our view, Article 17.5(i) does not require a complaining Member to use the words 'nullify' or 'impair' in a request for establishment. However, it must be clear from the request that an allegation of nullification or impairment is being made, and the request must explicitly indicate how benefits accruing to the complaining Member are being nullified or impaired.[393]
>
> In our view, a request for establishment that alleges violations of the ADA which, if demonstrated, will constitute a prima facie case of nullification or impairment under Article 3.8 of the DSU, contains a sufficient allegation of nullification or impairment for purposes of Article 17.5(i).[394]

3.11.5 Facts made Available

Article 17.5(ii) provides that the panel must examine the matter based on the facts made available in conformity with appropriate domestic procedures to the importing country authorities. Clearly, this means that the panel should not examine new evidence that did not form part of the administrative record of the investigation,[395] although it does not preclude the authorities from presenting the facts to the panel in a new format.[396]

---

[392] *Guatemala–Cement from Mexico I*, AB, para 75.
[393] *Mexico–HFCS from the United States*, Panel, para 7.26.
[394] *Mexico–HFCS from the United States*, Panel, para 7.28.
[395] *Guatemala–Cement from Mexico II*, Panel, para 8.19.
[396] *EC–Bed linen from India*, Panel, para 6.43.

In *Thailand–H-Beams*, the panel considered that the facts include confidential information submitted to the authorities:

In our view, this relates to all of the facts made available to the authorities of the import- ing Member, including any confidential information that the investigating authority would be prohibited from disclosing without permission pursuant to Article 6.5 of the ADA (to the extent that these form part of the record before a panel).[397]

This was later confirmed by the Appellate Body.[398]

In *Thailand–H-beams*, the AB further noted that Articles 17.5 and 17.6 place *limiting obligations* on panel review of administrative determinations.[399] In a sim- ilar vein, in *Mexico–HFCS 21.5*, the AB considered that Articles 17.5 and 17.6(i) did not authorize panels to engage in a new and independent fact-finding exercise.[400]

In *India–Steel plate*, the panel allowed India to submit affidavits from a former USDOC official,[401] overruling objections from the US that this violated Article 17.5(ii) because the affidavits had not been made available to the authorities during the administrative investigation.[402] In the view of the panel, the affidavits did not constitute new evidence, but rather should be seen as an 'expert opinion'.[403] In *United States–Hot rolled steel*[404] and *Egypt–Rebar*,[405] on the other hand, the panels took a strict line in not accepting new evidence.

3.11.6 Standard of Review

Article 17.6 contains the unique[406] standard of review applicable to anti-dumping disputes. According to Koulen,[407] this was the most controversial unresolved issue in the final days of the Uruguay Round and, in fact, particularly Article 17.6(ii) has remained subject to 'fierce controversy' until today.[408]

---

[397] *Thailand–H-Beams from Poland*, Panel, para 7.52.
[398] *Thailand–H-Beams from Poland*, AB, paras 114 and 118.
[399] *Thailand–H-Beams from Poland*, AB, para 114.
[400] *Mexico–HFCS from the United States*, 21.5 AB, para 84.
[401] *United States–Steel plate from India*, Panel, para 7.13.
[402] *United States–Steel plate from India*, Panel, para 7.10.
[403] WorldTradeLaw.net, *Dispute Settlement Commentary*, pp 13–14, checked on 23 April 2005, notes that the panel's finding on this point would appear to have broken new ground in terms of the scope of the evidence that may be submitted in a WTO anti-dumping dispute. In their view, the panel 'may have opened the door to arguments that other types of information, e.g., a new econometric analysis of the data on the record, are not new evidence and should be allowed in.'
[404] *United States–Hot rolled steel from Japan*, Panel, para 7.7.
[405] *Egypt–Rebar from Turkey*, Panel, para 7.20.
[406] Compare *United States–Lead and bismuth steel from the EC*, AB, para 50.
[407] Koulen, 'The New Anti-Dumping Code Through Its Negotiating History' in Bourgeois, Berrod and Gippini Fournier (eds), *The Uruguay Round Results* (1995) 151, 226.
[408] See, eg, Durling and Nicely, *Understanding the WTO Anti-Dumping Agreement: Negotiating History and Subsequent Interpretation* (2002) 585; and the discussion by various authors in (2003) 6 Journal of International Economic Law (2003).

As far as the panel's *assessment of the facts* of the matter is concerned, Article 17.6(i) instructs the panel to determine whether (1) the authorities' *establishment of the facts* was *proper* and whether their *evaluation* of those facts was (2) *unbiased and* (3) *objective*. If this was in fact the case, the panel may not overturn the evaluation, even though it might have reached a different conclusion.

It has been noted that the structure of Article 17.6(i) is critical:

Only if all three of these tests had been met, does the deferential standard of the second sentence come into play. It is therefore misleading to say that Article 17.6(i) requires deference to the authorities' evaluation. The deference only comes into play after the three elements have been established.[409]

17.6 In examining the matter referred to in paragraph 5:

(i) in its assessment of the facts of the matter, the panel shall determine whether the authorities' establishment of the facts was proper and whether their evaluation of those facts was unbiased and objective. If the establishment of the facts was proper and the evaluation was unbiased and objective, even though the panel might have reached a different conclusion, the evaluation shall not be overturned;

(ii) the panel shall interpret the relevant provisions of the Agreement in accordance with customary rules of interpretation of public international law. Where the panel finds that a relevant provision of the Agreement admits of more than one permissible interpretation, the panel shall find the authorities' measure to be in conformity with the Agreement if it rests upon one of those permissible interpretations.

In *Mexico–HFCS 21.5*, the AB set out that the obligations of Article 17.6(i) and 17.6(ii) are *cumulative*:

In other words, a panel must find a determination made by the ... authorities to be consistent with relevant provisions of the ADA if it finds that those ... authorities have properly established the facts and evaluated those facts in an unbiased and objective manner, and that the determination rests upon a 'permissible' interpretation of the relevant provisions.[410]

In *United States–Hot rolled steel*, the AB compared the standards laid out in Article 17.6(i) ADA and Article 11 DSU as regards the *assessment of the facts* and considered that there was no conflict between the two provisions. Although Article 17.6(i) did not include the word 'objective', in the view of the AB, it was inconceivable that the Article 17.6(i) assessment would not need to be objective.[411]

In *Thailand–H-beams*, the panel had considered that its examination of *proper establishment of the facts* included ascertaining whether the factual basis

[409] Durling and Nicely, *Understanding the WTO Anti-Dumping Agreement: Negotiating History and Subsequent Interpretation* (2002) 579.

[410] *Mexico–HFCS from the United States*, 21.5 AB, para 130.

[411] *United States–Hot rolled steel from Japan*, AB, para 55.

of the determination was discernible from the documents that were available to the interested parties in the course of the investigation and at the time of the final determination, and whether those documents reflected the actual underlying data.[412] On appeal, however, the AB disagreed with this interpretation:

Article 17.6(i) requires a panel, in its assessment of the facts of the matter, to determine whether the authorities' 'establishment of the facts' was 'proper'. The ordinary meaning of 'establishment' suggests an action to 'place beyond dispute; ascertain, demonstrate, prove'; the ordinary meaning of 'proper' suggests 'accurate' or 'correct'. Based on the ordinary meaning of these words, the proper establishment of the facts appears to have no logical link to whether those facts are disclosed to, or discernible by, the parties to an anti-dumping investigation prior to the final determination. Article 17.6(i) requires a panel also to examine whether the evaluation of those facts was 'unbiased and objective'. The ordinary meaning of the words 'unbiased' and 'objective' also appears to have no logical link to whether those facts are disclosed to, or discernible by, the parties to an anti-dumping investigation at the time of the final determination.

There is a clear connection between Articles 17.6(i) and 17.5(ii). The facts of the matter referred to in Article 17.6(i) are 'the facts made available in conformity with appropriate domestic procedures to the authorities of the importing Member' under Article 17.5(ii). Such facts do not exclude confidential facts made available to the authorities of the importing Member . . . The 'facts' referred to in Articles 17.5(ii) and 17.6(i) thus embrace 'all facts confidential and non-confidential', made available to the authorities of the importing Member in conformity with the domestic procedures of that Member. Article 17.6(i) places a limitation on the panel in the circumstances defined by the Article. The aim of Article 17.6(i) is to prevent a panel from 'second-guessing' a determination of a national authority when the establishment of the facts is proper and the evaluation of those facts is unbiased and objective. Whether evidence or reasoning is disclosed or made discernible to interested parties by the final determination is a matter of procedure and due process. These matters are very important, but they are comprehensively dealt with in other provisions, notably Articles 6 and 12 of the ADA.

Articles 17.5 and 17.6(i) require a panel to examine the facts made available to the investigating authority of the importing Member. These provisions do not prevent a panel from examining facts that were not disclosed to, or discernible by, the interested parties at the time of the final determination.[413]

Thus, the AB acknowledged the importance of the authorities' disclosing all relevant facts and reasoning to interested parties, but considered compliance

---

[412] *Thailand–H-Beams from Poland*, Panel, para 7.145.

[413] *Thailand–H-Beams from Poland*, AB, paras 114–118. Compare the discussion in Steger, 'Appellate Body Jurisprudence Relating to Trade Remedies', in *Peace Through Trade* (2004) 153, 194–196.

with these obligations of Articles 6[414] and 12[415] ADA issues. In the same case, the AB also considered that Article 17.6(i) did not preclude a panel from examining whether the injury determination was based on positive evidence and involved an objective examination in accordance with Article 3.1 ADA.[416]

In *Mexico–HFCS 21.5*, the AB considered that the proper establishment of the facts by the authorities includes both affirmative findings of events that took place during the investigation period and assumptions relating to such events made by the authorities in the course of their analyses. Such assumptions are inevitable in threat of injury [417] cases because future events can never be proven conclusively by facts.[418]

In *United States–Hot rolled steel*, the panel considered that the *proper establishment of the facts'* check involves determining whether the authorities collected relevant and reliable information concerning the issue in dispute. As such, it is a check of the investigative process.[419]

In the same case, the AB considered that Article 17(6)(i), although technically containing obligations imposed on the panel, effectively imposes the same obligations upon the authorities in the course of the investigation:[420]

Article 17.6(i) of the ADA ... states that the panel is to determine, first, whether the investigating authorities' 'establishment of the facts was proper' and, second, whether the authorities' 'evaluation of those facts was unbiased and objective' ... Although the text of Article 17.6(i) is couched in terms of an obligation on panels – panels 'shall' make these determinations – the provision, at the same time, in effect defines when investigating authorities can be considered to have acted inconsistently with the ADA in the course of their 'establishment' and 'evaluation' of the relevant facts. In other words, Article 17.6(i) sets forth the appropriate standard to be applied by panels in examining the WTO-consistency of the investigating authorities' establishment and evaluation of the facts under other provisions of the ADA. Thus, panels must assess if the establishment of the facts by the investigating authorities was proper and if the evaluation of those facts by those authorities was unbiased and objective. If these broad standards have not been met, a panel must hold the investigating authorities' establishment or evaluation of the facts to be inconsistent with the ADA.[421]

In two cases involving Argentina, *Argentina–Poultry* and *Argentina–Ceramic floor tiles*, the panels ruled that they would make their Article 17.6 (i) determination

---

[414] See sections 3.2.5.1 and 3.2.3, above.
[415] See section 3.6, above.
[416] *Thailand–H-Beams from Poland*, AB, para 137.
[417] See section 2.5, above.
[418] *Mexico–HFCS from the United States*, 21.5 AB, paras 84–85.
[419] *United States–Hot Rolled Steel from Japan*, Panel, para 7.26.
[420] Compare Czako, Human and Miranda, *A Handbook on Anti-Dumping Investigations* (2003) 30.
[421] *United States–Hot Rolled Steel from Japan*, AB, paras 55–56.

on the basis of the facts on the record at the time that the administrative determination was made, thereby rejecting *ex post facto* rationalizations.[422]

In *EC–Malleable cast iron tube or pipe fittings*, Brazil had expressed doubts about whether an internal note for the file, submitted to the panel by the EC in the course of the dispute settlement proceeding as Exhibit EC-12, actually formed part of the record in the underlying anti-dumping investigation and had requested the panel to find that the document was not properly before it. Brazil suspected, in other words, that the document had been made up *ex post*. The panel, however, had refused to do so. On appeal, Brazil claimed that the panel's assessment of the facts had not been proper under Article 17.6(i) because the panel had based its findings as to the contemporaneous nature of Exhibit EC-12 exclusively on unsubstantiated assertions from the EC which had been accepted by the panel on the basis of a presumption of good faith.[423] However, the AB found that the panel had not relied solely on the assertions of the EC, but had conducted an inquiry to verify the genuineness of Exhibit EC-12.[424] The AB considered that it was unable to conclude that the panel's assessment was in error because, based on its reading of the panel report, Brazil had failed to substantiate its claim that Exhibit EC-12 was not contemporaneous with the investigation.[425]

In *EC–Bed linen 21.5*, the AB rejected a claim by India that the panel had failed to comply with Article 17.6(i) by not seeking information from the EC *ex* Article 13 DSU.[426] The AB considered that Article 17.6(i) granted the panel a certain discretion:

... the discretion that panels enjoy as triers of fact under Article 11 of the DSU is equally relevant to cases governed ... by Article 17.6(i) ... Thus, as under Article 11 of the DSU, we 'will not interfere lightly with a panel's exercise of its discretion' under Article 17.6(i) ...[427]

Article 17.6(ii) requires the panel to interpret the relevant provisions of the ADA in accordance with customary rules of interpretation of public international law. Where the panel finds that a relevant provision of the ADA admits of more than one permissible interpretation, the panel shall find the authorities' measure to be in conformity with the ADA if it rests upon one of those permissible interpretations.

---

[422] *Argentina–Poultry from Brazil*, Panel, paras 7.48–7.49.
[423] *EC–Malleable cast iron tube or pipe fittings from Brazil*, AB, para 122.
[424] *EC–Malleable cast iron tube or pipe fittings from Brazil*, AB, paras 125–127.
[425] *EC–Malleable cast iron tube or pipe fittings from Brazil*, AB, para 128.
[426] *EC–Bed linen from India*, 21.5 AB, para 169.
[427] *EC–Bed linen from India*, 21.5 AB, para 169.

The first sentence of Article 17.6(ii) is commonly interpreted as referring to Articles 31 and 32 of the Vienna Convention on the Law of Treaties (VCLT):[428]

... under Article 17.6(ii) of the ADA, panels are obliged to determine whether a measure rests upon an interpretation of the relevant provisions of the ADA which is permissible under the rules of treaty interpretation in Articles 31 and 32 of the Vienna Convention. In other words, a permissible interpretation is one which is found to be appropriate after application of the pertinent rules of the Vienna Convention. We observe that the rules of treaty interpretation in Articles 31 and 32 of the Vienna Convention apply to any treaty, in any field of public international law, and not just to the WTO agreements. These rules of treaty interpretation impose certain common disciplines upon treaty interpreters, irrespective of the content of the treaty provision being examined and irrespective of the field of international law concerned.[429]

In *United States–Hot rolled steel*, the AB further noted that the first sentence of Article 17(6)(ii) is very similar to Article 3.2 DSU and that there is no conflict between the two provisions.[430] It has been observed that the second sentence of Article 17.6(ii) is inconsistent with the first sentence because Articles 31 and 32 VCLT envisage a single preferred interpretation, to be arrived at on the basis of the – self-contained – interpretational rules.[431]

Articles 31 and 32 VCLT
Article 31 General rule of interpretation

1. A treaty shall be interpreted in good faith in accordance with the ordinary meaning to be given to the terms of the treaty in their context and in the light of its objective and purpose.

2. The context for the purpose of the interpretation of a treaty shall comprise, in addition to the text, including its preamble and annexes:

(a) any agreement relating to the treaty which was made between all the parties in connection with the conclusion of the treaty;

(b) any instrument which was made by one or more parties in connection with the conclusion of the treaty and accepted by the other parties as an instrument related to the treaty.

---

[428] Compare Horlick and Clarke, 'Standards for Panels Reviewing Anti-Dumping Determinations under the GATT and the WTO', in Petersman (ed), *International Trade Law and the GATT/WTO Dispute Settlement System* (1997) 315, 319.

[429] *United States–Hot Rolled Steel from Japan*, AB, para 60.

[430] *United States–Hot rolled steel from Japan*, AB, para 57.

[431] Compare Durling, 'Deference, But Only When Due: WTO Review of Anti-Dumping Measures' (2003) 6 Journal of International Economic Law 125, 143; Durling and Nicely, *Understanding the WTO Anti-Dumping Agreement: Negotiating History and Subsequent Interpretation*,

3. There shall be taken into account, together with the context:

(a) any subsequent agreement between the parties regarding the interpretation of the treaty or the application of its provisions;

(b) any subsequent practice in the application of the treaty which establishes the agreement of the parties regarding its interpretation;

(c) any relevant rules of international law applicable in the relations between the parties.

4. A special meaning shall be given to a term if it is established that the parties so intended.

Article 32 Supplementary means of interpretation

Recourse may be had to supplementary means of interpretation, including the preparatory work of the treaty and the circumstances of its conclusion, in order to confirm the meaning resulting from the application of Article 31, or to determine the meaning when the interpretation according to Article 31:

(a) leaves the meaning ambiguous or obscure; or

(b) leads to a result which is manifestly absurd or unreasonable.[432]

In *United States–Hot rolled steel*, the AB stressed that Article 17.6(ii), second sentence, comes into play only after the rules of the VCLT have been applied and that it supplements, rather than replaces DSU Article 11.[433]

Thus far, panels and/or the AB have seldom concluded that more than one permissible interpretation existed,[434] a fact which has both been criticized[435] and applauded.[436]

(2002) 585; Croley and Jackson, 'WTO Dispute Procedures, Standard of Review, and Deference to National Governments' (1996) 90 American Journal of International Law 193, 201.

[432] Vienna Convention on the Law of Treaties, *http://www.un.org/law/ilc/text/treaties.htm*, checked on 16 April 2005.

[433] *United States–Hot rolled steel from Japan*, AB, paras 58–59. Compare WorldTradeLaw.net, *Dispute Settlement Commentary*, p 17 checked 23 April 2005; Durling, 'Deference, But Only When Due: WTO Review of Anti-Dumping Measures' (2003) 6 Journal of International Economic Law 125, 143.

[434] Compare Tarullo, 'The Hidden Costs of International Dispute Settlement: WTO Review of Domestic Anti-Dumping Decisions' (2002) 34 Law and Policy in International Business, 109, 113; Spamann, 'Standard of Review for World Trade Organization Panels in Trade Remedy Cases: a Critical Analysis' (2004) 38 Journal of World Trade 509, 511.

[435] See, eg, Tarullo, 'The Hidden Costs of International Dispute Settlement: WTO Review of Domestic Anti-Dumping Decisions' (2002) 34 Law and Policy in International Business 109, 113; Tarullo, 'Paved with Good Intentions: The Dynamic Effects of WTO Review of Anti-Dumping Action' (2003) 2 World Trade Review 373, 374; Greenwald, 'WTO Dispute Settlement: An Exercise in Trade Law Legislation' (2003) 6 Journal of International Economic Law 113, 117 who posits that ' . . . in the hands of the panels and the Appellate Body, Article 17.6 has quickly become a dead letter.' Compare Cunningham and Cribb, 'Dispute Settlement Through the Lens of "Free Flow of Trade": A Review of WTO Dispute Settlement of US Anti-Dumping and Countervailing Duty Measures' (2003) 6 Journal of International Economic Law 155, 161–164.

[436] See, eg, Durling, 'Deference, But Only When Due: WTO Review of Anti-Dumping Measures' (2003) 6 Journal of International Economic Law, 125–153.

In *EC–Bed linen*, the panel had found that while Article 2.2.2.(ii) did not mandate the exclusion of sales below cost, this did not mean that such exclusion was not permitted, as a result of which it had found that the EC's exclusion of such sales was a permissible interpretation.[437] On appeal, the AB overruled the panel on this point.[438] In the same case, the panel had found that the inter-model zeroing[439] practised by the EC did not constitute a permissible interpretation by the EC. On appeal, the AB agreed with the panel:

It appears clear to us from the emphatic and unqualified nature of this finding of inconsistency that the panel did not view the interpretation given by the European Communities of Article 2.4.2 of the ADA as a 'permissible interpretation' . . . Thus, the panel was not faced with a choice among multiple 'permissible' interpretations which would have required it, under Article 17.6(ii), to give deference to the interpretation relied upon by the European Communities. Rather, the panel was faced with a situation in which the interpretation relied upon by the European Communities was, to borrow a word from the European Communities, 'impermissible'.[440]

In the subsequent *EC–Bed linen 21.5* case, the AB considered that the Article 3.1 requirements that the injury determination must be based on positive evidence and involve an objective examination are not ambiguous and do not allow multiple permissible interpretations.[441]

In *United States–Hot rolled steel*, the AB upheld a panel finding that the USDOC's conclusion that a Japanese exporter had failed to 'cooperate' in the investigation did not rest on a permissible interpretation of the word 'cooperate'.[442] The AB also upheld a panel finding that the USDOC 99.5 per cent test was not permissible.[443] On the other hand, in that same case, the AB found that the reliance by the USDOC on downstream sales to calculate normal value rested upon an interpretation of Article 2.1 ADA that was in principle permissible.[444]

In *Egypt–Rebar from Turkey*, the panel considered Egypt's reading of Article 2.4 as not requiring the authorities to make an adjustment for credit costs in cases where normal value is based on constructed normal value 'not possible'.[445]

---

[437] *EC–Bed linen from India*, Panel, paras 6.83–6.87.
[438] *EC–Bed linen from India*, AB, para 83. See also section 1.3.2.2, above.
[439] See section 1.4.3.1, above.   [440] *EC–Bed linen from India*, AB, para 83.
[441] *EC–Bed linen from India*, 21.5 AB, para 118.
[442] *United States–Hot rolled steel from Japan*, AB, para 109. See also section 3.2.5.8, above.
[443] *United States–Hot rolled steel from Japan*, AB, para 158.
[444] *United States–Hot rolled steel from Japan*, AB, para 172. See also section 1.3.1.2, above.
[445] *Egypt–Rebar from Turkey*, Panel, para 7.351. Compare Tarullo, 'The Hidden Costs of International Dispute Settlement: WTO Review of Domestic Anti-Dumping Decisions' (2002) 34 Law and Policy in International Business 109, 143–144.

In *Argentina–Poultry*, the panel ruled that Argentina's interpretation of the domestic industry as producers representing an important, serious or significant portion (*in casu* 46 per cent) of total domestic production was permissible.[446] In the same case, the panel also implicitly considered it permissible to levy anti-dumping duties in the form of variable duties on the basis of the actual dumping margin prevailing at the time of duty collection.[447]

Article 17.7 provides that confidential information submitted to the Panel in a WTO dispute settlement proceeding shall not be disclosed without the formal authorization of the party which submitted it:

17.7 Confidential information provided to the panel shall not be disclosed without formal authorization from the person, body or authority providing such information. Where such information is requested from the panel but release of such information by the panel is not authorized, a non-confidential summary of the information, authorized by the person, body or authority providing the information, shall be provided.

3.12 Final Provisions

Article 18 provides that no specific action can be taken against dumping, except in accordance with the provisions of GATT 1994, as interpreted by the ADA. As GATT 1994 and the ADA effectively only authorize imposition of anti-dumping duties or acceptance of price undertakings, these are the only measures allowed[448]:

18.1 No specific action against dumping of exports form another Member can be taken except in accordance with the provisions of GATT 1994, as interpreted by this Agreement.[449]

In *United States–1916 Act*, the panel considered that footnote 24 to Article 18.1 does not prevent members from addressing the causes or effects of dumping through other trade policy instruments allowed under the WTO Agreement. However, when a law of a member addresses the type of price discrimination covered by Article VI and makes it the cause for the imposition of measures, the member has to abide by the requirements of Article VI and the ADA.[450] The

---

[446] *Argentina–Poultry from Brazil*, Panel, para 7.341. See also section 2.2, above.

[447] *Argentina–Poultry from Brazil*, Panel, para 7.361. See also section 3.3.3, above.

[448] Compare *United States–1916 Act–EC*, Panel, para 6.196.

[449] Fn 24 in ADA: This is not intended to preclude action under other relevant provisions of GATT 1994, as appropriate.

[450] *United States–1916 Act–EC*, Panel, para 6.199, upheld by the AB in *United States–1916 Act*, AB, para 123; *United States–CDSOA (Byrd amendment)*, AB, paras 261–262.

law at issue was the American 1916 Antidumping Act, which established a private right of action for American manufacturers against predatory pricing by foreign producers. The potential penalty envisaged by the statute consisted of payment of treble damages. This was clearly an action not contemplated by GATT 1994 or the ADA.

More complicated was the situation when a dispute settlement case was brought by a number of countries[451] against the American Continued Dumping and Subsidy Offset Act (CDSOA), better known as the Byrd Amendment. The CDSOA essentially provides that anti-dumping duties collected by the American authorities are paid back to the American industries which launched the application. The question therefore was whether such repayment constituted a *specific* action *against* dumping. The AB considered first that these two conditions operate together and complement each other.[452]

With regard to *specific* action, the AB considered that the action must be inextricably linked to, and strongly correlated with, a dumping determination:

In our view, the Panel was correct in finding that the CDSOA is a specific action related to dumping ... within the meaning of Article 18.1 of the ADA .... It is clear from the text of the CDSOA, in particular from Section 754(a) of the Tariff Act, that the CDSOA offset payments are inextricably linked to, and strongly correlated with, a determination of dumping, as defined in Article VI:1 of the GATT 1994 and in the ADA ... The language of the CDSOA is unequivocal. First, CDSOA offset payments can be made only if anti-dumping duties ... have been collected. Second, such duties can be collected only pursuant to an anti-dumping duty order ...

Third, an anti-dumping duty order can be imposed only following a determination of dumping, as defined in Article VI:1 of the GATT 1994 and in the ADA ... In the light of the above elements, we agree with the Panel that 'there is a clear, direct and unavoidable connection between the determination of dumping and CDSOA offset payments' ... In other words, it seems to us unassailable that CDSOA offset payments can be made only following a determination that the constituent elements of dumping ... are present. Therefore ... we find that the CDSOA is 'specific action' related to dumping ... within the meaning of Article 18.1 of the ADA ...[453]

The AB rejected the US argument that, in order to be specific within the meaning of Article 18.1, the measure must come into direct contact with the imported product, or entities connected to the imported good such as the importer, exporter or foreign producer.[454]

---

[451] Australia, Brazil, Canada, Chile, the EC, India, Indonesia, Japan, Korea, Mexico and Thailand.
[452] *United States–CDSOA (Byrd amendment)*, AB, para 236.
[453] *United States–CDSOA (Byrd amendment)*, AB, para 242.
[454] *United States–CDSOA (Byrd amendment)*, AB, para 253.

In ruling that the CDSOA also constituted a specific action *against* dumping, the AB considered that:

... it is necessary to assess whether the design and structure of a measure is such that the measure is 'opposed to', has an adverse bearing on, or, more specifically, has the effect of dissuading the practice of dumping ... , or creates an incentive to terminate such practices. In our view, the CDSOA has exactly those effects because of its design and structure.

The CDSOA effects a transfer of financial resources from the producers/exporters of dumped or subsidized goods to their domestic competitors. This is demonstrated by the following elements of the CDSOA regime. First, the CDSOA offset payments are financed from the anti-dumping ... duties paid by the foreign producers/exporters. Second, the CDSOA offset payments are made to an 'affected domestic producer', defined in Section 754(b) of the Tariff Act as 'a petitioner or interested party in support of the petition with respect to which an anti-dumping duty order, a finding under the Antidumping Act of 1921, ... has been entered' and that 'remains in operation'. In response to our questioning at the oral hearing, the United States confirmed that the 'affected domestic producers' which are eligible to receive payments under the CDSOA, are necessarily competitors of the foreign producers/exporters subject to an anti-dumping ... order. Third, under the implementing regulations issued by the United States Commissioner of Customs ('Customs') on 21 September 2001, the 'qualifying expenditures' of the affected domestic producers, for which the CDSOA offset payments are made, 'must be related to the production of the same product that is the subject of the related order or finding, with the exception of expenses incurred by associations which must relate to a specific case.' Fourth, Customs has confirmed that there is no statutory or regulatory requirement as to how a CDSOA offset payment to an affected domestic producer is to be spent, thus indicating that the recipients of CDSOA offset payments are entitled to use this money to bolster their competitive position vis-à-vis their competitors, including the foreign competitors subject to anti-dumping ... duties.[455]

As CDSOA offset payments were not definitive anti-dumping duties, provisional measures or price undertakings, the CDSOA violated Article 18.1 ADA.[456]

In *Mexico–Rice*, the panel closely followed these steps to reach a finding that a provision of the Mexican Foreign Trade Act requiring the authorities to – under certain circumstances[457] – impose fines on imports while the investigation is proceeding violated Article 18.1 ADA.[458]

---

[455] *United States–CDSOA (Byrd amendment)*, AB, paras 254–256.

[456] *United States–CDSOA (Byrd amendment)*, AB, paras 254–256. For criticism of the (panel) report, see Greenwald, 'WTO Dispute Settlement: An Exercise in Trade Law Legislation' (2003) 6 Journal of International Economic Law 113, 120–123.

[457] These circumstances are very similar to the critical circumstances discussed in section 3.4.2, above.   [458] *Mexico–Rice from the United States*, Panel, paras 7.278–7.279.

18.2 Reservations may not be entered in respect of any of the provisions of this Agreement without the consent of the other Members.

Article 18.3 is a transitional provision which covers the entry into force of the ADA. It provides that the ADA applies to investigations, and reviews of existing measures, initiated pursuant to applications made on or after 1 January 1995:

18.3 Subject to subparagraph 3.1 and 3.2, the provisions of this Agreement shall apply to investigations, and reviews of existing measures, initiated pursuant to applications which have been made on or after the date of entry into force for a Member of the WTO Agreement.

18.3.1 With respect to the calculation of margins of dumping in refund procedures under paragraph 3 of Article 9, the rules used in the most recent determination or review of dumping shall apply.

18.3.2 For the purposes of paragraph 3 of Article 11, existing anti-dumping measures shall be deemed to be imposed on a date not later than the date of entry into force for a Member of the WTO Agreement, except in cases in which the domestic legislation of a Member in force on that date already included a clause of the type provided for in that paragraph.

In *United States–DRAMS*, both parties agreed that Article 9.3.1 duty assessment procedures constitute 'reviews' within the meaning of Article 18.3.[459] However, a claim made by Korea concerning a DOC product scope determination made in 1993 in the original investigation was considered inadmissible by the panel because the ADA applied only to those parts of a pre-WTO measure that were included in the scope of a post-WTO review and there was no evidence that the product scope issue was re-visited during the review.[460]

Article 18.4 provides that each member shall take all necessary steps to ensure that its laws, regulations and administrative procedures are in conformity with the ADA provisions as of 1 January 2005:

18.4 Each Member shall take all necessary steps, of a general or particular character, to ensure, not later than the date of entry into force of the WTO Agreement for it, the conformity of its laws, regulations and administrative procedures with the provisions of this Agreement as they may apply for the Member in question.

In *United States–1916 Act*, the panel considered that when a law, regulation or administrative procedure of a member has been found incompatible with the provisions of the ADA, that member is *also* in breach of its obligations under

---

[459] *United States–DRAMS from Korea*, Panel, para 6.15.
[460] *United States–DRAMS from Korea*, Panel, para 6.17.

Article 18.4. As the panel had found that the 1916 Act violated Articles 1, 4.1, 5.1, 5.2, 5.4 and 18.1 ADA, the United States had therefore also violated Article 18.4 ADA.[461]

In *United States–Corrosion-resistant carbon steel flat products*, the AB broadly interpreted the phrase *laws, regulations and administrative procedures*:

Taken as a whole, the phrase 'laws, regulations and administrative procedures' seems to us to encompass the entire body of generally applicable rules, norms and standards adopted by members in connection with the conduct of anti-dumping proceedings.[462]

In a footnote, the AB observed that the scope of this phrase must be determined for purposes of WTO law on the basis of the content and the substance of the instrument in question and not merely on its form or nomenclature. The label given to the instrument under the member's domestic law is therefore not dispositive.[463] The AB's rationale was that any other interpretation would lead to the Article 18.4 obligations varying from member to member, depending on each member's domestic law and practice.

Partially relying on Article 18.4, the AB *implicitly* held that the American Sunset Policy Bulletin (SPB)[464] was a measure that may, as such, form the subject of dispute settlement under the ADA by overruling a panel finding that the SPB was not a mandatory legal instrument obligating a certain course of action.[465] In *United States–Oil country tubular goods*, the AB confirmed explicitly that the SPB was a measure subject to WTO dispute settlement and also clarified why it considered the SPB to be a measure:[466]

We note the argument of the United States that the SPB is not a legal instrument under United States law. This argument, however, is not relevant to the question before us. The issue is not whether the SPB is a legal instrument within the domestic legal system of the United States, but rather, whether the SPB is a measure that may be challenged within the WTO system ... Our mandate is confined to clarifying the provisions of the WTO Agreement and to determining whether the challenged measures are consistent with those provisions ... In our view, the SPB has normative value, as it provides administrative guidance and creates expectations among the public and among private

---

[461] *United States–1916 Act–Japan*, Panel, para 6.286. Compare *United States–Hot rolled steel from Japan*, Panel, paras 7.85–7.90; *US–CDSOA (Byrd amendment)*, AB, para 302.

[462] *United States–Corrosion-resistant carbon steel flat products from Japan*, AB, para 87.

[463] *United States–Corrosion-resistant carbon steel flat products from Japan*, AB, para 87.

[464] See also section 3.5.2, above.

[465] *United States–Corrosion-resistant carbon steel flat products from Japan*, AB, para 89.

[466] *United States–Oil country tubular goods from Argentina*, AB, para 186. Compare WorldTradeLaw.net, *Dispute Settlement Commentary on United States–Oil country tubular goods*, p 16, checked on 23 April 2005.

actors. It is intended to have general application, as it is to apply to all the sunset reviews conducted in the United States. It is also intended to have prospective application, as it is intended to apply to sunset reviews taking place after its issuance.[467]

In *United States–Steel plate*, the panel rejected India's claim that a *practice* may constitute an 'administrative procedure' in the sense of Article 18.4 ADA.[468] On the other hand, the AB in *United States–Hot rolled steel* noted that the 99.5 per cent test[469] constituted a 'consistent practice' of the USDOC which did not rest upon a permissible interpretation of the ADA,[470] thereby implicitly allowing it to be subject to WTO dispute settlement.

These reports have not yet answered the question whether internal guidelines, that are used by some anti-dumping administrations, fall within the scope of the phrase.[471] On the basis of the AB's rationale in *United States–Corrosion-resistant carbon steel flat products*,[472] this might possibly depend on whether the issues discussed in such internal guidelines are similar to the issues that other members address in their implementing regulations.

18.5 Each Member shall inform the Committee of any changes in its laws and regulations relevant to this Agreement and in the administration of such laws and regulations.

18.6 The Committee shall review annually the implementation and operation of this Agreement taking into account the objectives thereof. The Committee shall inform annually the Council for Trade in Goods of developments during the period covered by such reviews.

18.7 The Annexes to this Agreement constitute an integral part thereof.

---

[467] *United States–Oil country tubular goods from Argentina*, AB, para 187.

[468] *United States–Steel plate from India*, Panel, para 7.22. Compare *United States–Oil country tubular goods*, AB, para 220, where the AB noted: 'even assuming arguendo that a "practice" may be challenged as a "measure" in WTO dispute settlement-an issue on which we express no view here . . .'. WorldTradeLaw.net, *Dispute Settlement Commentary on United States–Oil country tubular goods*, p 17, checked on 23 April 2005, notes that the AB has sent conflicting signals on whether it will allow administrative practices to be subject to WTO dispute settlement.

[469] See section 1.3.1.2, above.

[470] *United States–Hot rolled steel from Japan*, AB, para 133.

[471] Compare WorldTradeLaw.net, *Dispute Settlement Commentary on United States–Oil country tubular goods*, p 16, checked on 23 April 2005.

[472] *United States–Corrosion-resistant carbon steel flat products from Japan*, AB, para 87.

Chapter 4

RESIDUAL ADA DISPUTE
SETTLEMENT ISSUES

Introduction

The Dispute Settlement Understanding (DSU) forms the core element of the dispute settlement system of the WTO. It applies to all disputes pertaining to the Agreements listed in its Appendix 1.[1] As early as in *Guatemala–Cement*,

---

[1] Art 1.1 DSU.

the Appellate Body noted that the special or additional rules and procedures of a particular Covered Agreement fit together with the generally applicable rules and procedures of the DSU to form a comprehensive, integrated dispute settlement for the WTO Agreement.[2] In that case, Article 17 ADA did *not* – as argued – *replace* the more general approach of the DSU; it is only in the specific circumstance where a provision of the DSU and a special (or additional) provision of another Covered Agreement – of its Appendix 2 – are mutually inconsistent, that the special or additional provision may be read to *prevail* over the provision of the DSU.[3]

Below we have identified and briefly reviewed a number of recurring conceptual topics directly or indirectly relating to dispute settlement in the area of the ADA that do not fit in with specific ADA articles.[4]

4.1 Exhaustion of Local/Administrative Remedies

The principle of exhaustion of *local* remedies would require that a party first pursue all administrative and judicial remedies available to it under the legislation of the importing country before recourse can be had to international dispute settlement; the principle of exhaustion of *administrative* remedies would require governments to only raise *claims* in WTO dispute settlement proceedings that have also been raised in administrative proceedings by the private parties involved.

While the literature is not conclusive on the question of exhaustion,[5] panel and AB rulings have increasingly established that these principles have no place in the context of WTO dispute settlement.

---

[2] *Guatemala–Cement*, AB, para 66.   [3] Art 1.2 DSU. *Guatemala–Cement*, AB, para 66.

[4] See for a more detailed analysis of these and other WTO dispute settlement issues Palmeter, and Mavroidis, *Dispute Settlement in the World Trade Organization: Practice and Procedure* (2nd edn, 2004); Steger, 'Appellate Body Jurisprudence Relating to Trade Remedies in Peace Through Trade (2004) 153–171.

[5] Generally speaking, authors would seem to accept that claims may be brought in WTO dispute settlement procedures before exhaustion of local and/or administrative remedies. See Petersmann, 'How to Promote the International Rule of Law?' (1998) 1 JIEL 25 at 35; Davey, 'Has the WTO Dispute Settlement System Exceeded its Authority?' (2001) 4 JIEL 79 at 104; Vermulst, Mavroidis and Waer, 'The Functioning of the Appellate Body After Four Years: Towards Rule Integrity' (1999) 33 JWT 1; and, for example, *United States–Anti-dumping duties on grey Portland cement and cement clinker from Mexico*, at para 5.11, ADP/82, 7 September 1992; or *United States–Imposition of anti-dumping duties on fresh and chilled Atlantic salmon from Norway*, para 590, ADP/87, 25 April 1994. For contrary views, see Martha, 'World Trade Disputes Settlement and the Exhaustion of Local Remedies Rule' (1996) 4 JWT 107; Kuyper, 'The New WTO Dispute Settlement System – The Impact on the European Community' (1995) 29 JWT 49, 65–68.

First of all, the DSU does not incorporate an obligation to the effect of exhaustion of local and/or administrative remedies.[6] This absence of an explicit exhaustion requirement fits with the absence of a legal interest requirement.[7] Second, the AB held in *Thailand–H-Beams* that a Panel may not go back to the administrative proceeding to examine whether certain claims were raised during the proceeding because there is not necessarily continuity between the claims made by private parties in the course of the administrative proceeding and the claims made by WTO members in WTO dispute settlement cases.[8]

Similarly, in *Argentina–Poultry*, the panel considered that the fact that an argument was not raised in the context of an investigation does not preclude a party from raising it at a later stage in a WTO panel proceeding.[9]

For WTO dispute settlement cases under the ADA, where the parties most directly involved in an administrative anti-dumping proceeding will virtually always be private companies while the party bringing a case to WTO dispute settlement necessarily will always be a government, this clarification is particularly welcome.

4.2 Consultations

Consultations constitute a mandatory 'safety-stop' before resorting to further action under the DSU. They form an important part of the process of clarifying the matter in dispute between parties. Indeed, it has been observed that a significant number of consultation requests have resulted in mutually acceptable solutions.[10]

If a WTO member requests consultations, the responding member should in principle reply within 10 days.[11] Consultations should then commence within 30 days. The requesting party may ask for the establishment of a Panel should these deadlines not be respected.[12] In case a third WTO member considers that it has a 'substantial interest' in the consultations, it has to notify the consulting countries involved as well as the DSB within 10 days of the date of circulation of the request for consultations.[13]

---

[6] Art 17.4 ADA could be considered as a 'sort-of' exhaustion of local remedies rule.

[7] See, for example, *EC–Bananas*, AB, para 135, where the EC argued that the US did not export bananas and therefore had no standing to bring a case. The Appellate Body found 'that a Member has broad discretion in deciding whether to bring a case against another Member under the DSU.'

[8] *Thailand–H-Beams from Poland*, AB, para 94.

[9] *Argentina–Poultry from Brazil*, Panel, para 7.146.

[10] Lacarte-Muró and Gappah, 'Developing Countries and the WTO Legal and Dispute Settlement System: A View from the Bench' (2000) 3 JIEL 395–401.   [11] Art 4.3 DSU.

[12] Art 4.3 DSU.   [13] Art 4.11 DSU.

Consultations should settle the dispute within 60 days after its request, failing which a panel may be requested; however, if parties jointly consider that, during the initial 60 days, consultations have failed to settle the dispute a panel may be requested earlier.

In those situations where consultations lead to a satisfactory adjustment of the matter they have obviously served their purpose. However, in situations where no mutually agreed solution is reached, the legal importance of consultations is often limited,[14] as the DSU provides that consultations are without prejudice to the rights of any member in any further proceedings.[15] While facts and information obtained during the consultation process may be and have been used by the parties and by the panel, such use is *probative* rather than *constitutive* in nature. The real cut-off point for the clear identification of the matter remains the request for the panel and, moreover, facts and information from the consultation stage may also be left aside by panels in cases where it deems that the value of such data is limited.[16]

4.3 Request for Establishment of a Panel

Once consultations have been concluded and a WTO member decides to proceed with dispute settlement, it will request the DSB in writing to establish a panel. This so-called request for establishment of a panel (REP) must be in writing, identify the specific measure at issue, and provide a summary of the legal basis of the complaint (the claims).[17] The measure at issue and the claims form the *matter*; this matter forms the basis for the terms of reference for a panel.[18]

---

[14] Where they have solved the differences of opinion with respect to some claims, but not to all, they have obviously still served *some* useful purpose.   [15] Art 4.6 DSU.

[16] See for example *EC–Bed Linen from India* where the panel did not rely on reports of the consultations (para 6.35) since it considered that they contained nothing new or substantive that was not otherwise before the panel (para 6.32) and were considered, at best, unnecessary (para 6.32). Similarly, in *Mexico–HFCS from the United States* the Panel 'did not consider it significant ... that Mexico may have made different arguments during the consultations.' See *Mexico–HFCS from the United States*, Panel, para 7.43. Compare also *Mexico–Rice from the United States*, Panel, para 7.41.

[17] Art 6.2 DSU.

[18] Compare *Guatamala–Cement from Mexico I*, AB, para 72. This is in line with older jurisprudence under the GATT. In *United States–Imposition of Anti-Dumping Duties on Imports of Fresh and Chilled Atlantic Salmon from Norway*, adopted 27 April 1994, BISD 41S/229, para 432, the panel found that 'the "*matter*" consisted of *the specific claims* stated by Norway ... with respect to *the imposition of these duties*'. Compare also *Brazil–Coconut from the Philippines*, AB at pp 19–20.

4.3.1 Multiple Measures

Nothing prevents a party from challenging multiple measures at the same time. For example, in _United States–Stainless steel plate in coils and stainless steel sheet and strip_ two anti-dumping duty orders issued by the US Department of Commerce were under consideration: one concerning _Stainless steel plate in coils_, and one concerning _Stainless steel sheet and strip in coils_.[19]

4.3.2 Co-complainants and Parallel Panels

Article 9.1 DSU allows one panel to examine complaints in cases where more than one WTO member requests the establishment of a panel related to the same matter. An example of this can be found in the case of the panel established by the DSB on 23 August 2001, concerning the _United States–CDSOA (Byrd Amendment)_ by _nine_ co-complainants: Australia, Brazil, Chile, the EC, India, Indonesia, Japan, Korea and Thailand.[20]

Alternatively, it is possible to establish _two_ panels concerning the same matter. In such case the same persons shall serve, to the extent possible, as panellists on each of the separate, parallel, panels.[21] See, for example, _United States–1916 Act (EC)_ and _United States–1916 Act (Japan)_.

4.3.3 Third Parties

According to Article 10.2 DSU the interests of third parties shall be fully taken into account during the panel process.[22] Thus, parties having a substantial interest in the matter but not wishing to be a co-complainant or request their own panel still have an opportunity to be heard (during the first meeting with the panel) and to make written submissions to the panel.[23] These submissions shall be given to the parties to the dispute and shall be reflected in the panel

---

[19] Anti-Dumping Duty Orders: _Certain Stainless Steel Plate in Coils from Belgium, Canada, Italy, the Republic of Korea, South Africa and Taiwan_, Federal Register Vol 64, No 98 at 27,757; and (Notice of) Anti-Dumping Duty Order: _Stainless Steel Sheet and Strip in Coils from the United Kingdom, Taiwan and South Korea_, Federal Register Vol 64, No 143 at 40,556–40,557.

[20] WT/DS217/5. Canada and Mexico also requested separate Panels to examine their complaints; see WT/DS234/12 and WT/DS234/13.   [21] Art 9.3 DSU.

[22] In order to participate in the proceeding, third parties must notify their interest at the DSB meeting where the panel is established or within 10 days thereafter in writing. The question has arisen whether this time period for notification should be shorter (five days) in cases with shorter time limits; while this five-day period was applied in some 21.5 proceedings such shortening seems not commonly accepted since members need time to decide whether or not to participate as a third party.

[23] Art 10.2 DSU. For example, in _EC–Bed Linen from India_ the US was third party and had its own views on the interpretation concerning the concept of domestic industry, see para 6.174. However, since India had raised no claims with respect to Art 4 ADA, the panel did not express itself on these views of the US, see para 6.175.

report. Third parties also receive the written submissions of the parties to the dispute.[24] Furthermore, Annex 3, paragraph 6 DSU provides that all third parties which have notified their interest in the dispute to the DSB shall be invited in writing to present their views during a session of the first substantive meeting of the panel set aside for that purpose. All such third parties may be present during the entirety of this session.

4.3.4 Matter, Claims and Arguments

Claims form the legal basis of the complaint with respect to the measure.[25] Together, the *measure* and the *claims* concerning that measure constitute *the matter referred to the DSB* (which forms the basis for a Panel's terms of reference). There is, in principle, no limit as to the number of claims that may be made with respect to one measure and, indeed, anti-dumping disputes often are multi-claim disputes.[26]

In turn, the distinction between *claims* and *arguments* was addressed in *EC–Bananas*, where the AB noted that there is a significant difference between the claims identified in the REP and the arguments supporting those claims.[27] While *claims* establish the panel's terms of reference under Article 7 of the DSU (together with the identified measure), *arguments* supporting those claims are set out and progressively clarified in the first written submissions, the rebuttal submissions and the first and second Panel meetings with the parties.[28]

Disagreements often arise with respect to the terms of reference after the applicant has filed its first submission. The respondent will normally check the submission against the REP and request a preliminary ruling in order to

---

[24] Art 10.3 DSU. The DSU is silent as to whether third parties may have access to the rebuttal submissions of the parties

[25] See, for example, *Thailand–H-Beams from Poland*, AB, at para 88:

...A defending party is entitled to know what case it has to answer, and what violations have been alleged so that it can begin preparing its defence... This requirement of due process is fundamental to ensuring a fair and orderly conduct of dispute settlement proceedings.

[26] See, eg, *Argentina–Poultry from Brazil*, Panel, where Brazil raised more than 40 claims. WorldTradeLaw.net, *Dispute Settlement Commentary on Argentina–Poultry from Brazil*, p 4, checked on 23 April 2005. Durling, 'Deference, But Only When Due: WTO Review of Anti-Dumping Measures' (2003) 6 Journal of International Economic Law 125, 130, provides an interesting table with the number of claims accepted and rejected at the panel stage and finds that of the 138 claims raised in the first 13 ADA panel proceedings (an average of slightly more than 10 claims per dispute), 69 were accepted and 69 rejected.

[27] *EC–Bananas*, AB, paras 141–145. Similarly, *Korea–Dairy Products from the EC*, AB, at para 123 clearly distinguishes claims from arguments.

[28] Indeed, there is no requirement that claims which are within the terms of reference must be raised in the first written submission; they can – in theory – also be raised at a later stage. See *EC–Bananas*, AB, para 147.

try to have the panel exclude claims that are not or not adequately addressed in the request for establishment.[29]

The Appellate Body, after having initially suggested in *EC–Bananas*[30] that it was sufficient to mention, in the REP, the articles of the Agreements alleged to have been violated, modified its views in *Korea–Dairy Products*. In that case the AB made clear that while identification of the articles is a minimum, it may not always be enough for the standard of Article 6.2 DSU,[31] particularly where articles contain multiple obligations. Thus, the question of whether the standard of Article 6.2 is met must be examined on a case-by-case basis. In resolving that question it must be taken into account whether the ability of the respondent to defend itself has been prejudiced.[32]

This ruling is particularly relevant for the ADA. The key articles – and, indeed, even paragraphs – of the ADA often contain multiple obligations. Thus, for example, Article 2 covering the dumping determination, Article 3 covering injury and causation and Article 6 covering due process may each form the basis for numerous claims. The AB has clearly established that where violations of such articles are alleged, a mere listing of the articles will almost certainly be insufficient and claims will need to be described in sufficient detail in the request for establishment. It is therefore recommendable for complainants to cite both articles and paragraphs and to provide a concise description of the alleged violations in the REP.[33]

The reasoning in *EC–Bananas* and *Korea–Dairy Products* was confirmed in *Thailand–H-Beams*:[34]

We are of the view that a complainant certainly takes a risk by not referring to the specific sub-paragraphs under which its claims of violation of an Article in a Covered Agreement fall. We note there are examples of more precise and informative Panel requests. We would certainly have preferred the Panel request in this case to have been more detailed in its treatment of Article 5 by at the very least identifying the specific

---

[29] See, eg, *United States–Oil country tubular goods from Argentina*; *EC–Malleable cast iron tube or pipe fittings from Brazil*; *Egypt–Rebar from Turkey*; *Argentina–Poultry from Brazil*; *EC–Bed Linen from India*; *Thailand–H-beams from Poland*; *Mexico–HFCS from the United States*.

[30] *EC–Bananas*, AB, para 141:

We accept the Panel's view that it was sufficient for the Complaining Parties to list the provisions of the specific agreements alleged to have been violated without setting out detailed arguments as to which specific aspects of the measures at issue relate to which specific provisions of those agreements.

[31] *Korea–Dairy Products*, AB, para 124.   [32] *Korea–Dairy Products*, AB, para 131.

[33] Compare *Argentina–Poultry from Brazil*, Panel, para 7.157, where the panel rejected one of Brazil's Art 6.2 claims on the ground that there was no reference to it in the REP.

[34] *Thailand–H-Beams from Poland*, Panel, para 7.23. See also the discussion in *United States–Oil country tubular goods from Argentina*, AB, paras 164–173.

sub-paragraphs of that Article that Poland was alleging had been violated. Ideally, there might also have been some narrative summarizing the legal basis of the complaint.

With respect to Article 3 ADA the AB accepted the panel's view that the REP went beyond a mere listing of that provision. With respect to Article 2 ADA, the AB was of the view that the lack of access to the confidential facts on the basis of which the Thai authorities based their determination of *injury* (Article 3) may have affected the precision with which Poland set out the claims in its REP.[35] Hence, it seems that the imprecision of Poland with respect to its claims on *dumping* could *de facto* be pardoned in view of the belated Thai information on *injury*; moreover, another mitigating circumstance appears to have been that Thailand's right of defence was not infringed.[36] The AB referred to these mitigating factors as 'the facts and circumstances of the case'.[37] In this regard the AB also specifically noted that Thailand requested neither a preliminary ruling with respect to Articles 2 and 3[38] nor any clarification, before Poland filed its first written submission.[39] Similarly, in light of 'the facts and circumstances' of the case, Poland's reference to Article 5 ADA was sufficient to meet the minimum requirements of Article 6.2 DSU.[40] The AB also noted that the procedural DSU rules should not be abused to develop litigation techniques.[41]

The AB jurisprudence enhances transparency and due process. Regrettably, however, the AB has left the door open for panels to make exceptions to the sensible rule on the ground that the respondent's right of defence is not impeded by doing so. The exception requires judgment calls by panels, and different panels may adopt different views. However, where specific articles are not mentioned in the REP, claims pertaining to those articles will be routinely rejected.[42]

4.4 Establishment and Composition of Panels

Once the REP has been made, the panel shall be established no later than at the DSB meeting following that at which the request first appeared on the agenda[43] – unless at that meeting the DSB decides by consensus not to

---

[35] *Thailand–H-Beams from Poland*, AB, para 91.
[36] *Thailand–H-Beams from Poland*, AB, para 95.
[37] *Thailand–H-Beams from Poland*, AB, para 92. One may wonder whether imprecision with respect to dumping claims is justified by the other party's belated information on injury.
[38] *Thailand–H-Beams from Poland*, AB, para 95.
[39] *Thailand–H-Beams from Poland*, AB, para 97.
[40] *Thailand–H-Beams from Poland*, AB, para 93.
[41] *Thailand–H-Beams from Poland*, Panel, para 97.
[42] See, eg, *Egypt–Rebar from Turkey*, Panel, para 7.141.   [43] Art 6.1 DSU.

establish a panel.[44] There is no compelling justification as to why panels cannot be established immediately upon request; the loss of time involved by waiting for the next DSB meeting seems unnecessary.

Article 8 DSU provides procedural guidance as to the composition of panels. Normally, panels consist of three members. If the parties to the dispute so agree within 10 days of the establishment of the panel, the membership of the panel may be raised to five.[45] This has never happened thus far.

Article 8.7 DSU provides that where there is no agreement on the panellists within 20 days of the date of establishment of a panel, the Director-General, at the request of either party – in consultation with the Chairman of the DSB and the Chairman of the relevant Council or Committee – shall appoint the panellists.[46] Article 8.10 DSU provides that when a dispute is between a developing country member and a developed country member, the panel shall include at least one panellist from a developing country member – if the developing country member so requests.

4.5 Function of Panels and Terms of Reference

In accordance with Article 11 DSU, the panel must make an objective assessment of the *matter* before it – including an objective assessment of the facts of the case and the applicability of and conformity with the relevant Covered Agreements, and make such other findings as will assist the DSB in making the recommendations or in giving the rulings provided for in the Covered Agreements.

Article 7 DSU deals with the terms of reference on the basis of which the panels must arrive at their findings. Unless agreed otherwise by the parties to the dispute within 20 days of the date of their establishment, panels shall have standard terms of reference.[47] Per Article 7.1 DSU these standard terms are:

Standard terms of reference for panels
To examine, in light of the relevant provisions in (name of the Covered Agreement(s) cited by the parties to the dispute), the matter referred to the DSB by (name of party) in document ... and to make such findings as will assist the DSB in making the recommendations or in giving the rulings provided for in that/those agreement(s).

---

[44] So far this has not happened.   [45] Art 8.5 DSU.
[46] See, for example, *EC–Bed Linen from India*; *Guatemala–Cement from Mexico II*; *United States–DRAMS from Korea*.   [47] Art 7.1 DSU.

Since the 'document' to which Article 7.1 refers is the REP, Article 7.1 underlines the importance of properly identifying the measure and claims in that document. Failure to do so undermines meaningful terms of reference, the importance of which was emphasized by the AB in *Brazil–Coconut*:

First, terms of reference fulfil an important due process objective – they give the parties and third parties sufficient information concerning the claims at issue in the dispute in order to allow them an opportunity to respond to the complainant's case. Second, they establish the jurisdiction of the Panel by defining the precise claims at issue in the dispute.[48]

4.6 Submissions to and Meetings with the Panel

Article 12 DSU, in conjunction with Appendix 3 of the DSU, sets forth the practical working procedures and timetable for the panel and the parties. The working procedures contained in that Appendix are relatively vague, but panels do have the power to establish their own working procedures.[49]

From the date of composition and agreement on the terms of reference, panels have in principle six months to provide their report;[50] in any case this period should not exceed nine months.[51]

Typically, the complaining party will have three to six weeks to provide its first written submission.[52] This first submission will form one of the most important elements on which the panel will decide since the submission normally contains all arguments in support of the claims.

The first written submission of the respondent forms the most important element of its defence, for which it will typically have only two to three weeks. This imbalance in time seems an unfair element in the typical working procedures – from an 'equality of arms' perspective. There seems no compelling argument why a respondent should have less time to provide its views as compared with a complainant which, moreover, would probably have started to prepare its first written submission before the REP had actually been filed.[53]

---

[48] *Brazil–Coconut from the Philippines*, AB, para 22.   [49] Art 12.1 DSU.

[50] Art 12.8 DSU.

[51] Art 12.9 DSU. The nine month period of Art 12.9 refers to the date of establishment of the panel until the date of circulation of the panel report to WTO members; this period is therefore counted on the basis of different reference dates than the six month period of Art 12.8. We note that there is no sanction on this deadline. For example, in *EC–Bananas* the examination of the panel took 12 months.   [52] Point 12 of App 3 to DSU (working procedures).

[53] Indeed, in light of Art 9.4 DSU one may wonder why three to six weeks are normally considered 'sufficient time' for a complainant while 'sufficient time' for a respondent is two to three weeks.

The first substantive meeting of the panel with the parties, which follows these first written submissions, constitutes a second crucial element in the dispute settlement proceeding. At this meeting both parties orally present their case and at that time the panel will have its first chance to put questions to the parties.[54] In addition, parties can put questions to each other. Following the meeting, these (and other) questions are often reproduced in writing.

The entire process is then 'repeated' in a second round of rebuttal submissions and a subsequent second meeting with the parties. Since this is the last chance for both parties to make their views known – apart from possible answers to follow-up questions – this second round has its own importance. It should be noted that the rebuttal submissions from both parties have to be filed simultaneously, which implies that a complainant can only react once (to the first written submission of the respondent) while the respondent has *de facto* two opportunities to provide a written defence against the first written submission of the applicant.

The practical effect of the imbalance in time periods for the first written submissions and the identical deadline for the rebuttal submissions is that some of the emphasis shifts towards the oral presentations in the first and second meetings with the panel. The complaining party will try to react to the first written submission of the respondent during the first meeting with the panel while both parties will react to each other's rebuttals during the second meeting with the panel.

One important practical aspect of the meetings of the parties with the panel is the parties' choice of representation, notably the use of non-governmental experts. The AB in *EC–Bananas* clarified that it is the sovereign right of a WTO member to determine the composition of its delegation in WTO dispute settlement proceedings. It found nothing in the WTO Agreement, the DSU or the working procedures, nor in customary international law or the prevailing practice of international tribunals, which would prevent a WTO member from determining the composition of its delegation in Appellate Body proceedings.[55] This ruling of the AB represented a significant break with past GATT practice where WTO members such as the US and the EC sometimes objected to other members' having outside legal counsel in the room during meetings with the panel. These objections under GATT practice would, if they had been endorsed under the WTO dispute settlement process,

---

[54] Point 8 of App 3 (working procedures) to the DSU.

[55] It may be noted that although technically the AB did not rule on the issue whether private counsel can participate in hearings during the Panel phase, it seems likely that the AB would overrule panels refusing such participation.

have disadvantaged smaller, less experienced members (indeed, the country concerned in *EC–Bananas* was Saint Lucia), which might not necessarily have sufficient in-house expertise.

In *Brazil–Aircraft 21.5 II*, a new question arose relating to the role of persons advising the government but which were not members of the official delegation.[56] Canada had shared submissions, statements and exhibits with lawyers of a private law firm.[57] The lawyers formed part of Canada's litigation team and were advisors to the Government of Canada, while a Canadian regional aircraft manufacturer had also retained the same law firm. The issue facing the panel was whether it was permissible for Canada to share Brazil's oral statement and other documents submitted to the panel in the meeting with these advisors, ie the members of the private law firm. The panel saw nothing in Article 1.2 of the DSU, or any other provision of the DSU, to suggest that confidential information may only be shared with members of the official delegation.[58] The panel also drew support from its working procedures, which imposed a confidentiality obligation on advisors outside the delegation. That provision would be pointless if it would be impermissible to share information with such advisors. Accordingly, the panel found that Canada had not acted inconsistently with the requirements of the DSU or the working procedures of the panel.

4.7 Confidentiality

The above-described situations concerning the composition of official delegations and their (outside) advisors illustrates the sensitivity of WTO members regarding confidentiality and the protection of business confidential information. Apart from the important prohibition on *ex parte* communications with the panel and the AB[59] which exists all through a dispute settlement proceeding, confidentiality surfaces at various stages and in various forms.

In the preliminary stages of a proceeding, confidentiality provisions safeguard the consultation stage[60] and proceedings involving good offices, conciliation

---

[56] *Brazil–Aircraft from Canada*, 21.5 Panel II, paras 3.1–3.15. See also Hernandez-Lopez, 'Recent Trends and Perspectives for Non-State Actor Participation in WTO Disputes' (2001) 35 JWT 499.

[57] Brazil did not submit any business confidential information and Canada mentioned that if such information had been submitted it would not have given this to the individuals of the litigation team.

[58] *Brazil–Aircraft from Canada*, 21.5 Panel II, para 3.7. The position of advisors – who are allowed access to the oral statement – is therefore different from that of observers wishing to attend a meeting with the panel; in *United States–Bismuth Steel* (para 6.2) such participation was not allowed.

[59] Art 18.1 DSU. [60] Art 4.6 DSU.

and mediation.[61] Article 18.2 directs itself to all involved in a panel and AB proceeding and sets forth certain basic principles surrounding confidentiality:

Article 18.2 DSU

Written submissions to the Panel or the Appellate Body shall be treated as confidential, but shall be made available to the parties to the dispute. Nothing in this Understanding shall preclude a party to a dispute from disclosing statements of its own positions to the public. Members shall treat as confidential information submitted by another Member to the Panel or the Appellate Body which that Member has designated as confidential. A party to a dispute shall also, upon request of a Member, provide a non-confidential summary of the information contained in its written submissions that could be disclosed to the public.

Article 14.1 DSU addresses the panel and adds that the deliberations of the panel shall be confidential. Article 13.1 DSU clarifies that confidential information, which is provided in response to a panel request, shall not be revealed without formal authorization from the individual, body, or authorities of the WTO member providing the information. Article 17.10 specifically deals with the Appellate Body stage.[62]

Articles 17.10 and 18.2 apply to all WTO members, and oblige them to maintain the confidentiality of any submissions or information submitted, or received.[63] The AB has also noted that these provisions oblige members to ensure that confidentiality is fully respected by any person that a member selects to act as its representative, counsel or consultant:

We would like to emphasize that all members of parties' delegations – whether or not they are government employees – are present as representatives of their governments, and as such are subject to the provisions of the DSU and of the standard working procedures, including Articles 18.1 and 18.2 of the DSU and paragraphs 2 and 3 of those procedures. In particular, parties are required to treat as confidential all submissions to the Panel and all information so designated by other Members; and, in addition, the Panel meets in closed session. Accordingly, we expect that all delegations will fully respect those obligations and will treat these proceedings with the utmost circumspection and discretion.[64]

---

[61] Art 5.2 DSU.

[62] As regards Art 17.10, the Appellate Body in *Canada–Civilian Aircraft from Brazil*, AB, para 143, clarified that the word *proceedings* in an Appellate Proceeding should be taken to include:

. . . any written submissions, legal memoranda, written responses to questions, and oral statements by the participants and the third participants; the conduct of the oral hearing before the Appellate Body, including any transcripts or tapes of that hearing; and the deliberations, the exchange of views and internal workings of the Appellate Body.

[63] *Canada–Civilian Aircraft from Brazil*, AB, para 145.
[64] *Canada–Civilian Aircraft from Brazil*, AB, para 145.

In addition to these general confidentiality provisions of the DSU, Article 17.7 ADA provides that confidential information provided to the panel shall not be disclosed without formal authorization from the person, body or authority providing such information.[65]

4.8 Burden of Proof

In general, WTO law provides that the burden of proof rests upon the party, whether complaining or defending, which asserts the affirmative of a particular claim or defence. If that party provides sufficient evidence to raise a presumption that what is claimed is true, the burden then shifts to the other party, which will fail unless it adduces sufficient evidence to rebut the presumption.[66] Thus, a claimant is obliged to present a *prima facie* case. The Appellate Body has defined a *prima facie* case as a case that, in the absence of effective refutation by the defending party, requires a panel, as a matter of law, to rule in favour of the complaining party presenting the *prima facie* case.[67]

It should be noted that certain provisions in the GATT, such as Articles XX and XI:1, contain so-called *affirmative defences*, in which the party invoking the *defence* has the burden of establishing it. In the context of the ADA, for example, one could argue that whereas Article 6.8 permits authorities to make determinations on the basis of the facts available, this is not so if the interested

---

[65] In *Thailand–H-Beams from Poland*, Panel, Thailand invoked this provision to submit certain confidential submissions only to the panel, but not to other parties. Poland and certain third parties argued that this constituted an *ex parte* communication and rested on a wrong reading of Art 17.7 ADA. The panel invited the parties to comment on this aspect. Basically, the question came down to the issue whether Art 17.7 ADA derogates from the general confidentiality provisions of the DSU and allows for a derogation to the prohibition on *ex parte* communications under specific circumstances, or whether the Article was merely a reflection of the general principles of confidentiality enshrined in the DSU (but not derogating from the prohibition on *ex parte* communications). The panel noted that the issue was a complex one (*Thailand–H-Beams from Poland*, Panel, Annex 4.1) but eventually was able avoid the question since the parties agreed on supplemental working procedures concerning such specific confidential information.

On appeal, the same proceeding addressed one further issue of confidentiality; in that instance the appellant submission of Thailand appeared not to have been treated in confidence by all parties involved. The Appellate Body noted that there was a *prima facie* case that the confidentiality provisions of Art 17.10 and 18.2 DSU might have been infringed (*Thailand–H-Beams from Poland*, AB paras 68 and 74.) As a result Poland accepted the withdrawal of its legal counsel and the Appellate Body rejected the *amicus curiae* brief which had used the confidential information (but which the AB did not find relevant to its task in any event).

[66] *United States–Shirts and Blouses*, AB, p 16. Confirmed in *EC–Hormones*, AB, para 109.

[67] *EC–Hormones*, AB, para 104.

party can prove that it acted to the best of its ability in the sense of point 5 of Annex II.

Burden of proof has been described as a procedural concept that speaks to the fair and orderly management and disposition of a dispute. As such, it must not be confused with the drawing of inferences from facts.[68]

For applicants challenging an anti-dumping measure, the burden of proof may constitute a more formidable hurdle than in other areas of WTO law. This is for two reasons. First, these types of cases are fact-rich and often fact-decisive. At the same time, the respondent, ie the WTO member that imposed the measure, often has a monopoly position as the possessor of *all* facts because of the confidentiality systems that prevail in most jurisdictions.[69] Such confidentiality systems preclude applicants from gaining access to factual information with regard to which confidential treatment has been claimed, either by the respondent member or its domestic industry.[70] Non-confidential summaries tend to be so vague as to be meaningless.

The problem is most acute with regard to the pre-initiation determination of standing,[71] not only because the determination relies entirely on confidential information supplied by the petitioning domestic industry and confidential analysis thereof by the domestic authorities, but also because often few details regarding this standing determination are provided in the notice of initiation of the proceeding.

Even though the standing provisions impose positive obligations on the administering authorities, panels have assigned the burden of proof of establishing a *prima facie* case to the applicant. The respondent therefore has the strategic advantage that it can decide whether to provide such information to the Panel and, if so, which portions. While a panel can resort to Article 13.1 of the DSU, it is often reluctant to do so in practice. And even if it does resort to Article 13.1 this does not always shed the necessary light on the questions to be resolved since parties do not always answer. These facts give respondents – with sole access to confidential information – an unfair advantage in WTO dispute settlement, which is disproportionately important in commercial defence cases and affects due process and fair play. In appropriate cases the burden of proof could be shifted to the *respondent*. Alternatively, the possibility could be created

---

[68] *Canada–Civilian Aircraft from Brazil*, AB, para 198.   [69] See section 3.2.5.6, above.
[70] Compare Horlick and Clarke, 'Standards for Panels Reviewing Anti-Dumping Determinations under the GATT and the WTO', in Petersman (ed), *International Trade Law and the GATT/WTO Dispute Settlement System* (1997) 315, 321 who make the same point with respect to the zeroing issue, as decided by the GATT panels in *EC–Audio tapes in cassettes from Japan* and *United States–Salmon from Norway*.   [71] See section 3.1.3, above.

for applicants and the panel to obtain access to the full confidential file in the course of the panel proceeding.[72] The release of such confidential information could be subject to appropriate confidentiality provisions, applicable to both panellists and members of delegations.

4.9 The Record

As anti-dumping cases invariably involve confidential company-specific information, an important issue is the *pool of information* that the panel should consider. A related, preliminary, question is when such information needs to be submitted to a panel.

The DSU does not specifically set forth a time limit as to *when* information (evidence) should be submitted. Article 12.1 directs a panel to follow the working procedures of the DSU. These working procedures specify in point 4 that parties to the dispute shall transmit to the panel, *before* the first substantive meeting, the written submissions in which they present the facts of the case and their arguments. In practice this requirement is not always interpreted strictly.[73]

As regards the question of *what* information can be considered, the DSU does not provide specific guidance. Obviously, the question of what information can be considered is closely related to the *standard of review* that must be applied.

Under Articles 12 and 13 DSU it is the responsibility of the panel to determine the admissibility and relevance of the evidence proffered by the parties to a dispute. Article 17.5(ii) of the ADA, discussed below, provides more specific guidance in the context of an anti-dumping proceeding.

One may conceptually envisage three widening circles of information, depending on who has access to the information. The smallest circle consists of information, either provided by interested parties to the authorities on a confidential basis, or emanating from the authorities themselves (internal working documents, records of deliberations, etc.). This information is available only to the administering authority. The intermediate circle would cover documents provided to interested parties by the administering authority,

---

[72] Currently, it happens often (*Mexico–HFCS from the United States*; *Thailand–H-Beams from Poland*; *United States–Wheat Gluten*) that the respondent, in trying to justify its measures, will wish to provide confidential information to the panel, but not to the opposing party. Such *ex parte* communications are not allowed. The respondent then has the choice to either withdraw the offer, or to provide the information to both the panel and the opposing party, if necessary, under specially drafted confidentiality provisions. The problem we signal *here*, however, is that the respondent will only proffer the information that suits its case.   [73] *Argentina–Footwear from the EC*, AB, para 79.

for example, disclosure comments, verification and hearing reports. The widest circle would consist of published determinations and other public information, theoretically available to all.

Panels have typically held that they will consider 'evidence on the record'. Clearly, this encompasses the second and third circle. The difficult question is whether information in the first circle forms part of the record.

The AB addressed this question in *Thailand–H-Beams* where it drew a distinction between the *evidence* that a panel may consider, and the procedural and evidentiary safeguards laid down in Articles 6 and 12 of the ADA.[74] In *Thailand–H-Beams* the AB did *not* find anything in Articles 3.1 and 17.6(i) that would preclude the authorities or panels reviewing the authorities' record, from taking into account confidential information not communicated to interested parties in the course of the administrative proceeding, thereby overruling the relevant panel finding.[75] On the other hand, the AB simultaneously noted that both Articles 6 and 12 ADA imposed important procedural and due process obligations upon authorities, which might form the basis for claims.[76] Thus, the AB emphasized the importance of possible Article 6 and Article 12 claims in such cases.

As regards what we termed the 'intermediate (second) circle' of evidence, a panel in an anti-dumping proceeding will find guidance in Article 17.5(ii) which provides that panels must examine the matter on the basis of the facts made available in conformity with appropriate domestic procedures to the authorities of the importing WTO member. For example, the panel in *US–Hot Rolled Steel* determined it may not consider *facts or evidence* presented to it by a WTO member in an attempt to demonstrate errors in the determination concerning questions that were investigated and decided by the authorities, unless these facts had been made available in conformity with the appropriate domestic procedures to the authorities of the investigating country during the investigation.[77] In *United States–Steel plate*, on the other hand, the panel did allow India to submit affidavits prepared by a former DOC official. In the view

---

[74] *Thailand–H-Beams from Poland*, AB, para 117.

[75] *Thailand–H-Beams from Poland*, AB, para 118. Compare *Egypt–Rebar from Turkey*, Panel, para 7.113.   [76] *Thailand–H-Beams from Poland*, AB, para 117.

[77] *United States–Hot rolled steel from Japan*, Panel, para 7.6. See also *Egypt–Rebar from Turkey*, Panel, para 7.21; *United States–CDSOA (Byrd Amendment)*, AB, paras 221–222; *United States–Softwood lumber from Canada II*, AB, para 9; *Guatemala–Cement from Mexico II*, Panel, para 8.19. WorldTradeLaw.net, *Dispute Settlement Commentary on Guatemala–Cement II*, p 25, checked on 23 April 2005, observes that the panel in that case broke its own rule by examining a notarial deed submitted by Mexico to the panel, which was not part of the record and had never been shown to the Guatemalan authorities in the course of the administrative proceeding.

of the panel, these affidavits did not constitute new evidence but rather 'something in the nature of expert opinion'.[78]

Other panels have ruled that they will not take into account *ex post* rationalizations submitted to the panel by the authorities in order to justify their administrative findings.[79]

4.10 Right to Seek Information/Adverse Inferences

Article 13 DSU provides that a panel shall have the right to seek information and technical advice from any individual or body, which it deems appropriate. The Article obliges members to respond promptly and fully to any such requests. As obvious as it seems, it should be pointed out that the AB has ruled that this right of the panel is a discretionary authority, not an obligation.[80] In this connection, the AB also noted that the panel has discretion *how* to seek expert advice.[81]

In practice, most panels have appeared reluctant to actively seek information beyond the record before them; one reason may be that the submissions of the parties tend to be fairly complete in the first place. Another likely explanation is that the panel phase still has relics of a diplomacy-based dispute settlement system where a panel may be reluctant to go beyond arguments made and evidence provided by the parties to the dispute.[82]

Problematic is the situation where panels *do* seek such information but members refuse to comply with such requests. In proceedings such as *Canada–Civilian Aircraft* and *US–Wheat Gluten*, members refused to comply with information requests of the panel. Nevertheless, this did not lead the panels to draw any specific '*adverse*' inference from the member's failure to cooperate. In both appeals, the AB refused to reverse the panel's refusal to draw adverse inferences. In both instances, however, the Appellate Body condemned the members who refused to provide information.

In *Canada–Civilian aircraft*, the Appellate Body found the justifications of Canada for its refusal to provide requested information 'less than

---

[78] *United States–Steel plate from India*, Panel, para 7.13. See also the discussion in WorldTradeLaw.net, *Dispute Settlement Commentary on United States–India Steel plate*, pp 12–13, checked on 23 April 2005.

[79] *Guatemala–Cement from Mexico II*; *Argentina–Ceramic floor tiles from Italy*; *Argentina–Poultry from Brazil*.   [80] *Argentina–Footwear from Italy*, AB, paras 84–86.

[81] *EC–Hormones*, AB, para 147.

[82] Indeed, in *Australia–Automotive Leather 21.5* where the panel did go beyond the arguments made (and findings sought) by the parties to the dispute, it was criticized not only by the parties concerned, but also by many other WTO members in the relevant DSB meeting.

persuasive'.[83] However, this did not mean that an adverse inference should automatically follow. The absence of such inference would only have been wrong if the panel had erred or abused its authority.[84]

In *United States–Wheat Gluten* a similar situation arose. The panel had requested that the US provide it with certain information. The US did not comply with this request and maintained that the information constituted business confidential information that it was entitled to withhold, under Article 3.2 of the ASG.[85] On appeal the EC posited that the failure to provide the requested information should have led the panel to draw adverse inferences with respect to a number of different issues, in particular 'productivity' and 'profits and losses'.[86] The Appellate Body criticized the United States for its failure to comply with the panel because such refusal seriously undermined the ability of a panel to make an objective assessment of the facts and the matter, as required by Article 11 of the DSU. As the panel had acknowledged that having had access to the information requested from the US would have facilitated an objective assessment of the facts, the AB deplored the conduct of the US.[87]

Subsequently, the Appellate Body explained in detail why it did not reverse the finding of the panel. First, it again recalled that the drawing of inferences is a discretionary task falling within a panel's duties under Article 11 of the DSU.[88] The Appellate Body then recalled that Article 11 of the DSU provides that a panel must draw inferences on the basis of all the facts of record. The refusal of a party to comply with a request for information by a panel under Article 13.1 is only one such fact although it is an 'important fact'. The panel had therefore correctly included other facts of record in order to make an objective assessment. Accordingly, the Appellate Body rejected the EC's argument that the panel erred in not drawing adverse inferences.[89]

The Appellate Body recalled that its task is not to redo the panel's assessment of the facts of record and decide what inferences it itself would draw from them. Rather, it must determine whether the panel improperly exercised its

---

[83] *Canada–Civilian Aircraft from Brazil*, AB, para 196. For a different perspective see Behboodi, 'Should' Means 'Shall': A Critical Analysis of the Obligation to Submit Information under Article 13.1 DSU in the Canada–Aircraft Case (2000) 3 JIEL 563. Behboodi notes at 569–570 that

...such refusals were never made outright, were clearly explained and placed in context, and were carefully balanced against other countervailing considerations, which, however, both the Panel and the Appellate Body elected to ignore.

[84] *Canada–Civilian Aircraft from Brazil*, AB, para 205.
[85] *United States–Wheat Gluten*, Panel, paras 8.7–8.12; and *United States–Wheat Gluten*, AB, para 168.
[86] *United States–Wheat Gluten*, AB, para 169.
[87] *United States–Wheat Gluten*, AB, para 171.
[88] *United States–Wheat Gluten*, AB, para 173.
[89] *United States–Wheat Gluten*, AB, para 174.

discretion under Article 11, by failing to draw certain inferences from the facts before it. In order for the AB to conduct such review, an appellant should at least:

- identify the facts on the record from which the panel should have drawn inferences;
- indicate the factual or legal inferences that the panel should have drawn from those facts; and
- explain why the failure of the panel to exercise its discretion by drawing these inferences amounts to an error of law under Article 11 of the DSU.[90]

The AB found that the EC had not met these three conditions because it had not been specific enough in identifying *which* facts supported a particular inference, *what inferences* should have been drawn and why the failure to draw inferences amounted to an error of law under Article 11 of the DSU.[91]

The AB has been criticized for its aversion to impose a 'penalty' on WTO members who do not comply with a panel's request for information.[92]

4.11 Amicus Curiae Briefs

Quite the reverse from the situation where a panel is not provided with the information it is looking for is the issue of *amicus curiae* briefs where panels, or the AB, are supplied with unsolicited information from parties which are not involved in the dispute. The AB held in *US–Shrimp* that such briefs may be submitted to a panel.[93] The practical impact of such briefs appears to have been limited thus far, although the practice raises important issues of principle, including the undermining of third party rights.[94]

Another occasion where *amicus curiae* briefs have led to controversy was in *Thailand–H-Beams* where it could be shown that the author of the *amicus curiae*

---

[90] *United States–Wheat Gluten*, AB, para 175.

[91] *United States–Wheat Gluten*, AB, para 176.

[92] Kuyper, 'The Appellate Body and the Facts' in Bronckers and Quick (eds), *New Directions in International Economic Law – Essays in Honour of John H. Jackson* (Kluwer, 2000) observes on p 321 that

[the] aversion from punishment or penalty is contradictory with the Appellate Body's eagerness to lay down a *duty* to provide requested information to the Panel. If such a duty is not obeyed, it would be quite normal that a punishment or penalty follows.

[93] *United States–Shrimp*, AB, para 108.

[94] Compare, eg, *EC–Bed Linen from India*, Panel, fn 10, where an *amicus curiae* brief was submitted but the panel did not take it into account, nor was it made available on the WTO website. See also, *United States–Softwood lumber from Canada I*, Panel, para 7.10, where the panel decided not to accept unsolicited *amicus curiae* submissions.

brief had had unauthorized access to the (confidential) appellant submission of Thailand.[95]

4.12 Judicial Economy

In *United States–Shirts and Blouses* the AB reconfirmed prior GATT panels' practice with respect to the principle of judicial economy as regards claims.[96] The AB held that a panel need only address those claims that must be addressed in order to resolve the matter in issue in the dispute.[97] Indeed, the AB considered that Article 3.2 DSU was not meant to encourage either panels or the Appellate Body to 'make law' by clarifying existing provisions of the WTO Agreement outside the context of resolving a particular dispute. In *EC–Poultry*, the AB clarified that judicial economy also extends to *arguments*.[98]

It should be noted, however, that the use of judicial economy is not unlimited; in *Australia–Salmon*, for example, the Appellate Body stated that to provide only a partial resolution of the matter at issue would be *false judicial economy*. A panel has to address those claims on which a finding is necessary to enable the DSB to make sufficiently precise recommendations and rulings so as to allow for prompt compliance by a member with those recommendations and rulings in order to ensure effective resolution of disputes to the benefit of all members.[99] These positions on judicial economy have been consistently applied since.[100]

While judicial economy is undoubtedly a traditional GATT principle and probably laudable in certain circumstances, it does increase, in conjunction with the lack of remand authority of the AB, the risk that the AB, faced with panel reasoning it does not agree with, is forced to interpret alternative provisions in both first and last resort.

The principle of judicial economy is a relic from the diplomacy-based GATT dispute settlement system, which should not have a place in the judicialized two-layered WTO system. In the absence of legislative guidance, parties might wish to exhort panels to rule on all claims, emphasizing the possibility of the panel being overruled by the AB on some points. In this sense, panel reports

---

[95] *Thailand–H-Beams from Poland*, AB, paras. 62–78. See also the discussion in World TradeLaw.net, *Dispute Settlement Commentary on Thailand–Steel*, pp 2–3, checked on 23 April 2005.

[96] Concerning judicial economy and other 'issue-avoidance techniques' see Davey, 'Has the WTO Dispute Settlement System Exceeded its Authority?' (2001) 4 JIEL 79.

[97] *United States–Shirts and Blouses*, AB, 21.   [98] *EC–Poultry*, AB, para 135.

[99] *Australia–Salmon*, AB, para 223.

[100] See for a recent case *Mexico–Rice from the United States*.

such as *Brazil–Aircraft 21.5 II*, where the panel *recognized but refused to apply* judicial economy, appear commendable.[101]

This conclusion seems especially pertinent in a situation where a material inconsistency claim is coupled to a public notice[102] claim. In the current system of judicial economy, where a panel rejects a substantive claim, it may also reject claims related to Article 12.2 on that issue.[103] Obversely, where the panel awards a claim, it might consider an Article 12.2 claim to be superfluous.[104] However, the substantive violation and the public notice violation are two separate issues. For example, if the Appellate Body were to overturn an affirmative panel finding on a substantive claim (for example an Article 3.4 inconsistency), a party would be left empty-handed, even though it did bring the concomitant Article 12 claim properly before the panel. Such logic may create a legal vacuum. Indeed, arguably because of this, parties have, on occasion, been forced to bring conditional appeals with respect to claims which the panel did not consider as a result of application of judicial economy.[105]

4.13 Interim Review

Before presenting its final report, the panel issues an interim report. Article 15 DSU deals with this interim review stage.[106] One can distinguish two phases in this stage. First the panel will issue the descriptive part focusing on factual aspects of the draft report (including the arguments of the parties).[107] Parties will have a certain period to comment on this factual part. After this phase, the panel will issue the interim report proper including the draft findings and conclusions of the panel.[108] Again, parties will have a certain period to comment on this interim report and they may also request a meeting with the panel to discuss the interim report. After these phases the panel will issue its final report which will include a discussion of the arguments made at the interim review stage.[109]

Parties will often focus on the factual (descriptive) part, with a view to getting the facts right in case of a possible appeal. By contrast, parties have been

---

[101] *Brazil–Aircraft from Canada*, Panel 21.5 II, paras 5.56 and 5.208.

[102] See section 3.6, above.   [103] For example, *EC–Bed Linen from India*.

[104] See section 3.6, above, and, for example, *EC–Bed Linen* paras 6.259 and 6.261. But see *Mexico–HFCS* where the Panel, in addition to the substantive claims, also ruled on the explanation claims; the Panel changed this approach in *Mexico–HFCS 21.5*, Panel.

[105] See, for example, *United States–Hot rolled steel from Japan*, AB, para 26.

[106] In addition, the working procedures will contain guidance as to the expected timeline in this connection.   [107] Art 15.1 DSU.

[108] Art 15.2 DSU.   [109] Art 15.3 DSU.

less inclined to challenge the findings and conclusions since there is the possibility for *appellate* review and because panels may not be inclined to change their mind at this stage.

4.14 Recommendations and Suggestions

Article 19.1 provides that where a panel or the Appellate Body conclude that a measure is inconsistent with a Covered Agreement, it shall recommend that the WTO member concerned bring the measure into conformity with that agreement. This is the only possible recommendation under the DSU. In addition, however, (non-legally binding) suggestions are possible.

WTO remedies are prospective (*ex nunc*) in nature. WTO law requires *cessation of wrongful conduct*, but not *reparations*.[110] On the basis of the same principle, as well as practical reasons,[111] WTO members such as the United States and the EC are opposed to revocation of measures or reimbursement of duties paid.[112]

A number of GATT AD[113] panels had recommended revocation of anti-dumping and countervailing measures as well as reimbursement of duties paid. In light of Article 19 DSU, such *recommendations* are no longer allowed. While *suggestions* to that effect are still possible, panels thus far have been reluctant to make such suggestions, rather limiting themselves to the Article 19 recommendation that the member concerned bring the measure into conformity with the Agreement found to have been violated.

In *Guatemala–Cement* and *Guatemala–Cement II*, however, the panel did suggest that Guatemala revoke the anti-dumping duties in light of the fundamental and pervasive nature of the violations found by the panel; however, in both cases it declined Mexico's request to recommend that Guatemala reimburse anti-dumping duties paid.[114] Similarly, in *Argentina–Poultry*, the panel suggested

---

[110]   See also Petersmann, 'How to Promote the International Rule of Law' (1998) JIEL 25.

[111]   Reimbursement would lead to a windfall profit for the importers, not necessarily the exporters; where exports have stopped as a result of the measure, reimbursement would not have any effect. See also Vermulst and Mizulin, 'Retroactivity of Remedies in the WTO' (2004) 1 Law and Economics in International Trade 53.

[112]   Palmeter and Mavroidis, *Dispute Settlement in the World Trade Organization: Practice and Procedure* (2nd edn 2004) 263.

[113]   *United States–Anti-Dumping Duties on Grey Portland Cement and Cement Clinker from Mexico*, paras 5.35–6.2, unadopted, ADP/82, 7 September 1992; *US–Imposition of Anti-Dumping Duties on imports of seamless stainless steel hollow products from Sweden*, paras 521–524, unadopted, ADP/47, 20 August 1990; *New Zealand–Imports of Electrical Transformers from Finland*, BISD. 32d Supp. at 70 (1986).

[114]   Even in *Guatemala–Cement from Guatemala II*, Panel, para 9.7, where the panel noted that Guatemala had maintained a WTO-inconsistent anti-dumping measure (on 16 counts) for a period of three and a half years, the panel declined to suggest that Guatemala refund the duties collected.

that Argentina repeal the measure 'in light of the nature and extent of the violations in this case.'[115] In *United States–Stainless steel plate in coils and stainless steel sheet and strip*, on the other hand, the panel refused to suggest that the United States revoke the order.[116] In *United States–Softwood lumber*, the panel took a similar approach.[117]

In *United States–1916 Act*, the panel suggested that one way for the United States to bring the Act in conformity with its WTO obligations would be to repeal it.[118] Similarly, in *United States–CDSOA (Byrd amendment)*, the panel suggested that the United States repeal the CDSOA.[119]

4.15 Adoption and Implementation

In order to provide sufficient time for the members to consider panel reports, the report cannot be adopted before 20 days after its circulation.[120] Article 16.2 DSU adds that if members have objections to the report, they will have to give their reasons in writing at least 10 days prior to the DSB meeting at which the panel report is to be considered[121]; in practice, however, it appears that any member will be allowed to express its views, regardless of whether the prior written notice was given. A panel report shall be adopted by the DSB within 60 days of the date of circulation to the WTO members, unless a party to the dispute notifies the DSB of its decision to appeal, or unless the DSB decides by consensus not to adopt the report.[122] An Appellate Body report shall be adopted by the DSB and unconditionally accepted by the parties to the dispute unless the DSB decides by consensus not to adopt the Appellate Body report within 30 days following its circulation to the members.[123] Once a panel report is adopted that recommends that a WTO member bring the measure into conformity with the Agreement found to have been violated, it is in first instance up to the member to decide how to do so.

---

[115] *Argentina–Poultry from Brazil*, Panel, para 8.7. The panel had also noted that the violations it had found were of a 'fundamental nature and pervasive.'

[116] *United States–Stainless steel plate in coils and stainless steel sheet and strip from Korea*, Panel, para 7.10.

[117] *United States–Softwood lumber from Canada*, Panel, para 8.8.

[118] *United States–1916 Act (Japan)*, Panel, para 6.292.

[119] *United States–CDSOA (Byrd amendment)*, Panel, para 8.6.   [120] Art 16.1 DSU.

[121] Art 16.2 DSU.   [122] Art 16.4 DSU.

[123] Art 17.14 DSU. This adoption procedure is without prejudice to the right of WTO members to express their views on an Appellate Body report. At this point the Report of the Panel which was appealed, and possibly amended by AB, is adopted simultaneously.

Article 21.1 DSU requires 'prompt compliance'[124] and at the DSB meeting
held within 30 days of adoption of the panel or Appellate Body report,[125] the
WTO member concerned must inform the DSB of its intentions in respect of
implementation. In situations where it is not practicable to implement immediately, that member shall have a reasonable period to do so. The Article then
lists three 'options' to determine such reasonable period.[126] The first option
requires the initiative of the member concerned and the approval of the
DSB.[127] The second option requires mutual agreement of the parties.[128]
Although the first two options are in theory hierarchical,[129] practice shows that
parties may first want to try to agree bilaterally on a reasonable period of time.
The third option is a fallback option in case neither the DSB nor the parties
can agree on a reasonable period. This third option provides for the possibility
of an arbitrator to determine the reasonable period of time. In case parties
cannot agree on an arbitrator within 10 days of referring the matter to arbitration, the Director-General shall appoint the arbitrator within another 10 days,
after consulting the parties.[130] Arbitration should last no longer than 90 days
after adoption of the DSB recommendations and rulings. Article 21.3(c)
provides as a guideline for the arbitrator that the reasonable period should
not exceed 15 months from the date of adoption of the panel or Appellate Body
report unless there are particular circumstances that would justify departure
from this guideline.[131]

In situations where there is disagreement as to the (level of) compliance
of the measures taken to comply with the recommendations and rulings of
the panel (or AB), such dispute shall be decided through recourse to dispute
settlement procedures.[132] In such situations, resort shall be had, wherever
possible, to the original panel. Such 21.5 Panels shall circulate their report
within 90 days of the matter being referred to it;[133] 21.5 panel reports may be
appealed to the AB.

---

[124] Paradoxically, the Art 21.3(c) arbitration procedure immediately largely emasculates the
promptness requirement by enabling an implementation period of as much as 15 months. If the
applicant party is not satisfied with the implementation, it may request the original Panel to
be re-convened. The Panel shall circulate its report within 90 days.

[125] Art 21.3, fn 11, provides that if no such meeting is scheduled, it will be held for such purpose.
[126] Art 21.3 DSU.   [127] Art 21.3(a) DSU.
[128] Art 21.3(b) DSU.
[129] Art 21.3(a) DSU provides that (b) only becomes applicable 'in the absence of such approval'.
[130] Art 21.3(c) DSU fn 12   [131] Art 21.3(c) DSU.
[132] Art 21.5 DSU. As the EC's request for an Article 21.5 procedure in the *EC–Bananas* case
showed, *either* party can initiate such action. See WT/DS27/40. Ecuador later filed its own request
(WT/DS27/41) but the DSB referred *both* requests to the original panel.
[133] In case the panel cannot meet this deadline it should inform the DSB in writing together with
the reasons for delay and the expected period within which it will submit its report.

As far as WTO dispute settlement cases against anti-dumping measures are concerned, the implementation stage thus far has not given rise to the type of high-visibility disputes and lack of implementation that has come up in other areas, such as the *Brazil–* and *Canada–Civil Aircraft* disputes, the *EC–Hormones* case and the *United States–FSC*. There has been need for the 21.5 procedures only twice, in *EC–Bed linen* and in *Mexico–HFCS*, and in both cases the members concerned implemented the findings of the 21.5 AB report, albeit after much time had passed. Because WTO remedies work only prospectively, this is, however, part of a more general problem.[134]

However, where anti-dumping disputes have involved challenges to statutory provisions, implementation has proven more cumbersome. The best example of this is *United States–CDSOA (Byrd amendment)*, where, as of the time of writing, the United States has not implemented the recommendation of the AB and various other countries have retaliated in return.

---

[134] See, eg, Durling, 'Deference, But Only When Due: WTO Review of Anti-Dumping Measures' (2003) 6 Journal of International Economic Law, 125, 146.

ANNEXES

ANNEX 1

Agreement on Implementation of Article VI
of the General Agreement on Tariffs and Trade 1994

Members hereby *agree* as follows:

PART I

Article 1. Principles

An anti-dumping measure shall be applied only under the circumstances provided for in Article VI of GATT 1994 and pursuant to investigations initiated[1] and conducted in accordance with the provisions of this Agreement. The following provisions govern the application of Article VI of GATT 1994 in so far as action is taken under anti-dumping legislation or regulations.

Article 2. Determination of Dumping

2.1 For the purpose of this Agreement, a product is to be considered as being dumped, i.e. introduced into the commerce of another country at less than its normal value, if the export price of the product exported from one country to another is less than the comparable price, in the ordinary course of trade, for the like product when destined for consumption in the exporting country.

2.2 When there are no sales of the like product in the ordinary course of trade in the domestic market of the exporting country or when, because of the particular market situation or the low volume of the sales in the domestic market of the exporting country[2], such sales do not permit a proper comparison, the margin of dumping shall be determined by comparison with a comparable price of the like product when exported to an appropriate third country, provided that this price is representative, or with the cost of production in the country of origin plus a reasonable amount for administrative, selling and general costs and for profits.

2.2.1 Sales of the like product in the domestic market of the exporting country or sales to a third country at prices below per unit (fixed and variable) costs of production plus

---

[1] The term 'initiated' as used in this Agreement means the procedural action by which a Member formally commences an investigation as provided in Article 5.

[2] Sales of the like product destined for consumption in the domestic market of the exporting country shall normally be considered a sufficient quantity for the determination of the normal value if such sales constitute 5 per cent or more of the sales of the product under consideration to the importing Member, provided that a lower ratio should be acceptable where the evidence demonstrates that domestic sales at such lower ratio are nonetheless of sufficient magnitude to provide for a proper comparison.

administrative, selling and general costs may be treated as not being in the ordinary course of trade by reason of price and may be disregarded in determining normal value only if the authorities[3] determine that such sales are made within an extended period of time[4] in substantial quantities[5] and are at prices which do not provide for the recovery of all costs within a reasonable period of time. If prices which are below per unit costs at the time of sale are above weighted average per unit costs for the period of investigation, such prices shall be considered to provide for recovery of costs within a reasonable period of time.

2.2.1.1 For the purpose of paragraph 2, costs shall normally be calculated on the basis of records kept by the exporter or producer under investigation, provided, that such records are in accordance with the generally accepted accounting principles of the exporting country and reasonably reflect the costs associated with the production and sale of the product under consideration. Authorities shall consider all available evidence on the proper allocation of costs, including that which is made available by the exporter or producer in the course of the investigation provided that such allocations have been historically utilized by the exporter or producer, in particular in relation to establishing appropriate amortization and depreciation periods and allowances for capital expenditures and other development costs. Unless already reflected in the cost allocations under this sub-paragraph, costs shall be adjusted appropriately for those non-recurring items of cost which benefit future and/or current production, or for circumstances in which costs during the period of investigation are affected by start-up operations.[6]

2.2.2 For the purpose of paragraph 2, the amounts for administrative, selling and general costs and for profits shall be based on actual data pertaining to production and sales in the ordinary course of trade of the like product by the exporter or producer under investigation. When such amounts cannot be determined on this basis, the amounts may be determined on the basis of:

(i) the actual amounts incurred and realized by the exporter or producer in question in respect of production and sales in the domestic market of the country of origin of the same general category of products;

(ii) the weighted average of the actual amounts incurred and realized by other exporters or producers subject to investigation in respect of production and sales of the like product in the domestic market of the country of origin;

---

[3] When in this Agreement the term 'authorities' is used, it shall be interpreted as meaning authorities at an appropriate senior level.

[4] The extended period of time should normally be one year but shall in no case be less than six months.

[5] Sales below per unit costs are made in substantial quantities when the authorities establish that the weighted average selling price of the transactions under consideration for the determination of the normal value is below the weighted average per unit costs, or that the volume of sales below per unit costs represents not less than 20 per cent of the volume sold in transactions under consideration for the determination of the normal value.

[6] The adjustment made for start-up operations shall reflect the costs at the end of the start-up period or, if that period extends beyond the period of investigation, the most recent costs which can reasonably be taken into account by the authorities during the investigation.

(iii) any other reasonable method, provided that the amount for profit so established shall not exceed the profit normally realized by other exporters or producers on sales of products of the same general category in the domestic market of the country of origin.

2.3 In cases where there is no export price or where it appears to the authorities concerned that the export price is unreliable because of association or a compensatory arrangement between the exporter and the importer or a third party, the export price may be constructed on the basis of the price at which the imported products are first resold to an independent buyer, or if the products are not resold to an independent buyer, or not resold in the condition as imported, on such reasonable basis as the authorities may determine.

2.4 A fair comparison shall be made between the export price and the normal value. This comparison shall be made at the same level of trade, normally at the ex-factory level, and in respect of sales made at as nearly as possible the same time. Due allowance shall be made in each case, on its merits, for differences which affect price comparability, including differences in conditions and terms of sale, taxation, levels of trade, quantities, physical characteristics, and any other differences which are also demonstrated to affect price comparability.[7] In the cases referred to in paragraph 3, allowances for costs, including duties and taxes, incurred between importation and resale, and for profits accruing, should also be made. If in these cases price comparability has been affected, the authorities shall establish the normal value at a level of trade equivalent to the level of trade of the constructed export price, or shall make due allowance as warranted under this paragraph. The authorities shall indicate to the parties in question what information is necessary to ensure a fair comparison and shall not impose an unreasonable burden of proof on those parties.

2.4.1 When the comparison under paragraph 4 requires a conversion of currencies, such conversion should be made using the rate of exchange on the date of sale,[8] provided that when a sale of foreign currency on forward markets is directly linked to the export sale involved, the rate of exchange in the forward sale shall be used. Fluctuations in exchange rates shall be ignored and in an investigation the authorities shall allow exporters at least 60 days to have adjusted their export prices to reflect sustained movements in exchange rates during the period of investigation.

2.4.2 Subject to the provisions governing fair comparison in paragraph 4, the existence of margins of dumping during the investigation phase shall normally be established on the basis of a comparison of a weighted average normal value with a weighted average of prices of all comparable export transactions or by a comparison of normal value and export prices on a transaction-to-transaction basis. A normal value established on a

---

[7] It is understood that some of the above factors may overlap, and authorities shall ensure that they do not duplicate adjustments that have been already made under this provision.

[8] Normally, the date of sale would be the date of contract, purchase order, order confirmation, or invoice, whichever establishes the material terms of sale.

weighted average basis may be compared to prices of individual export transactions if the authorities find a pattern of export prices which differ significantly among different purchasers, regions or time periods, and if an explanation is provided as to why such differences cannot be taken into account appropriately by the use of a weighted average-to-weighted average or transaction-to-transaction comparison.

2.5 In the case where products are not imported directly from the country of origin but are exported to the importing Member from an intermediate country, the price at which the products are sold from the country of export to the importing Member shall normally be compared with the comparable price in the country of export. However, comparison may be made with the price in the country of origin, if, for example, the products are merely trans-shipped through the country of export, or such products are not produced in the country of export, or there is no comparable price for them in the country of export.

2.6 Throughout this Agreement the term 'like product' ('produit similaire') shall be interpreted to mean a product which is identical, i.e. alike in all respects to the product under consideration, or in the absence of such a product, another product which, although not alike in all respects, has characteristics closely resembling those of the product under consideration.

2.7 This Article is without prejudice to the second Supplementary Provision to paragraph 1 of Article VI in Annex I to GATT 1994.

Article 3. Determination of Injury[9]

3.1 A determination of injury for purposes of Article VI of GATT 1994 shall be based on positive evidence and involve an objective examination of both (a) the volume of the dumped imports and the effect of the dumped imports on prices in the domestic market for like products, and (b) the consequent impact of these imports on domestic producers of such products.

3.2 With regard to the volume of the dumped imports, the investigating authorities shall consider whether there has been a significant increase in dumped imports, either in absolute terms or relative to production or consumption in the importing Member. With regard to the effect of the dumped imports on prices, the investigating authorities shall consider whether there has been a significant price undercutting by the dumped imports as compared with the price of a like product of the importing Member, or whether the effect of such imports is otherwise to depress prices to a significant degree or prevent price increases, which otherwise would have occurred, to a significant degree. No one or several of these factors can necessarily give decisive guidance.

---

[9] Under this Agreement the term 'injury' shall, unless otherwise specified, be taken to mean material injury to a domestic industry, threat of material injury to a domestic industry or material retardation of the establishment of such an industry and shall be interpreted in accordance with the provisions of this Article.

3.3 Where imports of a product from more than one country are simultaneously subject to anti-dumping investigations, the investigating authorities may cumulatively assess the effects of such imports only if they determine that (a) the margin of dumping established in relation to the imports from each country is more than de minimis as defined in paragraph 8 of Article 5 and the volume of imports from each country is not negligible and (b) a cumulative assessment of the effects of the imports is appropriate in light of the conditions of competition between the imported products and the conditions of competition between the imported products and the like domestic product.

3.4 The examination of the impact of the dumped imports on the domestic industry concerned shall include an evaluation of all relevant economic factors and indices having a bearing on the state of the industry, including actual and potential decline in sales, profits, output, market share, productivity, return on investments, or utilization of capacity; factors affecting domestic prices; the magnitude of the margin of dumping; actual and potential negative effects on cash flow, inventories, employment, wages, growth, ability to raise capital or investments. This list is not exhaustive, nor can one or several of these factors necessarily give decisive guidance.

3.5 It must be demonstrated that the dumped imports are, through the effects of dumping, as set forth in paragraphs 2 and 4, causing injury within the meaning of this Agreement. The demonstration of a causal relationship between the dumped imports and the injury to the domestic industry shall be based on an examination of all relevant evidence before the authorities. The authorities shall also examine any known factors other than the dumped imports which at the same time are injuring the domestic industry, and the injuries caused by these other factors must not be attributed to the dumped imports. Factors which may be relevant in this respect include inter alia the volume and prices of imports not sold at dumping prices, contraction in demand or changes in the patterns of consumption, trade restrictive practices of and competition between the foreign and domestic producers, developments in technology and the export performance and productivity of the domestic industry.

3.6 The effect of the dumped imports shall be assessed in relation to the domestic production of the like product when available data permit the separate identification of that production on the basis of such criteria as the production process, producers' sales and profits. If such separate identification of that production is not possible, the effects of the dumped imports shall be assessed by the examination of the production of the narrowest group or range of products, which includes the like product, for which the necessary information can be provided.

3.7 A determination of a threat of material injury shall be based on facts and not merely on allegation, conjecture or remote possibility. The change in circumstances which would create a situation in which the dumping would cause injury must be clearly foreseen and imminent.[10] In making a determination regarding the

---

[10] One example, though not an exclusive one, is that there is convincing reason to believe that there will be, in the near future, substantially increased importation of the product at dumped prices.

existence of a threat of material injury, the authorities should consider inter alia such factors as:

(i) a significant rate of increase of dumped imports into the domestic market indicating the likelihood of substantially increased importation;

(ii) sufficient freely disposable, or an imminent, substantial increase in, capacity of the exporter indicating the likelihood of substantially increased dumped exports to the importing Member's market, taking into account the availability of other export markets to absorb any additional exports;

(iii) whether imports are entering at prices that will have a significant depressing or suppressing effect on domestic prices, and would likely increase demand for further imports; and

(iv) inventories of the product being investigated.

No one of these factors by itself can necessarily give decisive guidance but the totality of the factors considered must lead to the conclusion that further dumped exports are imminent and that, unless protective action is taken, material injury would occur.

3.8 With respect to cases where injury is threatened by dumped imports, the application of anti-dumping measures shall be considered and decided with special care.

Article 4. Definition of Domestic Industry

4.1 For the purposes of this Agreement, the term 'domestic industry' shall be interpreted as referring to the domestic producers as a whole of the like products or to those of them whose collective output of the products constitutes a major proportion of the total domestic production of those products, except that:

(i) when producers are related[11] to the exporters or importers or are themselves importers of the allegedly dumped product, the term 'domestic industry' may be interpreted as referring to the rest of the producers;

(ii) in exceptional circumstances the territory of a Member may, for the production in question, be divided into two or more competitive markets and the producers within each market may be regarded as a separate industry if (a) the producers within such market sell all or almost all of their production of the product in question in that market, and (b) the demand in that market is not to any substantial degree supplied by producers of the product in question located elsewhere in the territory. In such circumstances, injury may be found to exist even where a major portion of the total domestic industry is not injured, provided there is a concentration of dumped imports into such an isolated market and provided

[11] For the purpose of this paragraph, producers shall be deemed to be related to exporters or importers only if (a) one of them directly or indirectly controls the other; or (b) both of them are directly or indirectly controlled by a third person; or (c) together they directly or indirectly control a third person, provided that there are grounds for believing or suspecting that the effect of the relationship is such as to cause the producer concerned to behave differently from non-related producers. For the purpose of this paragraph, one shall be deemed to control another when the former is legally or operationally in a position to exercise restraint or direction over the latter.

further that the dumped imports are causing injury to the producers of all or almost all of the production within such market.

4.2 When the domestic industry has been interpreted as referring to the producers in a certain area, i.e. a market as defined in paragraph 1 (ii), anti-dumping duties shall be levied[12] only on the products in question consigned for final consumption to that area. When the constitutional law of the importing Member does not permit the levying of anti-dumping duties on such a basis, the importing Member may levy the anti-dumping duties without limitation only if (a) the exporters shall have been given an opportunity to cease exporting at dumped prices to the area concerned or otherwise give assurances pursuant to Article 8 and adequate assurances in this regard have not been promptly given, and (b) such duties cannot be levied only on products of specific producers which supply the area in question.

4.3 Where two or more countries have reached under the provisions of paragraph 8(a) of Article XXIV of GATT 1994 such a level of integration that they have the characteristics of a single, unified market, the industry in the entire area of integration shall be taken to be the domestic industry referred to in paragraph 1.

4.4 The provisions of paragraph 6 of Article 3 shall be applicable to this Article.

Article 5. Initiation and Subsequent Investigation

5.1 Except as provided for in paragraph 6, an investigation to determine the existence, degree and effect of any alleged dumping shall be initiated upon a written application by or on behalf of the domestic industry.

5.2 An application under paragraph 1 shall include evidence of (a) dumping, (b) injury within the meaning of Article VI of GATT 1994 as interpreted by this Agreement and (c) a causal link between the dumped imports and the alleged injury. Simple assertion, unsubstantiated by relevant evidence, cannot be considered sufficient to meet the requirements of this paragraph. The application shall contain such information as is reasonably available to the applicant on the following:

(i) the identity of the applicant and a description of the volume and value of the domestic production of the like product by the applicant. Where a written application is made on behalf of the domestic industry, the application shall identify the industry on behalf of which the application is made by a list of all known domestic producers of the like product (or associations of domestic producers of the like product) and, to the extent possible, a description of the volume and value of domestic production of the like product accounted for by such producers;

(ii) a complete description of the allegedly dumped product, the names of the country or countries of origin or export in question, the identity of each known exporter or foreign producer and a list of known persons importing the product in question;

---

[12] As used in this Agreement 'levy' shall mean the definitive or final legal assessment or collection of a duty or tax.

(iii) information on prices at which the product in question is sold when destined for consumption in the domestic markets of the country or countries of origin or export (or, where appropriate, information on the prices at which the product is sold from the country or countries of origin or export to a third country or countries, or on the constructed value of the product) and information on export prices or, where appropriate, on the prices at which the product is first resold to an independent buyer in the territory of the importing Member.

(iv) information on the evolution of the volume of the allegedly dumped imports, the effect of these imports on prices of the like product in the domestic market and the consequent impact of the imports on the domestic industry, as demonstrated by relevant factors and indices having a bearing on the state of the domestic industry, such as those listed in paragraphs 2 and 4 of Article 3.

5.3 The authorities shall examine the accuracy and adequacy of the evidence provided in the application to determine whether there is sufficient evidence to justify the initiation of an investigation.

5.4 An investigation shall not be initiated pursuant to paragraph 1 unless the authorities have determined, on the basis of an examination of the degree of support for, or opposition to, the application expressed[13] by domestic producers of the like product, that the application has been made by or on behalf of the domestic industry.[14] The application shall be considered to have been made 'by or on behalf of the domestic industry' if it is supported by those domestic producers whose collective output constitutes more than 50 per cent of the total production of the like product produced by that portion of the domestic industry expressing either support for or opposition to the application. However, no investigation shall be initiated when domestic producers expressly supporting the application account for less than 25 per cent of total production of the like product produced by the domestic industry.

5.5 The authorities shall avoid, unless a decision has been made to initiate an investigation, any publicizing of the application for the initiation of an investigation. However, after receipt of a properly documented application and before proceeding to initiate an investigation, the authorities shall notify the government of the exporting Member concerned.

5.6 If, in special circumstances, the authorities concerned decide to initiate an investigation without having received a written application by or on behalf of a domestic industry for the initiation of such investigation, they shall proceed only if they have sufficient evidence of dumping, injury and a causal link, as described in paragraph 2, to justify the initiation of an investigation.

---

[13] In the case of fragmented industries involving an exceptionally large number of producers, authorities may determine support and opposition by using statistically valid sampling techniques.

[14] Members are aware that in the territory of certain Members employees of domestic producers of the like product or representatives of those employees may make or support an application for an investigation under paragraph 1.

5.7 The evidence of both dumping and injury shall be considered simultaneously *(a)* in the decision whether or not to initiate an investigation, and *(b)* thereafter, during the course of the investigation, starting on a date not later than the earliest date on which in accordance with the provisions of this Agreement provisional measures may be applied.

5.8 An application under paragraph 1 shall be rejected and an investigation shall be terminated promptly as soon as the authorities concerned are satisfied that there is not sufficient evidence of either dumping or of injury to justify proceeding with the case. There shall be immediate termination in cases where the authorities determine that the margin of dumping is *de minimis*, or that the volume of dumped imports, actual or potential, or the injury, is negligible. The margin of dumping shall be considered to be *de minimis* if this margin is less than 2 per cent, expressed as a percentage of the export price. The volume of dumped imports shall normally be regarded as negligible if the volume of dumped imports from a particular country is found to account for less than 3 per cent of imports of the like product in the importing Member, unless countries which individually account for less than 3 per cent of the imports of the like product in the importing Member collectively account for more than 7 per cent of imports of the like product in the importing Member.

5.9 An anti-dumping proceeding shall not hinder the procedures of customs clearance.

5.10 Investigations shall, except in special circumstances, be concluded within one year, and in no case more than 18 months, after their initiation.

Article 6. Evidence

6.1 All interested parties in an anti-dumping investigation shall be given notice of the information which the authorities require and ample opportunity to present in writing all evidence which they consider relevant in respect of the investigation in question.

6.1.1 Exporters or foreign producers receiving questionnaires used in an anti-dumping investigation shall be given at least 30 days for reply.[15] Due consideration should be given to any request for an extension of the 30-day period and, upon cause shown, such an extension should be granted whenever practicable.

6.1.2 Subject to the requirement to protect confidential information, evidence presented in writing by one interested party shall be made available promptly to other interested parties participating in the investigation.

6.1.3 As soon as an investigation has been initiated, the authorities shall provide the full text of the written application received under paragraph 1 of Article 5 to the known

---

[15] As a general rule, the time-limit for exporters shall be counted from the date of receipt of the questionnaire, which for this purpose shall be deemed to have been received one week from the date on which it was sent to the respondent or transmitted to the appropriate diplomatic representative of the exporting Member or, in the case of a separate customs territory Member of the WTO, an official representative of the exporting territory.

exporters[16] and to the authorities of the exporting Member and shall make it available, upon request, to other interested parties involved. Due regard shall be paid to the requirement for the protection of confidential information, as provided for in paragraph 5.

6.2 Throughout the anti-dumping investigation all interested parties shall have a full opportunity for the defence of their interests. To this end, the authorities shall, on request, provide opportunities for all interested parties to meet those parties with adverse interests, so that opposing views may be presented and rebuttal arguments offered. Provision of such opportunities must take account of the need to preserve confidentiality and of the convenience to the parties. There shall be no obligation on any party to attend a meeting, and failure to do so shall not be prejudicial to that party's case. Interested parties shall also have the right, on justification, to present other information orally.

6.3 Oral information provided under paragraph 2 shall be taken into account by the authorities only in so far as it is subsequently reproduced in writing and made available to other interested parties, as provided for in subparagraph 1.2.

6.4 The authorities shall whenever practicable provide timely opportunities for all interested parties to see all information that is relevant to the presentation of their cases, that is not confidential as defined in paragraph 5, and that is used by the authorities in an anti-dumping investigation, and to prepare presentations on the basis of this information.

6.5 Any information which is by nature confidential (for example, because its disclosure would be of significant competitive advantage to a competitor or because its disclosure would have a significantly adverse effect upon a person supplying the information or upon a person from whom that person acquired the information), or which is provided on a confidential basis by parties to an investigation shall, upon good cause shown, be treated as such by the authorities. Such information shall not be disclosed without specific permission of the party submitting it.[17]

6.5.1 The authorities shall require interested parties providing confidential information to furnish non-confidential summaries thereof. These summaries shall be in sufficient detail to permit a reasonable understanding of the substance of the information submitted in confidence. In exceptional circumstances, such parties may indicate that such information is not susceptible of summary. In such exceptional circumstances, a statement of the reasons why summarization is not possible must be provided.

6.5.2 If the authorities find that a request for confidentiality is not warranted and if the supplier of the information is either unwilling to make the information public or to authorize its disclosure in generalized or summary form, the authorities may

---

[16] It being understood that, where the number of exporters involved is particularly high, the full text of the written application should instead be provided only to the authorities of the exporting Member or to the relevant trade association.

[17] Members are aware that in the territory of certain Members disclosure pursuant to a narrowly-drawn protective order may be required.

disregard such information unless it can be demonstrated to their satisfaction from appropriate sources that the information is correct.[18]

6.6 Except in circumstances provided for in paragraph 8, the authorities shall during the course of an investigation satisfy themselves as to the accuracy of the information supplied by interested parties upon which their findings are based.

6.7 In order to verify information provided or to obtain further details, the authorities may carry out investigations in the territory of other Members as required, provided they obtain the agreement of the firms concerned and notify the representatives of the government of the Member in question, and unless that Member objects to the investigation. The procedures described in Annex I shall apply to investigations carried out in the territory of other Members. Subject to the requirement to protect confidential information, the authorities shall make the results of any such investigations available, or shall provide disclosure thereof pursuant to paragraph 9, to the firms to which they pertain and may make such results available to the applicants.

6.8 In cases in which any interested party refuses access to, or otherwise does not provide, necessary information within a reasonable period or significantly impedes the investigation, preliminary and final determinations, affirmative or negative, may be made on the basis of the facts available. The provisions of Annex II shall be observed in the application of this paragraph.

6.9 The authorities shall, before a final determination is made, inform all interested parties of the essential facts under consideration which form the basis for the decision whether to apply definitive measures. Such disclosure should take place in sufficient time for the parties to defend their interests.

6.10 The authorities shall, as a rule, determine an individual margin of dumping for each known exporter or producer concerned of the product under investigation. In cases where the number of exporters, producers, importers or types of products involved is so large as to make such a determination impracticable, the authorities may limit their examination either to a reasonable number of interested parties or products by using samples which are statistically valid on the basis of information available to the authorities at the time of the selection, or to the largest percentage of the volume of the exports from the country in question which can reasonably be investigated.

6.10.1 Any selection of exporters, producers, importers or types of products made under this paragraph shall preferably be chosen in consultation with and with the consent of the exporters, producers or importers concerned.

6.10.2 In cases where the authorities have limited their examination, as provided for in this paragraph, they shall nevertheless determine an individual margin of dumping for any exporter or producer not initially selected who submits the necessary information in time for that information to be considered during the course of the investigation, except where the number of exporters or producers is so large that individual examinations

---

[18] Members agree that requests for confidentiality should not be arbitrarily rejected.

would be unduly burdensome to the authorities and prevent the timely completion of the investigation. Voluntary responses shall not be discouraged.

6.11 For the purposes of this Agreement, 'interested parties' shall include:

(i) an exporter or foreign producer or the importer of a product subject to investigation, or a trade or business association a majority of the members of which are producers, exporters or importers of such product;

(ii) the government of the exporting Member; and

(iii) a producer of the like product in the importing Member or a trade and business association a majority of the members of which produce the like product in the territory of the importing Member.

This list shall not preclude Members from allowing domestic or foreign parties other than those mentioned above to be included as interested parties.

6.12 The authorities shall provide opportunities for industrial users of the product under investigation, and for representative consumer organizations in cases where the product is commonly sold at the retail level, to provide information which is relevant to the investigation regarding dumping, injury and causality.

6.13 The authorities shall take due account of any difficulties experienced by interested parties, in particular small companies, in supplying information requested, and shall provide any assistance practicable.

6.14 The procedures set out above are not intended to prevent the authorities of a Member from proceeding expeditiously with regard to initiating an investigation, reaching preliminary or final determinations, whether affirmative or negative, or from applying provisional or final measures, in accordance with relevant provisions of this Agreement.

Article 7. Provisional Measures

7.1 Provisional measures may be applied only if:

(i) an investigation has been initiated in accordance with the provisions of Article 5, a public notice has been given to that effect and interested parties have been given adequate opportunities to submit information and make comments;

(ii) a preliminary affirmative determination has been made of dumping and consequent injury to a domestic industry; and

(iii) the authorities concerned judge such measures necessary to prevent injury being caused during the investigation.

7.2 Provisional measures may take the form of a provisional duty or, preferably, a security – by cash deposit or bond – equal to the amount of the anti-dumping duty provisionally estimated, being not greater than the provisionally estimated margin of dumping. Withholding of appraisement is an appropriate provisional measure, provided that the normal duty and the estimated amount of the anti-dumping duty be indicated and as long as the withholding of appraisement is subject to the same conditions as other provisional measures.

7.3 Provisional measures shall not be applied sooner than 60 days from the date of initiation of the investigation.

7.4 The application of provisional measures shall be limited to as short a period as possible, not exceeding four months or, on decision of the authorities concerned, upon request by exporters representing a significant percentage of the trade involved, to a period not exceeding six months. When authorities, in the course of an investigation, examine whether a duty lower than the margin of dumping would be sufficient to remove injury, these periods may be six and nine months, respectively.

7.5 The relevant provisions of Article 9 shall be followed in the application of provisional measures.

Article 8. Price Undertakings

8.1 Proceedings may[19] be suspended or terminated without the imposition of provisional measures or anti-dumping duties upon receipt of satisfactory voluntary undertakings from any exporter to revise its prices or to cease exports to the area in question at dumped prices so that the authorities are satisfied that the injurious effect of the dumping is eliminated. Price increases under such undertakings shall not be higher than necessary to eliminate the margin of dumping. It is desirable that the price increases be less than the margin of dumping if such increases would be adequate to remove the injury to the domestic industry.

8.2 Price undertakings shall not be sought or accepted from exporters unless the authorities of the importing Member have made a preliminary affirmative determination of dumping and injury caused by such dumping.

8.3 Undertakings offered need not be accepted if the authorities consider their acceptance impractical, for example, if the number of actual or potential exporters is too great, or for other reasons, including reasons of general policy. Should the case arise and where practicable, the authorities shall provide to the exporter the reasons which have led them to consider acceptance of an undertaking as inappropriate, and shall, to the extent possible, give the exporter an opportunity to make comments thereon.

8.4 If an undertaking is accepted, the investigation of dumping and injury shall nevertheless be completed if the exporter so desires or the authorities so decide. In such a case, if a negative determination of dumping or injury is made, the undertaking shall automatically lapse, except in cases where such a determination is due in large part to the existence of a price undertaking. In such cases, the authorities may require that an undertaking be maintained for a reasonable period consistent with the provisions of this Agreement. In the event that an affirmative determination of dumping and injury is made, the undertaking shall continue consistent with its terms and the provisions of this Agreement.

---

[19] The word 'may' shall not be interpreted to allow the simultaneous continuation of proceedings with the implementation of price undertakings except as provided in paragraph 4.

8.5 Price undertakings may be suggested by the authorities of the importing Member, but no exporter shall be forced to enter into such undertakings. The fact that exporters do not offer such undertakings, or do not accept an invitation to do so, shall in no way prejudice the consideration of the case. However, the authorities are free to determine that a threat of injury is more likely to be realized if the dumped imports continue.

8.6 Authorities of an importing Member may require any exporter from whom an undertaking has been accepted to provide periodically information relevant to the fulfilment of such an undertaking and to permit verification of pertinent data. In case of violation of an undertaking, the authorities of the importing Member may take, under this Agreement in conformity with its provisions, expeditious actions which may constitute immediate application of provisional measures using the best information available. In such cases, definitive duties may be levied in accordance with this Agreement on products entered for consumption not more than 90 days before the application of such provisional measures, except that any such retroactive assessment shall not apply to imports entered before the violation of the undertaking.

Article 9. Imposition and Collection of Anti-Dumping Duties

9.1 The decision whether or not to impose an anti-dumping duty in cases where all requirements for the imposition have been fulfilled, and the decision whether the amount of the anti- dumping duty to be imposed shall be the full margin of dumping or less, are decisions to be made by the authorities of the importing Member. It is desirable that the imposition be permissive in the territory of all Members, and that the duty be less than the margin if such lesser duty would be adequate to remove the injury to the domestic industry.

9.2 When an anti-dumping duty is imposed in respect of any product, such anti-dumping duty shall be collected in the appropriate amounts in each case, on a non-discriminatory basis on imports of such product from all sources found to be dumped and causing injury, except as to imports from those sources from which price undertakings under the terms of this Agreement have been accepted. The authorities shall name the supplier or suppliers of the product concerned. If, however, several suppliers from the same country are involved, and it is impracticable to name all these suppliers, the authorities may name the supplying country concerned. If several suppliers from more than one country are involved, the authorities may name either all the suppliers involved, or, if this is impracticable, all the supplying countries involved.

9.3 The amount of the anti-dumping duty shall not exceed the margin of dumping as established under Article 2.

9.3.1 When the amount of the anti-dumping duty is assessed on a retrospective basis, the determination of the final liability for payment of anti-dumping duties shall take place as soon as possible, normally within 12 months, and in no case more than 18 months, after the date on which a request for a final assessment of the amount of the anti-dumping duty has been made.[20] Any refund shall be made promptly and normally in not more than 90 days following the determination of final liability made pursuant to this sub-paragraph. In any case, where a refund is not made within 90 days, the authorities shall provide an explanation if so requested.

9.3.2 When the amount of the anti-dumping duty is assessed on a prospective basis, provision shall be made for a prompt refund, upon request, of any duty paid in excess of the margin of dumping. A refund of any such duty paid in excess of the actual margin of dumping shall normally take place within 12 months, and in no case more than 18 months, after the date on which a request for a refund, duly supported by evidence, has been made by an importer of the product subject to the anti-dumping duty. The refund authorized should normally be made within 90 days of the above-noted decision.

9.3.3 In determining whether and to what extent a reimbursement should be made when the export price is constructed in accordance with paragraph 3 of Article 2, authorities should take account of any change in normal value, any change in costs incurred between importation and resale, and any movement in the resale price which is duly reflected in subsequent selling prices, and should calculate the export price with no deduction for the amount of anti-dumping duties paid when conclusive evidence of the above is provided.

9.4 When the authorities have limited their examination in accordance with the second sentence of paragraph 10 of Article 6, any anti-dumping duty applied to imports from exporters or producers not included in the examination shall not exceed:

(i) the weighted average margin of dumping established with respect to the selected exporters or producers or

(ii) where the liability for payment of anti-dumping duties is calculated on the basis of a prospective normal value, the difference between the weighted average normal value of the selected exporters or producers and the export prices of exporters or producers not individually examined,

provided that the authorities shall disregard for the purpose of this paragraph any zero and de minimis margins and margins established under the circumstances referred to in paragraph 8 of Article 6. The authorities shall apply individual duties or normal values to imports from any exporter or producer not included in the examination who has provided the necessary information during the course of the investigation, as provided for in subparagraph 10.2 of Article 6.

9.5 If a product is subject to anti-dumping duties in an importing Member, the authorities shall promptly carry out a review for the purpose of determining individual margins of dumping for any exporters or producers in the exporting country in question who have not exported the product to the importing Member during the period of

---

[20] It is understood that the observance of the time-limits mentioned in this subparagraph and in sub-paragraph 3.2 may not be possible where the product in question is subject to judicial review proceedings.

investigation, provided that these exporters or producers can show that they are not related to any of the exporters or producers in the exporting country who are subject to the anti-dumping duties on the product. Such a review shall be initiated and carried out on an accelerated basis, compared to normal duty assessment and review proceedings in the importing Member. No anti-dumping duties shall be levied on imports from such exporters or producers while the review is being carried out. The authorities may, however, withhold appraisement and/or request guarantees to ensure that, should such a review result in a determination of dumping in respect of such producers or exporters, anti-dumping duties can be levied retroactively to the date of the initiation of the review.

Article 10. Retroactivity

10.1 Provisional measures and anti-dumping duties shall only be applied to products which enter for consumption after the time when the decision taken under paragraph 1 of Article 7 and paragraph 1 of Article 9, respectively, enters into force, subject to the exceptions set out in this Article.

10.2 Where a final determination of injury (but not of a threat thereof or of a material retardation of the establishment of an industry) is made or, in the case of a final determination of a threat of injury, where the effect of the dumped imports would, in the absence of the provisional measures, have led to a determination of injury, anti-dumping duties may be levied retroactively for the period for which provisional measures, if any, have been applied.

10.3 If the definitive anti-dumping duty is higher than the provisional duty paid or payable, or the amount estimated for the purpose of the security, the difference shall not be collected. If the definitive duty is lower than the provisional duty paid or payable, or the amount estimated for the purpose of the security, the difference shall be reimbursed or the duty recalculated, as the case may be.

10.4 Except as provided in paragraph 2, where a determination of threat of injury or material retardation is made (but no injury has yet occurred) a definitive anti-dumping duty may be imposed only from the date of the determination of threat of injury or material retardation, and any cash deposit made during the period of the application of provisional measures shall be refunded and any bonds released in an expeditious manner.

10.5 Where a final determination is negative, any cash deposit made during the period of the application of provisional measures shall be refunded and any bonds released in an expeditious manner.

10.6 A definitive anti-dumping duty may be levied on products which were entered for consumption not more than 90 days prior to the date of application of provisional measures, when the authorities determine for the dumped product in question that:

(i) there is a history of dumping which caused injury or that the importer was, or should have been, aware that the exporter practises dumping and that such dumping would cause injury, and

(ii) the injury is caused by massive dumped imports of a product in a relatively short time which in light of the timing and the volume of the dumped imports and other circumstances (such as a rapid build-up of inventories of the imported product) is likely to seriously undermine the remedial effect of the definitive anti-dumping duty to be applied, provided that the importers concerned have been given an opportunity to comment.

10.7 The authorities may, after initiating an investigation, take such measures as the withholding of appraisement or assessment as may be necessary to collect anti-dumping duties retroactively, as provided for in paragraph 6, once they have sufficient evidence that the conditions set forth in that paragraph are satisfied.

10.8 No duties shall be levied retroactively pursuant to paragraph 6 on products entered for consumption prior to the date of initiation of the investigation.

Article 11. Duration and Review of Anti-Dumping Duties and Price Undertakings

11.1 An anti-dumping duty shall remain in force only as long as and to the extent necessary to counteract dumping which is causing injury.

11.2 The authorities shall review the need for the continued imposition of the duty, where warranted, on their own initiative or, provided that a reasonable period of time has elapsed since the imposition of the definitive anti-dumping duty, upon request by any interested party which submits positive information substantiating the need for a review.[21] Interested parties shall have the right to request the authorities to examine whether the continued imposition of the duty is necessary to offset dumping, whether the injury would be likely to continue or recur if the duty were removed or varied, or both. If, as a result of the review under this paragraph, the authorities determine that the anti-dumping duty is no longer warranted, it shall be terminated immediately.

11.3 Notwithstanding the provisions of paragraphs 1 and 2, any definitive anti-dumping duty shall be terminated on a date not later than five years from its imposition (or from the date of the most recent review under paragraph 2 if that review has covered both dumping and injury, or under this paragraph), unless the authorities determine, in a review initiated before that date on their own initiative or upon a duly substantiated request made by or on behalf of the domestic industry within a reasonable period of time prior to that date, that the expiry of the duty would be likely to lead to continuation or recurrence of dumping and injury.[22] The duty may remain in force pending the outcome of such a review.

---

[21] A determination of final liability for payment of anti-dumping duties, as provided for in paragraph 3 of Article 9, does not by itself constitute a review within the meaning of this Article.

[22] When the amount of the anti-dumping duty is assessed on a retrospective basis, a finding in the most recent assessment proceeding under subparagraph 3.1 of Article 9 that no duty is to be levied shall not by itself require the authorities to terminate the definitive duty.

11.4 The provisions of Article 6 regarding evidence and procedure shall apply to any review carried out under this Article. Any such review shall be carried out expeditiously and shall normally be concluded within 12 months of the date of initiation of the review.

11.5 The provisions of this Article shall apply mutatis mutandis to price undertakings accepted under Article 8.

Article 12. Public Notice and Explanation of Determinations

12.1 When the authorities are satisfied that there is sufficient evidence to justify the initiation of an anti-dumping investigation pursuant to Article 5, the Member or Members the products of which are subject to such investigation and other interested parties known to the investigating authorities to have an interest therein shall be notified and a public notice shall be given.

12.1.1 A public notice of the initiation of an investigation shall contain, or otherwise make available through a separate report,[23] adequate information on the following:

(i) the name of the exporting country or countries and the product involved;
(ii) the date of initiation of the investigation;
(iii) the basis on which dumping is alleged in the application;
(iv) a summary of the factors on which the allegation of injury is based;
(v) the address to which representations by interested parties should be directed;
(vi) the time-limits allowed to interested parties for making their views known.

12.2 Public notice shall be given of any preliminary or final determination, whether affirmative or negative, of any decision to accept an undertaking pursuant to Article 8, of the termination of such an undertaking, and of the termination of a definitive anti-dumping duty. Each such notice shall set forth, or otherwise make available through a separate report, in sufficient detail the findings and conclusions reached on all issues of fact and law considered material by the investigating authorities. All such notices and reports shall be forwarded to the Member or Members the products of which are subject to such determination or undertaking and to other interested parties known to have an interest therein.

12.2.1 A public notice of the imposition of provisional measures shall set forth, or otherwise make available through a separate report, sufficiently detailed explanations for the preliminary determinations on dumping and injury and shall refer to the matters of fact and law which have led to arguments being accepted or rejected. Such a notice or report shall, due regard being paid to the requirement for the protection of confidential information, contain in particular:

(i) the names of the suppliers, or when this is impracticable, the supplying countries involved;

---

[23] Where authorities provide information and explanations under the provisions of this Article in a separate report, they shall ensure that such report is readily available to the public.

(ii) a description of the product which is sufficient for customs purposes;

(iii) the margins of dumping established and a full explanation of the reasons for the methodology used in the establishment and comparison of the export price and the normal value under Article 2;

(iv) considerations relevant to the injury determination as set out in Article 3;

 (v) the main reasons leading to determination.

12.2.2 A public notice of conclusion or suspension of an investigation in the case of an affirmative determination providing for the imposition of a definitive duty or the acceptance of a price undertaking shall contain, or otherwise make available through a separate report, all relevant information on the matters of fact and law and reasons which have led to the imposition of final measures or the acceptance of a price undertaking, due regard being paid to the requirement for the protection of confidential information. In particular, the notice or report shall contain the information described in subparagraph 2.1, as well as the reasons for the acceptance or rejection of relevant arguments or claims made by the exporters and importers, and the basis for any decision made under subparagraph 10.2 of Article 6.

12.2.3 A public notice of the termination or suspension of an investigation following the acceptance of an undertaking pursuant to Article 8 shall include, or otherwise make available through a separate report, the non-confidential part of this undertaking.

12.3 The provisions of this Article shall apply mutatis mutandis to the initiation and completion of reviews pursuant to Article 11 and to decisions under Article 10 to apply duties retroactively.

Article 13. Judicial Review

Each Member whose national legislation contains provisions on anti-dumping measures shall maintain judicial, arbitral or administrative tribunals or procedures for the purpose inter alia of the prompt review of administrative actions to final determinations and reviews of determinations within the meaning of Article 11. Such tribunals or procedures shall be independent of the authorities responsible for the determination or review in question.

Article 14. Anti-Dumping Action on Behalf of a Third Country

14.1 An application for anti-dumping action on behalf of a third country shall be made by the authorities of the third country requesting action.

14.2 Such an application shall be supported by price information to show that the imports are being dumped and by detailed information to show that the alleged dumping is causing injury to the domestic industry concerned in the third country. The government of the third country shall afford all assistance to the authorities of the importing country to obtain any further information which the latter may require.

14.3 In considering such an application, the authorities of the importing country shall consider the effects of the alleged dumping on the industry concerned as a whole in the third country; that is to say, the injury shall not be assessed in relation only to the effect of the alleged dumping on the industry's exports to the importing country or even on the industry's total exports.

14.4 The decision whether or not to proceed with a case shall rest with the importing country. If the importing country decides that it is prepared to take action, the initiation of the approach to the Council for Trade in Goods seeking its approval for such action shall rest with the importing country.

Article 15. Developing Country Members

It is recognized that special regard must be given by developed country Members to the special situation of developing country Members when considering the application of anti-dumping measures under this Agreement. Possibilities of constructive remedies provided for by this Agreement shall be explored before applying anti-dumping duties where they would affect the essential interests of developing country Members.

PART II

Article 16. Committee on Anti-Dumping Practices

16.1 There is hereby established a Committee on Anti-Dumping Practices (referred to in this Agreement as the 'Committee') composed of representatives from each of the Members. The Committee shall elect its own Chairman and shall meet not less than twice a year and otherwise as envisaged by relevant provisions of this Agreement at the request of any Member. The Committee shall carry out responsibilities as assigned to it under this Agreement or by the Members and it shall afford Members the opportunity of consulting on any matters relating to the operation of the Agreement or the furtherance of its objectives. The WTO Secretariat shall act as the secretariat to the Committee.

16.2 The Committee may set up subsidiary bodies as appropriate.

16.3 In carrying out their functions, the Committee and any subsidiary bodies may consult with and seek information from any source they deem appropriate. However, before the Committee or a subsidiary body seeks such information from a source within the jurisdiction of a Member, it shall inform the Member involved. It shall obtain the consent of the Member and any firm to be consulted.

16.4 Members shall report without delay to the Committee all preliminary or final anti-dumping actions taken. Such reports shall be available in the Secretariat for inspection by other Members. Members shall also submit, on a semi-annual basis, reports of any anti-dumping actions taken within the preceding six months. The semi-annual reports shall be submitted on an agreed standard form.

16.5 Each Member shall notify the Committee (a) which of its authorities are competent to initiate and conduct investigations referred to in Article 5 and (b) its domestic procedures governing the initiation and conduct of such investigations.

Article 17. Consultation and Dispute Settlement

17.1 Except as otherwise provided herein, the Dispute Settlement Understanding is applicable to consultations and the settlement of disputes under this Agreement.

17.2 Each Member shall afford sympathetic consideration to, and shall afford adequate opportunity for consultation regarding, representations made by another Member with respect to any matter affecting the operation of this Agreement.

17.3 If any Member considers that any benefit accruing to it, directly or indirectly, under this Agreement is being nullified or impaired, or that the achievement of any objective is being impeded, by another Member or Members, it may, with a view to reaching a mutually satisfactory resolution of the matter, request in writing consultations with the Member or Members in question. Each Member shall afford sympathetic consideration to any request from another Member for consultation.

17.4 If the Member that requested consultations considers that the consultations pursuant to paragraph 3 have failed to achieve a mutually agreed solution, and if final action has been taken by the administering authorities of the importing Member to levy definitive anti-dumping duties or to accept price undertakings, it may refer the matter to the Dispute Settlement Body ('DSB'). When a provisional measure has a significant impact and the Member that requested consultations considers that the measure was taken contrary to the provisions of paragraph 1 of Article 7, that Member may also refer such matter to the DSB.

17.5 The DSB shall, at the request of the complaining party, establish a panel to examine the matter based upon:

(i) a written statement of the Member making the request indicating how a benefit accruing to it, directly or indirectly, under this Agreement has been nullified or impaired, or that the achieving of the objectives of the Agreement is being impeded, and

(ii) the facts made available in conformity with appropriate domestic procedures to the authorities of the importing Member.

17.6 In examining the matter referred to in paragraph 5:

(i) in its assessment of the facts of the matter, the panel shall determine whether the authorities' establishment of the facts was proper and whether their evaluation of those facts was unbiased and objective. If the establishment of the facts was proper and the evaluation was unbiased and objective, even though the panel might have reached a different conclusion, the evaluation shall not be overturned;

(ii) the panel shall interpret the relevant provisions of the Agreement in accordance with customary rules of interpretation of public international law. Where the panel finds that a relevant provision of the Agreement admits of more than one permissible interpretation, the panel shall find the authorities' measure to be in conformity with the Agreement if it rests upon one of those permissible interpretations.

17.7 Confidential information provided to the panel shall not be disclosed without formal authorization from the person, body or authority providing such information. Where such information is requested from the panel but release of such information by the panel is not authorized, a non-confidential summary of the information, authorized by the person, body or authority providing the information, shall be provided.

PART III

Article 18. Final Provisions

18.1 No specific action against dumping of exports form another Member can be taken except in accordance with the provisions of GATT 1994, as interpreted by this Agreement.[24]

18.2 Reservations may not be entered in respect of any of the provisions of this Agreement without the consent of the other Members.

18.3 Subject to subparagraph 3.1 and 3.2, the provisions of this Agreement shall apply to investigations, and reviews of existing measures, initiated pursuant to applications which have been made on or after the date of entry into force for a Member of the WTO Agreement.

18.3.1 With respect to the calculation of margins of dumping in refund procedures under paragraph 3 of Article 9, the rules used in the most recent determination or review of dumping shall apply.

18.3.2 For the purposes of paragraph 3 of Article 11, existing anti-dumping measures shall be deemed to be imposed on a date not later than the date of entry into force for a Member of the WTO Agreement, except in cases in which the domestic legislation of a Member in force on that date already included a clause of the type provided for in that paragraph.

18.4 Each Member shall take all necessary steps, of a general or particular character, to ensure, not later than the date of entry into force of the WTO Agreement for it, the conformity of its laws, regulations and administrative procedures with the provisions of this Agreement as they may apply for the Member in question.

18.5 Each Member shall inform the Committee of any changes in its laws and regulations relevant to this Agreement and in the administration of such laws and regulations.

18.6 The Committee shall review annually the implementation and operation of this Agreement taking into account the objectives thereof. The Committee shall inform annually the Council for Trade in Goods of developments during the period covered by such reviews.

18.7 The Annexes to this Agreement constitute an integral part thereof.

*

---

[24] This is not intended to preclude action under other relevant provisions of GATT 1994, as appropriate.

Annex I. Procedures for On-the-Spot Investigations Pursuant to Paragraph 7 of Article 6

1. Upon initiation of an investigation, the authorities of the exporting Member and the firms known to be concerned should be informed of the intention to carry out on-the-sport investigations.

2. If in exceptional circumstances it is intended to include non-governmental experts in the investigating team, the firms and the authorities of the exporting Member should be so informed. Such non-governmental experts should be subject to effective sanctions for breach of confidentiality requirements.

3. It should be standard practice to obtain explicit agreement of the firms concerned in the exporting Member before the visit is finally scheduled.

4. As soon as the agreement of the firms concerned has been obtained, the investigating authorities should notify the authorities of the exporting Member of the names and addresses of the firms to be visited and the dates agreed.

5. Sufficient advance notice should be given to the firms in question before the visit is made.

6. Visits to explain the questionnaire should only be made at the request of an exporting firm. Such a visit may only be made if (a) the authorities of the importing Member notify the representatives of the Member in question and (b) the latter do not object to the visit.

7. As the main purpose of the on-the-spot investigation is to verify information provided or to obtain further details, it should be carried out after the response to the questionnaire has been received unless the firm agrees to the contrary and the government of the exporting Member is informed by the investigating authorities of the anticipated visit and does not object to it; further, it should be standard practice prior to the visit to advise the firms concerned of the general nature of the information to be verified and of any further information which needs to be provided, though this should not preclude requests to be made on the spot for further details to be provided in the light of information obtained.

8. Enquiries or questions put by the authorities or firms of the exporting Members and essential to a successful on-the-sport investigation should, whenever possible, be answered before the visit is made.

Annex II. Best Information Available in Terms of Paragraph 8 of Article 6

1. As soon as possible after the initiation of the investigation, the investigating authorities should specify in detail the information required from any interested party, and the manner in which that information should be structured by the interested party in its response. The authorities should also ensure that the party is aware that if information is not supplied within a reasonable time, the authorities will be free to make determinations

on the basis of the facts available, including those contained in the application for the initiation of the investigation by the domestic industry.

2. The authorities may also request that an interested party provide its response in a particular medium (e.g. computer tape) or computer language. Where such a request is made, the authorities should consider the reasonable ability of the interested party to respond in the preferred medium or computer language, and should not request the party to use for its response a computer system other than that used by the party. The authority should not maintain a request for a computerized response if the interested party does not maintain computerized accounts and if presenting the response as requested would result in an unreasonable extra burden on the interested party, e.g. it would entail unreasonable additional cost and trouble. The authorities should not maintain a request for a response in a particular medium or computer language if the interested party does not maintain its computerized accounts in such medium or computer language and if presenting the response as requested would result in an unreasonable extra burden on the interested party, e.g. it would entail unreasonable additional cost and trouble.

3. All information which is verifiable, which is appropriately submitted so that it can be used in the investigation without undue difficulties, which is supplied in a timely fashion, and, where applicable, which is supplied in a medium or computer language requested by the authorities, should be taken into account when determinations are made. If a party does not respond in the preferred medium or computer language but the authorities find that the circumstances set out in paragraph 2 have been satisfied, the failure to respond in the preferred medium or computer language should not be considered to significantly impede the investigation.

4. Where the authorities do not have the ability to process information if provided in a particular medium (e.g. computer tape), the information should be supplied in the form of written material or any other form acceptable to the authorities.

5. Even though the information provided may not be ideal in all respects, this should not justify the authorities from disregarding it, provided the interested party has acted to the best of its ability.

6. If evidence or information is not accepted, the supplying party should be informed forthwith of the reasons therefor, and should have an opportunity to provide further explanations within a reasonable period, due account being taken of the time-limits of the investigation. If the explanations are considered by the authorities as not being satisfactory, the reasons for the rejection of such evidence or information should be given in any published determinations.

7. If the authorities have to base their findings, including those with respect to normal value, on information from a secondary source, including the information supplied in the application for the initiation of the investigation, they should do so with special circumspection. In such cases, the authorities should, where practicable, check the information from other independent sources at their disposal, such as published price

lists, official import statistics and customs returns, and from the information obtained from other interested parties during the investigation. It is clear, however, that if an interested party does not cooperate and thus relevant information is being withheld from the authorities, this situation could lead to a result which is less favourable to the party than if the party did cooperate.

Decision on anti-circumvention

Ministers,

Noting that while the problem of circumvention of anti-dumping duty measures formed part of the negotiations which preceded the Agreement on Implementation of Article VI of GATT 1994, negotiators were unable to agree on specific text,

Mindful of the desirability of the applicability of uniform rules in this area as soon as possible,

Decide to refer this matter to the Committee on Anti-Dumping Practices established under that Agreement for resolution.

*

Decision on review of Article 17.6 of the Agreement on Implementation of Article VI of the General Agreement on Tariffs and Trade 1994

Ministers decide as follows:

The standard of review in paragraph 6 of Article 17 of the Agreement on Implementation of Article VI of GATT 1994 shall be reviewed after a period of three years with a view to considering the question of whether it is capable of general application.

*

Declaration on dispute settlement pursuant to the Agreement on Implementation of Article VI of the General Agreement on Tariffs and Trade 1994 or Part V of the Agreement on subsidies and countervailing measures

Ministers recognize, with respect to dispute settlement pursuant to the Agreement on Implementation of Article VI of GATT 1994 or Part V of the Agreement on Subsidies and Countervailing Measures, the need for the consistent resolution of disputes arising from anti-dumping and countervailing duty measures.

ANNEX 2
Article VI GATT 1994

Article VI: Anti-dumping and Countervailing Duties

1. The contracting parties recognize that dumping, by which products of one country are introduced into the commerce of another country at less than the normal value of the products, is to be condemned if it causes or threatens material injury to an established industry in the territory of a contracting party or materially retards the establishment of a domestic industry. For the purposes of this Article, a product is to be considered as being introduced into the commerce of an importing country at less than its normal value, if the price of the product exported from one country to another

(a) is less than the comparable price, in the ordinary course of trade, for the like product when destined for consumption in the exporting country, or,

(b) in the absence of such domestic price, is less than either

    (i) the highest comparable price for the like product for export to any third country in the ordinary course of trade, or

    (ii) the cost of production of the product in the country of origin plus a reasonable addition for selling cost and profit.

Due allowance shall be made in each case for differences in conditions and terms of sale, for differences in taxation, and for other differences affecting price comparability.

2. In order to offset or prevent dumping, a contracting party may levy on any dumped product an anti-dumping duty not greater in amount than the margin of dumping in respect of such product. For the purposes of this Article, the margin of dumping is the price difference determined in accordance with the provisions of paragraph 1.

3. No countervailing duty shall be levied on any product of the territory of any contracting party imported into the territory of another contracting party in excess of an amount equal to the estimated bounty or subsidy determined to have been granted, directly or indirectly, on the manufacture, production or export of such product in the country of origin or exportation, including any special subsidy to the transportation of a particular product. The term 'countervailing duty' shall be understood to mean a special duty levied for the purpose of offsetting any bounty or subsidy bestowed, directly or indirectly, upon the manufacture, production or export of any merchandise.

4. No product of the territory of any contracting party imported into the territory of any other contracting party shall be subject to anti-dumping or countervailing duty by reason of the exemption of such product from duties or taxes borne by the like product when destined for consumption in the country of origin or exportation, or by reason of the refund of such duties or taxes.

5. No product of the territory of any contracting party imported into the territory of any other contracting party shall be subject to both anti-dumping and countervailing duties to compensate for the same situation of dumping or export subsidization.

6. *(a)* No contracting party shall levy any anti-dumping or countervailing duty on the importation of any product of the territory of another contracting party unless it determines that the effect of the dumping or subsidization, as the case may be, is such as to cause or threaten material injury to an established domestic industry, or is such as to retard materially the establishment of a domestic industry.

(b) The CONTRACTING PARTIES may waive the requirement of subparagraph *(a)* of this paragraph so as to permit a contracting party to levy an anti-dumping or countervailing duty on the importation of any product for the purpose of offsetting dumping or subsidization which causes or threatens material injury to an industry in the territory of another contracting party exporting the product concerned to the territory of the importing contracting party. The CONTRACTING PARTIES shall waive the requirements of sub-paragraph *(a)* of this paragraph, so as to permit the levying of a countervailing duty, in cases in which they find that a subsidy is causing or threatening material injury to an industry in the territory of another contracting party exporting the product concerned to the territory of the importing contracting party.

(c) In exceptional circumstances, however, where delay might cause damage which would be difficult to repair, a contracting party may levy a countervailing duty for the purpose referred to in sub-paragraph *(b)* of this paragraph without the prior approval of the CONTRACTING PARTIES; *Provided* that such action shall be reported immediately to the CONTRACTING PARTIES and that the countervailing duty shall be withdrawn promptly if the CONTRACTING PARTIES disapprove.

*

Ad Article VI

Paragraph 1

1. Hidden dumping by associated houses (that is, the sale by an importer at a price below that corresponding to the price invoiced by an exporter with whom the importer is associated, and also below the price in the exporting country) constitutes a form of price dumping with respect to which the margin of dumping may be calculated on the basis of the price at which the goods are resold by the importer.

2. It is recognized that, in the case of imports from a country which has a complete or substantially complete monopoly of its trade and where all domestic prices are fixed by the State, special difficulties may exist in determining price comparability for the purposes of paragraph 1, and in such cases importing contracting parties may find it necessary to take into account the possibility that a strict comparison with domestic prices in such a country may not always be appropriate.

Paragraphs 2 and 3

1. As in many other cases in customs administration, a contracting party may require reasonable security (bond or cash deposit) for the payment of anti-dumping or countervailing duty pending final determination of the facts in any case of suspected dumping or subsidization.

2. Multiple currency practices can in certain circumstances constitute a subsidy to exports which may be met by countervailing duties under paragraph 3 or can constitute a form of dumping by means of a partial depreciation of a country's currency which may be met by action under paragraph 2. By 'multiple currency practices' is meant practices by governments or sanctioned by governments.

Paragraph 6 (b)

Waivers under the provisions of this sub-paragraph shall be granted only on application by the contracting party proposing to levy an anti-dumping or countervailing duty, as the case may be.

ANNEX 3

Recommendations and other documents from the Committee on Anti-Dumping Practices

WORLD TRADE

ORGANIZATION

G/ADP/1
21 November 1995

(95-3635)

Committee on Anti-Dumping Practices

GUIDELINES FOR INFORMATION PROVIDED IN THE SEMI-ANNUAL REPORTS

ADOPTED BY THE COMMITTEE ON 30 OCTOBER 1995

[Footnotes omitted]

1. The information should always make clear which country is subject to the measure reported.

2. In order to systematically present data in the semi-annual reports, the names of the countries whose imports are subject to action must be organized in alphabetical order.

3. If any single country, e.g. Alpha in the illustrative report in the Annex, has more than one case, the different cases for this country must be organized in chronological order.

4. When imports of any particular product from more than one country are investigated, the names of the countries concerned should be provided separately, i.e. each product-country combination should be treated as one case. This is shown, for example, for product category 'machine tufted carpeting' in the illustrative report in the Annex.

5. As indicated by the titles for columns 4, 5 and 6 in the semi-annual report, the date when the measure is taken should always be provided.

6. Columns 4, 5 and 6 in the semi-annual reports should contain the dates on which measures entered into force rather than the dates on which findings were made.

7. The titles for columns 4, 5 and 6 also indicate that the dumping margins must be provided along with the dates for the measures reported in these columns. When there are several dumping margins, a range of the margins could be provided. The actual margins of dumping should be indicated for the preliminary and final duties mentioned in the reports.

8. If the rate of duty imposed is less than the dumping margin, then the rate of duty should also be provided along with the dumping margin. If the lower duty rate cannot be provided, this should be indicated by a footnote.

9. For the information in column 11, the reporting party should clarify the coverage of the data on 'Trade volume' that is provided, i.e. whether this data refers to the total trade volume of the subject product from the country under investigation, or to total trade volume from the country which is determined to be dumped, or some other notion of trade volume. The Committee could reach an agreement on the symbols to be used for indicating the coverage of such data.

10. When no information is provided under columns 11 to 13, then the reporting Party should give a reason for not providing such data. In this context, new symbols which could be used are 'CF' to denote confidentiality and 'n/a' to denote that the data is not provided because it may not be available or relevant in a situation of a review.

11. In columns 11 to 13, whenever relevant information is available it should be provided from the time when provisional measures are taken, and the information in these columns should be updated in order to provide the most recent relevant data pertinent to the latest decision point covered by the report, e.g. provisional measures or definitive duties.

12. For the information provided in columns 11 to 13, it would be desirable to indicate the time period for which the information is provided.

13. In column 14, the symbol 'TM' should be accompanied by the name of the third country whose market prices were used as a basis for calculations. The footnote to the table in the semi-annual report clearly indicates that such information should be specified in the report.

14. An initiation of a completely new investigation should be distinguished from the reopening of a suspended investigation or the opening of an investigation in the context of a review of an existing anti-dumping measure. This should be done by using the symbol (R) after the date of initiation for reviews or for reopening of a suspended investigation.

15. A list of the outstanding measures at the end of the reporting period and a list of measures revoked during the reporting period should be provided along with the other information in the report.

16. Provisional measures should never be listed in the annex 'All outstanding anti-dumping actions'. The measures listed in this annex should be divided into two categories: a first category comprising all definitive duties and a second category listing price undertakings.

17. The list of outstanding measures should contain measures in force at the end of the reporting period, i.e. the measure in force on 30 June or 31 December, rather than measures in force at the time of the submission of the report to the Committee.

18. The information on the measures in place at the end of the reporting period should include dates since the measures have been in place.

19. For further improving the transparency of the anti-dumping investigations, information on all cases pending at the end of the period should be reported even if there was no action taken during the period for which the report is provided.

20. The authorities should, as far as possible, compare the information in a semi-annual report with that provided in the previous report in order to correct past errors and to avoid any errors in the latest report.

21. Nothing in this format requires the notification of confidential information, including confidential business information.

WORLD TRADE

ORGANIZATION

G/ADP/2
21 November 1995

(95-3638)

Committee on Anti-Dumping Practices

MINIMUM INFORMATION TO BE PROVIDED UNDER ARTICLE 16.4 OF THE AGREEMENT IN THE REPORTS ON ALL PRELIMINARY OR FINAL ANTI-DUMPING ACTIONS

ADOPTED BY THE COMMITTEE ON 30 OCTOBER 1995

1. Title of the public notice regarding the action.

2. Date and place of publication.

3. Investigation (Regulation) Number and other notices relating to the same investigation (e.g. for initiation, provisional measure).

4. Margin(s) of dumping found and the basis of calculation.

5. Where anti-dumping measures are imposed, the product (including customs classification), origin (country/customs territory/firm), rate of duty and the effective date for each source of imports.

6. Where an undertaking is involved, the product, country/customs territory/firm, and effective date of the undertaking.

7. The period of investigation (dumping, injury).

8. Date of the dumping determination.

9. Date of the injury determination.

10. Type of injury found (material injury, threat, material retardation).

11. Volume and import penetration of dumped imports.

12. Effect on domestic prices of the like product (whether there was significant price undercutting/price suppression or depression).

13. Evidence on the impact on the domestic industry (i.e. the factors mentioned in Article 3:3 of the Agreement which were the basis for the finding regarding the impact on the domestic industry).

14. Evidence of causation of injury to domestic industry (the basis for determining the causation of injury, and other factors which might at the same time be causing injury to the domestic industry).

WORLD TRADE

ORGANIZATION

G/ADP/3
14 December 1995

(95-4075)

Committee on Anti-Dumping Practices

ORIGINAL: SPANISH

REQUEST FOR CONSULTATIONS UNDER
ARTICLE 17.3 OF THE AGREEMENT ON
IMPLEMENTATION OF ARTICLE VI OF
THE GENERAL AGREEMENT ON
TARIFFS AND TRADE 1994

The following communication, dated 6 December 1995, has been received from the Permanent Mission of Argentina.

In accordance with the provisions of Article 17, paragraph 3, of the Agreement on Implementation of Article VI of the General Agreement on Tariffs and Trade 1994, the Government of the Argentine Republic requests urgent consultations with the Government of Venezuela.

The measure which this request concerns is the investigation, for alleged dumping, currently being carried out by the Venezuelan Anti-Dumping and Subsidization Commission (CASS) into imports of oil country tubular goods (OCTG), of circular cross-section, with seam or seamless, whether or not complying with the American Petroleum Institute's technical standard, including production tubing and casing, solely in filleted/threaded and finished form and not as semi-finished (green) tubes, coming from and originating in the Argentine Republic.

On 5 June 1995, Grupo BPCA Tubulares Petroleros C.A. (BPCA) requested the Venezuelan Anti-Dumping and Subsidization Commission to initiate an anti-dumping investigation. In its application and the supplement thereto submitted a week later it claimed dumping of 'OCTG' coming from Argentina and Mexico and the existence of injury to the Venezuelan industry. On 15 June 1995, the Venezuelan authorities officially decided to open an investigation.

BCPA is a processing/finishing firm. Its main activity is importing unfinished ('green') tubing from such origins as Argentina and Mexico, processing and finishing these imported products and marketing the finished tubes, mainly on the Venezuelan market. BPCA limited its complaint to finished OCTG, and did not include unfinished tubes, which it presumably intended to continue importing.

In addition to BCPA, there are two other firms producing similar products in the Venezuelan industry, CONDUSID, which like BPCA is a processor/finisher of unfinished tubes, and SIDOR, the only integrated producer of finished OCTG in Venezuela.

CONDUSID (which represent 27 per cent of production) explicitly opposed the investigation by a note dated 5 June 1995, and subsequently submitted a formal reply acknowledging that there was no injury whatsoever resulting from the imports from Argentina and Mexico. SIDOR (which represents 38 per cent of production) never expressed support for the application.

.*/.*

On 21 August 1995, BPCA – the sole complainant – formally and unconditionally withdrew its complaint, stating that 'world market conditions and the internal situation on the Venezuelan market itself had changed, so that the objective situation that had led to the submission of the complaint had ceased to exist'. Following the formal withdrawal of the complaint by BPCA, no member of the Venezuelan industry supports the investigation.

The Government of Argentina believes that the investigation is inconsistent with, *inter alia*, the provisions of Articles 1, 3.1, 3.2, 3.3, 3.4, 3.5, 4.1, 5.1, 5.2, 5.4, 5.6 and 5.8 of the Agreement on Implementation of Article VI of the General Agreement on Tariffs and Trade 1994 and Article VI of the GATT.

In particular, it considers that the decision to continue the investigation *ex-officio* 'for reasons of public interest' has no basis in the Anti-Dumping Agreement and ignores a basic groundrule of the Anti-Dumping regime, namely that the complaint must have the support of the local industry.

Furthermore, it is clear that in accordance with Article 5.8 of the Agreement the national authorities must immediately terminate any investigation when they are satisfied that there is not sufficient evidence of injury to justify proceeding with the case, a condition which has existed from the moment the industry withdrew the complaint.

Without prejudice to the forgoing, and in the event that the Venezuelan authorities should apply provisional measures, the Government of the Argentine Republic reserves the right to avail itself of the provisions of paragraph 4 of Article 17 of the Anti-Dumping Agreement and Article 4 of the Understanding on Rules and Procedures Governing the Settlement of Disputes.

WORLD TRADE

ORGANIZATION

G/ADP/4
16 September 1996

(96-3615)

Committee on Anti-Dumping Practices

RULES OF PROCEDURE FOR MEETINGS OF THE COMMITTEE ON ANTI-DUMPING PRACTICES

APPROVED BY THE COUNCIL FOR TRADE IN GOODS ON 22 MAY 1996

Chapter I – Meetings

Rule 1

The Committee on Anti-Dumping Practices shall meet not less than twice a year in regular session, and otherwise as appropriate.

Rule 2

Meetings of the Committee on Anti-Dumping Practices shall be convened by the Director-General by a notice issued preferably three weeks, but in any case, not less than ten calendar days prior to the date set for the meeting. In the event that the tenth day falls on a weekend or a holiday, the notice shall be issued no later than the preceding WTO working day. Meetings may be convened with shorter notice for matters of significant importance or urgency at the request of a Member concurred in by the majority of the Members.

Chapter II – Agenda

Rule 3

A list of the items proposed for the agenda of the meeting shall be communicated to Members together with the convening notice for the meeting. It shall be open to any Member to suggest items for inclusion in the proposed agenda up to, and not including, the day on which the notice of the meeting is to be issued.

Rule 4

Requests for items to be placed on the agenda of a forthcoming meeting shall be communicated to the Secretariat in writing, together with the accompanying documentation to be issued in connection with that item. Documentation for consideration at a meeting shall be circulated preferably three weeks, but in any case not later than ten calendar days prior to the date set for the meeting.

Rule 5

Not applicable.

Rule 6

The first item of business at each meeting shall be the consideration and approval of the agenda. Representatives may suggest amendments to the proposed agenda, or additions to the agenda under 'Other Business'. Representatives shall provide the Chairperson or the Secretariat, and the other Members directly concerned, whenever possible, advance notice of items intended to be raised under 'Other Business'.

Rule 7

The Committee on Anti-Dumping Practices may amend the agenda or give priority to certain items at any time in the course of the meeting.

Chapter III – Representation

Rule 8

Each Member shall be represented by an accredited representative.

Rule 9

Each representative may be accompanied by such alternates and advisers as the representative may require.

Chapter IV – Observers

Rule 10

Representatives of States or separate customs territories may attend the meetings as observers on the invitation of the Committee on Anti-Dumping Practices in accordance with paragraphs 9 to 11 of the guidelines in Annex 2 to the Rules of Procedure of the General Council.

Rule 11

Representatives of international intergovernmental organizations may attend the meetings as observers on the invitation of the Committee on Anti-Dumping Practices in accordance with the guidelines in Annex 3 to the Rules of Procedure of the General Council.

Chapter V – Officers

Rule 12

The Committee on Anti-Dumping Practices shall elect a Chairperson* and may elect a Vice-Chairperson from among the representatives of Members. The election shall take place at the first regular meeting of the year and shall take effect at the end of the

---

* The Committee on Anti-Dumping Practices shall apply the relevant guidelines contained in the 'Guidelines for Appointment of Officers to WTO Bodies' (WT/L/31 dated 7 February 1995).

meeting. The Chairperson and Vice-Chairperson shall hold office until the end of the first regular meeting of the following year.

Rule 13

If the Chairperson is absent from any meeting or part thereof, the Vice-Chairperson shall perform the functions of the Chairperson. If no Vice-Chairperson was elected or if the Vice-Chairperson is not present, the Committee on Anti-Dumping Practices shall elect an interim Chairperson for that meeting or that part of the meeting.

Rule 14

If the Chairperson can no longer perform the functions of the office, the Committee on Anti-Dumping Practices shall designate the Vice-Chairperson referred to in Rule 12 or, if no Vice-Chairperson was elected, shall elect an interim Chairperson, to perform those functions pending the election of a new Chairperson.

Rule 15

The Chairperson shall normally participate in the proceedings as such and not as the representative of a Member. The Chairperson may, however, at any time request permission to act in the latter capacity.

Chapter VI – Conduct of business

Rule 16

Not applicable.

Rule 17

In addition to exercising the powers conferred elsewhere by these rules, the Chairperson shall declare the opening and closing of each meeting, shall direct the discussion, accord the right to speak, submit questions for decision, announce decisions, rule on points of order and, subject to these rules, have complete control of the proceedings. The Chairperson may also call a speaker to order if the remarks of the speaker are not relevant.

Rule 18

During the discussion of any matter, a representative may raise a point of order. In this case the Chairperson shall immediately state the ruling. If the ruling is challenged, the Chairperson shall immediately submit it for decision and it shall stand unless overruled.

Rule 19

During the discussion of any matter, a representative may move the adjournment of the debate. Any such motion shall have priority. In addition to the proponent of the motion, one representative may be allowed to speak in favour of, and two representatives against, the motion, after which the motion shall be submitted for decision immediately.

Rule 20

A representative may at any time move the closure of the debate. In addition to the proponent of the motion, not more than one representative may be granted permission to speak in favour of the motion and not more than two representatives may be granted permission to speak against the motion, after which the motion shall be submitted for decision immediately.

Rule 21

During the course of the debate, the Chairperson may announce the list of speakers and, with the consent of the meeting, declare the list closed. The Chairperson may, however, accord the right of reply to any representative if a speech delivered after the list has been declared closed makes this desirable.

Rule 22

The Chairperson, with the consent of the meeting, may limit the time allowed to each speaker.

Rule 23

Representatives shall endeavour, to the extent that a situation permits, to keep their oral statements brief. Representatives wishing to develop their position on a particular matter in fuller detail may circulate a written statement for distribution to Members, the summary of which, at the representative's request, may be reflected in the records of the Committee on Anti-Dumping Practices.

Rule 24

In order to expedite the conduct of business, the Chairperson may invite representatives that wish to express their support for a given proposal to show their hands, in order to be duly recorded in the records of the Committee on Anti-Dumping Practices as supporting statements; thus, only representatives with dissenting views or wishing to make explicit points or proposals would actually be invited to make a statement. This procedure shall only be applied in order to avoid undue repetition of points already made, and will not preclude any representative who so wishes from taking the floor.

Rule 25

Representatives should avoid unduly long debates under 'Other Business'. Discussions on substantive issues under 'Other Business' shall be avoided, and the Committee on Anti-Dumping Practices shall limit itself to taking note of the announcement by the sponsoring delegation, as well as any reactions to such an announcement by other delegations directly concerned.

Rule 26

While the Committee on Anti-Dumping Practices is not expected to take action in respect of an item introduced as 'Other Business', nothing shall prevent the Committee on Anti-Dumping Practices, if it so decides, to take action in respect of any such item at a particular meeting, or in respect of any item for which documentation was not circulated at least ten calendar days in advance.

Rule 27

Representatives should make every effort to avoid the repetition of a full debate at each meeting on any issue that has already been fully debated in the past and on which there appears to have been no change in Members' positions already on record.

Rule 28

Proposals and amendments to proposals shall normally be introduced in writing and circulated to all representatives not later than twelve hours before the commencement of the meeting at which they are to be discussed.

Rule 29

If two or more proposals are moved relating to the same question, the meeting shall first decide on the most far-reaching proposal and then on the next most far-reaching proposal and so on.

Rule 30

When an amendment is moved to a proposal, the amendment shall be submitted for decision first and, if it is adopted, the amended proposal shall then be submitted for decision.

Rule 31

When two or more amendments are moved to a proposal, the meeting shall decide first on the amendment farthest removed in substance from the original proposal, then, if necessary, on the amendment next farthest removed, and so on until all the amendments have been submitted for decision.

Rule 32

Parts of a proposal may be decided on separately if a representative requests that the proposal be divided.

Chapter VII – Decision-Making

Rule 33

Where a decision can not be arrived at by consensus, the matter at issue shall be referred to the Council for Trade in Goods.

Rule 34

Not applicable.

Chapter VIII – Languages

Rule 35

English, French and Spanish shall be the working languages.

Chapter IX – Records

Rule 36

Records of the discussions of the Committee on Anti-Dumping Practices shall be in the form of minutes.**

Chapter X – Publicity of meetings

Rule 37

The meetings of the Committee on Anti-Dumping Practices shall ordinarily be held in private. It may be decided that a particular meeting or meetings should be held in public.

Rule 38

After a private meeting has been held, the Chairperson may issue a communiqué to the Press.

Chapter XI – Revision

Rule 39

The Committee on Anti-Dumping Practices may decide at any time to revise these rules or any part of them.

** The customary practice under the GATT 1947, whereby representatives may, upon their request, verify those portions of the draft records containing their statements, prior to the issuance of such records, shall be continued.

WORLD TRADE

ORGANIZATION

G/ADP/5
3 November 1998

(98-4270)

Committee on Anti-Dumping Practices

RECOMMENDATION CONCERNING THE TIMING OF THE NOTIFICATION UNDER ARTICLE 5.5

ADOPTED BY THE COMMITTEE ON 29 OCTOBER 1998

The Committee notes that Article 5.5 of the Agreement on Implementation of Article VI of the GATT 1994 provides that 'The authorities shall avoid, unless a decision has been made to initiate an investigation, any publicizing of the application for the initiation of an investigation. However, after receipt of a properly documented application and before proceeding to initiate an investigation, the authorities shall notify the government of the exporting Member concerned'. The Committee considers that the second sentence of Article 5.5 calls for a notification to be made between two specific events, but does not establish any guidelines to determine more precisely when that notification must be made.

The Committee considers that guidelines for determining more precisely when the notification called for by the second sentence of Article 5.5 must be made would be useful. The Committee recognizes that different Members have different processes and deadlines for the examination of applications and the initiation of investigations. Thus, a specific guideline, establishing a date certain by which the notification should be made, might be unworkable. Nonetheless, the Committee considers that more general guidelines can be established.

In light of the above considerations, the Committee recommends that the notification required by the second sentence of Article 5.5 should be made as soon as possible after the receipt by the investigating authorities of a properly documented application, and as early as possible before the decision is taken regarding initiation of an investigation on the basis of that properly documented application.

WORLD TRADE	
	G/ADP/6
	16 May 2000
ORGANIZATION	
	(00-1992)

Committee on Anti-Dumping Practices

RECOMMENDATION CONCERNING THE PERIODS OF DATA COLLECTION FOR ANTI-DUMPING INVESTIGATIONS

ADOPTED BY THE COMMITTEE ON 5 MAY 2000

The Committee notes that although the Agreement on Implementation of Article VI of GATT 1994 refers to the period of data collection for dumping investigations when it refers to the 'period of investigation', it does not establish any specific period of investigation[1], nor does it establish guidelines for determining an appropriate period of investigation, for the examination of either dumping or injury.

The Committee considers that guidelines for determining what period or periods of data collection may be appropriate for the examination of dumping and of injury would be useful. The Committee also recognizes, however, that such guidelines do not preclude investigating authorities from taking account of the particular circumstances of a given investigation in setting the periods of data collection for both dumping and injury, to ensure that they are appropriate in each case.

In light of the foregoing considerations, the Committee recommends that with respect to original investigations to determine the existence of dumping and consequent injury -

1. As a general rule:

    (a) the period of data collection for dumping investigations normally should be twelve months, and in any case no less than six months,[1] ending as close to the date of initiation as is practicable;

    (b) the period of data collection for investigating sales below cost[1], and the period of data collection for dumping investigations, normally should coincide in a particular investigation;

    (c) the period of data collection for injury investigations normally should be at least three years, unless a party from whom data is being gathered has existed for a lesser period, and should include the entirety of the period of data collection for the dumping investigation;

---

[1] Footnote 4 of the Agreement does provide that, for purposes of determining whether sales below cost may be treated as not being in the ordinary course of trade, the 'extended period of time' within which such sales are made 'should normally be one year but shall in no case be less than six months'.

(d) In all cases the investigating authorities should set and make known in advance to interested parties the periods of time covered by the data collection, and may also set dates certain for completing collection and/or submission of data. If such dates are set, they should be made known to interested parties.

2. In establishing the specific periods of data collection in a particular investigation, investigating authorities may, if possible, consider practices of firms from which data will be sought concerning financial reporting and the effect this may have on the availability of accounting data. Other factors that may be considered include the characteristics of the product in question, including seasonality and cyclicality, and the existence of special order or customized sales.

3. In order to increase transparency of proceedings, investigating authorities should include in public notices or in the separate reports provided pursuant to Article 12.2 of the Agreement, an explanation of the reason for the selection of a particular period for data collection if it differs from that provided for in: paragraph 1 of this recommendation, national legislation, regulation, or established national guidelines.

WORLD TRADE

ORGANIZATION

G/ADP/7
1 May 2001

(01-2208)

Committee on Anti-Dumping Practices

RECOMMENDATION CONCERNING INDICATIVE LIST OF ELEMENTS RELEVANT TO A DECISION ON A REQUEST FOR EXTENSION OF TIME TO PROVIDE INFORMATION

ADOPTED BY THE COMMITTEE ON 26 APRIL 2001

The Committee notes the obligation to complete investigations within the time limits set out in Article 5.10 of the Agreement on Implementation of Article VI of GATT 1994 and the obligation to allow parties a full opportunity for the defense of their interests set out in Article 6.2 of that Agreement.

The Committee recognizes that investigating authorities gather information necessary to make determinations in an anti-dumping investigation through questionnaires and other requests for information, and establish deadlines for the submission of replies to such questionnaires and requests, as well as for other aspects of investigations, in order to ensure the orderly conduct and timely completion of the investigation. The Committee is mindful that each Member's investigating authority has discretion to grant or deny a particular request for extension of a particular deadline, in light of the facts and circumstances of the investigation at hand.

The Committee considers that a non-binding, non-exhaustive indicative list of elements relevant to a decision whether to grant or deny such a request for extension of time to respond to a questionnaire or other request for information would be useful. In light of the foregoing, the Committee considers that the following elements may be considered by an investigating authority in deciding whether to grant or deny a request for extension of time to provide information:

1. the time available for the conduct of the investigation and making the necessary determinations, including the time periods established in national legislation, regulations, and schedules governing the conduct of the investigation at hand, and whether the information can be considered in a subsequent phase of the investigation;

2. previous extension(s) of time granted to the same party in the same investigation;

3. the ability of the party from whom information is sought to respond to the request, in light of the nature and extent of the information requested, including the party's available resources, personnel, and technological capability;

4. any unusual burdens that will be incurred by the party being asked for information in searching for, identifying and/or compiling the information requested;

5. whether the party requesting the extension has provided a partial response to the request, or has previously provided information requested in the same investigation, although the absence of a partial response alone is not an appropriate basis for denial of a request;

6. any unforeseen circumstances affecting the ability of the party to provide the information requested within the time limit established;

7. whether other parties have been granted extensions of time for similar reasons during the same phase of the same investigation.

The decision whether to grant or deny a request for an extension of time to provide information should be made promptly, and if denied, the party making such a request should be informed of the reason for its denial.

WORLD TRADE

ORGANIZATION

G/ADP/8
18 May 2002

(02-6368)

Committee on Anti-Dumping Practices

CHAIRMAN'S REPORT TO THE COUNCIL FOR TRADE IN GOODS ON TRANSITIONAL REVIEW OF CHINA

[OMITTED]

WORLD TRADE

ORGANIZATION

G/ADP/9
29 November 2002

(02-6596)

Committee on Anti-Dumping Practices

RECOMMENDATION REGARDING ANNUAL REVIEWS OF THE ANTI-DUMPING AGREEMENT

ADOPTED BY THE COMMITTEE ON 27 NOVEMBER 2002

Paragraph 7.4 of the Ministerial Decision of 14 November 2001 on Implementation-Related Issues and Concerns states that the Ministerial Conference 'Takes note that Article 18.6 of the Agreement on the Implementation of Article VI of the General Agreement on Tariffs and Trade 1994 requires the Committee on Anti-Dumping Practices to review annually the implementation and operation of the Agreement taking into account the objectives thereof. The Committee on Anti-dumping Practices is instructed to draw up guidelines for the improvement of annual reviews and to report its views and recommendations to the General Council for subsequent decision within 12 months.'

Article 18.6 of the Agreement states: 'The Committee shall review annually the implementation and operation of this Agreement taking into account the objectives thereof. The Committee shall inform annually the Council for Trade in Goods of developments during the period covered by such reviews.'

The Committee considers that improvements in the reporting of anti-dumping activity under the Agreement and in the Committee's annual reviews are important to promoting transparency. Therefore, the Committee recommends the following improvements that would provide useful information to Members and the public, and would enhance transparency under the Agreement:

1. The Committee's annual report under Article 18.6 should include in the Summary of Anti-Dumping Actions [footnote omitted], in addition to the column currently included that lists the initiations reported by each Member, a comparable column listing the number of anti-dumping revocations reported by each Member during the reporting period. Where a Member has not provided such information, the report should note this omission. Members are already requested to report the number of revocations in a separate table as an annex to their semi-annual reports of anti-dumping activity. Consequently, such information should be included in the Article 18.6 annual report.

2. The Committee's Article 18.6 annual report should also include a chart comparing for each Member the number of preliminary and final measures reported in its semi-annual reports with the number of notices of preliminary and final measures the Member submitted to the Secretariat for the comparable period.

3. Developed country Members should include, when reporting anti-dumping actions in the semi-annual report that Members are required to submit under Article 16.4, the manner in which the obligations of Article 15 have been fulfilled. Without prejudice to the scope and application of Article 15, price undertakings and lesser duty rules are examples of constructive remedies that could be included in such Members' semi-annual reports. The Committee's annual report under Article 18.6 should include, in a separate table, a compilation of the information reported by each Member in this respect during the reporting period. Where a Member has not provided such information, the report should note this omission.

4. This recommendation does not prejudge the ability of Members to submit other proposals and to agree in the future on other recommendations aimed at improving annual reviews in the Committee on Anti-dumping Practices.

WORLD TRADE

ORGANIZATION

G/ADP/10
29 November 2002

(02-6587)

Committee on Anti-Dumping Practices

RECOMMENDATION CONCERNING THE TIME-PERIOD TO BE CONSIDERED IN MAKING A DETERMINATION OF NEGLIGIBLE IMPORT VOLUMES FOR PURPOSES OF ARTICLE 5.8 OF THE AGREEMENT

ADOPTED BY THE COMMITTEE ON 27 NOVEMBER 2002

The Committee notes that Article 5.8 of the Agreement on Implementation of Article VI of GATT 1994 provides that there shall be immediate termination in cases where the authorities determine that the volume of dumped imports, actual or potential, is negligible. Article 5.8 also defines the volume of dumped imports from a particular country that shall normally be regarded as negligible. However, it does not establish a period of time over which imports are to be counted in determining whether the volume of imports is negligible. The Committee considers that guidance regarding an appropriate time-period for that determination would be useful.

In light of the foregoing, the Committee recommends that, with respect to original investigations to determine the existence of dumping and consequent injury, whether the volume of dumped imports, actual or potential, from a particular country is regarded as negligible shall be determined with reference to the volume of dumped imports from that country during:

(a) the period of data collection for the dumping investigation; or

(b) the most recent 12 consecutive months prior to initiation for which data are available; or

(c) the most recent 12 consecutive months prior to the date on which the application was filed, for which data are available, provided that the lapse of time between the filing of the application and the initiation of the investigation is no longer than 90 days.

Not later than 60 days after the approval of this recommendation Members shall notify to the Committee on Anti-Dumping Practices which of the time-periods set out above, they will use in all investigations thereafter. If in any investigation the chosen methodology is not utilized, one of the two other methodologies shall be adopted, and an explanation shall be made in the public notice or separate public report of that investigation. Members which adopt the time-period mentioned in item (c) above shall also notify which of the other two time-periods they shall use in any case in which the lapse of time between the filing of the application and the initiation of the investigation is longer than 90 days, unless a Member's domestic law prohibits such a lapse.

WORLD TRADE

ORGANIZATION

G/ADP/11
18 December 2002

(02-6974)

Committee on Anti-Dumping Practices

CHAIRMAN'S REPORT ON THE COMMITTEE'S VIEWS AND RECOMMENDATIONS PURSUANT TO THE MANDATE TO THE COMMITTEE AND ITS WORKING GROUP ON IMPLEMENTATION IN THE DECISION ON IMPLEMENTATION-RELATED ISSUES AND CONCERNS ADOPTED ON 14 NOVEMBER 2001 AT THE DOHA MINISTERIAL CONFERENCE

Mr. Chairman, I am presenting this report to the General Council, on my own responsibility and without prejudice to the position of any Member, as Chairman of the Committee on Anti-Dumping Practices ('ADP Committee'). This report is submitted pursuant to paragraph 7.4 of the Decision on Implementation-Related Issues and Concerns adopted on 14 November 2001 at the Doha Ministerial Conference ('Ministerial Decision'), where Ministers agreed 'The Committee on Anti-Dumping Practices is instructed to draw up guidelines for the improvement of annual reviews and to report its views and recommendations to the General Council for subsequent decision within 12 months'.

I am also taking this opportunity, on my own responsibility and without prejudice to the position of any Member, to report on the activities of the Committee and its Working Group on Implementation pursuant to paragraphs 7.2 and 7.3 of the Ministerial Decision. Although neither of those paragraphs contains a specific obligation with respect to reporting, I consider it appropriate to take advantage of this opportunity to report to Members on all of the Committee's, and the Working Group's, efforts pursuant to the Ministerial Decision.

Paragraph 7.2 provides that Ministers recognize 'that Article 15 of the Agreement on the Implementation of Article VI of the General Agreement on Tariffs and Trade 1994 is a mandatory provision, the modalities for its application would benefit from clarification. Accordingly, the Committee on Anti-Dumping Practices is instructed, through its working group on Implementation, to examine this issue and to draw up appropriate recommendations within twelve months on how to operationalize this provision'. Paragraph 7.3 provides that Ministers take note 'Article 5.8 of the Agreement on the Implementation of Article VI of the General Agreement on Tariffs and Trade 1994 does not specify the time-frame to be used in determining the volume of dumped imports, and that this lack of specificity creates uncertainties in the implementation of the provision. The Committee on Anti-Dumping Practices is instructed, through its working group on Implementation, to study this issue and draw up recommendations within 12 months, with a view to ensuring the maximum possible predictability and objectivity in the application of time frames'.

Since establishing a framework for discussing the issues referred to the Committee and its Working Group on Implementation at a special meeting in December 2001, the Committee and Working Group have been engaged in discussing proposals on each of the three topics under disucssion. The Committee and Working Group have held a series of informal meetings, and I have also conducted informal consultations on numerous occasions. Members have submitted documents containing proposals, explanations, questions and answers, and draft recommendations, and have engaged actively in discussions. This process has led to a clarification and distillation of the issues. A technical summary, giving an overview of the main points in Members' proposals, questions and responses, and discussions, is attached to this report.

The discussions revealed that many Members recognize the importance of the issues raised. During the course of the discussions, delegations expressed their understanding, and, in some cases, support, in respect of some of the proposals or elements thereof. In addition, my perception is that many delegations, regardless of their views on the substance of the proposals made, found the discussions useful in furthering their understanding of the proposals and the technical issues involved, and of other Members' views concerning the proposals. This is confirmed by the high degree of constructive spirit with which Members engaged in the detailed discussions on these highly technical and complex issues.

As a result of the cooperative spirit shown by Members throughout the discussions, I am pleased to report that the Committee has adopted two recommendations with respect to implementation issues referred to it by Ministers.

First, with respect to the mandate in paragraph 7.4 of the Ministerial Decision, the Committee adopted, on 27 November, a recommendation regarding annual reviews of the Anti-Dumping Agreement, which has been circulated to Members in document G/ADP/9. In order to provide useful information to Members and the public, and to enhance transparency, the Committee has recommended that additional information, concerning the number of anti-dumping revocations reported by Members, be included in the annual report, that the annual report include a comparison of the number of preliminary and final actions reported by Members on an ad hoc basis and in their semi-annual reports, and that developed country Members should include in their semi-annual reports the manner in which the obligations of Article 15 of the Agreement have been fulfilled, which information will be compiled and included in a table in the Committee's annual report, including noting where Members have not provided such information. I believe that this additional information to be included in the Committee's annual reports will indeed improve those reports and promote transparency. I understand the Chairman intends to put this recommendation before Members for a decision by the General Council, and I strongly endorse its adoption.

Second, with respect to the mandate in paragraph 7.3 of the Ministerial Decision, the Committee adopted, on 27 November, a recommendation concerning the time-period to be considered in making a determination of negligible import volumes for purposes of Article 5.8 of the Agreement, which has been circulated to Members in document G/ADP/10. In order to provide guidance in this regard, the Committee has recommended that Members determine the volume of dumped imports with reference to one of three defined time periods, notify the Committee as to the chosen methodology to be used in all investigations, and if in any investigation the chosen methodology is not used, provide an explanation in the public notice or separate public report of that investigation. I believe that this recommendation, implemented by Members, will ensure predictability and objectivity in the application of time frames in anti-dumping investigations to determine negligible import volumes for purposes of Article 5.8.

This said, however, my sense is that there continue to exist substantially divergent views on the third implementation issue referred to the Committee and its Working Group, the matter of operationalizing Article 15 of the Agreement. Despite the many discussions, and the intensive efforts of a number of Members in consultations, I am unable to identify any significant basis for consensus on a recommendation by the Committee responsive to the mandate under which the discussions have been conducted. While the discussions have revealed areas of common ground among Members with respect to the proposals made, this has not proved adequate to attract support for a consensus on a recommendation on these areas. Certain delegations have expressed the view that the areas as to which there is some degree of common understanding are insufficient as a substantive matter to warrant a recommendation. Other delegations expressed disappointment in this regard, as they had hoped that the Committee might be in a position to formulate some sort of recommendations on some or all of the issues. It is clear, however, that the issues raised in the proposals, as developed and clarified through the discussions, may yet form the basis for further discussion, should any Member submit proposals concerning them for discussion in an appropriate forum.

In light of all this, I consider that, in the context of the mandate of Ministers to the Committee and its Working Group, the discussions of these issues have been taken as far as possible. I realize that what the Committee has succeeding in accomplishing may be less than was originally expected by some Members. However, to conclude on a positive note, I am pleased with the two recommendations that were adopted, and confident that they will improve the quality of the Committee's annual reports and the predictability and transparency of anti-dumping investigations. Moreover, I am convinced that the exchange of ideas has, in itself, been valuable, and the quality of the discussion and the information exchanged among Members supports my belief that we have usefully spent this time.

I would like to take this opportunity to thank the Members of the Committee for their active and cooperative engagement in this process, with each other and with me as

Chairman. I also would like to thank the previous Vice Chairperson of the Committee for her work on these issues, as well as the Secretariat for its support given to me in this process.

Finally, as the Committee has completed its work under the existing mandate, I would like to express the hope that Members will find useful the information in the technical report of the Committee's discussions on the matters referred to it and to its Working Group on Implementation by Ministers.

Cristian Espinosa Cañizares
Chairman
Committee on Anti-Dumping Practices
12 December 2002

WORLD TRADE

ORGANIZATION

G/ADP/12
11 November 2003

(03-6020)

Committee on Anti-Dumping Practices

CHAIRMAN'S REPORT TO THE COUNCIL FOR TRADE IN GOODS ON TRANSITIONAL REVIEW OF CHINA

[OMITTED]

WORLD TRADE

ORGANIZATION

G/ADP/13
23 November 2004

(04-5097)

Committee on Anti-Dumping Practices

CHAIRMAN'S REPORT TO THE COUNCIL FOR TRADE IN GOODS ON TRANSITIONAL REVIEW OF CHINA

[OMITTED]

ANNEX 4

WTO ADA Panel and Appellate Body Reports
In reverse chronological order

Panel Report	AB Report	Date & Reference	Applicant	Respondent	Third Parties
Mexico–Rice		6/6/2005 WT/DS295/R	US	Mexico	China, EC, Turkey
	US–Oil Country Tubular Goods	29/11/2004 WT/DS268/AB/R	Argentina, US	US, Argentina	EC, Japan, Korea, Mexico, the Separate Customs Territory of Taiwan, Penghu, Kinmen and Matsu
	US–Softwood lumber I	11/8/2004 WT/DS264/AB/R	Canada, US	US, Canada	EC, India, Japan
US–Oil Country Tubular Goods		16/7/2004 WT/DS268/R	Argentina	US	EC, Japan, Korea, Mexico, the Separate Custorms Territory of Taiwan, Penghu, Kinmen and Matsu
US–Softwood lumber II		13/4/2004 WT/DS264/R	Canada	US	EC, India, Japan
US–Softwood lumber I		22/3/2004 WT/DS277/R	Canada	US	EC, Japan, Korea
	US–Corrosion Resistant Steel	15/12/2003 WT/DS244/AB/R	Japan	US	Brazil, Chile, EC, India, Korea, Norway
US–Corrision Resistant Steel		14/8/2003 WT/DS244/R	Japan	US	Brazil, Canada, Chile, EC, India, Korea, Norway

(Continued)

Panel Report	AB Report	Date & Reference	Applicant	Respondent	Third Parties
	EC–Pipe fittings	22/7/2003 WT/DS219/AB/R	Brazil	EC	Chile, Japan Mexico, US
	US–CDSOA AD 21.3(c)	13/6/2003 WT/DS217/14 WT/DS234/22	US, Australia, Brazil, Canada, Chile, EC, India, Indonesia, Japan, Korea, Mexico, Thailand	Australia, Brazil, Canada, Chile, EC, India, Indonesia, Japan, Korea, Mexico, Thailand, US	
Argentina–Poultry		22/4/2003 WT/DS241/R	Brazil	Argentina	Canada, Chile, EC, Guatemala, Paraguay, US
	EC–Bed Linen 21.5	8/4/2003 WT/DS141/AB/RW	India	EC	Japan, Korea, US
EC–Pipe fittings		7/3/2003 WT/DS219/R	Brazil	EC	Chile, Japan, Mexico, US
	US–CDSOA	16/1/2003 WT/DS217/AB/R WT/DS234/AB/R	US	Australia, Brazil, Canada, Chile, EC, India, Indonesia, Japan, Korea, Mexico, Thailand, US	Argentina, Costa Rica, Hong Kong (China), Israel, Norway
EC–Bed Linen 21.5		29/11/2002 WT/DS141/RW	India	EC	Japan, Korea, US
US–CDSOA		16/9/2002 WT/DS217/R WT/DS234/R	Australia, Brazil, Canada, Chile, EC, India, Indonesia, Japan, Korea, Mexico, Thailand	US	Argentina, Australia, Brazil, Canada, Costa Rica, EC, Hong Kong (China), India, Indonesia, Israel, Japan Korea, Mexico, Norway, Thailand,
Egypt–Rebar		8/8/2002 WT/DS211/R	Turkey	Egypt	Chile, EC, Japan, US

(*Continued*)

Panel Report	AB Report	Date & Reference	Applicant	Respondent	Third Parties
US–Section 129(c)(1)		15/7/2002 WT/DS221/R	Canada	US	Chile, EC, India, Japan
US–India Steel Plate		28/6/2002 WT/DS206/R	India	US	Chile, EC, Japan
	US–Hot Rolled Steel 21.3(c)	19/2/2002 WT/DS184/13	Japan, US	US, Japan	
	Mexico–HFCS 21.5	22/10/2001 WT/DS132/AB/RW	Mexico	US	EC
Argentina–Floor Tiles		28/9/2001 WT/DS189/R	EC	Argentina	Japan, Turkey, US
	US–Hot Rolled Steel	24/7/2001 WT/DS184/AB/R	Japan, US	US, Japan	Brazil, Canada, Chile, EC, Korea
Mexico–HFCS 21.5		22/6/2001 WT/DS132/RW	US	Mexico	EC, Jamaica, Mauritius
	Thailand–H-Beams	12/3/2001 WT/DS122/AB/R	Thailand	Poland	EC, Japan, US
	EC–Bed Linen	1/3/2001 WT/DS141/AB/R	EC, India	India, EC	Egypt, Japan, US
US–Hot Rolled Steel		28/2/2001 WT/DS184/R	Japan	US	Brazil, Canada, Chile, EC, Korea
	US–1916 AD Act 21.3(c)	28/2/2001 WT/DS136/11 WT/DS162/14	EC, Japan	US	
US–Korea Steel Plate		22/12/2000 WT/DS179/R	Korea	US	EC, Japan
US–DRAMS 21.5		7/11/2000 WT/DS99/RW	Korea	US	EC
EC–Bed Linen		30/10/2000 WT/DS141/R	India	EC	Egypt, Japan, US
Guatemala–Cement II		24/10/2000 WT/DS156/R	Mexico	Guatemala	EC, Ecuador, El Salvador, Honduras, US
Thailand–H-Beams		28/9/2000 WT/DS122/R	Poland	Thailand	EC, Japan, US

(*Continued*)

Panel Report	AB Report	Date & Reference	Applicant	Respondent	Third Parties
	US–1916 AD Act	28/8/2000 WT/DS136/AB/R WT/DS162/AB/R	EC, Japan, US	US, EC, Japan	EC, India, Japan, Mexico
US–1916 AD Act		29/5/2000 WT/DS162/R	Japan	US	EC, India
US–1916 AD Act		31/3/2000 WT/DS136/R	EC	US	India, Japan, Mexico
Mexico– HFCS		28/1/2000 WT/DS132/R	US	Mexico	Jamaica, Mauritius
US–DRAMS		29/1/1999 WT/DS99/R	Korea	US	
	Guatemala– Cement I	2/11/1998 WT/DS60/AB/R	Guatemala	Mexico	US
Guatemala– Cement I		19/6/1998 WT/DS60/R	Mexico	Guatemala	Canada, El Salvador Honduras, US

Statistics

Table 8 – AD Measures: By Sector
From: 01/01/95 To: 31/12/04

Category	1995	1996	1997	1998	1999	2000	2001	2002	2003	2004	Totals
I	2	0	1	2	1	3	7	0	1	2	19
II	4	1	1	4	3	1	4	1	1	0	20
IV	6	5	1	3	1	2	2	0	1	0	21
V	0	1	2	3	1	5	11	8	1	10	42
VI	18	12	20	13	14	52	37	56	66	42	330
VII	10	10	13	14	25	23	11	24	48	21	199
VIII	0	0	1	0	0	0	0	0	0	0	1
IX	1	0	1	5	7	0	0	2	1	3	20
X	2	0	2	13	5	9	2	6	10	4	53
XI	4	8	9	1	21	24	8	29	2	14	120
XII	1	0	3	3	0	7	2	1	0	0	17
XIII	3	3	1	4	5	8	1	2	11	3	41
XV	49	24	45	59	82	79	64	59	63	38	562
XVI	8	17	16	29	3	13	11	15	9	6	127
XVII	1	5	1	0	1	0	1	2	2	0	13
XVIII	2	1	0	0	11	0	1	0	1	1	17
XX	7	3	7	3	3	5	2	6	4	4	44
. . .	1	0	0	4	1	1	2	1	0	0	10
Totals	119	90	124	160	184	232	166	212	221	148	1656

Index

About the Author

Edwin Vermulst has practised international trade law and policy in Washington DC and Brussels since 1985 and is a founding partner of Vermulst Verhaeghe & Graafsma Advocaten. He is a member of the Brussels bar. Mr Vermulst graduated from the University of Utrecht in 1983 and obtained LL.M. and SJD degrees from the University of Michigan Law School in 1984 and 1986.

Mr Vermulst was a WTO panellist and has been involved in WTO dispute settlement proceedings as a member of the delegation.

He has (co-)authored seven books, including landmark comparative analyses of the anti-dumping systems of Australia, Canada, the EC and the United States with Professor John Jackson in 1989 and of rules of origin with Jacques Bourgeois and Paul Waer in 1994, and also numerous articles. Most recently, in the TEN project, he compared and analysed problems in the anti-dumping systems of 10 leading users, together with Gary Horlick.

Mr Vermulst is a Member of the Faculty of the World Trade Institute in Bern and teaches at the Amsterdam Law School.

He is the Editor of the Journal of World Trade and Co-editor-in-Chief of Law and Economics in International Trade.

Mr Vermulst is invariably selected as a leading trade practitioner by publications such as *Who's Who in Trade, Legal 500, Chambers Global* and the *Rushford Report.*

Lightning Source UK Ltd.
Milton Keynes UK
UKOW030627170312

189125UK00001B/50/P